Adolescents, Media, and the Law

American Psychology-Law Society Series

Series Editor
Ronald Roesch

Editorial Board
Gail S. Goodman
Thomas Grisso
Craig Haney
Kirk Heilbrun
John Monahan
Marlene Moretti
Edward P. Mulvey
J. Don Read
N. Dickon Reppucci
Gary L. Wells
Lawrence S. Wrightsman
Patricia A. Zapf

Books in the Series

Trial Consulting
Amy J. Posey and Lawrence S. Wrightsman

Death by Design: Capital Punishment as a Social Psychological System
Craig Haney

Psychological Injuries: Forensic Assessment, Treatment, and Law
William J. Koch, Kevin S. Douglas, Tonia L. Nicholls, and Melanie L. O'Neill

Emergency Department Treatment of the Psychiatric Patient:
Policy Issues and Legal Requirements
Susan Stefan

The Psychology of the Supreme Court
Lawrence S. Wrightsman

Proving the Unprovable
Christopher Slobogin

Adolescents, Media, and the Law
Roger J.R. Levesque

Adolescents, Media, and the Law

*What Developmental Science Reveals
and Free Speech Requires*

Roger J.R. Levesque

OXFORD
UNIVERSITY PRESS

2007

OXFORD
UNIVERSITY PRESS

Oxford University Press, Inc., publishes works that further
Oxford University's objective of excellence
in research, scholarship, and education.

Oxford New York
Auckland Cape Town Dar es Salaam Hong Kong Karachi
Kuala Lumpur Madrid Melbourne Mexico City Nairobi
New Delhi Shanghai Taipei Toronto

With offices in
Argentina Austria Brazil Chile Czech Republic France Greece
Guatemala Hungary Italy Japan Poland Portugal Singapore
South Korea Switzerland Thailand Turkey Ukraine Vietnam

Copyright © 2007 by Oxford University Press, Inc.

Published by Oxford University Press, Inc.
198 Madison Avenue, New York, New York 10016

www.oup.com

Oxford is a registered trademark of Oxford University Press

Library of Congress Cataloging-in-Publication Data
Levesque, Roger J.R.
Adolescents, media, and the law : what developmental science reveals
and free speech requires / Roger J.R. Levesque.
p. cm. — (American psychology-law society series)
Includes bibliographical references and index.
ISBN 978-0-19-532044-2
1. Mass media and youth—United States. 2. Teenagers—United States—Attitudes.
3. Mass media—Social aspects—United States. I. Title.
HQ799.2.M35L48 2007
302.230835—dc22   2006038796

9 8 7 6 5 4 3 2 1
Printed in the United States of America
on acid-free paper

For Helen and our children
Emma, William, Thomas, Henry, and Marc

Series Foreword

This book series is sponsored by the American Psychology-Law Society (APLS). APLS is an interdisciplinary organization devoted to scholarship, practice, and public service in psychology and law. Its goals include advancing the contributions of psychology to the understanding of law and legal institutions through basic and applied research; promoting the education of psychologists in matters of law and the education of legal personnel in matters of psychology; and informing the psychological and legal communities and the general public of current research, educational, and service activities in the field of psychology and law. APLS membership includes psychologists from the academic research and clinical practice communities as well as members of the legal community. Research and practice is represented in both the civil and criminal legal arenas. APLS has chosen Oxford University Press as a strategic partner because of its commitment to scholarship, quality, and the international dissemination of ideas. These strengths will help APLS reach its goal of educating the psychology and legal professions and the general public about important developments in psychology and law. The focus of the book series reflects the diversity of the field of psychology and law, as we will publish books on a broad range of topics.

I am pleased to include Roger Levesque's latest book in this series. His focus on the impact of media on adolescents is particularly timely. As he notes in his introductory chapter, today's adolescents are inundated with a wide variety of media, more so than any prior generation. Television, video games, movies, Internet, and MP3 players play an increasing dominant role in the lives of many youth. Unlike prior generations, adolescents are considerably more autonomous, typically interacting with the media with little or no adult supervision.

Media clearly play an important role in shaping adolescent identity, behavior, and health. Levesque's perspective is that the media can have both positive and negative effects on adolescent behavior and he is interested in understanding these effects in the context of adolescent development. He cautions us to not view the relationship of media and adolescent development in a narrow and simplistic manner. Indeed, while he acknowledges that the research on media effects has provided useful information about its impact, he is clear that the research falls short in aiding our understanding of the multiple factors that shape adolescent development. Research tends to focus on simple relationships between the media and a given behavior, such as aggression, ignoring the multidimensional influences on adolescent development.

Professor Levesque notes that the media's impact on prosocial behavior may be more powerful than its negative impact. Unfortunately, a substantial amount of the research focuses on the negative effects. He presents concise, clear summaries of what the research tells us about the impact of the media in four areas: violence, body images, smoking, and sexuality. He identifies gaps in our knowledge and provides directions for future research. He points to many contradictory findings and notes that we have insufficient information about long-term effects. His conclusion that there is evidence of negative effects in each of these areas will not be surprising to most.

This review of research is important in that it supports the conclusion that society should be concerned about the impact of media on adolescent development. It provides the basis for his analysis of how society should respond to this concern. He notes that the dominant response has been censorship to restrict access of adolescents to certain media. Parents are, of course, expected to be the primary mechanism for restricting access. As Levesque points out, this may be viable with young children but generally fails with adolescents. Following a stimulating and thoughtful discussion of free speech rights, he concludes that the current legal approaches to limit adolescent rights also fail to address the concerns, and he concludes that the legal system's adult-centered approach has negatively impacted the constitutional rights of adolescents. Levesque proposes a creative alternative, one that would not restrict adolescent access but rather would foster self-governance and increased civic participation. Rather than focusing on media as a source of negative influence, his approach seeks to promote the development of competency through access to information. His analysis and recommendations will be of interest to adolescents, parents, teachers, school administrators, community leaders, and policy makers, and I expect they will provide the foundation for stimulating and valuable discussion about the role of media in our society.

Ronald Roesch
American Psychology-Law Society

Acknowledgments

In a book I published in this series a few years ago, I thanked the editor, Ronald Roesch, for having provided exceptional editorial comments and having suggested potential areas of research. I need to thank Professor Roesch again, for it was his comments and suggestions that led me to envision this book. I, again, have gained much from his insights and support. His hard work, especially his close editing, certainly has made this book much better (and shorter!) than it would have been if I had worked without his guidance. It has been a real treat to work with someone whose work epitomizes the best of good editing and, more importantly, good role modeling.

Contents

Adolescents, Media, and the Law

1

Introduction
Adolescence and the Media in Changing Times

Adolescents live in a saturated and rapidly changing media environment and are inundated by what our Constitution deems "speech." The emergence and development of new communication technologies deeply infiltrate adolescents' lives. Innovations in media technologies offer a continuous diet of highly vivid, on-demand, and increasingly interactive audiovisual images (R. E. Anderson, 2002). Not surprisingly, today's adolescents spend more time with more media and massive amounts of information than any generation before them. For example, typical junior high students spend more waking hours with media than with anything else: 11- to 14-year-olds dedicate more than 6.5 hours per day to media, and because they use several media simultaneously, they encounter almost 8 hours per day of media content (Roberts & Foehr, 2004). This infusion and its eventual influence on adolescents' lives, of course, grows exponentially when we consider that the media's numerous devices, images, and communications similarly inundate those with whom adolescents interact. Modern information technology offers adolescents not only more speech but also more ways to deliver speech that then becomes part of everyday experiences, fanning the media's impact beyond particular moments of exposure.

Adolescents are more than exposed to the new media and mass information environment—they pay attention to it. Adolescents seek and acquire information through a heady number of different media. More types of new media appear as traditional media evolve. Each medium offers adolescents numerous choices, and different genres allow them to individualize information to accommodate their tastes. Television markets, for example, now include literally hundreds of channels that reach the most isolated locations. Some of those channels now target adolescents, while other channels are targeted by adolescents who seek adult materials (especially those deemed "adolescent"). Although illustrative, the television media now actually constitute a fraction of adolescents' consumed media. The media industry also targets audio and video systems to adolescents, and those increasingly portable and miniaturized technologies allow adolescents to spread media content to the extent that adolescents themselves become a media source. Cell phones, instant messaging, e-mail, and webcams facilitate adolescents' continuous mediated contact with others. Just as technologies allow people to merge and easily exchange information, the technologies themselves also merge. Cell phones have Internet capacities that, like personal computers, serve as gateways to seemingly limitless human information. These new capacities also link to older media, as televisions now link to the Internet. Media of all kinds infuse adolescents' environments with information, both wanted and unwanted.

Technological changes now more easily allow adolescents to interact actively with and create their own media environments, a power fraught with consequences. The flourishing of adolescents' media environments affects the kinds of information available to adolescents, how they interpret that information, and how they integrate information into their belief systems. Interactive media transforms listening and viewing audiences into active participants; video games and even televised broadcasts become interactive as they request adolescents' calls and e-mails. These changes add new dimensions to potential influences; adolescents have always interacted with their informational environments, but those environments now appear much more responsive and appealing to adolescents' desires. These obvious changes gain significance as they highlight transformations in the social context of media use. Adolescents' media use no longer involves a family experience; media exposure and use have become increasingly private activities. It long has been noted that adolescents have access to numerous media technologies in their bedrooms and places outside of adult supervision, but adolescents' private uses of media take on new dimensions as they continue to expand through increasing access to traditional and emerging technologies (Calvert, Jordan, & Cocking, 2002; Roberts & Foehr, 2004). As a result, the increasing number and capacities of media available offer adolescents even more autonomy in their media selection and even more freedom from adult comment about the messages they receive. Like adults, adolescents have become active, increasingly free, and highly individualized receivers of media information. Regrettably, adolescents are not adults, and the new media that foster privatization and individualization of media use also introduce new forces in adolescents' developmental environments that challenge traditional social and legal tendencies to treat adolescents like children.

The Developmental Significance of Changing Media Environments

Important consequences emerge from the manner in which electronic media create information independence through the amounts and kinds of information, ideas, and images made easily available for adolescents. The transforming landscape of media environments yields changes in the development of adolescents' sense of self. We know, for example, that certain types of media content, such as portrayals of violence (Huesmann, Moise-Titus, Podolski, & Eron, 2003), drug use (K. M. Thompson, 2005), and sexuality (J. D. Brown, 2002; Ward, 2003), as well as the media's push toward various forms of consumerism (Chaplin & John, 2005; Gunter, Oates, & Blades, 2005; Valkenburg, 2000), potentially play powerful roles in identity development. Evidence from literally thousands of empirical studies leaves no doubt that information emanating from various media influences adolescents' developing sense of self. Leading media researchers now list mass media as equal in importance to most other socializing agents, including such traditional institutions as parents, schools, and churches (Calvert, 1999; Christenson & Roberts, 1998; Strasburger & Wilson, 2002). The new media even allow adolescents to form multiple and virtual social selves through identity experiments (Valkenburg, Schouten, & Peter, 2005).

The new information independence and its potential relationship to an adolescent's developing sense of self gain significance to the extent that they allow adolescents to shape and accomplish their developmental tasks. Adolescence, for example, represents a shift from immersion in the family to increasing connections with the larger social world, from parent-defined to self-and peer-influenced identity and values. Although adolescents are much more attached to their families than popular images suggest, adolescents experience the developmental task of identity development by negotiating relationships with their outer world as they explore and experience a wide variety of social relationships. Thus, when teens get online, they do so for social functions. They look to spend time talking to people via e-mail, immersing themselves in chat groups, and locating information (Hellenga, 2002). These interactions under such unique social conditions—perceived by adolescents as risk free and experienced relatively anonymously from adults—hold great potential for changing the experience of adolescence. Providing adolescents with opportunities to manage developmental needs certainly constitutes the most significant promise of modern communication systems.

The promise of adolescents' encounters with the new media certainly contributes to considerable hope among professionals committed to adolescents' healthy development. For example, adolescents typically experience difficulties accessing a wide panoply of traditional health services. E-health, the use of technological advances to improve access, quality, safety, and efficiency of healthcare, holds the potential to help fill gaps. The Internet combines positive features of traditional lay and professional, personal and impersonal sources. Although it is unlikely to supplant the role of trusted peers and adults and may not allow access to information as easily as many may have hoped, the Internet already plays an important role in adolescents' repertory of health information sources (Gray, Klein, Noyce, Sesselberg & Cantrill, 2005). Adolescents explore their own values and identities, and they struggle with issues that may not be easily discussed with parents and peers. Although variations in adolescents' access to quality and privacy impact the extent to which the Internet allows for offering mutual support, fostering social networks, and obtaining answers to specific health concerns (Skinner, Biscope, & Poland, 2003), it does seem that the Internet can nurture interactions that contain the key ingredients of successful helping relationships—those that provide information and emotional support for healthy development in relatively safe and anonymous ways.

The promise of new uses for emerging technologies complements well-established research that already documents the media's potential, but often ignored, benefits. For example, a recent review that combined statistical results from numerous studies, a technique known as meta-analysis, examined and compared the magnitude of the effects of watching antisocial and prosocial behaviors (Mares & Woodard, 2005). Analysis of the magnitude of the effects, measured as "effect sizes," indicated that the effect size of prosocial television viewing on prosocial behavior was .63. These are impressive results given that the most widely employed guidelines view an effect size of .10 as small, .30 as medium, and .50 as large (Rosenthal & DiMatteo, 2001). Although impressive in and of itself, the findings were even more impressive when compared to the effect sizes of violent television viewing on antisocial behavior. The prosocial effect size actually was *twice* the size of the effect for antisocial behavior, which was .30, an effect size considered both significant and moderate. Although these figures may not mean much to those unaccustomed to such statistical analyses, these figures are quite impressive. Medical studies, for example, revealed a .03 effect size of aspirin on reducing the risk of heart attacks; these effect sizes were sufficient enough proof for the government to authorize the drug manufacturer to state that aspirin can prevent heart attacks and for the manufacturer to stop the test and provide all participants with aspirin (Rosenthal, 1990). The most recent analyses accumulating current knowledge of media effects, then, point to the conclusion that the media actually can have greater positive effects than negative effects.

The potential harm accruing to adolescents who lack media access also reveals the remarkable extent to which adolescents can benefit from access to modern media. Some of the more pernicious effects of media may befall those who lack access. Leading commentators conclude that the digital divide between relatively wealthy and poor families continues to worsen *both* at school and at home (Attewell, 2001). Indeed, even when computers and rapid home Internet access is provided at no cost for low-income adolescents and their families, we still see little use of the Internet's communication tools, and important ethnic differences still contribute to digital divides (Jackson, et al., 2006). This is not surprising. Like adults, adolescents who lack resources to engage available informational environments (Bucy & Newhagen, 2004), even if they have access to computers at school or at home, run the risk of missing out on the kind of information necessary to function successfully in today's world. This divide certainly has important developmental consequences. Our information society evolves rapidly and inevitably sustains rapid social change that rests on two powerful forces: increased intercultural interaction and an economic system that treats knowledge as a commodity. Together, these transformations have major implications for adolescents' skills, learning strategies, and developing sense of self. The explosion of knowledge means an inability to retain knowledge in fields and a focus on being able to obtain, organize, manage, and critically evaluate information. The expansive, global reach of media technology increasingly requires the ability to operate in a global society, and the ability rests on the inner and social resources available to engage information.

Regrettably, the new information independence in a global information society also makes adolescents subject to encountering the media's risks. Much popular interest centers on the Internet's facilitation of crimes against adolescents. Without doubt, the Internet's connections to others render some adolescents subject to deception, which may lead to victimization online and to aggressive solicitations offline (Finkelhor, Mitchell, & Wolak, 2000). Although the stereotype of Internet crimes centers on unknown adults meeting juvenile victims online, Internet use equally plays a role in crimes against minors by family members and acquaintances. Offenders who commit sex crimes against family members and acquaintances, for example, increasingly use the Internet as a tool to seduce or groom victims; store or disseminate sexual images of victims; arrange meetings, communicate, and reward victims; or advertise or sell victims (Mitchell, Finkelhor, & Wolak, 2005a). In addition, adolescents actually are much more likely to be aggressors of Internet victimizations than they are likely to be targets (Ybarra & Mitchell, 2004). Whether the media simply exacerbate or provide an outlet for adolescents' difficulties remains to be determined. But the new media still figure in the harms that adolescents face.

The new media actually seem to facilitate known forms of harms rather than create new crimes. This rule seems to apply to risks that do not only come from others. As with any activity that may be damaging if excessively exploited, adolescents who spend too much time online run the risks of losing their friends, their mental health, or their social skills, or even of becoming online delinquents. Adolescents' use of Internet chat rooms, for example, associates with psychological distress, a difficult living environment, and a higher likelihood of risky behaviors (Beebe, Asche, Harrison, & Quinlan, 2004). On average, however, boys and girls alike tend to describe their online social interactions as (1) occurring in private settings such as e-mail and instant messages, (2) involving friends who are also part of their daily, offline lives, and (3) devoting themselves to fairly ordinary yet intimate topics (e.g., friends, gossip; Gross, 2004). Despite the belief that the Internet allows for exploring different selves, adolescents who pretend online tend to do so to play jokes on friends rather than to explore a desired or future identity (Gross, 2004). Even cutting-edge media, then, seem simply to extend adolescents' normal interactions and behaviors, which, for some adolescents, may become abnormal.

Although the media may not exacerbate new harms, contributing to existing harms certainly constitutes one of the media's greatest hazards. Longitudinal studies now link even a modest diet of television watching (less than two hours a day) during childhood and adolescence to adverse health indicators that include obesity, poor fitness, smoking, and raised cholesterol levels (Hancox, Milne, &

Poulton, 2004). Numerous studies report negative relationships between media exposure and various measures of adolescents' academic performance for television (Neuman, 1995), music media (Christenson & Roberts, 1998), and for video games and computer games (Leiberman, Chaffee, & Roberts, 1988). Recent reviews also report distinct negative effects of various media on scholastic performance (see Shin, 2004). In addition and despite complaints about television's portrayal of irresponsible behaviors, portrayals of recklessness continue unabated and without consequences, as revealed by research that tracks violence, risky sex, and the use of drugs, alcohol, and tobacco (Will, Porter, Geller, & DePasquale, 2005). The effect of these portrayals goes beyond the obvious. A recent meta-analysis of studies examining adolescents' viewing of violent television found that such viewing had its greatest "antisocial" effect on nonviolent and nonaggressive activities, with the largest effect on the reduction in family discussions, which had an effect size of 2.33, an extremely high effect. This was followed by role stereotyping (.90 effect), less socializing (.75 effect), materialism (.40), and passivity (.36; Mares & Woodard, 2005). There is no paucity of research linking the wide variety of media to an even wider variety of negative effects.

Although voluminous, the research on media effects often is not as conclusive and robust as many would hope. Research still tends to be cross-sectional and correlational, and many studies claiming to be predictive actually fail to use longitudinal data. In addition, research has yet to document effectively the links between aggression and crime, just like other areas of research have yet to link certain media to actual outcomes. This makes it difficult to draw firm conclusions about the factors that are responsible for variations in developmental outcomes and media use. For example, a recent search of published work examining the effects of media violence on children and adolescents revealed five meta-analytic reviews and one quasi-systematic review (Browne & Hamilton-Giachritsis, 2005). The review concluded that evidence consistently shows that violent imagery in television, film, video, and computer games has substantial short-term effects on arousal, thoughts, and emotions—all of which increases the likelihood of aggressive or fearful behavior in younger children, especially in boys. The evidence, however, becomes inconsistent when considering older children and teenagers, and long-term outcomes for all ages. Researchers continue to highlight the multifactorial nature of aggression, the methodological difficulties of showing causation, and the weak evidence from correlational studies linking media violence directly to crime. If these limitations apply to the most studied area of media effects on adolescents, they certainly may well apply to others, including those indicating positive effects. These limitations may not counsel against the utility of such research, but they do reveal the need to place research in appropriate perspective.

More problematic than limitations inherent in existing research, though, are studies that investigate a wide variety of factors and report findings that suggest contradictory implications. For example, a meta-analysis of the effects of sexualized images on aggressive behavior actually found an inverse relationship between portrayals of nudity and aggressive behavior (Allen, D'Alessio, & Bezgel, 1995). The accumulation of experimental results reveals a small, but still significant (−0.14), effect indicating that greater exposure to nudity associates with lower levels of aggressive or antisocial behavior. As expected, analyses of erotica without violence reported higher effects (0.17), and those limited to violent erotica revealed even higher effects (0.22). These studies reveal that evaluations of risk and harm inevitably lead to certain judgments and subjective interpretations that go to the heart of evaluations of the meaningfulness of research findings.

Research limitations and potentially contradictory findings, which are amplified even more if we take (as we do in the next several chapters) a broader look at media effects on adolescent development, complicate efforts to respond to adolescents' media environments. The already impressive volume of research, however, renders it unlikely that more research will lead to dramatically different views about the role the media plays in adolescents' broader informational environments. The major concern involves how to maximize existing media research and developmental understandings to further society's unquestioned need to guide adolescents toward optimal health and responsible citizenship while still respecting adolescents' right to develop their own sense of self.

The Failures and Challenges Facing Social and Policy Responses

Despite the complexity of media effects, both positive and negative, censorship remains the dominant response to shaping adolescents' media environment. We will examine these responses more closely throughout the last three chapters. For now it is important to note that typical responses to dealing with media effects predominantly leave matters to parents, and, if not parents, then to the media industry itself. This essentially means that the legal system directly sets the limit to what should be available for adults (e.g., it would prohibit child pornography and other obscene materials from circulating) and then generally leaves it to parents, those acting as parents, and the media industry itself to limit adolescents' access to what is available in the marketplace. If research reveals anything, it is that these efforts remain far from satisfactory. The pervasiveness of media in adolescents' lives, often including materials meant for mature audiences, serves as a testament to the failed response. Equally indicative of the failed response is the media's role in adolescents' overall informational environments—the manner in which the media influence parents, peers, and social institutions that shape adolescents' views and responses to information. The legal system has yet to respond adequately to these realities.

By far, the most dominant social response to dealing with problematic (and good) media seeks to increase parental involvement in their children's media exposure. Although such responses may work well for young children, they may not work so well with adolescents. The most studied interventions, which actually are surprisingly sparse, examine the benefits of parents' approaches to mediating children's violent television viewing. One recent study examined the effects of factual mediation, which provides children with facts about a violent program's production techniques, and evaluative mediation, which provides negative evaluations of the programs' characters. The findings revealed that evaluative mediation was the most effective strategy for promoting positive outcomes, particularly for younger children (5- to 7-year olds, as opposed to 10- to 12-year olds). Importantly, factual mediation had either no effect or actually increased some children's vulnerability to media violence (Nathanson, 2004). During adolescence, however, parental efforts to mediate the effects of televised violence and sex may well backfire. A survey of both parents and students indicated that restrictive mediation, a mode dominating the adolescent period, related to less positive attitudes toward parents, more positive attitudes toward the content, and more viewing of the content with friends (Nathanson, 2002). Perhaps even more distressing given popular pleas to have parents spend more time with their children's media, coviewing relates to both more positive attitudes toward and viewing of television violence and sex (Nathanson, 2002). Encouraging parents to take part in their adolescents' media, including attempts to control it, remains far from an optimal solution.

Other important lines of research also reveal the limitations of relying on parents' censorship. Studies show that parents may have rules in place that restrict certain television programs and media, but it is unclear whether parents provide the socially acceptable answer, whether adolescents acknowledge the rules, and whether parents consistently enforce them. In addition, parents clearly have tools at their disposal that can limit their children's access to media, such as the V-Chip to block out television programs and filters to block unwanted Internet access. Yet, only a very small percentage of parents install or activate the new devices, with even fewer using blocking devices for television (Jordan, 2004) than the Internet (Mitchell, Finkelhor, & Wolak, 2005b). These findings are not surprising. Parents' technological skills tend to lag behind those of adolescents, and adolescents' media savviness actually increases their role and power in family decision-making processes (Belch, Krentler, & Willis-Flurry, 2005). Even greater use of new blocking devices, though, would not necessarily lead to dramatic reductions in adolescents' access to targeted materials. For example, the use of filtering and blocking software only leads to a modest reduction in unwanted exposure to what parents are most concerned about—sexual materials—and various other forms of parental supervision actually do not associate with any reduction in exposure (Mitchell, Finkelhor, & Wolak, 2003). Further, meta-analyses of experiments testing the effects of ratings on children's interest in programs reveal that ratings indicating restricted or controversial content have a deterrent effect for children under age 8 but that by age 11, and especially for boys, the ratings elicit an enticement effect (Bushman & Cantor, 2003). These striking experimental results reveal a trend that gains considerable support from other types of research. Although studies of the impact of anti-violence media productions do reveal some effectiveness, they also document a prevalence of unanticipated "boomerang" effects (Cantor & Wilson, 2003). Censorship efforts are far from foolproof and may actually result in antithetical effects.

The potential positive and negative risks associated with the media's fostering of information independence takes on even greater urgency as parents can no longer exert as much control over their adolescents' access to media messages. For example, society evinces concern about television violence; and it does seem that controlling violence on television may help limit access to violent media images. But, by the time children reach adolescence, television no longer dominates their media environment and other media offer violent images and potentially problematic information. For example, adolescents are attracted to adult entertainment, and the Internet greatly simplifies access to adult pastimes such as gambling and sexual interaction. But even readily accessible media, like video, computer and Internet games, tend to be dominated by violent content (Gentile & Anderson, 2003). These games have particular appeal to adolescents. For example, video games provide a gratifying context for the experience of emotions. The fact that gamers are largely in control of the game implies that they can voluntarily select the emotional situations they confront. This freedom attracts adolescents who are in the midst of constructing their identities. For them, the violent game provides a safe, private laboratory where they can experience different emotions, including those that are controversial and problematic in ordinary life (Jansz, 2005).

Industry self-regulation, the other dominant approach to dealing with media identified as potentially harmful (Campbell, 1999), has yet to result in the effective curtailment of media exposure to adolescents. The television industry evinces an inability to regulate itself as forcefully as its own standards suggest it should. Sexual content and graphic violence and vulgar language are more prevalent than ever before. Since the enactment of the Communications Act of 1934, the FCC has had the unquestioned authority to license broadcast stations in accordance with the public interest, convenience, and necessity. This has meant that it can control, within important limits, broadcast indecency. Despite this mandate, the FCC has been rather inadequate in overseeing the television industry if we take as evidence, as we will see in chapters 2 and 4, the rise in sexualized and violent content on television. These patterns find parallels throughout the media industry. Most notably, the Federal Trade Commission's report, *Marketing Violent Entertainment to Children: A Fourth Follow-up Review of Industry Practices in the Motion Picture, Music Recording & Electronic Game Industries* (2004), recently revealed illustrative findings. Just under half the movie theaters admitted children ages 13 to 16 to R-rated films even when not accompanied by an adult. The surveys also revealed that unaccompanied children ages 13 to 16 were able to buy both explicit recordings and Mature-rated electronic games 85% of the time. Of the 44 movies rated R for violence the commission selected for its study, the commission found that 80% were targeted to children under 17. Of the 55 music recordings with explicit content labels the commission selected for its review, the commission found that all were targeted to children under 17. Of the 118 electronic games with a Mature rating for violence the commission selected for its study, 70% targeted children under 17. The report concluded that while the entertainment industry has taken important steps to identify content that may be inappropriate for minors, the companies in those industries still routinely target children under 17 in their marketing of products that their own ratings systems deem inappropriate or in need of parental caution due to violent content. These studies are quite significant in and of themselves, but they gain even greater significance given that violent content coincides with other content that would be deemed problematic for young audiences. The media industry markets a continuous diet of problematic materials.

The focus on parents and industry self-regulation may appear odd given the media's potential impact on adolescent development. The accumulation of evidence indicating the media's harmful effects certainly tempts parents, policy makers, and commentators to limit, if not outright ban, adolescents from exposure to adult media deemed problematic. Although appealing and apparently rational, such censorship increasingly results in challenging and fruitless endeavors. We have noted a strong focus on self-regulation. Despite criticisms of such approaches, they actually seem to provide the most viable approach given our current commitment to First Amendment freedoms.

Concerns about sexualized and violent media, two forms of media content receiving considerable empirical attention, certainly lead to numerous legislative hearings, policy statements and calls to action. They also result in surprisingly little legislative action; and action that does end up legislated actually tends to be found unconstitutional. In almost every case involving indecent speech, for example, the courts address the most obvious purpose of attempted restrictions on such speech: the need to protect children. Free speech jurisprudence is peppered with cases that go at great lengths to craft out special constitutional protections for children (see, *New York v. Ferber*, 1982; *Ginsberg v. New York*, 1968). However, concern for shielding minors from indecent speech erodes when it conflicts with adults' speech rights. A long line of cases supports rejecting measures that shield minors from indecent speech if they have a restraining effect on the ability of adults to access such speech (for the leading case, see *Butler v. Michigan*, 1957). Consequently, the child protection interest frequently loses out to the idea that burdens on adults' speech are tantamount to unconstitutional infringements.

Recent cases simply extend prior efforts and provide the media with unprecedented protection from censorship. Whereas the broadcasting and telephone industries undoubtedly have been the target of some important regulatory efforts to suppress indecent speech, there is no doubt that the most prominent and significant attempt in recent years focuses on the relatively new technologies of cable television and the Internet. Because it is older and (for now) more pervasive, cable television particularly has been the target of a number of regulatory initiatives over the past two decades, which have produced two significant Supreme Court cases since the mid-1990s: *Denver Area Educational Telecommunications Consortium v. FCC* (1996) and *United States v. Playboy Entertainment Group* (2000). Both cases limited efforts to control the discretion of the cable industry. Efforts to limit the Internet also generally have been ruled unconstitutional even when done in the name of child protection. Congress, the courts, and commentators have contemplated various ways to address the problem of children's access to sexually explicit materials on the Internet, spanning the spectrum from purely technological solutions to purely legislative regulatory regimes. Most notable, in *Ashcroft v. ACLU* (2004), the Supreme Court assessed and upheld a preliminary injunction against Congress's most recent legislation in this arena, the Child Online Protection Act (COPA) (2000), finding that claims of unconstitutionality are likely to prevail. The doctrines supporting these cases, as we will see in chapters 6 and 7, suggest that reversals are unlikely to come any time soon. The media enjoy increasingly expansive protections as they more deeply infiltrate our lives.

Efforts to control the media industry more directly through litigation also remain pervasively unfruitful. Despite increasing concern about the effects of media violence on child consumers, courts essentially have foreclosed the possibility of media company liability for the violent content of their child-entertainment products. Courts have decided the media-violence causation issue in favor of the media industry, and violent media products have received broad First Amendment protections (for a review of recent cases, see Proman, 2004). As a result, plaintiffs in media-violence suits are nearly foreclosed from presenting a genuine issue of material fact regarding causation because, even if the First Amendment does not bar particular suits, courts have concluded that media violence cannot, under virtually any circumstances, lead directly to violent behavior in children. Therefore, media companies are held to owe no duty to third parties injured by youths under the influence of violent media products. Furthermore, courts find that aggressive behavior after exposure to violent media products is an unforeseeable, superseding intervening cause of injury that cannot point to liability. These legal interpretations result in considerable protection for the media.

The above tensions and failures are obviously problematic for adolescents, families, and broader society. Commentators readily blame the media, families, and adolescents themselves when adolescents do not comport by societal ideals. Yet, the problem runs much deeper. It most fundamentally involves how the legal system, reflecting dominant societal beliefs, approaches adolescents' rights. As with other areas of adolescents' lives, adolescents' inability to reach healthy outcomes has as much to do with the failure to take adolescents' rights seriously as it does with the failures of key socializing institutions. For example, the legal system assumes that parents are the primary sources of sexual guidance for their children and that parents control their children's access to sexual information (Levesque, 2000). Yet, the assumption bears little resemblance to reality. Parents do not necessarily provide timely, clear, or even accurate information. Many parents lack the information and the ability to deliver the information even if they had it. Adolescents actually seem to know more about certain sexual risks and their negative outcomes than their parents do (see American Social Health Association, 1996) and parents pervasively lack the comfort level necessary to communicate about these issues with their children (Brindis, 2002). In addition, parents oftentimes fail to control the information their adolescents receive.

In fact, adolescents generally rank parents behind peers, schools, and popular media as primary sources of information and guidance, and parents increasingly limit their own roles as sexuality educators as their children reach and pass through adolescence (Sutton, Brown, Wilson, & Klein, 2002). Likewise, society charges schools to take the role of parents when parents fail, and the legal system assumes that schools counter parental inadequacies. Again, the legal assumption does not necessarily reflect reality. Schools pervasively fail to develop programs that provide adolescents with accurate information about sex and sexuality; schools do not even do so even when they have the power, ability, and mandate to do so (Levesque, 2003). Despite earlier moves toward comprehensive sexuality education, the last decade has witnessed a marked retrenchment away from a more comprehensive treatment of adolescent sexuality toward a much greater reliance on abstinence (Landry, Kaeser, & Richards, 1999). That movement away from more comprehensive sexuality education programs directly responds to legal mandates and shifting political winds that move in the opposite direction of what the best available evidence suggests would be more effective and would more realistically reflect the sexual lives of most adolescents. The effect of these realities and legal assumptions seems quite dramatic. When parents and schools fail to respond to adolescents' needs, adolescents fail to develop the necessary skills and capacities to engage in the types of relationships that society would accept as responsible (see Levesque, 2002b). Adolescents are not given the necessary information and appropriate guidance about how to mature successfully free from even the negative aspects of sexual activity.

The limitations in institutional efforts to address adolescents' media access, and the potential risks for harm and benefits of accessing massive informational environments, highlights the significance of socializing adolescents in the responsible use of technology and information. This socialization poses unique challenges for the legal system. To what extent should the legal system limit adults' access to media in the name of protecting adolescents? What is the government's role in providing adolescents with access to media? How can the government limit adolescents' media access? To what extent do parents retain the right to control their adolescents' media environments when it seems that they may not be effective gate-keepers? Why provide the media industry wide protection from government regulation? What types of media rights do adolescents possess? Are adolescents' media rights distinguishable from the Constitutions' broader free speech rights? How seriously should we take scientific evidence? Why do regulatory failures increase in the presence of a parallel increase in evidence that the media constitute such a potentially powerful source of harm? How can the legal system engage in harm reduction while still respecting the rights of adolescents, parents, and other adults? How can the legal system foster more proactive approaches to adolescents' media environments? Without doubt, questions continue to mount and make us wonder whether the dominant responses to adolescents' media environments simply rest on inaccurate assumptions and misperceptions that bog down efforts to shape more effectively adolescents' informational environments. Should that be the case, then it remains to be determined what our legal system would look like if it recognized adolescents' peculiar position in society and embraced their developmental needs as the starting point for an adolescent jurisprudence rather than, as we will see is the case in free speech jurisprudence, taking the rights of adults as foundational standards. That is precisely the goal of this text.

The Chapters Ahead

Although the topic of adolescents and media naturally garners much attention, research tends to focus on specific problem areas, such as violence or sexuality, without attempting to understand the confluence of forces that shape adolescents' media environments. The legal system tends to act similarly. Specifically, one can critique much of the research and law in this field for the lack of consideration paid to the contexts of adolescents' lives and their role in shaping adolescents' identities, choices, and world views. Researchers often "control for" these contextual factors rather than embrace them as integral components of their empirical models. As we will see, the legal system tends to do the same as it broadly grants adults the power to control adolescents' media rights and then tries to address particular issues, like violence, sexuality, and drug use, in a piecemeal fashion. These somewhat narrow approaches actually are quite understandable given the complexity of media use and adolescent development. They do, however, complicate our inquiry and require us to go beyond media research and media law—we turn to broader research on adolescent development and First Amendment law. As a result, we must first examine key exemplars of media research relating to adolescent development to identify trends and place that research in the context of adolescent development. Then we examine free speech rights of both adults and adolescents, an examination that leads us to explore what the developmental sciences tell us about how individuals develop in ways that further these rationales for our society's firm commitment to free speech rights. We do so to begin envisioning the factors that would contribute to an adolescent jurisprudence that recognizes and responds to adolescents' needs as well as those of their families and modern civil society envisioned by our Constitution.

Part I begins the empirical exploration. Given the nature of existing research, the analysis necessarily focuses on content deemed problematic. Thus, chapters 2 through 5 focus on research relating to violence, sexuality, smoking, and body image. These factors were chosen simply because they are the most frequently examined areas of media research dealing with adolescent development. The exemplars of media research also were chosen because the issues they address are, not surprisingly, of great concern to society and of considerable interest to adolescents themselves. In addition to examining trends in relevant media research findings, we place those findings in the context of adolescent development and of the media's potential role in responding more effectively to concerns. Where research allows us to do so, we seek to place the media's role within adolescents' broader informational environments. As we will see, each major area of media research has important strengths and weaknesses, and those qualities help shed light on research gaps and provide us with strong indicators of the nature of the media's role in adolescents' overall informational environments. Together, the chapters serve as a necessary and appropriate springboard for re-examining the legal regulation of adolescents' informational environments. They provide a representative analysis of what we know, don't know, and should know about the place of the media in adolescents' marketplace of ideas.

Part II turns our analyses to the law. We begin, in chapter 6, by examining how the law regulates everyone's speech, speech for adults as well as for adolescents. Those analyses reveal an expanding protection of free speech rights, much of which directly involves media and informational environments. After detailing the rationales for protecting speech, we examine the key limits the Constitution places on speech. The limits are important to consider given that they provide the ultimate standard on which to judge everyone's free speech. Importantly, chapter 6 continues and examines often ignored aspects of free speech jurisprudence, such as the right to information. Chapter 7 moves the analysis directly to the regulation of adolescents' media environments. We find surprisingly few regulations. We do find, however, a general rule that bestows considerable control of adolescents' rights to media on parents and those acting as parents; we also find what we will call "harmful to minors laws." Given the limited development of adolescents' media rights, we necessarily turn and take a broader look at adolescents' free speech rights. Although the analysis may seem tangential, this broader view and understanding of adolescents' rights is necessary if we are to address adolescents' media environments in a more comprehensive fashion. The analysis situates the media in their proper place, as part of adolescents' broader informational environments structured by families, peers, schools and other socializing institutions. As a result, we look at adolescents' freedom of expression and right to information as highlighted by leading areas of Supreme Court jurisprudence.

Chapter 8 concludes our analyses by examining the implications of social science findings and free speech jurisprudence for the development of a First Amendment jurisprudence for adolescents. The discussion reframes the current piecemeal approaches to adolescents' media and free speech rights, which tend to compare adolescents to adults. Rather than offering adults' experiences as the benchmark from which to determine whether the legal system should recognize and respect adolescents' rights, the analyses look at the constitutional principles that govern free speech rights to develop principles that would foster the development of legal rules that remain faithful to the Constitution's plain dictate that everyone deserves its protections. To do so, we begin by accounting for the need and failure to consider the changing role of adolescents' informational environments. We then reexamine the traditionally accepted free speech principles guiding First Amendment jurisprudence—engaging markets of ideas, fostering civic engagement, and nurturing self-fulfillment—in light of what they mean for adolescents and their development. We end by enumerating principles that would allow for reaching fidelity to free speech principles guiding the Constitution's approach to informational environments. The analysis emphasizes how responses affirming adolescents' rights still further the deep, historically tested rationales for regulating adolescents' development and environments. Those important commitments, it is argued, need not detract from reform efforts that would prepare both adolescents and their social environment for an increasingly changing and challenging world.

Part I

THE DEVELOPMENTAL SCIENCE OF MEDIA
EFFECTS: EXEMPLARS OF RESEARCH

2

Adolescent Aggression and the Media

Over the past forty years, researchers in the fields of psychology and broadcasting have produced an impressive amount of empirical literature investigating the influence of media exposure on aggressive and violent tendencies. These researchers typically conclude that exposure to media violence, especially violent television and even sometimes simply television, associates with aggression (Gentile, 2003). The vast majority of these researchers also find that media violence plays a causal role in fostering aggression (see Bushman & Anderson, 2001). Despite some criticisms that the research does not support alleged causal claims (Ferguson, 2002; J. L. Freedman, 2002; Fowles, 1999), it seems increasingly clear that the media can powerfully influence adolescents' aggression, violence, and even criminal behavior.

Researchers present a remarkably consistent, yet highly nuanced, empirical picture. Most notable, their research tends to show that media effects are subtle and cumulative, rather than obvious and direct; for example, the effects can be short term but are likely to be long term (Bushman & Anderson, 2001). Research also indicates that media effects tend to result in minor rather than severe behavior; for example, violence in the media most likely contributes more to disrespectful and aggressive behavior than to murder (Potter, 1999; Kuntsche, 2004), an unsurprising finding given the low base rates (occurrence) of severe behaviors. Studies further reveal that media effects influence viewers in different rather than identical ways: the media influence one's environment, which in turn, influences individuals who also influence their environments (Bandura, 1994, 2001). Thus, the media have predictable and general effects, and different forms of media can increase the likelihood of aggressive or violent behavior without being the necessary, sufficient, most recent, or primary cause of aggressiveness or violence. A look at empirical studies reveals that researchers know these limitations quite well as they offer very carefully worded conclusions (e.g., C. A. Anderson & Bushman, 2002).

Carefully chosen conclusions are necessary given our understanding of adolescent aggression and violence and the emerging belief that the media play an often subtle role in adolescent development. These behaviors emerge from many sources, and the media figure prominently in discussions of their broadest causes. For example, researchers have identified key factors that increase children's and teens' risk for becoming involved in serious violence during the teenage years (United States Department of Health and Human Services [USDHHS], 2001c). For children under 13, the most important factors include early involvement in serious criminal behavior, early substance use, being male, a history of physical aggression toward others, low parent education levels or poverty, and parent involvement in illegal activities. Once a child becomes a teenager, different factors predict involvement in serious violence. Friends and peers are much more important predictors for teens, as are friendships with antisocial or delinquent peers, membership in a gang, and involvement in other criminal activity. Typically, the more risk factors that are present, the greater a child's or teen's likelihood of becoming involved in serious violence. Researchers also have begun to identify protective factors, such as a commitment to school and a negative attitude toward criminal behavior, that may shield children and teens, even in the presence of a number of risk factors. These risk and protective factors have yet to be examined as systematically with more general forms of aggression, such as bullying and victimization, that may seem less visible but still exert significant harmful effects on adolescents' lives (see Olson, 2004). Researchers point to the balancing of risk and protective factors to explain aggressive and violent tendencies (Corrado, Roesch, Hart, & Gierowski, 2002). As we will see, it is in the balancing that the media seem to occupy an important role. This is not to argue that some media may not have direct, immediate effects; media pose greater risks for some than for others. But, researchers now emphasize that the developmental influence of the media derives from the manner in which they operate as a broad socializing force that shapes risk and protective factors, more than as a direct contributor to violence.

Unlike researchers, commentators frequently ignore or play down the complexities of the media's influence on adolescents' aggressive behavior. For example, popular press and policy calls for action tend to overstate findings on relationships between media violence and violent criminal behavior (see Savage, 2004), when we know that important differences exist between broad concepts like aggression, violence, and crime. Importantly and to counter criticisms, professional groups' position statements on the effect of media violence often allow important wiggle room, as evidenced by the most recent joint statement by six leading professional organizations that focus on public health issues: the American Psychological Association, the American Academy of Pediatrics, the American Academy of Family Physicians, the American Psychiatric Association, the American Medical Association, and the American Academy of Child and Adolescent Psychiatry. These influential public health organizations signed a joint statement attesting to the dangers of media violence: "At this time, well over 1,000 studies . . . point overwhelmingly to a causal connection between media violence and aggressive behavior in some children" (American Academy of Pediatrics, 2000, p. 1). The health groups' overall message is causal. But the carefully phrased and qualified language acceptable to social scientists, such as the inclusion of "some," considerably limits the claim. Although calls often muffle forceful language, they (quite appropriately) evoke considerable interest in the place of media violence in adolescent development. As a result, the media's actual role may be misunderstood, but the media now occupy an important role in efforts to identify the causes of aggression and prevent its consequences.

Few doubt that the rising interest in the media's influence on adolescent aggression and violence is well placed. Adolescents commit considerable violence. Yearly, about one in nine murders are committed by youth under 18. On average, about five youths are arrested for murder in this country each day (a total of 1,176 in 1999; Fox & Zawitz, 2001). Adolescents also are victims of violence from a wide variety of sources. Murder is the second leading cause of death for this age group. In 2002, there were over 2000 homicides among youth aged 10–19. The focus on murder should not detract from other ways youth engage in violence. Youth under 18 accounted for about one in six violent crime arrests in 1999 (Snyder, 2000). Leading national surveys reveal that for every teen arrested, at least ten have engaged in violence that could have seriously injured or killed another person (USDHHS, 2001c). Reviews of surveys reveal that between 30–40% of male teens and 16–32% of female teens report they have committed a serious violent offense by the age of 17 (USDHHS, 2001c). One in five victims of serious violent crime is between the ages of 12 and 17 (Snyder & Sickmund, 1999). Youth aged 12–17 are three times as likely as adults to be victims of simple assault and twice as likely to be victims of serious violent crimes (USDHHS, 2001c). About one in twenty high school seniors reveals that they have been injured with a weapon in the past year, and almost one in seven reports that someone has injured them on purpose without a weapon (Institute for Social Research, University of Michigan, 1999).

Adolescents also are perpetrators and victims of aggression, much of which could be viewed as violent. Aggression encompasses a wide range of activities, including bullying, threatening remarks, physical fights, assaults with or without weapons, and suicide. For example, suicide remains the third leading cause of death among teenagers—over 1,500 teens kill themselves each year (Centers for Disease Control and Prevention, 2005a). More than one in three high school students report that they have been in a physical fight in the past year, and about one in nine of those students required medical attention for their injuries (Institute for Social Research, University of Michigan, 1999). More than one in six sixth to tenth graders reveal that they are bullied sometimes, and more than one in twelve disclose that they are bullied once a week or more (Nansel et al. 2001). These forms of aggression may not count as the violence found in reports of adolescent violence, but they are of significance to adolescents' daily lives and often go unnoticed. Much violence and aggression remains unreported or simply accepted as part of normal adolescent development (Levesque, 2002b).

The wide attention paid to media violence in politics, popular press, and empirical studies, coupled by the significance of aggression and violence in the lives of adolescents, renders this area of research essential to understanding the media's role in adolescent development and its consequences. Understanding how to respond to media violence and its effects requires a close look at the strengths and weaknesses of the empirical literature and an effort to integrate that literature with possible responses. To do so, this chapter explores the nature of media violence and its particular influence on adolescents and their development. That review reveals the immense power the media potentially play in adolescent development, including the power not only to shape aggressive and violent dispositions but also to address violence and foster nonviolent relationships. To introduce the media's socializing force, this chapter also pays attention to factors that moderate and mediate media effects, although research only recently has turned to these considerations. That is, we consider the factors that shape how the media influence adolescents, since the media do not act alone. Together, findings reveal the need to reconsider how best to prepare adolescents to respond to violent media.

Media's Violent Images

Researchers have produced numerous comprehensive reports on the nature of the media's violent images. Over the last three decades, the most systematic research examining the amount of violence in various media has centered on television violence (see Potter, 1999). The National Television Violence Study (NTVS; Wilson et al., 1997; Wilson et al., 1998), for example, included all program genres except news programming from twenty-three broadcast and cable channels over a 20-week period ranging from October to June during 1994 through 1997. The massive study reported percentages of the main types of violent content as a function of program genre and contextual variables. The survey rated the violent content variables according to three levels of analysis: the program, the scene, and the violent interaction. Given their comprehensiveness and level of details, these are rather impressive studies.

The NTVS study found that 61% of programs on television contain some violence, with movie (89%), drama (75%), and children's television (67%) containing the programs with the highest percentages of violence (Wilson et al., 1998). Thirty-two percent of all television genres contained excessive violence, which was defined as nine or more acts of violence in a given program, with movies (59%), dramas (40%), and children's television (31%) containing the most. The NTVS also revealed much about the nature of televised violence, with much of the aggression appearing as glamorized, trivialized, and sanitized. For example, 44% of the interactions involved perpetrators who have attractive qualities worth emulating. Approximately 40% of violent programs contain humor, either in the form of humor used by characters involved in the violence or humor directed at the violence. Approximately 45% of all programs containing violence feature no immediate punishment or condemnation for the violence; about 84% reveal no long-term consequences. Almost 45% of all programs present characters that are never or rarely punished for their aggressive actions. Violence also is sanitized. Only 16% of violent programs depict the long-term, realistic consequences of violence; of all violent scenes, 86% feature no blood or gore.

More recently developed forms of entertainment media for youth can be even more graphic and violent than what appears on television. This seems particularly true of video games. A recent study, for example, analyzed the violent content of sixty of the most popular video games from three gaming systems: Nintendo 64, Sega DreamCast, and Sony PlayStation (Smith, 2003). Adapting the coding scheme from the NTVS, the study showed that mature-audience games are more likely to feature violence than are those rated for general audiences and that, when compared to general audience games, mature-audience games are more likely not only to feature child perpetrators but also to justify acts of repeated and graphic gun violence. These types of studies gain significance to the extent that they underestimate exposure to violence and aggression given that the majority of the most popular games are extremely violent in nature: they involve brutal mass killings as the primary strategy for winning games and contain extremely gory graphics (e.g., C. A. Anderson & Bushman, 2001; Bartholow & Anderson, 2002; Funk et al., 1999). By the mid 1990s, for example, only 10% of video games available for the home market were identified as violent in nature, but the violent games—particularly *Mortal Kombat* and *Street Fighter II* —overwhelmingly dominated the market (Kent, 2001).

Music videos, an important part of adolescents' media experiences, also contain considerable violence. The literature, however, offers some discrepancies as to the amount of violence contained in music videos. For example, some reports indicate that, overall, about 15% of the videos on popular cable music channels (e.g., MTV, VH-1, BET) contain violence (e.g., Durant, Rich et al., 1997; Smith & Boyson, 2002). On the other hand, findings from the NTVS indicated that 53% of music videos contained violent scenes (Wilson et al., 1997; Wilson et al., 1998). This apparent discrepancy could be a function of different methods of coding what constitutes violence and differences in the examined music genres. For example, whereas nearly a third of rap and heavy metal music videos contain violence, less than 10% of adult contemporary and rhythm and blues videos do (Strasburger & Wilson, 2002). Despite wide variations in estimates of violence depicted in music videos, violence actually does appear quite frequently even if we only take the lowest estimates.

In considering exposure to violence, it is important to recognize adolescents' viewing patterns. As we already have seen, violence does not reach everyone equally, and adolescents differentially seek out different media with different levels of violence. Violence on television is illustrative. One large study examined high school students' exposure to television programming with aggressive content and explored whether consumption of aggressive television varied by sex and ethnicity (Yoon & Somers, 2003). Definitions of both direct and indirect aggression were used to rate television programs, and the participants' exposure to both was assessed. In this regard, note that indirect aggression involves aggression where the intent can be hidden, harm is inflicted circuitously, and the perpetrator is left undetected by the victim; examples include socially ostracizing behaviors such as leaving the victim out of activities, refusing to talk to them, and gossiping about them behind their back. The researchers found that everyone was highly exposed to violence, although girls watched more television programs containing indirect aggression. The study also noted the important finding that exposure to aggressive television content peaked in grade ten and fell sharply thereafter. These findings highlight the important consideration that early and mid-adolescence constitutes an important developmental stage to consider and that all youth are exposed to the media's aggressive images. These findings also reveal the challenges faced by efforts to understand the effects of media portrayals of violence.

Effects of Media Portrayals of Violence

Researchers use several methodologies to study the effects of media violence on aggression and violence. Each approach has its strengths and limitations, and no single approach provides definite answers to complex problems. Taken together, however, the different methodologies suggest important conclusions about the influence of media violence on adolescent behavior. By using each method as a framework, this section sketches the nature of available evidence examining the effects of media violence.

Experimental Studies

Experimental studies randomly assign participants either to receive a treatment (e.g., play a violent video game) or to serve in a control group (e.g., play an exciting, but not violent, video game). Media research often involves experiments in a laboratory, although some experiments are held in more naturalistic field settings. This method arguably offers the best way to establish cause-and-effect relationships given that researchers may manipulate variables of interest while holding all other variables constant. This method, however, tends to permit only a focus on minor physical aggression, verbal aggression, aggressive emotions, and aggressive thoughts, rather than long-term behavior and violence or even criminal behavior. Yet, the numerous laboratory and field experiments that have examined the effect of exposure to violent behavior provide generally unambiguous examinations between media violence and aggression, and they pervasively report positive links. Studies generally conclude that media violence can foster aggressive thoughts and actions, and these may contribute to violence. Equally importantly, experimental studies provide us with nuanced findings that help us understand broad claims about media-violence effects.

Numerous important findings emerge from laboratory and field experimental studies. In laboratory settings, children (both boys and girls) exposed to violent behavior on film or television behave more aggressively immediately afterward. The typical research paradigm involves randomly selected participants who are shown either a violent or nonviolent short film and are observed afterward as they interact with each other. This paradigm was used in the now classic studies that showed children different films and examined how they would respond to a Bobo doll (an inflated punching bag). Those studies revealed that viewing violence can cause short-term aggressive behavior in some children (Bandura, 1965). The studies concluded that participants who view the violent film clips consistently tend to behave more aggressively toward each other or toward surrogate objects. In these settings, exposure to violent film scenes clearly causes some children to engage in more aggressive behavior.

Numerous studies since the classic studies have revealed that viewing violence in the media can influence an individual's subsequent aggression, and some now examine how media violence may even effect indirect aggression. One recent study, for example, examined the immediate effect of viewing indirect and direct aggression on subsequent indirect aggression among 199 children who ranged from 11 to 14 years of age (Coyne, Archer, & Eslea, 2004). This study showed participants an indirect-, direct-, or no-aggression video and measured their subsequent indirect aggression by negative evaluation of a confederate and responses to a vignette. Participants viewing indirect or direct aggression provided a more negative evaluation of and gave less money to a confederate than participants viewing no aggression. Participants viewing indirect aggression gave less money to the confederate than those viewing direct aggression. Participants viewing indirect aggression gave more indirectly aggressive responses to an ambiguous situation, and participants viewing direct aggression gave more directly aggressive responses. Experimental studies like these reveal that even viewing indirect aggression in the media can produce an immediate impact on subsequent aggression.

Evidence from field studies also clearly indicates that the amount of television and film violence a child regularly watches positively relates to the child's aggressiveness. Several experiments have shown that emotionally or physically excited viewers are especially apt to be stimulated aggressively by violent scenes (for a review, see Berkowitz, 1993). Evidence also suggests that youth who are predisposed to be aggressive and who recently have been aroused or provoked are somewhat more susceptible to these effects than others. Aggressive boys who view violent films act more aggressively than nonaggressive boys who view the same violent film (see, e.g., Josephson, 1987). Importantly, the increased effects due to predispositions do not mean that those who are less predisposed are immune from media influences. Youth who watch more violence on television and in the movies behave more violently and express beliefs more accepting of aggressive behavior. Further support for the finding that no group is immune comes from research indicating that simply thinking about violent words in-

creases the risk for physical aggression against others (Carver, Ganellen, Froming, & Chambers, 1983). Findings like these lead researchers to conclude that
violent media places individuals at higher risk of violence to the extent that the
risk of physically aggressive behavior against other people increases among those
who hold aggressive thoughts and that violent media also has immediate effects
on aggressive thoughts or emotions (Bushman & Anderson, 2001).

Although much research focuses on children and early adolescents, randomized experiments also reveal that exposure to media violence can cause
immediate increases in aggressive thought and tolerance for aggression in late
adolescence. Now-classic studies have shown that college students who have
watched violent sex scenes report an increased acceptance of physical aggression toward women (Malamuth & Check, 1981). More recently, college students
randomly assigned to view short violent film segments display more aggressive
thoughts (Bushman, 1998) or more aggressive emotions (C. A. Anderson, 1997).
Both college-aged males and females who view a series of violent films exhibit
significantly more hostility than others who view nonviolent films (Zillmann &
Weaver, 1999), findings that are important given that feelings of hostility predispose individuals to behave aggressively or violently because they are more
inclined to interpret ambiguous interactions as hostile encounters and respond
accordingly (cf, Zillmann, 1979). Similarly, exposure to media violence can lead
to physical assaults by teenage boys, at least in the short run. Studies supporting this view actually involved delinquent boys in out-of-home care who were
differently exposed to violent or nonviolent films; as expected, those exposed to
violent films engaged in significantly more physical assaults (Parke, Berkowitz,
Leyens, West, & Sebastian, 1977). These latter studies remain rather impressive
in that they revealed how violent movies can generate serious physical aggression even in settings that have officially prescribed rules against disruptive behavior. These studies also reinforce those that highlighted the important role of
predispositions.

Several important studies have examined how music videos affect adolescents' aggressive thinking and attitudes. Experimental studies with adolescents, for example, reveal that merely viewing nonviolent rap music videos with
sexually subordinate images of women significantly increases adolescent girls'
acceptance of teen dating violence when compared with adolescents who are
not exposed to the music videos (Johnson, Adams, Ashburn, & Reed, 1995).
Similarly, exposing males to nonerotic violent music videos leads to a significant increase in adversarial sexual beliefs and negative affect (Peterson & Pfost,
1989), and exposure to music videos that display stereotypic sex role behavior
renders students more likely to accept such behavior (Hansen, 1989). Exposure
to violent rap music videos increases the endorsement of violent behavior in response to hypothetical conflict situations (Johnson, Jackson, & Gatto, 1995). Not
surprisingly, college students who are shown rock music videos with antisocial
themes report a greater acceptance of antisocial behavior when compared with
students who are not shown antisocial rock music videos (Hansen & Hansen,
1990). These findings parallel recent studies that reveal how songs with violent

lyrics increase aggressive thoughts and affect behavior. For example, rap music that includes misogynistic lyrics associates with aggression toward women in the laboratory (Barongan & Nagayama Hall, 1995). Such findings are rather impressive and challenging to obtain given that some song genres have nearly incomprehensible lyrics to those who are unfamiliar with them (C. A. Anderson, Carnagey, & Eubanks, 2003). Experimental studies reveal, then, that watching violent videos and listening to aggressive music creates attitudes and beliefs that are accepting of violence, at least in the short term.

Important meta-analyses now confirm and demonstrate the robustness of experimental results examining relationships between the observation of dramatic television or film violence and the commission of aggressive behavior. Recall that a meta-analysis provides a quantitative review of relevant research on a given topic in a way that summarizes the results from several separate studies. The statistical technique allows for combining individual studies to yield a picture of the overall pattern across different investigations. The analyses result in numerical estimates of the size of an effect across all the studies taken together. As expected, several meta-analyses now have computed the effect sizes for randomized experiments investigating the influence of television and film violence on aggression. One of the most highly cited studies reported moderate to large average effect sizes (Paik & Comstock, 1994). Notably, the effect sizes were larger for laboratory studies (.87) than for field studies (.62), for time-series studies (.39), or for surveys (.38). The results held for individuals of all ages, but were greater for preschool children and college students than for older children, adolescents, and adults. Also importantly, the effect size was greater for cartoons than for other forms of violence, and greater for programs involving erotica alone and those combining erotica and violence than for those involving violence alone. The study concluded that effect sizes are smaller for more serious outcomes than for less serious outcomes. Interestingly, new studies tend to find higher effect sizes. A more recent, large-scale analysis reports a steady increase in the effect between media violence and aggressive behavior (Bushman & Anderson, 2001).

Randomized experiments examining the effects of video games reveal findings similar to those obtained in investigations of television and movie violence. For example, college students who have played a violent video game subsequently deliver more than 2.5 times as many high-intensity punishments as those who played a nonviolent video game, a finding significant for both men and women (Bartholow & Anderson, 2002). Similarly, research has long indicated that participants who play violent video games generate more aggressive thoughts (Calvert & Tan, 1994). The finding has been replicated to include a wide range of ways to index aggressive thinking, ranging from time taken to read aggressive and nonaggressive words to profiling hostile explanations for hypothetical unpleasant interpersonal events (Kirsh, 1998; C. A. Anderson & Dill, 2000; Bushman & Anderson, 2002). These findings are supported by research assessing physical aggression between boys who have played either a violent or a nonviolent video game and finding that those who play the violent video game are more physically aggressive across several measures of physical aggression (Irwin & Gross, 1995). These are rather impressive results that take on even greater significance from recent experiments that seek to separate out violent content from other arousal or affective properties of video games, such as levels of frustration, difficulty, and enjoyment. Those experiments demonstrate that the effects of violent video games on aggression are independent of the games' effects on arousal or affect (C. A. Anderson et al., 2004).

The above findings reveal research trends found in a meta-analysis of existing empirical research on the effects of violent video games. That analysis found that the effect of violent video games on aggression positively associates with type of game violence and negatively relates to time spent playing the games (Sherry, 2001). Although the meta-analyses revealed that the video-game effects are smaller than those that have been found with television violence on aggression, the results gain increasing significance. These meta-analytic results firmly suggest significant links between repeated exposure to violent video games with aggressive and violent behavior in the real world. Meta-analyses of violent video game effects support the conclusion that exposure to violent video games increases the likelihood of engaging in aggression. The most recent meta-analysis culled experimental, field, and cross-sectional studies and found that exposure relates to significant increases in aggressive behavior, aggressive affect, aggressive cognitions, and physiological arousal (C. A. Anderson et al., 2004). Results also indicated that video exposure significantly relates to decreases in prosocial, helping behavior.

The meta-analytic findings gain considerable significance given the increasing time adolescents spend playing video games, the high rates of violence in video games, and users' active participation. Recent research reveals the depth of the effect and its close association with aggression. For example, laboratory experiments with college students who play the violent video game *Doom* find that those students associate themselves with aggressive traits and actions (Uhlmann & Swanson, 2004). Self-reported prior exposure to violent video games predicts automatic aggressive self-concept, above and beyond self-reported aggression, suggesting that playing violent video games can lead to the automatic learning of aggressive self-views (Uhlmann & Swanson, 2004). These findings gain support from other experimental studies indicating that prior video game use and violent video game exposure promote hostile thoughts (Tamborini et al., 2004). Together, these studies certainly point to the need to consider the role video games and similar media can play in fostering aggressive behavior.

Correlational Studies

Correlational studies provide a one-point-in-time snapshot of the relation between individuals' consumption of media violence and their aggressive behavior. Unlike experimental studies, these studies tend to include measures of more serious forms of physical aggression. Regrettably, correlational studies tend not to be as conclusive as experimental studies because they can only conclude that the amount of television and film violence that adolescents regularly watch correlates with their current physical aggression, verbal aggression, and aggressive thoughts. As a result, these studies do not indicate whether media violence causes aggression, whether aggressive adolescents are attracted to media violence, or whether some other factors predispose the same adolescents to both watch more violence and behave more aggressively than their peers. Despite these limitations, correlational studies do complement experimental and other more conclusive types of research. These studies' samples typically are more representative and their results reflect more natural, real-world behaviors. Despite the focus on merely stating relationships and not excluding potentially confounding factors, this approach often leads to rather impressive findings. This different methodological approach actually produces many of the same patterns that have been produced in laboratory experiments.

Correlational research reveals links between viewing violent media and adolescents' aggressive behavior, including physically aggressive acts serious enough to be considered violent. For example, early research reported significant correlations for over 2000 male and female high school and junior high school students who viewed television violence; these students' four favorite television programs correlated .11 with their aggressiveness and .16 with their more serious aggressive delinquency (McIntyre & Teevan, 1972). Similarly, another important study reported correlations between television violence viewing and aggression of .32 for seventh- and tenth-grade boys and .30 for girls of the same age, a study that included correlations with fighting and hitting and other measures of aggressive behavioral delinquency (McLeod, Atkin, & Chaffee, 1972). Yet another early study of 12- to 17-year-old males reported 49% more violent actions in the past six months by heavy television violence viewers than by light violence viewers (Belson, 1978). These studies, and many more since them, conclude that a positive correlation exists between viewing violence on television and aggressive behavior. Together, however, the studies suggest that correlations tend to be higher for elementary school children than for teenagers and adults, and this remains especially the case when research assesses general aggression (see C. A. Anderson et al., 2003).

Correlational studies have yet to report systematically the effects of exposure to violent music videos or music lyrics on aggressive behavior. Existing research, however, does suggest links. For example, children who watch more MTV than do their peers tend to be involved in more physical fights when they are in the third through fifth grades; they also tend to be rated by peers and teachers as more verbally aggressive, more relationally aggressive, and more physically aggressive than other children (Roberts, Chirstenson, & Gentile, 2003). Similarly, the music adolescents listen to relates to their maladaptive behaviors. Most notably, students who prefer rap and heavy metal music report more hostile attitudes than students who favor other music genres (Rubin, West, & Mitchell, 2001), and preference for rap and heavy metal links to behavioral problems in school, drug use, arrests, and sexual activity (Took & Weiss, 1994). Correlational studies do reveal that links exist between violent music videos and maladaptive attitudes, such as the acceptance of violence, although these studies do not present direct evidence to explain those connections.

Correlational surveys that measure associations between time spent playing violent video games and aggression report significant relationships. Eighth and ninth graders who expose themselves to greater amounts of video game violence are more hostile, report getting into arguments with teachers more frequently, and are more likely to be involved in physical fights (Gentile, Lynch, Linder, & Walsh, 2004). College students' self-reports of acts of aggressive delinquent behavior within the past year correlate with measures of recent exposure to violent video games (C. A. Anderson & Dill, 2000). Importantly, the magnitude of such relationships sinks but remains significant when analyses control for antisocial personality, gender, and time spent playing any type of video game.

Correlational research also has begun to examine both video game playing and television use. For example, a national representative sample of 4,222 adolescents answered questions on the frequency of television viewing, electronic game playing, feeling unsafe at school, bullying others, hitting others, and fighting with others (Kuntsche, 2004). For the total sample, all bivariate relationships between television viewing or electronic game playing and each violence-related variable were significant. With the exception of excessive electronic game playing among girls, the study found that electronic media are thought to lead not directly to real-life violence but to hostility and indirect violence.

Comprehensive meta-analyses of correlational studies, the most recent of which is over ten years old, reveal that viewing television positively and significantly correlates with aggressive behavior (Paik & Comstock, 1994). Meta-analyses also have examined the impact of viewing on actual physical aggression against another person. The effect size for these studies, which included 200 tests of hypotheses, were essentially the same for these studies as for all surveys combined: $r = .20$ (with r of .19 for all studies), a size considered significant and moderate. Together, these studies present rather compelling evidence that frequent viewing of violence in the media associates with comparatively high levels of aggressive behavior.

Longitudinal Studies

Longitudinal studies help us determine how adolescents' habitual consumption of violence influences their violent and aggressive behavior later in life. As such, this method can test the plausibility of long-term predisposing effects between media violence viewing and aggression more directly than correlational studies and can help determine whether experimental studies generalize to the real world. Although longitudinal nonexperimental data do not provide a strong test of causation, they can help compare the relative plausibility of alternative causal perspectives. Several different groups of investigators have conducted studies on different samples of children and teens, and their investigations report strong connections between early exposure to media violence and subsequent aggressive behavior. Together, longitudinal studies highlight the media's impact on physical aggression and provide some of the most powerful evidence indicating that the media impacts adolescents.

In what leading researchers deem the first longitudinal study in this area, initiated in 1960 with 856 youth, researchers found that boys' early childhood viewing of violence on television statistically related to their aggressive and antisocial behavior 10 years later, after they had graduated from high school (Eron, Huesmann, Lefkowitz, & Walder, 1972). The results are impressive in that the relationship remained significant even after the authors controlled for initial aggressiveness, social class, IQ, parents' aggressiveness, parents' nurturance and punishment, and other relevant variables (Lefkowitz, Eron, Walder, & Huesmann, 1977). Importantly, aggressiveness at age 8 did not predict viewing violence at age 18, a finding indicating that the effects of violent viewing do not seem to be a consequence of highly aggressive youth liking to watch more violence than their less aggressive counterparts. Also important, the overall links were significant only for boys; the findings reveal no relations between exposure to television violence and aggressive girl's aggressive behavior.

A second groundbreaking longitudinal study of children in five countries examined representative samples of children who grew from 7 to 8 or from 8 to 11 years of age (Huesmann & Eron, 1986; Huesmann, Lagerspetz, & Eron, 1984; Huesmann et al., 2003). The 3-year study revealed that the television viewing habits of children as young as first graders predicted subsequent childhood aggression, and the prediction remained even after controlling for initial levels of aggression. In contrast to the earlier longitudinal study, this effect was obtained for both boys and girls. Despite overall effects, considerable differences were found among the countries and between boys and girls in them. Effects were found even in countries without large amounts of violent programming, such as Israel, Finland, and Poland (Huesmann & Eron, 1986). Although the synchronous correlations were positive in all countries, the longitudinal effect of violence viewing on aggression was not significant for girls in Finland or for all children in the Netherlands. Similarly, in the United States, significance was reached only for girls, while the opposite was true for Poland. In Israel, there were significant effects for children living in a city but not for children raised on a kibbutz. As a result, these findings reveal some relationships between violent television viewing and aggression, but that relationship appears erratic and moderate, and that relationship clearly does not appear causal for all viewers (for a review of these studies, see Moeller, 2001).

The lack of support for causal relationships in the cross-national studies reveals the importance of examining factors that may influence the relationship between media exposure and aggressive behavior. We will return to identifying important factors below, but for now note several general findings revealed by these cross-national studies (Huesmann & Eron, 1986). In most countries, the more aggressive children also watched more television, preferred more violent programs, identified more with aggressive characters, and perceived television violence as more like real life than did the less aggressive children. The combination of extensive exposure to violence coupled with identification with aggressive characters was a particularly potent predictor of subsequent aggression for many children. Results from the United States illustrate well the complexities (Huesmann & Eron, 1986; Huesmann et al.,1984). Girls' viewing of television violence has a significant effect on their later aggression even after taking into account their early levels of aggression, socio-economic status, and academic achievement. For boys, those who had watched violent programming frequently in their early childhood and who also reported a strong identification with aggressive television characters were generally regarded as more aggressive.

A 15-year follow-up of the U.S. sample confirmed links between exposure to media violence and aggression (Huesmann et al., 2003). Most notable, the results reveal a delayed effect of media violence on serious physical aggression. Significant correlates were found between television violence viewing during childhood and a general measure of aggression (including physical, verbal, and indirect), as well as measures of physical aggression or violence. Adults who viewed more violent programs in childhood, compared to those who viewed them less often, committed significantly more acts of physical aggression. Importantly, high aggressiveness during childhood did not contribute to frequent viewing of television violence later, but frequent exposure to television violence during childhood resulted in high levels of aggressive behavior later. These latter two findings were similar for both men and women. Importantly, the effects of frequent childhood exposure to television violence on later aggression remained significant even when the researchers controlled for parents' education and children's achievement.

Other important longitudinal studies support the finding that television viewing may have adverse effects on adults, a population that actually has not been studied as much as adolescents or children. One notable longitudinal study examined television viewing habits in adolescence (at age 14) and early adulthood (at age 22) and their effects on later violent behavior (at age 30; Johnson, Cohen, Smailes, Kasen, & Brook, 2002). Although the analysis used total amount of television viewing, rather than focusing on violent programming, the study revealed several significant findings. Television viewing at age 14 significantly predicted assault and fighting behavior at 16 or 22 years of age. The significance remained even after controlling statistically for family income, parental education, verbal intelligence, childhood neglect, neighborhood characteristics, peer aggression, and school violence. Television viewing at age 22 also significantly predicted assault and fighting at age 30. Although the results varied in terms of effect size differences for males versus females at different time periods and for different measures of aggression, the general finding remained that viewing violence during adolescence influences outcomes much later than previously studied. These rather impressive results are the first from a longitudinal study to link adolescent television habits to adult aggression.

A few longitudinal studies have seemed to produce results at odds with the thesis that viewing violence in the media causes aggression. Reviews of these studies, however, view them as weak and inconsistent rather than discrepant (for a review, see Huesmann & Miller, 1994). For example, the National Broadcasting

Company's 3-year longitudinal study of middle childhood reported significant regression coefficients for only two out of the fifteen critical tests of their causal theories for boys, and reported three out of the fifteen critical tests as significant for girls (Milavsky, Kessler, Stipp, & Rubens, 1982). The results did not go unchallenged. Researchers note, for example, that an additional ten results were in the predicted direction for boys and, for girls, an additional seven were in the predicted direction. Similarly, positive correlations between television violence and aggression were observed at each point in time. In addition, researchers have reexamined the data and reached a conclusion opposite to that of the original authors: the data does support links between early exposure to media violence and later aggressive behavior (see Comstock & Strasburger, 1990). Studies that point to the lack of media effects on adolescents' aggression appear equivocal and, equally interestingly, subject to considerable efforts to determine how the findings fit with the general theme that media violence actually does contribute to effects.

Taken together, available evidence supports the general conclusion that longitudinal research supports the claim that exposure to media violence does increase the risk of aggressive responses. Meta-analyses devoted to examining the results of longitudinal studies find significant overall small effect sizes ($r = .17$; C. A. Anderson & Bushman, 2002). Given the wide variety of violent media images and outcome measures, researchers often describe these findings as rather impressive. These studies affirm the conclusion that high levels of exposure to violent television during childhood can promote aggression in later childhood, adolescence, and even young adulthood. Available evidence reveals that early exposure to a lot of media violence can later increase aggression, even after controlling for prior levels of aggressiveness, parenting, social class and intellectual functioning. That evidence appears stronger than evidence suggesting that more aggressive children tend to watch more violence than their less aggressive peers. These findings also reveal that the increased aggression, when indexed in adulthood, includes very serious forms of aggression and violence.

The Significance and Limitations of Effects Research

Exposure to media violence influences adolescents' behaviors. Meta-analyses have examined the effects of media violence across all major types of media that have been studied. Studies reveal considerable convergence of effects across studied media types. The most recent and comprehensive analysis (C. A. Anderson & Bushman, 2001, for example, revealed the following results. Average effect sizes were .23 for 124 laboratory experiments involving 7,305 participants; .19 for 28 field experiments involving 1,976 participants; .18 for 86 cross-sectional studies involving 37,341 participants; and .17 for 42 longitudinal studies involving 4,975 participants. Together, these analyses establish rather impressive results. Statistical evidence finds that exposure to media violence significantly associates with aggression and violence.

Although impressive, the conclusions remain fraught with complexities and controversies. First, definitions of media violence present important issues. The most accepted definition is one that was used by the NTVS (Wilson et al., 1998). That ongoing study defines media violence as:

> Any overt depiction of a credible threat of physical force or the actual use of such force intended to physically harm an animate being or group of beings. Violence also includes certain depictions of physically harmful consequences against an animate being or group that occur as a result of unseen violent means. Thus there are three primary types of violent depictions: credible threats, behavioral acts, and harmful consequences. (p. 41)

Researchers generally agree with the definition provided in the NTVS, but they do not necessarily use it in their own research (see Bartholow, Dill, Anderson, & Lindsay, 2003). In addition, researchers' definitions do not necessarily comport with popular perceptions of what constitutes violence in the media. For example, the public seems more concerned with being shocked by what they watch (e.g., they do not consider cartoon violence as especially problematic), while researchers are concerned that the public will be harmed by what they watch, whether or not it is perceived as shocking (e.g., researchers do consider cartoon violence as especially problematic; Potter, 1999). These divergences render eventual agreement unlikely and challenge efforts to gain more effective responses to findings.

Second, when considering the influence of different media on adolescents, it is important to distinguish among aggression, violence, and criminality. The empirical focus still remains on aggression and not necessarily violence, let alone crime itself. The point is of significance. Several have expressed skepticism regarding links between aggression and violence (see Zimring & Hawkins, 1997). The skepticism is appropriate when considering, for example, the extension of laboratory aggression to criminal behavior. Although there may be a link between the two, the place of law, social disapproval, socialization, and formal punishment in the manner society defines and responds to criminal aggression arguably makes it qualitatively different from laboratory-induced aggression.

Third, establishing causation is particularly problematic. The laboratory studies arguably help establish causality. Yet, they retain important limitations. Most notably, these studies may have sponsor effects or demand characteristics that might lead participants to believe that they should act aggressively. Similarly, some situations might be qualitatively different from actual physical aggression in real life and lead to the expectation, as when playing with Bobo dolls, that the props are meant for aggressive actions. Likewise, the effects of aggression experienced in laboratory settings are rather different than those felt in real life (e.g., Bobo dolls smile and bounce back when hit). Although researchers have made important attempts to address some of these concerns, issues of external validity remain. In addition to issues of external validity, causation remains problematic because media violence, depending on how it is defined, is rampant, and adolescents' aggressive and even violent behaviors (depending on how they are defined) also are considerably rampant. Adolescents, particularly in later adolescence, constitute an unusually violent group. That violence and law-breaking behavior is so common to adolescence is seen in the well-established research examining adolescence-limited and life-course persistent behaviors (Moffit, Caspi, Harrington, & Milne, 2002). Yet, it is not clear how much violent media materials youth are exposed to during adolescence, nor is it clear how early experiences impact the adolescent period, or even the adult period (although it is well recognized that adults as a group are not as aggressive and violent as adolescents and even children—again, depending on adopted definitions).

Despite limitations, it appears fair to conclude that a vast amount of research has been conducted to determine whether media exposure causes aggression and violence. Many of these studies support the causation hypothesis. The results of numerous meta-analyses are rather impressive. These analyses essentially average the effect sizes of multiple studies and allow researchers to ask whether particular factors significantly link to particular outcomes, which allows for establishing links between exposure to violence and violent behavior. Nevertheless, many inconsistencies exist, and significant questions still remain regarding the internal and external validity of this research, thus raising questions about the effects of media on adolescents' everyday lives.

Theoretical Understandings of the Media's Effects on Adolescents' Aggression

Evidence that media violence may cause aggressive or violent behavior, coupled by concern about the need to prevent or limit the effects of media violence, has led researchers to theorize the psychological processes that could explain those effects. The very rich theoretical domain provides numerous theories to help us understand why the empirical evidence may make sense. Several important theoretical perspectives, many of which were formulated long before the recent rise in media-effects research, support empirical conclusions regarding the effects of dramatic media violence on aggressive behavior.

Dominant models used to understand the influence of the media stem from the social-cognitive, information-processing models that focus on the particular ways people perceive, think, learn, and eventually interact with their social world. These models explain the processes through which exposure to violence in the mass media could cause both long- and short-term increases in aggressive and violent behavior. Some of the theorized processes contribute to both kinds of effects, although some focus on how the media contribute to either the long-term or short-term effects. For example, the long-term observational learning of beliefs and biases supporting aggression fosters long-term effects. Priming, excitation transfer, or imitation of specific behaviors best account for short-term effects. Together, these models help explain much of the psychological processes by which media violence might contribute to aggression. Some researchers recently have proposed integrative models of aggression, of which general aggression model (GAM) has received the most attention (see C. A. Anderson & Bushman, 2002). As expected from a psychological model that seeks to unify prior approaches, GAM focuses both on individual and situational factors that may influence aggression; considers how emotions, cognitions, and arousal interact to produce aggression; and accounts for the initial development as well as the persistence of aggressive behavior. Rather than focus on the new broader integrative models that bring together existing theories, this analysis focuses on component models that would provide the foundational basis for explaining media influences.

Long-Term Effects

Social-cognitive observational-learning theory arguably emerges as the most dominant theory that helps explain the long-term effects of exposure to media violence. The long-term effects are seen as acquired through observational learning of three social-cognitive structures: schemas about a hostile world, aggressive scripts for social problem solving, and normative beliefs about the acceptability of aggression (Bushman & Huesmann, 2001). Together, these cognitive structures (beliefs, attitudes, and interpretational biases) help account for the manner in which very young children imitate behaviors they witness. For example, the theory posits that violent programming provides children with cognitive scripts (mental routines stored in memory to guide perceptions), interpretations, and behaviors that encourage aggressive behavior. Once learned, scripts can be retrieved from memory. Their retrieval depends on the similarity between the fictional event and a real-life situation, as well as on the circumstances surrounding the initial encoding of the script. When retrieved, an aggressive script may be reinforced and broadened to new sets of circumstances. Because the impact of the aggressive script can be exponential, repeated exposure to media violence can lead to developing sets of cognitive scripts that emphasize aggression as a typical response to social situations. The centrality and significance of schemas to understand media violence's effects is highlighted by research indicating that schemas about violence seem more important than actual content. Television viewers, for example, rely much more on their personal schema than on program content in constructing their interpretations of violence (Potter, Pashupati, Pekurny, Hoffman, & Davis, 2002). In addition, although viewers may share the same story schema, they appear to make different judgments on the schema elements, and hence their judgments about violence vary.

Developmental research reveals well how social learning could increase aggressiveness. Research involving young children provides strong evidence that the observation of specific aggressive behaviors around them increases children's likelihood of behaving in that manner (Bandura, 1977). Although aggressive behaviors in children 2 to 4 years old generally appear spontaneously (Tremblay, 2000), observing specific aggressive behaviors at that age leads children to acquire more coordinated aggressive scripts for social problem solving and counteracts environmental forces that would help children avoid aggression. As children mature, their social scripts acquired through observation of family, peers, community, and the mass media become more complex, abstracted, and automatic (Huesmann, 1988). This development coincides with children's development of more elaborate social-cognitive schemas about their world. In particular, extensive observation of violence leads children to bias their world schemas toward attributing hostility to others' actions (Comstock & Paik, 1991; Gerbner, Gross, Morgan, & Signorielli, 1994). Such attributions, in turn, increase the likelihood of aggressive behavior (Dodge, Pettit, Bates, & Valente, 1995). As children further mature, normative beliefs about the appropriateness of social behaviors crystallize and begin to act as filters to limit inappropriate social behaviors (Huesmann & Guerra, 1997). Children's own behaviors influence the normative beliefs they develop, but so do observations of the behaviors of those around them, including those observed in the mass media (Huesmann, 1999; Huesmann, Guerra, Zelli, & Miller, 1992). Social-cognitive observational-learning theory, then, posits long-term effects of exposure to violence that arise from the influence of exposure on the development of aggressive problem-solving scripts, hostile attributional biases, and normative beliefs approving of aggression.

Much of the above-described manner of learning takes place without awareness or intention. Observational-learning theory posits that the likelihood that viewers will acquire an observed behavior increases when viewers perceive the model performing the behavior as similar to or attractive to them, when viewers identify with the model, when the context is realistic, and when rewards follow the viewed behavior (Bandura, 1977). Importantly, none of these factors are necessary conditions to foster media-violence effects. Most notably, cartoon characters in television or video games are not very realistic, yet exposure to such media increases the possibility of aggressive behavior. Although not all the conditions noted above are necessary, behavior persists largely because of its schedule of reinforcements. Whether observational learning leads to long-term effects of media violence partly depends on the imitated behaviors' consequences. Rewards or punishments may come from specific individuals, such as peers, teachers, and parents. Or, individuals may vicariously experience rewards or punishments from what other persons receive for imitating the portrayed behavior. Theoretically, long-term consequences of observations of violent behaviors can arise in the absence of an awareness of their influence. Repeated observations of aggressive and violent behaviors should increase the likelihood that individuals will incorporate aggressive scripts into their repertoires of social scripts (sets of "rules" for how to interpret, understand, and deal with a variety of situations), especially if viewers experience reinforcement for their own use of those scripts.

The above processes are very similar to those hypothesized by cultivation theory. Given its relevance to explaining other types of media effects, we will return to this theory in later chapters. For now, it is important to note that the theory suggests that the media tend to produce a very small, consistent set of different messages (in this instance, several images that relate to aggression). When exposed over time, viewers come to believe that media messages reflect the real world. For example, exposure to heavy amounts of television can lead people to overestimate amounts of crime and victimization and perceive the world as a violent place (Gerbner, Gross, Jackson-Beeck, Jeffries-Fox, & Signorielli, 1978). As a result, overestimations can produce several effects, including feelings of fear, anxiety, and suspicion (Morgan & Shanahan, 1997). These feelings, in turn, may lead individuals to respond in more defensive ways. Much research supports the view that media content may temporarily increase the accessibility of information, which in turn allows that information to influence related judgments or behaviors (Roskos-Ewoldsen, Roskos-Ewoldsen, & Carpenter, 2002). If this priming occurs frequently during long periods of time, it increases accessibility to the feeling, a point of considerable significance given that chronically accessible information most likely chronically influences perceptions and behaviors (Roskos-Ewoldsen et al., 2002).

Desensitization theory provides another related way to understand long-term effects. In this context, desensitization refers to a reduction in distress-related physiological reactivity to observations or thoughts of violence. In terms of media violence, emotional desensitization occurs when people who watch media violence no longer respond with as much unpleasant physiological arousal as they did initially. Viewing a lot of violence can lead people to become emotionally desensitized and therefore less likely to experience negative emotional reactions to real life aggression. The negative emotional responses people otherwise would have to violence no longer inhibits thinking about violence, condoning violence, or acting violently. This desensitization can result in a heightened likelihood of violent thoughts and behaviors with repeated exposure to violence; such negative emotional responses lead to habituation and further contribute to desensitization (Huesmann et al., 2003).

Desensitization theory finds considerable empirical support. Research reveals that media violence initially provokes fear, anxiety, and sleep disturbances (e.g., Cantor, 2001; Harrison & Cantor, 1999). However, violent media are typically consumed in conditions of relaxation and pleasure, and with no apparent adverse consequences for consumers. As such, repeated exposure may cause the initial adverse reactions to fade, such that people become less responsive to real violence. A number of studies support this basic premise, in that participants exposed to violent media (e.g., "slasher" films, televised police action, or violent boxing matches) are less physiologically aroused by subsequent real-world violence than are participants exposed to nonviolent media (e.g., Gentile & Anderson, 2003). But we have yet to conclude whether those reactions actually lead to violent behavior. Nevertheless, research has now well established that, compared to less aggressive college students, aggressive college students do tend to experience decreased arousal when exposed to repeated scenes of violence (C. A. Anderson et al., 2003).

The systematic-desensitization approach also suggests that repeated exposure to increasingly gory and realistic portrayals of violence in video games may desensitize people to violence in the real world. Research has found that, after considering real-life violence exposure, media-violence exposure, empathy, and attitudes towards violence, only exposure to video game violence predicts lower empathy, a finding that leads researchers to conclude that the active nature of playing video games, intense engagement, and the tendency to be translated into fantasy play may explain apparent desensitization (Funk, Bechtoldt-Baldacci, Pasold, & Baumgardner, 2004). These studies support the conclusion that violent media may alter cognitive, affective, and behavioral processes, possibly leading to desensitization.

Shorter-Term Effects

The processes theorized as determining long-term effects of media violence might also explain the shorter-term relations between exposure to violence and aggressive behavior. However, a few other processes have been widely discussed as playing a role in short-term relations. Two theories dominate this area of research: cognitive-priming theory and excitation-transfer theory.

Cognitive-priming theory posits that ideas are partially primed (cued) by associated stimuli in the environment and that this activation accounts for the short-term effects of media violence (Berkowitz, 1984). The theory holds that exposure to violent scenes can activate sets of associations related to aggressive thoughts or emotions that become aggressive primes. These primes then filter and bias subsequent perceptions, since aggressive primes or cues make aggressive schemas more easily available for use in processing other incoming information. If aggressive schemas are primed while certain events occur (such as an ambiguous provocation), the new events are more likely to be interpreted as involving aggression, thereby increasing the likelihood of an aggressive response. Thus, the theory suggests that viewing violence might provide adolescents with cognitive scripts for violence that are activated when they encounter a real-life situation that involves some aspect of the script.

Researchers have demonstrated that priming effects relate to aggression. For example, the mere presence of a weapon within a person's visual field typically increases aggressive thoughts and aggressive behavior (Bartholow, Anderson, Benjamin, & Carnagey, 2005). Priming theory views the reason for this increase as a simple result of the pairing of the observed stimulus (the weapon) with past observations of violence or the violence inherently suggested by the stimulus, which activates memory traces for aggressive scripts, schemas, and beliefs sufficiently to increase the probability of their use. Not surprisingly, a provocation that follows a priming stimulus is more likely to stimulate aggression as a result of the priming. Importantly, encounters with some event or stimulus can prime, or activate, related concepts and ideas in a person's memory even without the person being aware of this influence, and this lack of awareness helps account for the automatic nature of aggressive behavior. An important study showed boys either a violent film in which a walkie-talkie was used or a nonviolent film (Josephson, 1987). Following the film, the boys were interviewed by someone holding either a walkie-talkie or microphone. Consistent with the priming hypothesis, adolescents who were considered initially aggressive revealed greater aggression when they saw the violent film and the walkie-talkie afterward. Although this effect is short-lived, the primed script, schema, or belief may have been acquired before and in a completely different context. Importantly, the study also supports the cognitive script view in that the boys who were more initially aggressive seemed more likely to be disinhibited by the exposure to violence.

Excitation-transfer theory, the second dominant theory used to explain short-term effects, maintains that the arousing nature of media violence accounts for the media's contribution to aggression (Zillmann, 1991). Although real-world or media violence may not be appealing, it can be arousing for most adolescents. Violence tends to increase heart rate, the skin's conductance of electricity, and other physiological indicators of arousal. To the extent that observed violence arouses viewers, the observed violence can increase aggression in at least two ways. First, arousal can energize or strengthen an individual's dominant action tendencies. Aggression can result, for example, when a person is provoked or otherwise instigated to aggress at a time of increased arousal. The increased general arousal stimulated by the observed violence may simply reach a peak that reduces the ability of inhibiting mechanisms (such as normative beliefs) to restrain aggression (Berkowitz, 1993). Second, the propensity to behave aggressively increases when an aroused person misattributes arousal to a provocation by someone else. This excitation transfer occurs when a subsequent provocation may be perceived as more severe than it is because the emotional response stimulated by the observed violence is misattributed as being due to the provocation (Zillmann, 1979, 1983). Such excitation transfer could account for a more intense aggressive response in the short run. As recently found, playing a violent video game for as little as 10 minutes increases the player's automatic association of themselves with aggressive actions and traits, and having a history of exposure to violent video games positively associates with aggressive views of the self (Uhlmann & Swanson, 2004). This type of research suggests that frequent exposure to violent media followed by provoking events could lead to an increase in the viewers' aggressive social encounters, which in turn can affect their self-images and the aggressiveness of their social environments. We already have seen that people tend to react more violently to provocations immediately after watching exciting movies than they do at other times. In fact, this has been a criticism of media violence research: the ensuing violent behavior may be due to excitation, not necessarily to the violence (see J. L. Freedman, 2002). Given the difficulties of teasing out excitement from violence, it does seem reasonable to conclude that excitement plays a role in explaining violent media effects.

Significance of Theoretical Approaches to Media Effects

Theoretical understandings of media effects lend considerable support to empirical findings. Indeed, the robustness of media research lies just as much with empirical findings indicating a causal relationship as it does with attempts to understand the mechanisms by which exposure evokes consequences. A substantial body of psychological theory explains well the processes through which exposure to violence in the mass media could cause both short- and long-term increases in aggressive and violent behavior.

Viewers learn the appropriateness of behaviors in different circumstances, as a function of the degree to which the actions are depicted as effective versus ineffective, rewarded versus punished, or generally resulting in positive versus negative outcomes. The social learning and social cognitive theories provide important constructs to help us understand behavioral choices. In addition, they help account for the acquisition of novel aggressive behavior even in the absence of immediate rewards. Although different, the theoretical processes are not mutually exclusive. Observational learning, desensitization, priming, and excitation transfer all may contribute simultaneously to the stimulation of aggression by the observation of violence. Similarly, priming effects may be seen as short-term, but repeated priming may make schemas chronically accessible. Frequently primed aggression-related thoughts, emotions, and behavioral scripts become automatically and chronically accessible. As they become part of the normal internal state of the individual, they increase the chances that social encounters will be interpreted in an aggressive-biased way and translate into aggressive encounters (e.g., C. A. Anderson & Huesmann, 2003). This automatization process changes short-lived increases in aggression-biased perceptions into relatively long-lasting aggression-based perceptual filters.

Numerous other theories have been advanced, some of which have earned more support than others. For example, catharsis theory predicts that viewing violence should be followed by reductions in aggression (Feshbach & Singer, 1971; Fowles, 1999). It seems, however, that the weight of the evidence does not support any such negative relation (see Huesmann, Eron, Berkowitz, & Chaffee, 1991; Paik & Comstock, 1994). On the other hand, some theoretical perspectives explain long-term relations between exposure to violence and aggression without hypothesizing any direct effect of violence viewing on aggression. Most notably, social-comparison theory suggests that aggressive children feel happier and more justified if they believe that others also commit aggression, and viewing media violence makes them feel happier because it convinces them of others' aggressivity (Huesmann, 1988). The usual assumption is that aggressive children simply enjoy watching media violence more than other children do (Fowles, 1999; Goldstein, 1998).

The complexity revealed by the leading theory of observational learning emphasizes that responses to the media are parts of larger responses to one's environment. What matters in terms of media influence is the extent to which the social environment responds to actions that imitate the media. The media do not function alone. These models highlight complexity as they reveal not only why exposure to violent media increases aggressiveness and violent behavior but also why numerous factors might exacerbate or mitigate effects. We know, for example, that severe aggressive and violent behavior seldom occurs in the absence of multiple predisposing and precipitating factors such as neurophysiological abnormalities, poor child rearing, socioeconomic deprivation, poor peer relations, attitudes and beliefs supporting aggression, drug and alcohol abuse, frustration and provocation, and numerous other factors. Exposure to media violence appears to be one such long-term predisposing and short-term precipitating factor. Accepted theories, then, point to the need to consider particular adolescents' media environments and other influences and factors that shape their development.

Placing the Media in the Context of Adolescent Development

Research does not support a simple, unidirectional causal sequence in which viewing media violence clearly contributes to aggressive and violent behavior. This leads us to the need to turn to factors that would mediate the relationship, particularly those that relate to the adolescent period. Media influence exerted on adolescents' aggression interacts with a range of other individual, family, peer, and community-level factors. As with all other concerns adolescents face, a look at the epidemiology of violence identifies multiple and interrelated factors which seem to predict the strategies adolescents adopt. This section examines key factors identified by research and the manner these factors relate to the relative power of various media in influencing adolescents' susceptibility to aggressive and violent behavior. As expected, adolescents are not affected equally by media violence, and not all portrayals of media violence foster the same effect. This expectation makes it important to examine the characteristics of individuals, of media content, and of social environments that may increase or decrease the influence of media violence on aggressive behavior.

Developmental Characteristics

Age emerges as one of the most important moderators of how individuals interpret and react to violent media content. Important theories support the claim. For example, developmental theory suggests that younger children, whose social scripts, schemas, and beliefs are less crystallized than those of older children, should be more sensitive to violent media influences. Likewise, observational-learning theory suggests that the viewer's age can influence the extent to which he or she identifies with the depicted aggressive characters, which may in turn influence learning and enactment of the observed aggression.

As theorized, research does support the conclusion that the media-violence effect is largest for children less than 5 years old. This was, for example, the finding from a highly regarded meta-analysis (Paik & Comstock, 1994). Importantly, age effects do not necessarily dwindle. The over-all size of effects for college-aged students in experimental studies, for example, matches or exceeds that of 6- to 11-year-olds. The meta-analysis further revealed that research using experiments, for example, finds that the effect sizes decrease between the preschool and adult years, but that they increase among those of college age. Effect sizes from surveys are the highest for adults and preschoolers.

The full developmental spectrum has yet to be fully understood. Recent studies reveal a larger longitudinal effect of overall television viewing time (not only television violence) on assault and fighting behavior at age 30 than at the ages of 16 and 22 (Johnson, Cohen, Smailes, Kasen, & Brook, 2002). These findings, however, are difficult to interpret simply because comparisons do not control for the different outcome measures used in research with children and adults, with the former focusing on aggressive behavior and the latter on aggressive thoughts. Yet, longitudinal studies that do use the same behavioral measures of aggression on the same participants at different ages reveal significant effects for children (8-year-olds) and not for young adults (19-year-olds; see Eron et al., 1972). Although clearly important steps in understanding the effects of media, the research still leaves unanswered which measures would best capture links between the media and aggressive behavior.

Together, the findings actually reveal surprising results. One would probably have expected to find less media influence as individuals mature and acquire an enhanced ability to comprehend, analyze, and react critically to the media. This does not appear to be the case. The content of the media changes and remains influential. And, media exposure in adolescence seems to evince sleeper effects.

Familial and Peer Influences

How cultural, environmental, and situational factors moderate the impact of media violence remains surprisingly underinvestigated. Most notable, much remains speculative about the role that those close to adolescents—families and peers—play in impacting the media's influence on adolescents. Although research remains tentative, important findings have emerged.

Given the powerful role parents can play in fostering aggressive and violent behavior in adolescents, the potential role of families in the moderation of the media's influence on adolescents is of considerable interest. Familial influences potentially take three forms. First, they may involve the possible effects of parents' characteristics. Second, they may involve parents' efforts to control access to media and what parents do with their children when they view violence. Lastly, the media may impact familial relationships. Existing research examining the moderating effects of parents on children's aggression tends to support only the second consideration.

How parents control their children's viewing and what parents do when their children view violence, rather than who the parents are, appear to be more important in mitigating the effects of observing violence. Studies examining parents' characteristics as possible moderators find little evidence that several parental characteristics actually matter. Studies have examined whether, for example, parents' aggressiveness, coldness, personality, or viewing habits increase or decrease the effects of exposure to violence. Research reveals little evidence of moderating effects (Huesmann et al., 2003). Parents' efforts to control adolescents' responses to media, however, have been found influential. Research suggests that any negative effects of television viewing can to some extent be attenuated if parents watch and discuss television shows with their children. Generally, it has been argued that when parents take an active, mediating approach toward television viewing by their children—for example, by including regular commentaries and examining the media's realistic portrayals, justifications for violence, and other issues that impact learning—adolescents are less likely to be inappropriately influenced by media content. Research examining the influence of television supports this claim in samples of young children. For example, early research has found that when parents take an active, mediating approach that shapes how television could influence learning, their children are less likely to be influenced badly by media content (Singer & Singer, 1986). Researchers have found that children whose parents discuss the inappropriateness of television violence with them or restrict access to violent television report lower aggressive tendencies than children whose parents do not discuss television violence or restrict access to violent television shows (Nathanson, 1999). Other research indicates that either type of parental intervention may decrease the importance children give to violent television. That lower importance, in turn, may lower children's aggressive attitudes (C. A. Anderson et al., 2003). These findings should not be surprising. Parents' television habits and child-rearing practices influence a child's television habits (Comstock & Paik, 1991) as well as a child's orientation to the world. Such early parenting factors as harsh punishment, rejection of the child, and lack of discipline are well known to influence children's subsequent aggression (Tremblay, 2000).

Although research demonstrates that parents can protect their children from harmful media effects by engaging in parental mediation, parental influences may wane when their children reach adolescence and increase peer interactions. Parents retain influence throughout their children's lives, but peers also become especially important and influential during adolescence. Surprisingly, very little mass communication research has considered the role of peers in shaping the effects of media violence on adolescents. One recent study took a first look at peer mediation of antisocial television and found that it occurs more frequently and is more potent than parental mediation (Nathanson, 2001). In addition, peer mediation promotes more positive orientations toward antisocial television, which in turn leads to greater aggression. Whereas parental mediation can inhibit negative media effects, peer meditation seems to facilitate harmful outcomes.

Research also has examined the impact of viewing violent media on family relationships. A national sample of children aged 6 to 12 examined the relative merits of three theoretical perspectives on the relation between family conflict and children's use of television and electronic games with violent content (Vandewater, Lee, & Shim, 2005). The study examined three hypotheses: (1) the family-context hypothesis, whereby family conflict positively relates to violent electronic media use because family tensions will be reflected in children's interest in media with violent content; (2) the reaction hypothesis, whereby family conflict positively relates to nonviolent media use because children seek out nonviolent media content as a reaction against conflict in their family environment; and (3) the escape hypothesis, whereby family conflict positively relates to total electronic media use because children use media to escape family conflict regardless of content. Results only supported the family-context hypothesis. Interest in violent media reflects family tensions that create situations that foster media effects.

The most striking findings relating to family influence comes from a meta-analysis of studies that examined the relationship between violent television viewing and measures of both prosocial and antisocial behavior (Hearold, 1986). The study found that viewing violent television had its greatest "antisocial" effect on nonviolent and nonaggressive activities, with the largest effect being on the reduction in family discussions, which had an effect size of 2.33, a very high effect. The study also reported effects on role stereotyping (.90), less socializing (.75), materialism (.40), and passivity (.36). Together, these findings reveal the important influence the media have on shaping social relationships.

Psychological Influences

Different types of people seek out different types of media content that elicit different meanings for different people. Studies have examined numerous psychological factors that may influence the effects of exposure to violent media. For example, research that finds no conclusive direct link between exposure and aggression does find that individual viewer characteristics (e.g., motivation to view aggressive media) make direct and indirect links between audience predictors and aggression outcomes (Haridakis & Rubin, 2003). Of the many potential variables to consider, two have received a considerable amount of attention: aggressive dispositions and identification with media characters. Research generally supports the conclusion that individual characteristics and expectations mediate the impact of exposure to media violence.

Individuals deemed characteristically more aggressive than their peers tend to present a lower threshold for a media-violence-induced activation of aggressive behavior. Research generally reveals that highly aggressive individuals show greater aggressive behavior, attitudes, emotions, and beliefs after exposure to media violence than their relatively less aggressive counterparts (Bushman, 1995). Importantly, these findings do not mean that violent media do not affect relatively nonaggressive children. Children with low levels of earlier aggression, as well as their highly aggressive peers, show significant effects of media violence on later aggression (Gentile & Anderson, 2003; Huesmann et al., 2003). In addition, some findings reveal that less aggressive individuals are more affected by media violence than are more aggressive individuals (C. A. Anderson, 1997). These findings do not discount the possibility that selective exposure may be at work. Adolescents with a predisposition toward aggressive behavior (regardless of whether they actually are aggressive) might find violent media more interesting and therefore use more of it than children with lower predispositions toward aggression. A recent study of the relationship between video-game playing and aggression found that children who preferred violent video games were more aggressive than children who did not, thus suggesting the possibility of a selective exposure effect (Wiegman & van Schie, 1998). Despite the need for more conclusive evidence, existing research does support the general rule that different types of people seek out different types of media content and that such content differently affects them.

Adolescents are more likely to behave aggressively if they identify with aggressive characters or perceive violent scenes as realistic. This is unsurprising given theoretical assumptions that those characteristics increase the likelihood that individuals have aggressive ideas, primed by the observed violence, to imitate the character or to acquire aggressive scripts or schemas. Research supports the claim. Children who thought that violent shows they watched were realistic or those who identified with aggressive television characters had higher average scores on verbal and physical aggression 1 year after they were interviewed, and they also had higher composite scores of aggression when they were interviewed 15 years later (Huesmann et al., 2003). Those most at risk were those who had both watched violence and identified with the violent characters. The finding that more realistic portrayals are more likely to increase viewers' aggression than those presented in a more fictionalized fashion does not mean, however, that fictional violence is not linked to aggressive behavior; even unrealistic violence links to aggression (C. A. Anderson et al., 2003). These findings support well the view that adolescents' predispositions likely impact the media's influence.

Media Content Characteristics

We already have seen that the portrayal of violence can alter the meaning of violence and moderate viewers' cognitive, emotional, and behavioral responses. Identification with aggressive perpetrators, as we have seen, increases the risk that adolescents will be influenced by the aggression. In this regard, characteristics of the aggressive perpetrator play an important role. Research has long shown that viewers are particularly likely to be influenced by aggressive characters portrayed as similar to themselves based on such characteristics as age, gender, and race (Bandura, 1994). Research also indicates, however, that difference may be important. A perpetrator's overall attractiveness, power, and charisma actually may be more important than similarity to the viewer (C. A. Anderson et al., 2003).

Portrayals of violence's consequences also likely impact the influence of media violence. Theoretically, the portrayal of justified violence renders viewers more likely to believe the appropriateness of their own aggressive responses to a perceived offense. As a result, they are more likely to engage in aggressive behavior. Experimental research does reveal that observing justified violence does increase the likelihood that angered participants will assault individuals who have provoked them (C. A. Anderson et al., 2003). Similarly, rewarding the perpetrators for aggressive actions may increase the likelihood the viewers will model the aggressiveness. Again, experimental studies reveal that rewarded violence increases the risk that viewers will behave aggressively (C. A. Anderson, et al., 2003). Similarly, showing the effects of violence on victims may reduce the risk of aggression. Findings in this area are inconclusive, but some do support the claim that viewing the negative consequences of actions leads viewers to respond less aggressively. Again, however, violence need not necessarily be justified or rewarded to increase aggressiveness in viewers; violence simply may contribute to learning aggressive thoughts and behaviors. Indeed, even viewing the negative consequences of violence may lead to desensitization; viewers who show less negative emotional reactions to violence are more likely to behave aggressively than those who show more negative reactions (C. A. Anderson et al., 2003).

In addition to the consequences of violence, exposure to sexuality in the media also contributes to aggressive and violent behavior. Two meta-analyses examined the effect sizes for exposure to explicitly sexual treatments in experimental studies, and both report some of the largest effect sizes in research on media effects. One analysis examined only sexually explicit portrayals (Allen, D'Alessio, & Bezgel, 1995). That analysis reported an overall effect size for exposure to all types of pornography—it pooled together exposure to nudity, nonviolent sexual behavior, and violent sexual behavior—and found a small, but still statistically significant, effect size ($r = .13$). As expected, analyses of erotica without violence reported higher effects ($r = .17$), and those limited to violent erotica revealed even higher effects ($r = .22$). Less expected, though, was the finding that portrayals of nudity (absent sex and violent sex) had a negative effect on aggressive or antisocial behavior ($r = -.14$). The second meta-analysis examined sexually explicit as well as violent portrayals (Paik & Comstock, 1994). The analysis revealed even higher effect sizes for violent erotica ($r = .60$), which was higher than any of the other effects, such as exposure to television and film violence, which produced a small effect size ($r = .31$). The analyses reported an effect size for erotica without violence that also was quite substantial and higher than the general exposure to violence ($r = .46$). The results reveal that sexual portrayals alone contribute to aggressiveness, and that when combined with violence, they are more likely to contribute to aggressive or violent outcomes.

The above findings, however, may not mean much unless media are actually aimed at younger audiences. It actually appears that they are. For example, a recent study examined the perpetrators of violence on American television in terms of their chronological age and compared the amount and nature of violence committed by child and teen characters to that committed by adult characters (Wilson, Colvin, & Smith, 2002). The results suggest that younger perpetrators are depicted in several ways that pose risks for the child viewer. Compared to adult perpetrators, child perpetrators are more often portrayed as attractive, are less likely to be punished for aggression, and engage in violence that results in fewer negative consequences to their victims. In addition, these younger characters are disproportionately featured on the very programs and channels that are targeted to the child audience. In considering media effects, then, it does seem that the characteristics of the media must be a source of concern.

Sex Differences and Similarities

Gender remains one of the most important factors researchers consider in their examinations of media influences. Remarkably, when it comes to media violence, researchers report little differences in media effects for females and males (Paik & Comstock, 1994). Both females and males are affected by violence in the media. Meta-analyses reveal effect sizes similar for both genders in the method that most closely represents real-life, everyday associations: surveys (females, $r = .19$; males, $r = .18$). Experiments also reveal similar effect sizes, but the size is somewhat greater for males (females, $r = .30$; males, $r = .44$).

Important studies reveal considerable similarities between both sexes' responses to media violence. A recent study of children growing up between 1977 and 1995, for example, reported similar effect sizes for males and females over 15 years old (Huesmann et al., 2003). The study found that, for both male and female participants, more childhood exposure to television violence, greater childhood identification with same-sex aggressive television characters, and a stronger childhood belief that violent shows tell about life "just like it is" predicted more adult aggression regardless of how aggressive participants were as children. It is particularly interesting that the longitudinal results were of about the same magnitude for female as for male participants. Earlier longitudinal studies, such as those conducted in 1960–1970 (Eron, Huesmann, Lefkowitz, & Walder, 1972) and 1960–1982 (Huesmann, 1986) had found only longitudinal effects for boys.

Despite similarities in effects, some gender differences do emerge in the kinds of aggression associated with early childhood exposure to media violence. Most notably, longitudinal studies reveal that early exposure to violence predicts increased use of indirect aggression for girls when they become adults (Huesmann et al., 2003). Likewise, early exposure to media violence exhibits a stronger relation to physical violence for boys when they become adults (Huesmann et al., 2003). Early television violence viewing correlates with adult physical aggression for both male and female participants but correlates with adult indirect aggression only for female participants. Another important finding relates to identification with aggressive characters. Although identification with same-sex aggressive television characters and the perception that violent television shows tell about life "like it is" predicts adult aggression for both genders, these factors exacerbate the effect of television-violence viewing only for male participants (Huesmann et al., 2003). Boys who viewed television violence and identified with male aggressive television characters or perceived television violence as true to life most at risk for adult aggression. The same gender difference had been found earlier for the childhood data relating television viewing to subsequent adolescent aggression (Huesmann & Eron, 1986): identification was a moderator for boys but not for girls.

That the media may impact different forms of violence is not surprising given the consistent sex differences found in the literature on aggression; indirect aggression is more characteristic of females and more acceptable for them

(Moretti, Odgers, & Jackson, 2004). The lack of a finding of a relation between exposure to media violence and female aggression in earlier longitudinal studies may have been due to the failure to measure indirect aggression sufficiently in those studies. Similarly, important changes in social norms for appropriate female behavior may have disinhibited female aggression, and the increase in aggressive female models in movies and television might have engendered a stronger observational-learning effect. The combination of these two factors may have led to an increase in the size of the effect for female participants, making detection easier. It is not that girls were not subject to the observational effect in earlier years. Indeed, they were, as the laboratory experiments showed (Paik & Comstock, 1994). Rather, their normative beliefs about appropriate female roles seem to have inhibited their use of the learned aggressive behaviors or aggressive scripts. This explanation agrees with the information-processing perspectives that posit that learned scripts for aggressive behavior are not followed if they violate individuals' normative beliefs about what is appropriate for them.

Significance and Limitations of Influences Research

Numerous factors can influence the extent to which media violence will effect aggressive emotions, thoughts, and actions. There exists, however, a surprising lack of systematic research on mediators and moderators of the media's influence on adolescents. Although important studies have been conducted, much remains to be investigated. For example, when adolescents form attitudes and beliefs and take action as a result of their exposure to media content, they also discuss the media with peers, and their responses may ultimately be shaped by those interactions. Surprisingly, research has yet to disentangle this potential effect. Yet another important limitation involves the extent to which research seems to focus on the effects of each medium separately. This is problematic to the extent that adolescents are exposed to violent materials from a variety of media sources that potentially are more powerful and interactive than has been the case when much of the research was conducted. Research that focuses on the interactive and cumulative effects of numerous combined media remains necessary.

The findings and theories we have discussed, however, suggest that the social environment and the adolescents' own dispositions will likely influence the effects of the media. The weight of the influence would increase to the extent that factors would, for example, alter the chances that the adolescents will identify with aggressive characters, alter the adolescents' perceptions of the scene's reality, or alter the chances that the adolescents will watch violence. Despite the need to control for factors, however, it is important to note that media effects remain. Some studies reveal the effects even after controlling for potential confounding factors. For example, one leading study assessed television viewing and aggressive behavior over a 17-year interval in a community sample of 707 individuals (Johnson, et al., 2002). There was a significant association between the amount of time spent watching television during adolescence and early adulthood and the likelihood of subsequent aggressive acts against others. This association remained significant after previous aggressive behavior, childhood neglect, family income, neighborhood violence, parental education, and psychiatric disorders were controlled statistically. And, as we have seen, the effects remain in studies that examine the impact of moderators and mediators (Huesmann et al., 2003).

Findings highlight the reality that media violence can affect any child from any family. Research supports observational learning, habituation or desensitization, priming, and excitation-transfer theories. The media affect not only violence-prone youth. Theory supported by this research suggests that violence in the media increases the likelihood of a child growing up to behave more aggressively in some situations. The violent films and television programs that probably have the most deleterious effects on children are not always the ones that adults and critics believe are the most violent. Overall, these results suggest that both males and females from all social strata and all levels of initial aggressiveness are placed at increased risk for the development of adult aggressive and violent behavior when they experience a high and steady diet of violent media in early childhood. The obvious follow-up question is whether society can do anything to prevent or at least moderate this effect.

Modifying Media Influences on Adolescents' Aggressive Tendencies

Although important questions remain to be resolved about the exact extent and nature of the effects of observed violence on aggressive and violent behavior and its importance relative to other causal factors, compelling evidence does reveal that adolescents' habitual exposure to violence in the media does have lasting effects on their propensity to behave aggressively and violently. This raises the concern whether research can help develop and test interventions that parents, schools, communities, and the government can promote that will mitigate these long-term effects. In this section, we explore research that examines ways to reduce the effects of media violence on aggressive attitudes and behaviors. Somewhat surprisingly, intervention efforts seeking to modify the media's influences tend not to address explicitly the media link to violence. Instead, the common forms of intervention seek to change views of media violence.

The first approach that seeks to uncover effective interventions uses experimental settings to study interventions done just prior to or during the viewing of violent programs. Experiments generally conclude that adults' comments can influence early adolescents' actions and attitudes after viewing violence (Cantor & Wilson, 2003). A recent experiment with 5- to 7- and 10- to 12-year-old children is illustrative (Nathanson, 2004). The experiment compared two approaches to mediating children's violent television viewing. Factual mediation provided children with facts about a violent program's production techniques. Evaluative mediation provided negative evaluations of the program's characters. The study found evaluative mediation the most effective strategy for promoting positive outcomes, particularly for younger children. Factual mediation had either no effect or actually increased some children's vulnerability to media violence. The study's conclusions comport with other well-established research findings. Generally, adults' encouragement to empathize with victims of violence lowers levels of aggressiveness and adults' criticisms of portrayals of violence lower elements of aggressiveness compared to conditions when adults provide no commentary, remain neutral, or approve of the violence (Nathanson & Cantor, 2000).

The experimental findings are subject to important limitations, but the findings gain support from other methods. For example, all experimental methods used proxies to measure aggressive behavior, such as attitudes toward violence. Further, none of the experiments examines long-term intervention effects. Yet, the findings remain important to the extent that some recent studies reveal the significant, but perhaps unintended, effects of parental mediation. For example, a survey of both parents and students was conducted to explore the relationship between parental mediation of televised violence and sex and adolescents' attitudes toward their parents, perceptions of their parents' attitudes toward them, attitudes toward the mediated content, and amount of viewing of the mediated content with friends (Nathanson, 2002). As expected, simply coviewing has no impact or actually increases adolescents' positive attitudes toward the media. In this case, coviewing related to both more positive attitudes toward and actual viewing of television violence and sex. Also importantly, the results indicated that restrictive mediation related to *less* positive attitudes toward parents, *more* positive attitudes toward the content, and *more* viewing of the content with friends.

The second approach used to investigate interventions involves media literacy efforts developed for school settings. These programs seek to increase the ability to understand, analyze, and evaluate messages encountered in the mass media (J. A. Brown, 2001). The approach posits that the development of critical-thinking skills will empower students and render them less vulnerable to the media's harmful effects. Despite a wide variety of approaches, these programs explicitly deal with media violence as they include efforts to increase adolescents' understanding of media effects, the role the media plays in their lives, the nature of media stories, and elements of media production.

Research reveals that media literacy can help children deal more effectively with media violence. Again, however, the majority of relevant research has been conducted with preadolescents (ages 9–12). That research highlights the need to use imaginative and indirect approaches that avoid simple lectures about reality and fantasy and instead encourage critical thinking and personal involvement in portrayals of media violence (see Vooijs & van der Voort, 1993). Importantly, given the recent push in media literacy programs to include teaching production skills (see J. A. Brown, 2001), such programs may backfire when dealing with issues of violence. Perhaps not surprisingly, involvement in creating entertainment violence may inadvertently legitimize antisocial behavior and encourage aggressive behavior (see Doolittle, 1980).

As with other interventions, media literacy approaches have important limitations. They tend not to measure actual aggressive behavior; rather, they measure interpretations of or attitudes toward media violence. In addition, although the majority of efforts do report cognitive changes in interpretations of violence (especially for young children), the interventions generally fail to modify the enjoyment of or exposure to violence programming (see Rosenkoetter, Rosenkoetter, Ozretich, & Acock, 2004; Vooijs & van der Voort, 1993). These limitations would appear important in that reducing media exposure (through curricular programs that focus on management of media use) without targeting violence actually can reduce antisocial behavior even in the absence of instruction about media-violence effects (Robinson, Wilde, Navracruz, Haydel, & Varady, 2001). Yet another important limitation of interventions involves the pervasive failure to assess long-term effects. Studies that do examine the long-term effects of media literacy programs relating to violence show that intervention effects disappear over time (Vooijs & van der Voort, 1993).

A third major form of intervention makes use of media productions to address youth violence. By using television programs, movies, advertisements, and documentaries, this approach seeks to highlight problems associated with violence. Unlike other approaches, this area of research intervention targets mid-to-late teens or college students. This age group has been found to hold strong attitudes that are more resistant to change than those of young children or preadolescents. Nevertheless, this area of research does report noteworthy findings. Focusing on the consequences to the victim seems to be more effective than focusing on the perpetrator of violence (Winkel & deKluever, 1997). For example, a victim-focused documentary significantly reduced acceptance of rape myths and of coerced sex among 15- and 16-year-old boys and girls, but a perpetrator-focused documentary unexpectedly strengthened boys' acceptance of macho behavior, coerced sex, and rape myths (Winkel & deKluever, 1997). Focusing on perpetrators seems problematic unless perpetrators can be shown as remorseful and suffering (Wilson et al., 1998). Although some studies find that encouraging student participation and personal involvement does not make much difference (Linz, Fuson, & Donnerstein, 1990), the emerging consensus is that the impact of antiviolence media productions are stronger when accompanied by student participation (Wilson et al., 1998) than when viewed without such support (Biocca et al., 1997). Importantly, messages that remain ambiguous or that are presented from multiple perspectives may be misinterpreted by certain viewers. This important pattern emerges in research projects that unintentionally reinforce the attitudes and behaviors targeted for change. Such boomerang effects have been found in efforts to change attitudes toward sexual violence (Wilson, Linz, Donnerstein, & Stipp, 1992; Winkel & deKleuver, 1997).

Again, however, existing research remains limited. Research still pervasively involves short-term interventions. The studies still focus on attitudes, such as acceptance of rape myths, acceptance of interpersonal violence (Winkel & deKleuver, 1997), the perceived seriousness of date rape (Wilson et al., 1992), attitudes about aggression (Biocca et al., 1997), and levels of empathy (Wilson et al., 1998). Overall, the research may be informative. But, considerably more research is needed if we are to derive firm, usable conclusions.

A last approach simply seeks to limit exposure to violent media. The easiest way to reduce the effects of media violence on children, of course, is to reduce children's exposure to such violence. Prevention programs aimed at reducing exposure could obviously be targeted either at the production sources of the violence or at the individual viewing the violence. In a society with strong protections for free speech, it is probably always going to be easier to target prevention efforts at viewers than producers. Such intervention efforts gain increasing significance in light of the reality that media violence permeates society.

Although the efforts seem well-targeted, efforts that simply aim to prevent access to certain media appear problematic and even somewhat futile. The futility derives from several factors. As we have seen, violence is ubiquitous in today's media. In addition, simply restricting adolescents' access to media violence may backfire in that it may make adolescents more interested in the content than if parents had not restricted it (Nathanson, 2002). Similarly, restrictive ratings and advisories may lead to "forbidden fruit" effects whereby labeling materials inappropriate for youth increases its attractiveness (Bushman & Cantor, 2003). Parents may actually not limit their children's access. Despite industry ratings of video games, a recent survey revealed that 90% of teens in grades eight through twelve reported that their parents never check the ratings of video games before allowing them to be purchased, and only 1% had ever prevented a purchase based on a game's rating (see Gentile & Walsh, 2002). Part of the failure also rests with industry. Ratings provided by the video game industry often do not match those provided by parents or their game-playing kids (C. A. Anderson & Bushman, 2001; Funk, Flores, Buchman, & Germann, 1999; Walsh & Gentile, 2001). The difficulties of reducing exposure to media violence make other interventions important.

Studies of intervention efforts reveal important points worthy of close consideration. A clear generalization that emerges is the need to tailor interventions to specific needs of the audience or parts of the audience. Overall, the effectiveness of the three types of interventions appears highly variable, and age and gender differences are quite prominent. The findings suggest that we need more research to determine the best approaches to developing parental interventions, media literacy strategies, and prosocial media presentations for reducing youth violence. Yet, it does seem that the exposure of early adolescents and children appears of greatest concern. The social value of reductions in the exposure of adults and even older teenagers appears small compared to the social value of reducing younger children's exposure.

Conclusions

The media expose adolescents to a great deal of violence. The vast majority of research examining links between media violence and adolescent aggression focuses on television. Associational studies indicate a positive relationship between viewing television violence and adolescent aggression. Meta-analyses indicate that the effect of television violence is in the small to medium range. Similar findings emerge for other media. Together, evidence points to the finding that the typical portrayal of violence in the media leads to the development of unrealistic and unhealthy attitudes toward violence and aggression. Evidence also suggests that the influence of media systems operates through two pathways. In the direct pathway, they promote changes by informing, enabling, motivating, and guiding media consumers. In the socially mediated pathway, media influences link consumers to social networks and community settings that provide incentives or disincentives for desired change.

Despite these relationships, the media most likely do not directly cause adolescents' aggression. Instead, whatever effects media violence might have on adolescents' aggression are likely mediated by the adolescents' own characteristics as well as those of their families, peers, and communities. The media likely contribute to aggressive behavior in circuitous ways. For example, adolescents who are predisposed toward aggression are likely to simply enjoy violent media. As initially aggressive children experience this media, their views of violence as normal may be affirmed, they may learn additional aggressive scripts, and the ensuing arousal may reduce inhibitions regarding aggression, all of which increases the risk of behavioral aggression. These outcomes are even more likely if the adolescent lives in a family environment that tends to exacerbate the negative effects of media exposure. And, as research suggests, it is likely that adolescents at the greatest risk for violence and aggression also experience family situations that are the least likely to reduce the potentially negative effects of media exposure. Adolescents who are not predisposed to aggression may also be affected by media violence. This is likely to be the case when they are exposed, for example, to significant amounts of television and live in families with minimal parental involvement and ineffective child-rearing techniques. Viewing violent media increases the perception of violence as acceptable, shapes the development of new aggressive scripts and behaviors, and reduces inhibitions toward aggression. Even the initially nonaggressive adolescent might become aggressive.

These developmental tendencies reveal the important point that it is possible that viewing violence on television might have little or no negative effect on adolescents. The problematic effects of media violence are likely to be attenuated if adolescents find themselves in environments that do not support what we know to be links to violence. That is, adolescents are less likely to become violent or aggressive, even if exposed to problematic media, if their environment exerts a reasonable amount of control and if socializing institutions, like families and schools, can engage in effective mediation and maintain positive emotional relationships. This agentic view—one which understands adolescents as active participants in their media environments that influence their thoughts, emotions and actions—highlights the need to address adolescents' overall information environment if we are to respond effectively to the media's increasingly powerful influence on adolescent development.

3

Adolescents' Body Images and the Media

Adolescents increasingly experience, and place themselves at risk for, unhealthy physical development. Nationally, approximately 14% of high school students are overweight and another 15% are at risk for being overweight (Grunbaum et al., 2004). The problem seems especially alarming when focusing on extremes, on adolescents who are not merely overweight but actually obese. Among adolescents, obesity remains the most common nutritional disease in the United States, and the number of obese adolescents has grown by 75% over the past three decades, with some estimates revealing that up to 25% of adolescents currently are obese (Troiano, Flegal, Kuczmarski, Campbell, & Johnson, 1995; Stice, Cameron, Hayward, Taylor, & Killen, 1999). Overall, prevalence estimates for dysfunctional eating range form 7–33% for both adolescent boys and girls (Neumark-Sztainer & Hannan, 2000). These estimates mean that about one in four adolescents experiences weight problems, a number high enough to be viewed as an epidemic in need of a "Call to Action" from the U.S. Surgeon General (United States Department of Health and Human Services, 2001b).

Although studies and statistics often fail to differentiate well between a range of eating dysfunctions, the problem's magnitude renders it difficult to discount. Eating pathologies, including threshold and subthreshold anorexia nervosa, bulimia nervosa, and binge-eating disorder, constitute some of the most prevalent psychiatric problems for adolescents, and they are harms marked by chronicity and relapse (Fairburn, Cooper, Doll, Norman, & O'Connor, 2000; Lewinsohn, Striegel-Moore, & Seeley, 2000). Research reveals that the extremes of eating pathologies, as evidenced by eating disorders and eating-disorder symptomatology, particularly afflict adolescent girls and do so at higher rates than boys (American Psychiatric Association, 2000; Smolak & Murnen, 2001). Yet, boys also reveal dysfunctional responses to weight concerns. Fully one third of adolescent boys want a leaner body (e.g., Furnham & Calnan, 1998; McCabe & Ricciardelli, 2001a; Neumark-Sztainer, Story, Falkner, Beuhring, & Resnick, 1999; Ricciardelli & McCabe, 2001a), and males tend to be fairly evenly divided between those who want to lose weight and those who want to gain it (Raudenbush & Zellner, 1997). As a result, adolescent boys are more likely to develop behavioral problems associated with the pursuit of muscularity (Drewnowski, Kennedy, Kurth, & Krahn, 1995; Ricciardelli & McCabe, 2004) and are more likely to use anabolic steroids and evidence other negative attitudes and behaviors associated with muscle dysmorphia (Labre, 2002; Pope, Phillips, & Olivardia, 2000). The conclusion drawn from these findings is that both male and female adolescents engage in behaviors to alter their body size and shape, and they suffer for doing so.

Weight concerns do not only affect adolescents with extreme problems. Even adolescents without objective weight problems reveal unhealthy attitudes toward weight. Nearly half (44%) of adolescents report trying to lose weight, with the prevalence of trying to lose weight higher among female (59%) than male (29%) high school students (Grunbaum et al., 2004). Although those numbers may seem to reflect appropriate responses to real problems in light of the rise in weight dysfunctions among American adolescents, adolescents (like adults) who try to control their weight typically do so ineffectively and actually may be placing themselves at risk for harm. Dieting or restricting food intake to lose or control weight among adolescent girls frequently precedes eating dysfunctions (Polivy & Herman, 2002; Ricciardelli & McCabe, 2004). One in four adolescents (27%) reports unhealthy weight-control behaviors, such as fasting, overeating, using diet pills, vomiting, and ingesting laxatives (see Paxton, Valois, Drane, & Wanzer, 2004). Although estimates vary widely, they indicate that 12–26% of adolescent boys and 38–50% of girls try to lose weight by dieting and other more extreme methods (Ricciardelli & McCabe, 2004). National surveys of high school students reveal that, within the time frame of 30 days, 6% of students had vomited or taken laxatives to lose weight or to keep from gaining weight and 9% of students had taken diet pills, powders, or liquids without a doctor's advice to lose weight or to keep from gaining weight (Grunbaum et al., 2004). Others engage in similarly unhealthy practices that go unnoticed as ways to control weight, such as excessive physical exercise and smoking (Tomeo, Field, & Berkey, 1999). Nationwide and again within a 30-day time frame, 57% of students exercise to lose weight or to keep from gaining weight and 15% of high school students smoke one or more cigarettes every day (Grunbaum et al., 2004). Exercising to lose weight in itself is not pathological. However, several individuals who use exercise as a weight-loss strategy go to pathological extremes and develop exercise dependence (Cockerill & Riddington, 1996). Five percent of both adolescent boys and girls can be classified as being exercise dependent, with an additional 15% of boys and 19% of girls being classified as at risk of exercise dependence (Ricciardelli & McCabe, 2004). Elevated dieting and radical weight-loss efforts reported by adolescents, especially elevated incidental exercise, appetite suppressant, laxative use, vomiting, and binge eating are more likely to result in weight gain than in weight loss (Stice et al., 1999).

Weight-related concerns contribute to many negative outcomes, both during and after adolescence. Unhealthy efforts to control weight mean that weight management efforts associate with adverse psychological health. Adolescents concerned with their weight and shape experience body-image dissatisfaction and distortion, low self-esteem, depression, and general psychiatric distress (French, Perry, Leon, & Fulkerson, 1995; Ross & Ivis, 1999). Perhaps even more troublesome, some unhealthy eating behaviors, such as overeating, associate with suicide risk, with one recent study indicating that more than one fourth of girls (29%) and boys (28%) who meet criteria for binge eating syndrome report that they have attempted suicide (Ackard, Neumark-Sztainer, Story, & Perry, 2003). Eating pathology during adolescence increases the risk for future onset of obesity, depressive disorders, suicide attempts, anxiety disorders, substance abuse, and health problems (J. G. Johnson, Cohen, Kasen, & Brook, 2002; Stice, Cameron, Killen, Hayward, & Taylor, 1999; Stice, Hayward, et al., 2000). The potentially negative effects of poor body images tend to last well beyond adolescence and actually become exacerbated during adulthood (Newman et al., 1996; Patton, Selzer, Coffey, Carlin, & Wolfe, 1999). Importantly, this means that morbidity and mortality due to weight-related disorders and problems occur more frequently during adulthood but that the antecedents that trigger these concerns arise during adolescence (see Dietz, 1998). Less than a third of individuals with eating disorders ever receive treatment (Fairburn et al., 2000; J. G. Johnson, Cohen, Kasen et al., 2002), and treatment produces symptom remission for only 40–60% of patients (Telch, Agras, & Linehan, 2001; Wilfley et al., 2002).

Given the potentially dramatic consequences of weight concerns, much effort aims to address them during adolescence with the hope of better understanding the dynamics and causes of weight-controlling efforts and of developing effective preventive efforts. Researchers describe many influences as formative in the development and maintenance of shape- and weight-related concerns. By far, body-image satisfaction receives the most attention in the study of adolescence, with research seeking to understand the nature of adolescents' body image and factors influencing its development (Littleton & Ollendick, 2003). Three factors foster this interest. First, a large portion of adolescents, especially girls, report significant body dissatisfaction (Thompson, Heinberg, Altabe, & Tantleff-Dunn, 1999). Second, dissatisfaction with one's body image increases the risk for subsequent onset of eating pathology and disorders (Attie & Brooks-Gunn, 1989; Killen et al., 1996), and we just have seen the potential pervasiveness and destructiveness of such pathologies. Third, body image serves as a potent risk factor that predicts depression, low self-esteem, emotional distress, appearance rumination, and unnecessary cosmetic surgery (Ohring, Graber, & Brooks-Gunn, 2002; Thompson, Heinberg, et al., 1999; Byely, Archibald, Graber, & Brooks-Gunn, 2000; Stice & Bearman, 2001; Wertheim, Koerner, & Paxton,

2001; Stice, Hayward, et al., 2000). In brief, adolescents' body image contributes to major public health hazards for society and adolescents themselves. The factors linked to negative body image reveal the challenges of addressing body shape and size concerns during adolescence. Properly addressing these concerns proves difficult simply because of the nature of adolescence itself. The adolescent transition necessarily involves the need to come to terms with biological changes that impact adolescents' physical and emotional health. Adolescents experience a unique combination of physical maturation, including increases in adipose (fat) for girls (e.g., Ackard & Peterson, 2001), social emphasis on appearance (e.g., Harter, 1999), focus on social comparison (Jones, 2001), significance of peers (Berndt, 1996), and search for identity (Erikson, 1968). In essence, weight and shape concerns pose particular challenges because adolescents experience them as they are negotiating normative concerns associated with the adolescent transition.

The bulk of research on adolescents' body image has focused on disorders and on the factors that contribute to adolescents' body images. Many factors actually have been identified, such as teasing or critical comments about one's appearance from parents, siblings, or peers; early pubertal maturation; sexual maltreatment; psychiatric disturbance; physical shape and mass; academic pressures; and elevated social comparison tendencies (Thompson & Heinberg, 1999; Ricciardelli & McCabe, 2004). Although research has not determined decisively the relative influence of these potential factors, research examining adolescent development in this area increasingly plays down these factors and centers attention on the media as the most important contributor to body-image disturbance and eating dysfunctions.

Given all the possible factors influencing adolescents' development of weight and shape concerns, it actually is not that unreasonable that research focuses on the media. Media researchers and developmentalists view the mass media as the most potent and pervasive communicators of sociocultural standards of body images. The media's role in sociocultural standard setting emerges as significant given the current focus on sociocultural explanations for eating dysfunctions and body-image disorders. Those explanations, not surprisingly, accord media—particularly television and fashion magazines—a dominant role (Cash & Pruzinsky, 2002; Thompson & Smolak, 2001). Perhaps more importantly, adolescents themselves note the media's influence, and that influence comports with our understanding of adolescence. Most notably, the early teen years, 13–15, are the years in which adolescents subjectively perceive the media to have a greater influence on their body image, more so than adolescents who are younger or older (Polce-Lynch, Meyers, Kliewer, & Kilmartin, 2001). Those years also happen to be important years in body-image development, in that body dissatisfaction increases significantly between the ages of 13 and 15 (Rosenblum & Lewis, 1999). These findings suggest that external cues, such as the media and social feedback, have their greatest impact on body image during early adolescence (13–15 years). Importantly, longitudinal research has found that body dissatisfaction stabilizes between ages 15 and 18 (Jones, Vigfusdottir, & Lee, 2004; Stice

& Whitenton, 2002) or actually shows a positive increase in satisfaction for girls (Attie & Brooks-Gunn, 1989) and a stabilization or decrease in body dissatisfaction for boys (Rosenblum & Lewis, 1999; Jones, 2004). This research suggests, then, that physical, social, and psychological changes during adolescence stabilize rather quickly and influence the extent to which adolescents seek and feel like they receive external cues that often derive from media.

This chapter examines research on the media's impact on adolescents' weight and shape images. In terms of addressing concerns about adolescents' body images, we find that researchers often center on the media's pervasive and largely unattainable standards of weight and beauty in the forms of muscularity and thinness. The argument made by researchers, as we will see, is that those standards tend to complicate and negatively influence adolescents' task of developing and maintaining a positive body image, especially for girls (van Hoeken, Lucas, & Hoek, 1998) but increasingly for boys (Labre, 2002). This leads researchers to focus on the internalization of media ideals and on how internalization works during the adolescent period. That focus, however, also means an effort to determine the extent to which adolescents have access to and use media and the ways by which society can modify the media's negative impact on adolescent development.

Media Body Images and Their Effects

We already have seen in previous chapters that adolescents are, in many ways, overexposed to media. This exposure becomes significant to the extent that the quantity and nature of relevant information found in mainstream media portrays images of the body. Content analyses of body depictions reveal that television reflects the thin ideal of feminine beauty for girls and of lean muscularity for boys. For example, underweight women are overrepresented in comparison to the general population (Fouts & Burggraff, 1999). Similarly, the media, especially magazines and increasingly television, focus on dense, muscular, lean, and increasingly unattainable male body ideals, which is now described as a culture of muscularity (Agliata & Tantleff-Dunn, 2004). Likewise, a preponderance of commercials also touts the benefits of weight loss, muscle gain, and beauty aids (Downs & Harrison, 1985). Together, these messages suggest high rewards for thinness, weight, loss and muscularity (Owen & Laurel-Seller, 2000). As a result, these depictions offer stereotypical views for boys and girls and difficult-to-attain body shapes.

Considering the impact of these portrayals means determining how adolescents use them. Researchers reveal well how the media infiltrate adolescents' attitudes toward their bodies. The bulk of concern about media influence on body image focuses on the advertising and editorial content of fashion magazines simply because those are most relevant to adolescent girls (Malkin, Wornian, & Chrisler, 1999). That research suggests that young women are frequently exposed to messages and images that reinforce the body ideal, which become the standards of thinness and beauty for defining oneself and others (Pesa, Syre &

Jones, 2000). Girls, in particular, have a greater likelihood of being negatively affected by the feminine ideal, and this is more pronounced when their bodies are undergoing dramatic changes and when adult definitions of "beauty" become relevant social norms (Martin & Gentry, 1997). Much research has focused on determining the validity of these suggested links, what constitutes appropriate empirical evidence, and how to assess direct and indirect links.

Correlational Research

Numerous studies document associations between adolescents' media use and their concerns about weight and body image (Thompson, Heinberg, et al., 1999). For example, girls' body dissatisfaction relates to reading fashion magazines at least twice a week (Field, Camargo, et al., 1999) and to reading magazines that feature thin models and dieting information (Harrison & Cantor, 1997). Importantly, the link does not seem spurious. Teenage girls who read magazines on a regular basis view them as an important source of beauty and fitness information (Levine & Smolak, 1996). Self-reported influences of magazine advertisements and articles on personal conceptions of ideal body shapes significantly account for variation in weight management behavior, disordered eating, and drive for thinness in adolescent girls (Levine, Smolak, Moodey, Shuman, & Hessen, 1994). Researchers continue to find that teenage girls endorse their ideal as the models found in fashion magazines aimed at teenage girls, and the ideal they describe is clearly in the anorexic range (Thompson & Heinberg, 1999).

Findings from the magazine-exposure literature parallel findings from television exposure. A girl's body dissatisfaction positively correlates with her watching soap operas, music videos (Tiggeman & Pickering, 1996), and television programs featuring thin main characters (Botta, 1999). Middle-school-aged girls who perceive more television influence on the importance of attractiveness report greater body-image dissatisfaction, use of weight management techniques, and pathological beliefs about eating (see Thompson & Heinberg, 1999). Perceived media pressure to lose weight also has been found to associate with weight loss strategies in adolescent boys (Ricciardelli & McCabe, 2001b). Although adolescents may recognize the influence of television, they are not necessarily aware of the extent of the effect. Adolescents generally are not unaware of the unrealistic nature of media portrayals, but a surprising number are not. Surveys indicate, for example, that 71% of adolescent girls ages 16 and 17 believe that female actors on television are unrealistically thin, which leaves over one fourth unaware that the vast majority of female television characters are thinner than the average American woman (Thompson & Heinberg, 1999). Many adolescents do not seem to realize the potentially pathological nature of influences on them.

Experimental Research

Controlled laboratory experiments have examined the effects of viewing magazine ads or photos of models on ratings of body satisfaction or physical attractiveness. These studies typically expose some participants to neutral images (cars or models of neutral weight) or to images of ideal body types in order to gauge their immediate psychological impact. Several reviews conclude that controlled experiments do not support a straightforward relationship between media and negative body images (Levine & Smolak, 1996, 1998). Yet, we still can cull important suggestions from these experimental findings.

Reviews of experimental research reveal that many factors shape the media's influence on viewers. For example, one study reveals that a 3-minute exposure to twelve photographs of models taken from popular women's magazines led to transitory increases in depression, stress, guilt, shame, insecurity, and body-image dissatisfaction that were not evident for controls who viewed photographs of average-sized models (Stice & Shaw, 1994). Importantly, women with eating disorders are even more likely to demonstrate negative effects following exposure to photographs of models from popular fashion magazines (Waller, Hamilton, & Shaw, 1992). Yet, other studies report no immediate effect of thin media images on body satisfaction. Comparing the influence of thin models versus control images, some studies find no significant differences in body satisfaction (Champion & Furnham, 1999) or body self-perception (Martin & Kennedy, 1993).

Controlled experiments also have examined the role of internalization as a dispositional factor linking exposure to heightened distress. That research also reveals complicated effects of media exposure. For example, some studies expose participants to videotapes of commercials, with experimental groups viewing stimuli emphasizing societal ideals of thinness and attractiveness. These studies find that college students who view the materials focusing on ideals rather than on neutral subjects report increases in dissatisfaction with both weight and overall appearance when they possess high dispositional levels of internalization. In contrast, those with low dispositional levels of internalization actually reveal decreases in dissatisfaction with both weight and overall appearance following exposure to the experimental tapes portraying body ideals (Heinberg & Thompson, 1995). Satisfied adolescents seem actually to benefit from biased media. In conducting separate analyses of satisfied and dissatisfied participants, some researchers have found that the satisfied participants felt thinner after viewing advertising focused on thin body image than did the satisfied participants in the control condition of neutral images (Posavac, Posavac, & Posavac, 1998). Dispositional levels of internalization of societal ideals for thinness and attractiveness moderate the effect of societal ideals.

Given the complex findings of controlled experiments, meta-analytic techniques have offered much-needed clarity. One highly cited meta-analysis has examined findings gleaned from twenty-five experimental manipulations of the thin ideal on the body image of women and girls. The analysis revealed small but consistent effects, indicating that female participants have a lower body satisfaction after viewing thin media images than after viewing images of average-size models, plus-size models, or inanimate objects like cars or houses (Groescz, Levine, & Murnen, 2002). Importantly, the analysis found that few studies had measured dispositional body dissatisfaction before exposing participants to images of the thin ideal. But, those that did measure dispositional dissatisfaction suggest that the negative effect of those images is enhanced when the subjects exposed to them are vulnerable because they have already internalized the slender ideal of beauty.

Meta-analyses revealed two other critical points about the effects of media, points that reveal the importance of popular media for adolescents. First, the effects appeared to be greatest with only a few exposures, not with ten or more exposures. This finding, coupled with the finding of dispositional dissatisfaction, suggests that the experimental effect is seen most clearly in the activation—not the cultivation—of a thinness schema in females who are highly motivated and cognitively prepared to think about themselves in relation to weight, shape, and beauty. Second, the effects were greater among younger teen girls than women and among those with initially low levels of body satisfaction. Together, these findings make the fundamental point that the glorification of slenderness has the most deleterious effect during or immediately after the early adolescent transition and that the effect is particularly strong on girls who are entering that transition already possessing a strong investment in thinness and beauty (see also Levine & Smolak, 1998).

Experiments have examined the effects of a thin ideal portrayed on television. Generally, those that have compared the effects of appearance-related commercials with other commercials reported adverse effects on at least some participants. Girls and women exposed to appearance-related commercials, such as those that depict women as sex objects, expressed greater anger, anxiety, and depression (Cattarin, Thompson, Thomas, & Williams, 2000; Hargreaves & Tiggemann, 2002a; Heargreaves & Tiggemann, 2003; Heinberg & Thompson, 1995; Lavine, Sweeny, & Wagner, 1999). They also rated beauty characteristics as being more important to attract the opposite sex (Tan, 1979). They further reported a greater tendency to compare themselves with models in the advertisements (Cattarin et al., 2000). Importantly, not all experiments show negative effects. One study, for example, exposed sorority members to product commercials either rated as highly body-image or neutral-image oriented; the body-image commercials reduced body-size overestimations and made young women feel less depressed (Myers & Biocca, 1992). These results show complexity and, again, the need to consider viewers' dispositions. The conflicting results lead to the conclusion that those who are at risk are more likely to experience negative responses, but the studies actually did not examine who or why individuals would be at risk.

Some experimental research has focused on males. Research that has exposed older adolescents to television advertisements containing ideal male images or neutral images indicate that those exposed to ideal images became significantly more depressed and had higher levels of muscle dissatisfaction than those exposed to neutral television ads (Agliata & Tantleff-Dunn, 2004). These findings are consistent with research on later adolescence which finds that, when boys experience body dissatisfaction, it is often due to sociocultural pressures that encourage larger, excessively muscular, and powerful bodies (Cohane & Pope, 2001; Pope & Gruber, 1997). Importantly, the media actually may play a larger role in male's body image concerns than previously thought. This is made even more possible by the way males tend to find visual materials more evocative than females do (Barthel, 1992). But the findings may not necessarily result from seeing male bodies but from boys' viewing female bodies. Research has examined the influence of viewing stereotypical images of women on men. A leading study found that, compared to men exposed to neutral advertisements, men exposed to advertisements that portrayed women as sex objects rated their own bodies as thinner (Lavine et al., 1999). Viewing sexist ads also led to larger discrepancies between actual and ideal body size, with men preferring a larger body and chest, and overestimations of the ideal male size selected by their male peers. It was argued that television advertisements may impact males' body images via messages that lead to inaccurate stereotyped perceptions of the ideal and negative self-appraisals. These provocative findings reveal that the media clearly evoke reactions in how males view their own bodies.

The Significance and Limitations of Effects Research

The above media and developmental research findings reveal important developments in the study of media effects, but the findings are not without limitations. In fact, the research remains quite limited. The bulk of research examining the influence of media is correlational in nature and the direction of relationships remains unclear. As a result, we do not know whether exposure to media is an etiological factor in body-image and eating disturbance or whether individuals with eating pathologies or body-image disturbances choose to expose themselves to such images at a higher rate than their less distressed counterparts. Evidence from controlled experiments also has been criticized (Levine & Smolak, 1996; Thompson, Heinberg, et al., 1999). The effects of brief exposures on body image may be short-lived and confined to conditions that may not reflect adolescents' everyday experiences with media. In addition, the method appears ill suited to test the effects of cumulative media exposure. Given that we do not necessarily know what these findings mean for extremes of weight and shape concerns, we know even less about the influence of media on adolescents without extreme responses to the media's portrayal of body images. Some efforts have sought to examine the media's impact by using longitudinal methods, but those studies typically only examine effects over a few months (Jones, 2004). This is further complicated by research that notes how the media give people what they already want (Raphael & Lacey, 1992). Even those claims, however, do not necessarily erase the reinforcing nature of media portrayals. Most likely, the relationship between mass media and body image is complex, reciprocal, and defined by many moderating factors.

Understanding Media Effects on Adolescents' Body Images

The findings we have examined thus far may be deemed suggestive, but they do reveal a consistent link between media exposure and how adolescents feel about their bodies. The general proposition is that efforts to reduce the discrepancy between actual body size and ideal body image often result in negative outcomes. This proposition, however, does not explain as well why the media influence some adolescents more than others. For the purpose of understanding the media's potentially powerful impact during adolescence and on particular adolescents, two explanations appear especially compelling: self-schema theory and social-comparison theory. These theories and their supporting research gain considerable meaningfulness when placed in the context of adolescent development and media effects.

Internalized Schema Effects

The schema approach seeks to explain why the media influence some people more than others. More specifically, researchers have borrowed from self-schema theory and have developed the concept of appearance schemas. These schemas are learned beliefs, assumptions, and generalizations about one's appearance and its implications (see Thompson, Heinberg, et al., 1999). For example, individuals' schematics for a dimension such as body-image investment may be primed by exposure to ideals of attractiveness and, in turn, process and react more negatively to appearance stimuli than those who are aschematic (do not have a particular schema) on that dimension (Lavin & Cash, 2001). These schemas can be activated by appearance-related cues, and, when activated, influence subsequent emotions and information processing. Importantly, while we all possess these schemas, we do not possess them to the same degree (Markus, Hamill, & Sentis, 1987). Some who are high in appearance schematicity invest more heavily in their appearance compared with others, just as, for example, some children who invest more in gendered appearances do so because they have more salient and elaborated gender schemas than others (Ruble & Martin, 1998). Individuals differ in the strength, elaboration, and accessibility of these schemas. In particular, the impact of appearance-related information on perceptions, affect, and behavior may be especially strong for individuals who develop highly elaborate schemata linking issues of appearance with implications for the self (Hargreaves & Tiggemann, 2002b). Thus, individuals are likely to invest differently in their bodies depending on appearance schematicity, and they are likely to be satisfied quite differently.

Body schemas in the development of the self appear quite important to adolescents given their developmental task of coming to terms with rapid body changes and the importance adolescents attach to visual media. Since adolescents readily admit that media influences their behaviors, it is not surprising to find that the degree to which individuals accept or internalize socially defined standards for weight and attractiveness, referred to as thin-ideal internalization, emerges as an important mediator of the relationship between media exposure and disturbances in their body image as well as eating dysfunctions (Thompson, Heinberg, et al., 1999). Various measures of this construct assess the extent to which individuals wish to look like fashion models or media celebrities, compare their own body to media figures, and use the media to learn about attractiveness (Cusumano & Thompson, 2001; Thompson & Stice, 2001). This commitment made by individuals to socially defined ideals of attractiveness appears to undermine body satisfaction to the extent that most individuals necessarily find it quite difficult, if not impossible, to attain ideals (Thompson & Stice, 2001).

The linkage between internalized appearance ideals and body dissatisfaction receives substantial empirical support. A greater commitment to appearance ideals associates with heightened body dissatisfaction in cross-sectional studies of girls and boys (Cusumano & Thompson, 2001; Jones et al., 2004; Smolak, Levine, & Thompson, 2001) and college women (Cusumano & Thompson, 1997; Stice, Schupak-Neuberg, Shaw, & Stein, 1994). For example, wanting to look like people portrayed in media is among the strongest predictors of adolescents' concerns about weight (Field et al., 2001; Taylor et al., 1998) and greatly increases the odds of becoming a constant dieter (Field et al., 2001). In addition, thin-ideal internalization mediates the relationship between eating disorder symptoms and exposure to ideal body images in magazines and television. That is, media exposure to print media and television leads to the internalization of slender-ideal body shape which, in turn, leads to body dissatisfaction and eating-disordered symptoms (Stice et al., 1994). Not surprisingly, it is not the exposure to total media, such as television, that relates to body-image disturbance but rather exposure to particular programs, such as soap operas, movies, and music videos (Tiggemann & Pickering, 1996). This finding has been replicated more recently for music videos (Borzekowski, Robinson, & Killen, 2000), for "ideal body" programs (Van Den Bulck, 2000), and for fashion magazines (Harrison & Cantor, 1997; Tiggemann, 2003). Thus, the internalization of a stringent and essentially unattainable ideal of beauty can lead to body dissatisfaction, negative affect, low self-esteem, or even eating disorders (Thompson & Stice, 2001).

The suggestion that those at risk are more likely to experience negative responses to media focusing on ideal body types receives support from the only study that longitudinally examined the impact of magazines. That study randomly assigned adolescent girls to a 15-month subscription for *Seventeen* magazine or to a nonsubscription condition (Stice, Spangler, & Agras, 2001). The subscribers spent more time reading *Seventeen* than did the comparison group, 21 versus 15 total hours. But the study did not find effects for the magazine subscription on any of the negative outcomes measured. However, girls who lacked adequate social support reported increased body dissatisfaction, dieting behaviors, and bulimic symptoms. In addition, those who were subscribed reported increased negative effect if they had initially high body dissatisfaction. Although important, this area of study remains quite limited to the extent that longitudinal studies have yet to focus on the prospective role of internalized appearance ideals for boys.

The above research findings, as we have noted, focus on girls' experiences and tends to approach body-image concerns from girls' perspectives. The impact of media exposure on adolescent males' body images, however, increasingly becomes an area of inquiry (Pope et al., 2000). That research examines how the media industry subjects males to a culture of muscularity, a focus on dense, muscular, lean, and increasingly unattainable male body ideals (Agliata & Tantleff-Dunn, 2004). Not surprisingly, research that has exposed older adolescents to television advertisements containing ideal male images or neutral images indicated that those exposed to ideal images became significantly more depressed and had higher levels of muscle dissatisfaction than those exposed to neutral television ads (Agliata & Tantleff-Dunn, 2004). Importantly, unlike research with women, this research found no evidence supporting the notion that those high in dispositional disturbance (those who noted higher discrepancies between self and ideal images) differed from those in low dispositional disturbance in terms of the influence of ideal advertisements. This means that males may not internalize and process sociocultural pressures of appearance through the same schema-driven processes as females; males may not filter messages like women do. Importantly, although recent research still confirms that girls compared with boys report greater internalization of appearance ideals (Cusumano & Thompson, 2001), internalization has been related to lower body esteem during early adolescence for both boys and girls (Smolak et al., 2001). These findings are consistent with research examining older adolescents that finds that boys who experience body dissatisfaction tend to do so because of sociocultural pressures that encourage larger, excessively muscular, and powerful bodies (Cohane & Pope, 2001; Pope & Gruber, 1997).

Social-Comparison Effects

Social comparison refers to the cognitive judgments that people make about their own attributes compared with those of others and has been an important psychological process connected to self-evaluation (Wood, 1989). Social-comparison theorists typically distinguish three types of motives for social comparison: self-evaluation, self-improvement, and self- (or ego-) enhancement (Wood, 1989). The purpose of comparison has an impact. Although information gathered through social comparison can theoretically enhance or detract from self-regard, an interesting aspect of research on appearance social comparison has been its consistent linkage with negative self-evaluation. Most notable, one group of researchers found that early adolescents (in this instance 9- to 14-year-olds) who were instructed to compare their own physical attractiveness to that of slender models (for the purposes of self-evaluation) felt less physically attractive afterward (Martin & Gentry, 1997). Conversely, girls instructed to think about slender models in ways that inspire self-improvement or enhance the girls' perceptions of their own personal beauty felt more physically attractive after seeing the models. With music videos, it was shown that viewing thin ideal images produces more self-reported actual comparison among young women (Tiggemann & Slater, 2003). Further, it was shown that the level of comparison processing mediates the effect of video images on body dissatisfaction (Tiggemann & Slater, 2003).

Whether the targets of comparison have been peers or celebrities, appearance social comparison has been associated with elevated body dissatisfaction in cross-sectional studies of adolescent boys and girls (Jones, 2001; Schutz, Paxton, & Wertheim, 2002) and of college women (Thompson, Coovert, & Stormer, 1999; van den Berg, Thompson, Obremski-Brandon, & Coovert, 2002). These findings are important in light of research indicating that early-adolescent girls are more likely to compare themselves to slender models, and girls with low self-esteem and poor body images are more likely to seek out and enjoy advertisements with slender, attractive models (Martin & Gentry, 1997; Martin & Kennedy, 1993); early-adolescent girls who read fashion magazines and compare themselves to portrayed models report greater body dissatisfaction and higher levels of disordered eating (Field, Cheung, et al., 1999). Longitudinal studies have replicated these findings (Jones, 2004).

Findings examining links to social comparison are buttressed by the mechanisms through which the ideal body types contribute to disturbance. These mechanisms highlight the significance of social comparison as the prime factor in the development and maintenance of body-image disturbance (Smolak, Levine, & Gralen, 1993). Females report appearance-related peer-group comparisons to be the most influential on body image (Heinberg & Thompson, 1992). This is not to say that mass media is not influential, for the media have been identified as the most influential force in forming, strengthening, and activating stereotypes (Lavine et al., 1999). Males, on the other hand, place a greater emphasis on comparison with celebrities (Heinberg & Thompson, 1992). During adolescence, especially early adolescence, when social comparison plays a more significant role in self-perception, girls who do not have the ideal body shape agonize about their bodies (Levine & Smolak, 1998). When coupled with certain family and personality dynamics, these conditions can induce dangerous eating disorders, such as anorexia nervosa and bulimia nervosa (Polivy & Herman, 1999). One study that examined these issues longitudinally (over a few months) found that the self-evaluative process of social comparison significantly contributes to change in body dissatisfaction among adolescent girls (Jones, 2004). Although previous cross-sectional research has established a linkage between social comparison and body image (Schutz, Paxton, & Wertheim, 2002), this is one of the only studies to provide confirming longitudinal evidence.

A possible explanation for the prominence of social comparison as a significant predictor comes from research on individual differences in the use of social comparison. Individuals with low self-esteem and more uncertain self-evaluations, especially when the self-evaluations are personally important, report more use of social comparison (Lyubomirsky & Ross, 1997; Pelham & Wachsmuth, 1995). The descriptions of uncertainty and low self-esteem are reminiscent of the characteristics frequently associated with adolescent girls, especially within the appearance arena (Harter, 1999). Indeed, research has demonstrated that girls use social comparison more regularly than do boys (Jones, 2001). That finding has been extended by longitudinal research demonstrating that individual differences among girls in the frequency of social comparison have prospective consequences for undermining an appreciation for body image as girls persistently stand in judgment on themselves (Jones, 2004).

Significance and Limitations of Effects Research

Self-schema theory and social-comparison theory provide important insight to our efforts to understand the media's potentially powerful role in shaping adolescents' views about their bodies and responses to those views. Internalized appearance ideals and appearance social comparisons appear to be central psychological factors that account for body dissatisfaction. The internalized appearance-ideals factor represents the adoption of societal appearance ideals as a personal goal and standard. Social comparison, on the other hand, represents the evaluative process that involves both seeking information and making judgments about the self relative to others. Existing research reveals that both factors clearly play a role in adolescents' perceptions of who they are, as well as in the media's role in that perception. But research has yet to investigate how those factors work together, and how they work over time.

Placing the Media in the Context of Adolescent Development

As noted at the beginning of our discussion, the media industry constitutes only one element of an appearance culture that potentially shapes adolescents' internalization of appearance ideals and body shapes. Research has sought to address the impact of peers, families, and individual characteristics. Regrettably, research tends to view these factors either in isolation or aggregated together in a manner that prohibits comparing the contribution of one factor to another. Yet, the current findings, coupled with our understanding of the adolescent period, still provide us with a clearer view of the media's role in adolescents' weight and shape concerns.

Family and Peer Influences

Two areas of study are particularly relevant to an understanding of adolescents' concerns about their weight and shape. One approach proposes that media predispose individuals to eating disturbances when messages are condoned and reinforced by family and peers. The negative impact of this predisposition is felt when it occurs in the setting of low self-esteem—a poorly developed self-concept—and perceptions of having problematic weight (Stice, Shaw, & Nemeroff, 1998). Another view suggests that predispositions are shaped and maintained by family and peer modeling of weight concerns. Those predispositions interact with adolescents' developmental changes, such as pubertal changes and academic stress. Social contexts of messages of ideals may then lead to disordered eating (Levine & Smolak, 1998; Thompson, Heinberg, et al., 1999). Regrettably, research does not allow us to accept or reject either of these approaches. Research does, however, provide us with a picture of the influences of families and peers on adolescents' weight and shape concerns.

As with any socialization matter during adolescence, peers clearly can play a potentially powerful role. As children enter adolescence, peer relationships play an increasingly powerful role in their well-being and adjustment (Hartup, 1996). During adolescence, friends create a social world governed by norms and expectations that reflect and shape behaviors and attitudes in arenas such as academic performance, drug use and smoking, and antisocial activities (Capaldi, Dishion, Stoolmiller, & Yoerger, 2001; Urberg, Degirmencioglu, & Pilgrim, 1997). In addition, friends and peer pressure can play a powerful role in encouraging and sustaining dieting (Levine, Smolak, & Hayden, 1994; Paxton, Schutz, Wertheim, & Muir, 1999). Peers also seem to exert some pressure among adolescent girls who adopt extreme weight-loss behaviors, such as when bulimics report being pressured by their peers to engage in both binging and purging (Stice, Nemeroff, & Shaw, 1996). Given that reality, an understanding of body-image disturbance necessarily requires considering the contribution of peers to the internalization of media influences and body images.

Little research focuses on the contribution of the peer-appearance context to prospective change in body dissatisfaction. Although existing research has included friend and peer pressure as a factor in the development of body dissatisfaction and eating disorders for girls (Paxton et al., 1999), researchers typically aggregate peer influences with other sources of social-cultural pressure (Stice & Whitenton, 2002; Thompson, Heinberg, et al., 1999; Wertheim, Martin, Prior, Sanson, & Smart, 2001). Yet research in the area of peer relationships verifies the importance of peers during adolescence and the need to distinguish conceptually and empirically between friends and other peers (Bukowski, Hoza, & Boivin, 1993).

Research that directly compares peer and media images reveals that media images, in their own right, actually have limited direct impact when tested in a multidimensional model (see Cusumano & Thompson, 1997; Jones et al., 2004). The findings that place more focus on peers than media do not necessarily mean that the media exert no influence. To the contrary, those findings reveal that how media is used, such as with peers, indicates the media's impact. In considering peer influence, it would seem that two aspects of peer experiences would contribute to internalization and body image: appearance conversations with friends and appearance criticisms and pressures from peers.

Just as adolescents who become deviant have been seen as obtaining deviance training with their friends, adolescents also engage in "appearance training" with their friends. Conversations about clothes, looks, and attractiveness provide the everyday context for processing information relevant to appearance concerns. The friendship context is of special importance for body-image development because of the sheer amount of time spent with same-sex friends, the value placed on friendships (Berndt, 1996), and the ways in which friends create an appearance culture with shared norms and expectations (Paxton et al., 1999). Conversations with friends about appearance direct attention to appearance-related issues, reinforce the value and importance of appearance to close friends, and promote the construction of appearance ideals. Adolescents, both boys and girls, who report engaging in more frequent conversations about appearance with friends are more likely to endorse greater internalization that, in turn, relates to greater feelings of dissatisfaction with one's own body (Jones et al., 2004). These benign conversations with friends provide a major context within which to value and amplify appearance concerns as they highlight appearance as an important attribute, support the construction of appearance norms and ideals, and encourage evaluating the self relative to others on physical attributes. Girls and boys who report more frequent conversations with their friends about appearance also report greater internalized appearance ideals and body dissatisfaction (Jones et al., 2004). Importantly, conformity to appearance ideals links to the perceived social benefit of peer acceptance. For example, high school girls who thought that their peer relationships would improve through weight loss also felt negatively about their bodies (Paxton et al., 1999). Adolescents experience more dissatisfaction with their body images if they believe that their relationships with peers would improve as a result of appearance changes (Jones, 2004). Longitudinal research reveals that body dissatisfaction does not, in itself, generate a negative cycle among girls by enhancing social-comparison processes that serve to perpetuate body dissatisfaction. Rather it is the social context, particularly the appearance training that goes on in the conversations with friends, that encourages appearance social comparison and leads to change in body dissatisfaction (Jones, 2004). These findings are buttressed by research indicting that middle-school-aged girls who perceive higher peer influence and more television influence on the importance of attractiveness report greater body-image dissatisfaction, use of weight management techniques, and pathological beliefs about eating (see Thompson & Heinberg, 1999). Thus, adolescents who endorse popular media and who have appropriate comparison targets regarding attractiveness may be more vulnerable to media influence.

The place of peer criticism about appearance also is a well-documented characteristic of adolescence (Eder, Evans, & Parker, 1995). The experience of being a target of appearance criticisms from peers can reinforce the value of appearance to peers and highlight specific desirable appearance attributes. And, the absence of such attributes presumably serves as the basis for the criticism. Peer appearance criticism, then, does more than generate a direct and potent experience with negative evaluations of one's own body by another. It also potentially contributes to internalization by reflecting features of the appearance culture among peers. Researchers have long documented links between critical appearance comments and negative body image for pre-adolescent girls up to those in late adolescence (Levine, Smolak, & Hayden, 1994; Thompson, Heinberg, et al., 1999). Several cross-sectional studies of adolescents have confirmed a positive linkage between teasing and body dissatisfaction for boys and girls (Barker & Galambos, 2003; Jones et al., 2004; Levine et al., 1994; Lunner et al., 2000; Paxton et al., 1999; van den Berg, Wertheim, Thompson, & Paxton, 2002; Wertheim et al., 2001). These findings are supported by research indicating that critical comments from peers rarely occur for most students, but when they do occur, they emerge as strong, direct predictors of body dissatisfaction and also emerge as strong predictors of internalization of body-image types, which in turn impact body image. This reflects findings from late adolescents who have described teasing episodes from their childhood and adolescence: peers in general (62%) and friends (47%) were the most commonly recalled perpetrators, but it was peers in general who were endorsed most frequently as the worst teasers (Rieves & Cash, 1996). Importantly, where research does reveal that girls are more embedded in an appearance culture and feel less satisfied with their body images, boys report greater peer criticism about their bodies and express greater changes in body dissatisfaction (Jones et al., 2004).

Although research examining the development of body images during the adolescent period does focus heavily on the relative influence of peers and friends, it is important to consider how parents potentially play a powerful role in their children's socialization. Family members, particularly mothers, are perceived as the primary socialization agents who transmit messages to adolescents regarding their appearance and eating practices. For example, through modeling and encouragement from their mothers, girls with eating disorders are more likely to be rewarded for engaging in these behaviors than girls who did not experience eating disorders (Pike & Rodin, 1991; Moreno & Thelen, 1993; Keel, Heatherton, Harnden, & Hornig, 1997). When not focusing on extremes, other familial sources of influence emerge as significant. Fathers are perceived to have a greater influence on their daughters' attitudes, and mothers are perceived to have a greater influence on their sons' attitudes (McCabe & Vincent, 2003). For boys, mothers exert a strong influence on body image, whereas fathers have a strong influence on levels of exercise and eating (Ricciardelli, McCabe, & Banfield, 2000). Mothers influence through positive comments, whereas fathers influence through criticism. Only one study appears to have examined actual messages from mothers and fathers and their influence on adolescent boys. Mothers may be more accepting of dieting as a weight-loss strategy, whereas fathers may be more accepting of alternative strategies such as exercise (Wertheim, et al., 2002). Cross-sectional studies have shown that parents exert their influence by modeling and by directly encouraging body-change strategies in both adolescent boys and girls (McCabe & Ricciardelli, 2003a; Ricciardelli & McCabe, 2001b; Vincent & McCabe, 2000). Longitudinal studies also found that boys who reported that it was important for their fathers that they not be fat were more likely to become constant dieters over a 1-year period (Field et al., 2001). Weight loss strategies in adolescent boys over an 8-month period have been found to be weakly predicted by both perceived parental and peer pressure to lose weight (McCabe & Ricciardelli, 2003a; Ricciardelli & McCabe, 2003). In addition, parents' views of diets and eating concerns may not be the strongest influence on disordered eating among adolescents; parents' psychopathological traits appear more influential (Steiger, Stotland, Trottier, & Ghadiriam, 1996; Olivardia, Pope, & Hudson, 2000; Swarr & Richards, 1996).

Few studies have examined the combined effects of family, peers, and the media within a single research design. One study assessed eating behavior, body satisfaction, and concern about being slender among 385 girls aged 10 to 14 years (Levine et al., 1994). The authors found that the media and teasing and criticism by the family were the strongest predictors of body dissatisfaction and drive for thinness. Family and peers, but not the media, were found to be the strongest influences on bulimic symptomatology among young adult women. Another important study found that this influence took place through social reinforcement and modeling, a finding supported by earlier research (Stice, 1998). Yet another found that peers were the strongest influence on weight concerns among high school girls, although the media also significantly influenced concerns about weight (Taylor et al., 1998). Bulimic symptoms relate to perceived pressure to be thin from family, friends, dating partners, and the media (Irving, 1990; Stice, Ziemba, Margolis, & Flick, 1996). These seemingly contradictory findings reveal the significance of media for general dissatisfaction and the even more significant role families and peers play in more dysfunctional responses to body images.

Together, the above findings reveal the important role played by social support. The support of peers, friends, and family often figures prominently in adolescents' general health. Not surprisingly, theorists have suggested that a lack of social support may play an important role in promoting body-image and eating disturbances (Stice, Presnell, & Spangler, 2002; Swarr & Richards, 1996). In support of those propositions, mounting indirect evidence buttresses the assertion that social support may be related to body dissatisfaction. Research suggests that deficits in social support predicted eating pathology onset (Stice et al., 2002). Social support has been found to mitigate the adverse effects of sociocultural pressures to be thin on the subsequent development of body dissatisfaction (Stice, Presnell, & Bearman, 2001), and deficits in perceived social support predict increased body dissatisfaction (Stice & Whitenton, 2002). Researchers have suggested that positive family and peer relationships may serve as a protective factor against developing eating disorders (Archibald, Graber, & Brooks-Gunn, 1999). Much, however, depends on the conceptualization of support. Three cross-sectional studies have found an association between weight concerns and poor parent relations. One study found that concerns about overeating associated with lower perceived intimacy with the father, whereas concerns about undereating related to lower perceived intimacy with both the father and mother (Mueller et al., 1995). Another study found that binge eating and purging moderately associated with family problems (Lock, Reisel, & Steiner, 2001). Finally, another found that disordered eating associated with perceived low family communication, low parental caring, and low peer support (Neumark-Sztainer, Story, Hannan, Beuhring, & Resnick, 2000). Yet, cross-sectional studies (Vincent & McCabe, 2000; Wertheim et al., 1992; Wichstrom, 2000) and one longitudinal study (Ricciardelli & McCabe, 2003) have found no evidence for the relationship between parent and peer relations and attitudes and behaviors associated with boys' disordered eating.

The above findings are consistent with the proposition that acceptance in their immediate social network might help adolescents feel more positively about themselves and their bodies and render them more resilient to media and other sociocultural pressures. The perception that they are accepted and appreciated in their immediate social environment is thought to help adolescents feel more positively about themselves and their bodies. Perceived social support may also buffer adolescents from the myriad pressures to conform to the culturally defined thin ideal or body muscularity that putatively fosters body dissatisfaction. Popular media operates through social relationships.

Biological Influences

Body mass remains the most consistent biological characteristic related to body image satisfaction. Cross-sectional (Jones et al., 2004; van den Berg, Thompson, et al., 2002; Field et al., 2001) and longitudinal research (Cattarin & Thompson, 1994; Stice & Whitenton, 2002; Striegel-Moore et al., 2000) reveals that both girls and boys who have greater body mass express heightened body dissatisfaction. Although elevated adiposity emerges as one of the most potent predictors of increases in body dissatisfaction (Stice & Whitenton, 2002; Jones, 2004), the findings do seem to vary based on sociocultural factors. We know that links between body mass and satisfaction are less pronounced in groups of girls from higher social classes (Byely et al., 2000; Stice & Bearman, 2001; Stice & Whitenton, 2002). In addition, the longitudinal studies that have examined the hypothesized direct relation between body mass and change in body dissatisfaction have found support mainly for girls (Jones, 2004). Prospective, longitudinal studies reveal that issues associated with muscularity rather than weight are of central importance for boys (Jones, 2004). Boys who are in early adolescence evidence a desire to increase body bulk, but others evidence a desire to increase muscle tone (McCabe & Ricciardelli, 2001a). Several studies have found a higher body mass index (BMI) to be associated weakly with dieting and other weight loss behaviors among adolescent males (see Ricciardelli & McCabe, 2004). As with girls, it seems that higher BMI for boys also increases body dissatisfaction and social pressure to be thin, which putatively lead to dieting, negative affect, and elevated risk for eating pathology (Stice, 2002). The importance that boys attach to weight loss may also be different from the meaning it has for adolescent girls. Weight loss for boys may be associated with decreasing body fat and increasing muscle leanness, whereas for girls it may be focused on slimness. Overall, these findings have been interpreted as providing additional support for the assertion that the greater the degree of departure from the current thin ideal for girls and muscularity for boys, the greater the body dissatisfaction (Graber, Brooks-Gunn, Paikoff, & Warren, 1994; Jones, 2004).

Although both pubertal development and negative affect have been linked to body dissatisfaction, dieting behaviors, and binge eating, researchers have yet to untangle the role of pubertal development in body-change strategies. With pubertal development, girls experience a normative increase in body fat that may move them further away from society's ideal body shape for a woman. Those developments support consistent findings that associate puberty with higher levels of body dissatisfaction and disordered eating among girls (e.g., Attie & Brooks-Gunn, 1989; Keel, Fulkerson, & Leon, 1997; Swarr & Richards, 1996). In contrast to puberty in girls, puberty moves the majority of boys closer to society's ideal body shape for boys. Those developments help explain why the three studies that included boys failed to find any relationship between pubertal development and disordered eating (e.g., Keel et al., 1997; Leon, Fulkerson, Perry, & Early-Zald, 1995; Vincent & McCabe, 2000). They also help explain why three other cross-sectional studies (McCabe & Ricciardelli, 2001b, 2003b; McCabe, Ricciardelli, & Finemore, 2002) and three longitudinal studies found no association between pubertal growth and strategies to weight loss and binge-eating behavior (Leon et al., 1995; Ricciardelli & McCabe, 2003). Although pubertal development for boys may be related more closely to strategies to increase weight, it also links to an effort to increase muscle tone. The focus on muscle tone has been used to explain why one cross-sectional study found that boys who reported that they had reached puberty were significantly more likely than prepubertal boys to try to lose weight (O'Dea & Abraham, 1999) and another finding that the prevalence of purging in boys was associated with the stage of pubertal development (Field, Camargo, et al., 1999). Together, these studies do not point to an important role for puberty's effect on body-change strategies.

Pubertal timing, rather than puberty itself, appears to be a salient factor for determining whether puberty will be associated with any adjustment difficulties (e.g., Graber, Lewinsohn, Seeley, & Brooks-Gunn, 1997). From a developmental deviance perspective, experiencing puberty out of synchrony with peers may foster feelings of alienation and depression (e.g., Petersen & Taylor, 1980). Early-maturing girls have been found to be at the greatest risk of body dissatisfaction (e.g., Blyth, Simmons, & Zakin, 1985; Siegel, Yancey, Aneshensel, & Schuler, 1999; Simmons & Blyth, 1987; Williams & Currie, 2000), and they also tend to be less popular with their peers and have poorer self-esteem and higher levels of depression (e.g., Blyth et al., 1985; Stice, Presnell, & Bearman, 2001). Conversely, late-maturing boys have been found to be more likely to experience higher levels of body dissatisfaction (Blyth et al., 1981; R. Freedman, 1990; Siegel, et al., 1999), are less popular with their peers, have more conflict with their parents, and display more depressive symptoms (Blyth et al., 1981; Siegel et al., 1999). Yet, cross-sectional (Wichstrom, 1995) and prospective (Wichstrom, 2000) studies reveal no association between pubertal timing and eating dysfunctions. These findings suggest that the effects of pubertal timing on disordered eating may be mediated or moderated by body dissatisfaction and other individual factors for both adolescent girls and boys.

Studies that included factors such as parent, peer, and body influences, in addition to media, report important findings indicating the media's minor role. Two studies that have examined all of these factors found that media is not a strong predictor of body-image and body-change strategies for either boys or girls. Although these findings are at variance with past studies, they may be due to the inclusion of a range of other factors in the regression equations, which may have explained the variance that has previously been attributed to the influences of the media (McCabe, & Ricciardelli, 2003a). Parents were more important sociocultural transmitters of messages for both adolescent boys and girls than were peers or the media. However, both male and female friends played a role in predicting body-change strategies for adolescent girls and, to a lesser extent, for adolescent boys. This role was greater for female friends than it was for male friends. Consistent with the findings with parents, the feedback primarily affected either extreme body-change strategies (e.g., binge eating, use of food supplements) or strategies that moved the adolescent away from the sociocultural ideal (McCabe & Ricciardelli, 2003b). These are quite interesting findings suggesting that the media may be important, but its importance pales in comparison to other factors influencing adolescents' lives.

Psychological Influences

A third group of variables that has been studied as either correlates or risk factors in the development of disordered eating are often grouped together as psychological or individual variables. These variables, which have been primarily studied among adolescent girls, include body dissatisfaction and other body-image concerns, negative affect, low self-esteem, perfectionism, impulsivity, gender-related personality traits, and inadequate coping skills (e.g., Murnen & Smolak, 1997; Polivy & Herman, 2002; Shisslak & Crago, 2001; Stice, 2002; Striegel-Moore & Steiner-Adair, 1998). We already have seen the significance of body-image concerns and focus on other factors. The other factors are worth examining, although research has yet to pinpoint the media's role in how they may influence adolescents' views of their bodies.

Negative affect is one of the main individual variables that researchers have found to be associated with both body dissatisfaction and disordered eating in adolescent girls; however, there is an ongoing debate about the directional and causal nature of this relationship. Negative affect encompasses mood states such as depression, stress, shame, inadequacy, guilt, and helplessness (Watson, Clark, & Tellegen, 1988). A number of theorists and researchers have argued that girls used both dieting and binge eating to regulate and/or alleviate negative affect. The majority of cross-sectional studies have found evidence for a weak to moderate relationship between negative affect and disordered eating, even for adolescent boys (e.g., Keel, Klump, Leon, & Fulkerson, 1998; Lock et al., 2001; McCabe & Ricciardelli, 2001b, 2003b; Mueller et al., 1995; Neumark-Sztainer & Hannan, 2000; Neumark-Sztainer et al. 2000; Ricciardelli & McCabe, 2001b;

Ross & Ivis, 1999; Tomori & Rus-Makovec, 2000; Wichstrom, 1995). Prospective studies have also examined the relationship between negative affect and disordered eating among adolescents and have reported negative affect as one of the main variables to predict disordered eating over a 3- to 4-year period (Leon, Fulkerson, Perry, Keel, & Klump, 1999), although not all prospective studies find significant results (see Stice, Akutagawa, Gaggar, & Agras, 2000; Ricciardelli & McCabe, 2003).

Data suggest that boys and girls who are bulimic or anorexic suffer from highly distorted body images and depression and are likely to have been abused. Two studies reveal a weak association between disordered eating and both sexual and physical abuse, which had occurred during childhood in both adolescent girls and boys (Lock et al., 2001; Neumark-Sztainer et al., 2000). The authors interpreted the findings as suggesting that disordered eating in some adolescent boys and girls may develop in response to past trauma. In these instances, boys may develop an internalizing coping style that closely resembles that seen in adolescent girls, who become more at risk for depression, anxiety, and eating disorders. These are important health issues and could be addressed by clearer and more focused health programs in schools that directly assess teen's perceptions of their bodies and other factors associated with eating disorders. The potential role of the media in influencing these factors, however, has yet to be examined systematically. We will see in chapter 5, though, that the media can play an important role in sexual development.

In the past decade, sexual orientation, particularly for adult men, also has been identified as an individual risk factor contributing to the development of disordered eating attitudes and behavior. Several studies have found that adult gay men are more concerned with body weight and shape, report higher levels of body dissatisfaction, higher levels of dieting, and greater bulimic symptoms than do heterosexual men (e.g., Boroughs & Thompson, 2002); studies have reported mixed findings for adult women (e.g., Epel, Spanakos, Kasl-Godley, & Brownell, 1996; Heffernan, 1994; Lakkis, Ricciardelli, & Williams, 1999). Although adolescents have been included in some of the past studies (e.g., Williamson & Hartley, 1998), those that have focused on adolescents (primarily boys) find weak effects indicating that, for example, adolescent boys from grade seven to twelve who were gay were more likely to report weight concerns, poorer body image, dieting, binge eating, and purging than nongay boys (French, Story, Remafedi, Resnick, & Blum, 1996); some studies also report no association between sexual orientation and disordered eating for adolescent boys between 12 and 19 years old (Lock et al., 2001). These studies are actually difficult to interpret given that gay identity is not always well defined during adolescence and adolescents actually are not especially interested in neatly categorizing their sexual orientation (Savin-Williams, 2005). But it does appear that sexuality may well influence the relationship between body image and disordered eating, and as such may reveal the media's potential role.

Other psychological factors that have been studied in relation to adolescents' disordered eating and related behaviors include low self-esteem, perfectionism, interpersonal distrust, low interoceptive awareness, and the use of alcohol and other drugs. Although these variables have been studied less extensively among boys than in girls, the same relationships have been found for both genders. For example, the majority of studies reveal a relationship between self-esteem and various indicators of disordered eating. An overall weak to moderate association has been found between low self-esteem and concerns about eating (Mueller et al., 1995), binge eating (Ross & Ivis, 1999; Tomori & Rus-Makovec, 2000), and dieting and the binge-purge cycle (French et al., 2001; Neumark-Sztainer & Hannan, 2000). And, again, we may have a hunch that the media influence these factors, but research has yet to support those hunches.

The level of alcohol and other drug use among both adolescent girls and boys is often ignored but has been found to be moderately related to binge eating is (e.g., French et al., 2001; Neumark-Sztainer & Hannan, 2000; Ross & Ivis, 1999; Tomori & Rus-Makovec, 2000; Williams & Ricciardelli, 2003). Both binge eating and high levels of substance use are viewed as mood-altering appetitive behaviors and involve an overreliance on negative styles of self-control that involve passivity and bullying (Williams & Ricciardelli, 2003). Support for this view also has come from an important study that found extreme weight loss methods to associate with other health-compromising behaviors related to high impulsivity, including both boys and girls' drug use, delinquency, suicide attempts, unprotected intercourse, and multiple sexual partners (Neumark-Sztainer, Story, & French, 1996). As we will see in the next chapter, these factors appear highly influenced by the media, but the extent to which the media influence, for example, links between alcohol use and weight and shape strategies remains to be determined.

The Significance and Limitations of Influences Research

One of the major limitations of this area of research is that few longitudinal evaluations have examined the different variables associated with disordered eating and either body and shape problems. This limitation means that it is not possible to separate causes from consequences, so that many of the variables identified as determinants may well be consequences. The possibility that many of the observed relationships are bidirectional also has received no empirical investigation. For example, symptoms associated with disordered eating and muscle dysmorphia may predict negative affect and poorer psychosocial functioning in other areas of boys' lives, such as forming intimate relationships and developing a career path; however, studies have yet to test these relationships. Equally problematic, our understanding of links is hampered by how the few existing longitudinal studies only have tracked adolescents from 2 months to 1 year, an important point given that it may well be that some of the identified risk factors may have a greater predictive impact in early and later adulthood than during adolescence. A firmer understanding of this phenomenon seems necessary if we are to understand more clearly the media's role.

Although many propose biopsychosocial models, they have yet to be taken seriously. This failure is important beyond the need to determine how different factors work together to produce negative outcomes. Similarly important would be studies that examine the role of protective factors in the development of disordered eating and the pursuit of muscularity, as most researchers have only targeted potential risk factors. Our understanding of influences on body images certainly lends itself to the identification of several potential protective factors in the development of disordered eating for adolescents. These include being self-directed and assertive, successfully performing multiple roles, coping well with stressful situations, having a high self-esteem, being a member of a family in which there is a low focus on weight and attractiveness, having a close but not too close relationship with parents who accept a diverse range of body shapes and sizes, and enjoying close relationships with friends or romantic partners who are relatively unconcerned with weight and who provide social support (Shisslak & Crago, 2001). Although these factors may make sense to consider given the research we have just reviewed, these factors have yet to be studied, as does the media's role in shaping these factors.

Modifying Media Influences on Adolescents' Weight and Shape Strategies

Concerns about adolescents' weight and shape have lead to two often unrelated prevention efforts. One series of prevention programs focuses on the media's role in fostering ideals and helping adolescents counter these ideals. Another series of programs focuses more directly on body image, especially in an effort to prevent eating disorders. Both of these types of programs are important to consider, given that media messages do not emanate alone but rather are influenced by adolescents' broader informational environments.

Media-Focused Programs

Researchers have proposed possible interventions specifically targeting the negative effect of mass media messages promoting ideals that foster adolescents' inappropriate responses. Efforts include helping adolescents to become more discriminating in their use of the mass media, developing strategies to reduce social comparison, and addressing undiscriminating acceptance of the media's presentation of ideals (Shaw & Waller, 1995). Overall, interventions that teach adolescents to be more critical consumers of media have shown effectiveness in reducing thin-ideal internalization (Irving, DuPen, & Berel, 1998; Thompson & Heinberg, 1999). These interventions also have effectively mitigated the impact of media images on body dissatisfaction. For example, one study found that female college students with negative body images who were given a 7-minute psychoeducational presentation involving media analysis were less likely to engage in social comparison and less likely to be negatively affected by images of slender beauty than were students who saw the same images without prior inoculation (Posavac, Posavac, & Weigel, 2001). Interventions that have been deemed more effective are those that emphasize the artificial, carefully crafted nature of media images with the diversity of women's shapes and weights (Levine, Piran, & Stoddard, 1999).

The mass media also may provide one of the most successful venues for primary prevention of eating disorders. These strategies target children and adolescents with the hopes of preventing later development of eating disorders, and some evaluations have focused on nutrition, dieting, body esteem, exercise, and reduction of the stigma regarding obesity (Levine, 1999; Levine & Smolak, 1998). This area of research, however, has only recently focused on media issues and has yet to produce encouraging results beyond pilot research (see, for example, Stice, Mazotti, Weibel, & Agras, 2000). Generally, these interventions increase knowledge, but that knowledge leads to little effect on body image or eating-related attitudes and behaviors (Smolak, Levine, & Schermer, 1998). For example, researchers have concluded that brief single-session eating disorder prevention interventions, which are typically 1 hour in length, are insufficient to produce lasting attitudinal and behavioral change because these types of programs rarely produce effects (Martz & Bazzini, 1999). As a result, and more generally, research finds psychoeducational content ineffective in producing behavioral change (Clarke, Hawkins, Murphy, & Sheeber, 1993; Larimer & Cronce, 2002). The most successful approaches focus on eating disorders. Eating disorder prevention programs that produced the most promising effects include cognitive interventions that alter maladaptive attitudes, such as thin-ideal internalization or body dissatisfaction, and behavioral interventions that alter maladaptive behaviors, such as fasting and overeating (Stice & Shaw, 2004).

Little research has explored how parents can mediate the negative effects of media. One recent study, which should be seen as suggestive at this point, examined several forms of parental mediation and adolescents' television processing, emotions while viewing, and body-image disturbance. The survey of both parents and adolescents (at two stages) revealed that most traditional measures of parental mediation were *not* significantly related to any adolescent outcomes (Nathanson & Botta, 2003). Perhaps more importantly, data revealed that parental mediation of incidental content regarding characters' appearance and body size—even if it criticized the television images—actually encouraged deep processing of the images and negative emotions, which in turn led to indicators of body-image disturbance.

Reviews of preventive efforts reveal the insufficiency of simply asking adolescents to reject problematic media. Effective programs encourage skill development and the desire to resist pressures, such as those for attractiveness and thinness. These are rather challenging goals given that peers, families, and others reinforce the socialization of media. These realities suggest a need to move toward more comprehensive prevention efforts that focus on adolescents' experiences.

Dysfunction-Focused Programs

Eating disorder prevention programs have undergone rapid transformations, so much so that reviews now discern three generations (see Stice & Shaw, 2004). The first generation of eating disorder prevention programs delivered didactic psychoeducational material about eating disorders in universal interventions involving all available adolescents. This type of intervention rested on the assumption that information about the adverse effects of eating disorders would deter individuals from initiating these maladaptive behaviors. The second generation of prevention programs also was universal in focus and didactic in format but included components focusing on resistance of sociocultural pressures for thinness and healthy weight-control behaviors. These interventions were guided by the assumption that sociocultural pressures play a key role in the etiology of eating pathology and that adolescents turned to radical dieting and compensatory behaviors primarily for weight-control purposes. The third generation of interventions has included selective programs that target high-risk individuals with interactive exercises that focus on risk factors that have been shown to predict the onset of eating pathology (e.g., body dissatisfaction).

The quick development in generations of programs may appear promising, but the changes actually emerged because of the pervasive failure of early efforts. Reviews examining the first two generations of prevention research, which include media efforts, report discouraging findings and pervasive ineffectiveness (e.g., Littleton & Ollendick, 2003; Levine & Smolak, 2001; Striegel-Moore & Steiner-Adair, 1998). Empirical and theoretical reviews identifying the failures and successes of those studies, however, report encouraging results to the extent that they tell us what not to do. Equally importantly, meta-analyses of the findings from trials published since 2000 offer cause for optimism in that they do report significant findings supporting the effectiveness of new prevention efforts (Stice & Shaw, 2004).

Reviews reveal a number of suggestions that may be used to enhance the efficacy of eating disorder prevention programs. They suggest a need to avoid focusing solely on increasing knowledge of eating disorders and nutritional information, given that mere knowledge does not lead to changes in behavior and attitudes and that psychoeducational content fails to produce behavioral change (Clarke et al., 1993). Results also reveal a need to foster participant interaction. This emerges because simply adding alternative strategies to psychoeducational efforts yields disappointing results if the delivery format remains didactic rather than interactive. Theoretically, participants in interactive programs show greater intervention effects because this format helps them become engaged in the program content, which facilitates skill acquisition and attitudinal change. Interactive programs also are more likely to involve exercises that allow participants to apply the skills taught in the intervention, which should facilitate skill acquisition (Stice & Shaw, 2004).

These findings echo the conclusions drawn from other prevention areas that psychoeducational interventions by themselves generally are ineffective in producing behavioral change (e.g., Larimer & Cronce, 2002). In addition, interventions that target established risk factors for eating pathology will be more effective than those that focus on nonestablished risk factors (Stice, Mazotti, et al., 2000; Stice & Shaw, 2004). Selective programs that are offered to high-risk participants are more effective than universal programs that are offered to all available participants, a point highlighted by the finding that several universal prevention programs are more effective for subgroups of high-risk participants than for the full sample (Buddeberg-Fischer, Klaghofer, Gnam, & Buddeberg, 1998; Stewart, Carter, Drinkwater, Hainsworth, & Fairburn, 2001). Similarly, reviews also reveal the need to continue programs across school years beyond just a few sessions added on to school curricular. Brief single-session eating disorder prevention interventions, which are typically 1 hour in length, are insufficient to produce lasting attitudinal and behavioral change because these types of programs rarely produce effects (Martz & Bazzini, 1999). In the end, however, these suggestions only offer reason for hope; they have yet to become part of programs demonstrating effectiveness.

Conclusions

Body image emerges as a critical concern for adolescents, and we now know that it links to many problems associated with the adolescent period. Current research seeks to identify the risk factors for body dissatisfaction itself in order to provide a better understanding of the complex ways in which social, psychological, and biological changes influence adolescents' body-image development. It is the focus on body image that leads researchers to identify the media as a potent socializer of adolescents' attitudes and behaviors regarding their physical development.

Although research investigating the media's place in the development of adolescents' body image historically has focused on girls, research increasingly examines the media's influence on boys' body images. These developments reflect a changing view of the impact of body images, as well as of the media industry itself. Earlier research on the development of body dissatisfaction primarily focused on females because of the higher prevalence of their body dissatisfaction and related adjustment problems. The extent of body dissatisfaction among adolescent girls has frequently been explained by the greater sociocultural emphasis on physical attractiveness for women and an increasingly prominent "culture of thinness" often promoted by the media. Although body dissatisfaction has typically been less evident among males, the desire to develop muscularity has emerged as an important concern and associates with body dissatisfaction among adolescent boys. Popular media convey stereotypes of the ideal male body as much as it does of the female body, and we are beginning to learn that stereotypical images of females actually influence the development of boys' own body images. Problematic media images result in negative consequences for both adolescent males and females.

Theories developed to help us understand the media's role in shaping adolescents' body images and their appearance schemas provide important insights.

These theories offer considerable support for the claim that media images do influence adolescent development. Perhaps more importantly, however, they reveal possible areas for intervention. Body-image interventions, for example, can target appearance schemas by challenging underlying attitudes and beliefs about appearance while also encouraging the development of adaptive self-schemas in other nonappearance related domains. Interventions also may use the media to provide information on problematic means of achieving the idealized body size, such as fasting, overexercising, and purgative techniques. Theories and research on the impact of the media and the development of dysfunctional beliefs also highlight what has been missing in efforts to address problems associated with media images. Prevention programs have most frequently focused on media literacy and person-based issues and ignored the roles of parents and peers. We have seen that internalization and body-image satisfaction depends considerably on peer appearance culture. As a result, greater attention should be given to helping adolescents understand the ways by which their appearance conversations serve to create and reinforce standards that can augment the internalization of appearance ideals and undermine body-image satisfaction. When dealing with extremes of weight concerns, parents appear to be a dominant influencing factor and research focus. In fact, research on eating disorders tends to not even explore the significance of the media. Instead, research focuses on family dynamics and ignores how the media factor in adolescents' pathological development. Yet, as we have seen, the focus on family responses to media images may be quite relevant, with even incidental comments about body images leading to adolescents' negative views of their own bodies. Our understanding of body dissatisfaction reveals the need to consider how the media work with other socializing influences in adolescents' lives. Much unlike other areas of research on media effects, then, this area of research has yet to move more decisively into directions that take into account adolescents' broader informational environments. Judging from what we have learned from other contexts, this research would appear quite significant and necessary if we are to address more effectively the true place of the media in adolescents' body-image development.

The need to consider adolescents' broader informational environment gains considerable support when we step back and consider the manner research findings tend to reveal something often left unsaid: the need to focus on tolerance, social support, and the media's role in shaping other aspects of adolescent development. Intervention is needed not only to help adolescents understand media images and social pressure but also to help them learn not to criticize others. Much of the research now points to deficits in perceived social support as the best predictor of increased body dissatisfaction. This is consistent with the assertion that acceptance in one's immediate social network might help adolescents feel more positively about themselves and their bodies and render them more resilient to sociocultural pressures to be thin or muscular. Results suggest the need to direct greater attention to the role of social support deficits in promoting body-image disturbances. Regrettably, research has yet to consider forthrightly these sources of developmental influences. Similarly, we know about the significance of media images not directly implicating body images, such as those relating to sex roles and aggressive behavior. These influences clearly may be shaped by the media and directly deal with the extent to which they and their environments exhibit tolerance; yet, as we have seen, research on media violence ignores issues of body image (and vice versa) even though these developmental concerns clearly relate to one another. Taken together, then, research in this area of adolescent development and media influence underscores the need to focus on much more than media images of bodies if we are ever to address how the media's portrayals of bodies influence adolescent development.

4

Adolescent Smoking and the Media

Many social problems link to the media's influence on adolescents. The most lethal, health-related actions adolescents take—in terms of those that result in the leading cause of death in the United States—involve the initiation and habituation of smoking (Centers for Disease Control and Prevention, 1998). In addition to potentially hastening their own deaths, adolescents who initiate and continue smoking at an early age place themselves at an increased risk for developing a broad array of long-term serious health problems, including chronic lung disease, heart disease, stroke, and many types of cancer (e.g., lungs, larynx, esophagus, mouth, and bladder; Centers for Disease Control and Prevention, 2005b). These risks actually are well recognized. As the health consequences of tobacco smoking have become more apparent, governments have regulated the types of promotion available to tobacco manufacturers. Regulations now strictly limit young adolescents' access to tobacco products and seek to control the media's efforts to encourage adolescents' tobacco use. Attempts to reduce the impact of the tobacco industry's promotions highlight the challenges faced by efforts that seek to limit, but not ban, types of media portrayals of tobacco use. As we will see, the effort reveals the need to address more subtle initiatives and images that avert regulation and may well reach and influence adolescents even more effectively than materials deemed inappropriate.

Recognition that the adolescent period plays a role in smoking's negative health consequences acknowledges an important reality. Cigarette smoking relates to the adolescent period in numerous ways. The vast majority of smokers report their first tobacco use during adolescence (Centers for Disease Control and Prevention, 1998). Nearly 90% of adult smokers indicate that they first started smoking before the age of 18 (Backinger, Fagan, Matthews, & Grana, 2003), and the average age of first use is 15 (Burns & Johnson, 2001). Over half of high school students have tried smoking, and over a quarter of high school students report regular smoking; of these, regular smokers are an average of 13 years old, and 10 is the average age at which they smoked their first whole cigarette (Maney, Vasey, Mahoney, Gates, & Higham-Gardill, 2004). These ages are of considerable significance given that they predict eventual smoking patterns. Most notably, adolescents who experiment with cigarette smoking are likely to progress to daily smoking (Lamkin, Davis, & Kamen, 1998). Adolescents who initiate smoking at earlier ages use larger amounts of tobacco, use it over longer periods of time, and experience more difficulty quitting than youth who begin smoking later in life (Everett et al., 1999; Breslau & Peterson, 1996). Indeed, adolescents also are less likely to quit during their lifetime if they initiated tobacco use at younger ages (Everett et al., 1999). Cigarette smoking involves the entire age range of the adolescent period, and involving early ages means increasing the risk of negative outcomes.

Prevalence of youth tobacco use remains quite high. Population estimates for persons under the age of 18 indicate that every day 5,500 youth try cigarettes for the first time, and nearly 3,000 more youth become daily smokers (Gilpin, Choi, Berry & Pierce, 1999). National surveys reveal that, in 2000, the 30-day prevalence of smoking was 11% among grade 6–8 students (ages 11 to 14 years of age) and 28% among grade 9–12 students (15 to 17 years of age) (Centers for Disease Control and Prevention, 2000). In fact, by the age of 18, approximately two-thirds of high school students have tried smoking with peak experimentation occurring between the ages of 13 and 16 years (Duncan, Tidlesley, Duncan, & Hops, 1995). Although cigarettes are the predominant form of tobacco use by youth and young adults, both populations use other forms of tobacco that probably are unknown to most adults. These include the well-known forms such as cigars and smokeless tobacco as well as less-known types like bidis and kreteks. Smokeless tobacco includes both chewing tobacco and snuff; bidis are flavored cigarettes primarily from India; and kreteks are cigarettes that contain both cloves and tobacco. Thirty-five per cent of high school students report using any form of tobacco within the past 30 days. In 2000, U.S. high school students reported current use of the following tobacco products in these percentages: cigarettes (28%), smokeless tobacco (6.6%), cigars (14.8%), pipes (3.3%), bidis (4.1%), and kreteks (4.2%; Centers for Disease Control and Prevention, 2002). These high rates reveal that no other problem behavior reaches such high prevalence levels of health risk and links to negative effects.

These high rates and varieties of tobacco use have not been ignored by research investigating links between the media and adolescence, but several gaps in research challenge efforts to understand properly the media's role in adolescent smoking. For example, given cigarette use patterns, efforts have been made to discourage adolescents from initiating smoking and to encourage adolescents to quit smoking. Indeed, current research investigating the place of the media in adolescence reveals a heavy focus on tobacco use cessation and prevention. Yet, the links between smoking and the media seem assumed, even though we do not understand very well how smoking in the media influences adolescents' development and environments, which would in turn influence smoking patterns. In addition, although the law formally regulates this type of media and considerable social consensus supports the view that the media play a strong role in adolescents' smoking habits, research only has begun to address how the media industry itself could be used to influence adolescents' attitudes and behaviors involving tobacco use. This chapter explores those issues.

We first examine the media's smoking images and their potential effects. We then move to understand how the media affect adolescents' smoking, place smoking in the context of adolescent development, and then examine efforts to limit adolescents' smoking strategies and the media's potential role. Although at times the more general terms *tobacco use* and *smoking* are used, in all cases, the presented analyses refer to cigarette smoking unless otherwise indicated. Overall, the analysis points to the need to consider the peculiarities of adolescent development and their social environment to understand the media's influence and to harness media effects in intended ways.

Media Smoking Images and Their Effects

The current understanding of the place of the media in the development of adolescents' smoking strategies reveals media images that are both highly restricted yet ubiquitous. The saturation of smoking images remains even though the government highly regulates the tobacco industry. Restrictions in the form of policies and formal industry agreements limit media advertising efforts seeking to market products directly to adolescents and children (L. H. Glantz, 1997; Gostin, Arno, & Brandt, 1997). Despite these restrictions, the media still present many images of tobacco use and, equally importantly, find alternative methods of tobacco promotion. It may well be, as several claim, that marketing efforts involve an intentional skirting of regulations (Hoek, 1999). But, tobacco clearly remains part of our popular culture and, as such, the media likely reflect those realities. The central concern becomes the extent to which tobacco is portrayed, how it is portrayed, and the effects of those portrayals on adolescents and their social environment.

Media Images of Smoking

Interest in the cultural dissemination of smoking in the media typically centers on the portrayals of smoking in films. Popular movies often have been at the center of research and continue to be so given that they were the direct focus of the Master Settlement Agreement between the States' Attorneys General and the tobacco industry. Among other efforts, that settlement had ruled out the paid placement of cigarettes in movies (National Association of Attorneys General, 1998). Yet, analyses of tobacco portrayals in movies that compare images before and after the settlement reveal that tobacco images still infuse the media. A recent study, for example, examined the top grossing PG-13 movies from the two years before the 1998 settlement (1996 and 1997) and the 2 years after (1999 and 2000) the settlement and found that the average amount of time tobacco products were in use on the screen actually increased by 50% (Ng & Dakake, 2002). The rates at which tobacco appears per minute of film during the 1990s are similar to those observed in the 1960s, despite a dip in the 1980s (Stockwell & Glantz, 1997). Despite a general lack of research, then, several studies actually have described how smoking is portrayed in movies and have concluded that portrayals of smoking continue and actually have increased (Everett, Schnuth, & Tribble, 1998; Wakefield, Flay, Nichter, & Giovino, 2003).

Several additional research findings make the appearance of tobacco in movies important to note. First, these findings reveal the challenges faced by efforts to limit media exposure to adolescents. With or without regulations, portrayals of smoking in popular films occur with much more frequency than expected on the basis of the actual prevalence of smoking (Stockwell & Glantz, 1997; Hazan & Glantz, 1995). Second, only a small fraction of movie portrayals of tobacco use present antismoking messages. For example, the top twenty highest-grossing films in each year from 1990 to 1996 averaged 5 minutes of tobacco incidents, of which only 43 seconds involved negative portrayals. Third, films marketed to young audiences portray tobacco use. Tobacco use occurred in two-thirds of children's G-rated animated films from 1937 to 1997; and all of the films in that category that were released in 1996–1997 depicted tobacco use (Goldstein, Sobel, & Newman, 1999). Together, this research reveals that the presentation of smoking tends to spin positive views and reaches all audiences. The research also indicates that current media portrayals contradict efforts to limit exposure to children and ensure that individuals make responsible decisions regarding tobacco use.

Many studies support the above findings and also describe the types of portrayals. For example, studies that have examined the depiction of smoking in movies report that smokers are depicted more positively than nonsmokers and that Hollywood's portrayal of smoking tends to ignore the negative consequences and correlates of smoking (McIntosh, Bazzini, Smith, & Wayne, 1998). Movies aimed at young audiences are more likely to have positive portrayals of smoking than movies aimed at mature audiences (Escamilla, Crdock, & Kawachi, 2000). These film portrayals of tobacco may lead some to conclude that they have to do as much with product placement as it does with the actor's status on film and efforts to highlight character information. The reality remains that tobacco images appear very frequently in movies, especially those aimed at young audiences.

As we have learned in earlier chapters, movies distinctly present an important media for adolescents, but other forms of media also reach adolescents and shape their attitudes and development. Yet, few examinations detail the prevalence and nature of portrayals in other media. We do know, however, that portrayal rates are quite high and that the media often frames images in ways that appeal to adolescents.

Arguably the most important area of research other than research focusing on movie images deals with the portrayals of smoking in magazines. As expected, smoking images are rampant, both in advertising and incidental portrayals, but studies surveying this area do not pinpoint prevalence rates as well as research examining films (see Gray, Amos, & Currie, 1996). Unlike the above research, however, researchers in this area have examined adolescents' responses to tobacco images. The inclusion of cigarettes in magazine images influences how adolescents rate pictures. For example, a group of researchers reported that smoking images are rated as more "druggy," wild, and depressed, and nonsmoking images as more healthy, rich, nice, fashionable, slim, and attractive (Amos, Currie, Gray, & Elton, 1998). Such findings reveal that what cigarettes signify varies considerably in different images, and that variation depends on the prominence of the cigarette, presence of other cues such as types of clothes and background, and the "strength" of the image (Gray, Amos, & Currie, 1997).

Studies also report that, despite the variation, perception varies with observer characteristics. Smokers and nonsmokers rate themselves in the same way that they differentiated between smokers and nonsmokers in the photographs (e.g., smoking-related attributes are considered desirable by smokers). These effects are strongest for 15- to 16-year-old boys, as compared to girls as well as older or younger adolescents (Amos et al., 1998; Gray, Amos, & Currie, 1997). These are important findings. Yet, apart from magazine research, no work has examined the mediating role of viewer characteristics in determining differential viewer effects in electronic and print media images (Wakefield et al., 2003).

Rather surprisingly, little research has examined the place of smoking in the television media. Evidence that does exist reveals unequivocal results as to whether television serves as an important medium for the diffusion of smoking images. Music videos, for example, constitute an important source of media that brings smoking directly to adolescents. Music videos broadcast on network television present smoking in 12% of country music videos and 26% of those broadcast on MTV (Durant, Romes et al., 1997). Research examining tobacco use on prime-time television also reveals that 24% of programs contain tobacco events; and the only study to do so, conducted in 1992, found that 92% of these events were pro-tobacco (Hazan & Glantz, 1995). More recent research that focuses more broadly on prime-time television rather than music videos, however, reveals much fewer tobacco portrayals. One study compared the prevalence of tobacco users among characters on prime-time with rates of use in the United States. It found that results for prime-time television characters versus those for the U.S. population (respectively) were 2.5% versus 28.9%. The authors concluded that, contrary to prevailing beliefs, tobacco users are uncommon on prime-time television and are less prevalent than in the U.S. population (Long, O'Connor, Gerbner, & Concato, 2002).

Other media, such as the electronic media, have yet to attract much attention from researchers. Only one study has built on content analyses of smoking in the popular media by examining Internet sites. Although the study did not try to determine the prevalence of tobacco images, it did examine sites devoted to smoking culture and lifestyles (Watson, Clarkson, Donovan, & Giles-Corti, 2003). That research revealed that the Internet provides easy access to sites with photographs that depict smoking. Somewhat unexpectedly, however, the study found that many sites featured women, with fully one third of sites containing partial or full nudity (Watson et al., 2003). Researchers found the high level of nudity and sexualization of smoking as rather notable given estimates that only 1.5% of Internet content contains pornography (Lawrence & Giles, 1999). Despite the high sexualization, identified sites were easily accessible to youth. None of the sites required age verification procedures that are commonly available on the Internet to prevent underage youth from viewing age-inappropriate content. Some actually placed "warnings" in ways that would lure adolescents to the site; and some contained advertising that the United States has banned on television and radio since the early 1970s. None of the sites featured the U.S. Surgeon General's warnings about the health hazards of smoking. The authors concluded that the sites portrayed only positive aspects of smoking, such as links between sexuality and smoking behavior, and none of its drawbacks.

Effects of Media Portrayals of Smoking

The extent to which images are portrayed and how they are portrayed constitutes only one aspect of research that seeks to understand the media's place in adolescents' smoking strategies. Arguably the more important concern involves whether, how, and the extent to which media portrayals shape adolescents' attitudes and behaviors. Given the significance of this concern, it is surprising to find lack of concrete findings. Yet, it is encouraging to find that important research actually has addressed specifically whether viewing smoking in the media actually affects adolescents' smoking behavior.

The most recognizable and influential research in this area examined young children's responses to cigarette advertising. The seminal study specifically focused on the influence of advertising on very young children, aged 3 to 6 years, by examining brand logo recognition in a sample of 229 children in two preschools in Georgia (Fischer, Schwartz, Richard, & Goldstein, 1991). Researchers asked each child to match a logo with a picture of products using twenty-two brand logos, ten with products targeted to children, five representing cigarette brands, and seven with logos targeted to adults. As expected, the Disney Channel logo recognition was higher for subjects aged 3, 4, and 5. By age 6, however, children all equally recognized and correctly matched the silhouette of Mickey Mouse and the face of Old Joe Camel; they did so independent of the use of cigarettes in their homes. The researchers concluded that these findings clearly linked media efforts with knowledge about smoking.

Although the findings from the Georgia study were impressive and received considerable popular press, the research left open the extent to which recognition would influence actual smoking behavior. Studies examining awareness and attitudes toward cigarette advertising support a compelling argument that advertising influences children's smoking. However, they do not make the necessary link that would reveal how awareness of or exposure to cigarette advertisements contributes to changes in youths' smoking behavior. The correlation has been used to imply a causal link between consumption and exposure to advertising, as well as between recognition and smoking behavior. As we now know, such leaps in the interpretation of data are questionable; the causal links may exist, but such conclusions cannot be had from existing research.

Research that does examine the influence of brand recognition reveals that recognition does not necessarily encourage expected behaviors. Studies published after the first recognition studies reached some important conclusions regarding the impact of advertising on children. For example, one study found that the use of trade characters in advertising leads to brand recognition among 3- to 8-year-olds, but not to liking the product or desiring to purchase it (Henke, 1995). In addition, the study noted that the children were aware that cigarette advertisements were targeted to adults. Other research has found that exposure to cartoon trade characters in cigarette advertising did not improve attitudes toward the product category among young children (Mizerski, 1995). More recently, it was found that eighth graders were skeptical about trade characters (Joe Camel and The Marlboro Man) and that many react negatively to them (Phillips & Stavchansky, 1999). Collectively, these findings reveal important limits in the influence of trade characters on children and adolescents. The studies do not, however, reveal firm conclusions about the long-term influence of aggressive advertising.

More recent studies have sought to establish the existence of a causal relationship between exposure to advertising for cigarettes and youths' smoking behavior. One notable naturalistic study focused on in-store promotional advertising. A carefully drawn national sample of 202 schools identified over 3,000 smokers. The researchers then matched convenience stores within a 1-mile radius of the selected schools and related the cigarette brands that were advertised most in each store to the brands the youths smoked. The findings indicated that where the convenience stores had more advertising for Marlboros, the youths were more likely to smoke Marlboros, and where the convenience stores had more advertising for Camels, the youths were more likely to smoke Camels (Wakefield, Ruel, Chaloupka, Slater, & Kaufman, 2002). These studies parallel those of three longitudinal studies that have demonstrated that adolescents who own promotional items (hats, banners, etc.) are more susceptible to tobacco use and more likely to become smokers (Biener & Seigel, 2000; Pierce, Choi, Gilpin, Farkas, & Berry, 1998; Sargent et al., 2000).

These are quite rigorous studies. One of those studies, for example, linked advertising and exposure to promotional tobacco items to later smoking as it found that adolescents who had a favorite cigarette advertisement in 1993, compared with those who did not, were twice as likely either to have started smoking by 1996 or to be willing to start; and adolescents who owned or were willing to own a promotional item were three times as likely to have started smoking by 1996 or to be willing to start (Pierce et al., 1998). The authors concluded that these findings provide the first longitudinal evidence that tobacco promotional activities causally relate to the onset of smoking. These findings gain significance to the extent that adolescents have a high level of participation in tobacco promotion, with 35% of 12- to 17-year-olds participating in campaigns by owning promotional items (Coytaux, Altman, & Slade, 1995).

Many other studies have linked tobacco marketing with an increased risk of smoking uptake in adolescents. For example, owning tobacco promotional items and being able to recall cigarette advertisements can double the odds that an adolescent will become an established smoker (Biener & Siegel, 2000). Movie images, like commercial advertising, associate smoking with celebrities and depict it as an attractive behavior (Basil, 1997). In popular contemporary movies, smoking is frequently associated with characteristics many adolescents find appealing, such as toughness, sexiness, and rebelliousness (Dalton et al., 2002). Strong associations exist between receptivity to tobacco industry promotions and openness to smoking. Adolescents who purchase or receive tobacco promotional items and are willing to use or wear promotional items are more open to smoking (Mowery, Farrelly, Gable, Wells, & Haviland, 2004). Restricted advertising does not close other channels for advertising.

Another line of research involved a laboratory experiment that focused on the relationships among advertising, peer influence, and adolescents' intentions to smoke. When exposed to peers who smoked, those who had previously been exposed to cigarette advertising expressed greater intentions to smoke than those who had not been exposed to cigarette advertising. Moreover, those who were exposed to the cigarette advertising condition were more likely to view smokers more positively ("fun," "well-liked," "sexy," "cool," etc.; Pechmann & Knight, 2002). Importantly, the study also examined the relative influence of the media and peers. Both factors remained strong predictors and were even better predictors of adolescents' intention to smoke when they were factored together (Pechmann & Knight, 2002). The research obviously remains limited to the extent that it focuses on the intent to smoke, but the intent to smoke does link to eventual smoking (Pierce, Choi, Gilpin, Farkas, & Merrit, 1996). Together, these studies have been interpreted as supporting a causal relationship between exposure to smoking advertisements and adolescents' smoking.

The above research finds support from numerous studies that consider the influence of various advertising and marketing techniques on susceptibility to smoking. An important study reveals the significance of advertising as it considered its influence in light of adolescents' relative exposure to a social environment where peers, siblings, and parents smoked. That study examined data from 3,536 adolescents who had never smoked to determine factors that would impact their susceptibility to smoking (Evans, Farkas, Gilpin, Berry, & Pierce, 1995). The study surveyed two indices: (1) a 5-point index of an individual's receptivity to advertising as evidenced by recognition of advertising messages, having a favorite advertisement, naming a brand he or she might buy, owning a tobacco-related promotional item, and willingness to use a tobacco-related promotional item; and (2) an index classifying the individual's reported exposure to family and peer smoking. The relationship of receptivity to advertising and susceptibility to smoking was stronger than the relationship of family or peer smoking and susceptibility, suggesting that advertising exerts a more powerful influence than exposure to peer or family smoking. Importantly, the findings indicated that nonsmokers exposed to peers, siblings, and parents who smoked were more than twice as likely to be susceptible to smoking, but nonsmokers who were highly receptive to tobacco marketing were almost four times as likely to be susceptible to smoking. These striking findings highlight the powerful role that media, by itself, can play in influencing whether adolescents eventually smoke.

Longitudinal studies, which follow people over time and monitor changes in smoking behavior while simultaneously measuring exposure (to movies showing smoking, in this case), provide the strongest evidence for causality that can be obtained in a population-based study. To determine whether exposure to movie smoking predicts smoking initiation in adolescents, a longitudinal study surveyed adolescents who had never previously tried smoking (Dalton et al, 2003). After controlling for a wide variety of other effects—grade in school, sex, school, friend smoking, sibling smoking, parent smoking, receptivity to tobacco promotions, school performance, sensation-seeking propensity, rebelliousness, self-esteem, parent's education, authoritative parenting, and perception of parental disapproval of smoking—the study attributed 52.2% of smoking initiation in the 10- to 14-year-olds to seeing smoking in movies. This effect is stronger than the effect of traditional cigarette advertising and promotion, which has been shown to account for 34% of new experimentation (Pierce et al., 1998). These findings suggest that the effect of smoking in movies is a more powerful force than overt advertising, a conclusion emerging from the most convincing evidence to date that smoking in movies promotes initiation of smoking in adolescence, and that this effect is quite large.

Results reveal that viewing smoking in movies strongly predicts whether or not adolescents initiate smoking, and the effect increases significantly with greater exposure. Adolescents who viewed the most smoking in movies were almost three times more likely to initiate smoking than those with the least amount of exposure. The magnitude of this association comports with the results of cross-sectional studies of adolescents (Sargent et al., 2001). It also is consistent with the results of other cross-sectional studies that have linked actor smoking with adolescent smoking. Such studies found that adolescents were more likely to have tried smoking if their favorite movie stars smoked on screen (Distefan, Gilpin, Sargent, & Pierce, 1999; Tickle, Sargent, Dalton, Beach, & Heatherton, 2001). It further is consistent with research reporting that exposure to smoking in movies associates with smoking experimentation, even after controlling for the effects of other social influences, parenting, and personality characteristics of the child (Sargent et al., 2001).

Evidence may reveal that smoking in movies nearly triples the relative risk that an adolescent who views those movies will start smoking. But these estimates only reveal part of the whole story. Like cigarette advertising and promotion (Pierce, Distefan, Jackson, White, & Gilpin, 2002), the effects of smoking in movies are strongest in children whose parents are the best role models. Children of nonsmoking parents who are in the top quartile of exposure to smoking in movies are 4.1 times as likely to smoke as those in the lowest exposure quartile. This effect is substantially stronger than the increase by 1.6 times between these two exposure groups in children of smoking parents (Glantz, 2003). The data suggest that children with nonsmoking parents are especially susceptible to the effect of movie smoking exposure (Dalton et al., 2003). Explaining this disparity remains a challenge. Children with parents who smoke might have a more realistic view of smoking, so they are less likely to be influenced by the glamorous portrayal of smoking in movies. However, an equally plausible explanation is that children with parents who smoke are already at a higher risk for smoking initiation, which makes other social influences less likely to raise their risk. Although incompletely understood, the interaction still reveals the media's potentially powerful influence.

Another important longitudinal study, conducted between 1996 and 1999, involved a representative sample of California adolescents who were initially aged 12 to 15 years (Distefan, Pierce, & Gilpin, 2004). At baseline, adolescents who reported that they had never smoked were asked to nominate their two favorite male and female movie stars. Researchers reviewed the most popular stars' movies in the 3 years before baseline and recorded whether or not the star smoked on-screen. Adolescent smoking status was reassessed 3 years later. Adolescents with a favorite star who smoked on-screen were significantly more likely to have smoked by the follow-up interview. Importantly, the study also found that adolescents who had never smoked but had friends who smoked were approximately twice as likely to have smoked by the follow-up interview as those who reported no smoking among family or friends. Adolescents who were highly receptive to tobacco advertising and promotions were twice as likely as those who were minimally receptive to have smoked by the follow-up interview (Distefan et al., 2004). The study concluded that adolescent girls who had a favorite star who smoked in movies released between 1994 and 1996, before the baseline survey, had more than 80% increased odds of smoking by the time of the follow-up interview relative to those whose favorite star did not smoke on-screen. Importantly, the researchers found a lack of effect among boys, which they attributed, in part, to a stronger influence of their receptivity to other tobacco advertising and promotional practices.

Few researchers have used experimental methods to examine the impact of media on adolescents, but the one that has reveals that adolescents are more likely to report positive attitudes toward smoking after seeing smoking portrayed in movies. That study examined how on-screen smoking might influence young viewers (Pechmann & Shih, 1999). The study compared the responses of ninth graders to movies with smoking scenes left intact with those where professionals had edited out those scenes. Compared with smoking scenes that did not feature smoking, smoking scenes positively aroused young viewers (as measured on a seven-point scale from "boring" to "exciting") and increased their intent to smoke. In addition, those who saw the movie with the smoking scenes were more likely to regard those who smoke (including themselves, if they were to smoke) as smarter, more successful, more fit, and athletic. However, and rather importantly, showing teenagers an antismoking advertisement before the movie nullified these effects. This area of research remains largely unchartered, but the evidence certainly appears quite consistent with the overall view that the media can influence attitudes toward smoking and, eventually, smoking behaviors themselves.

The Significance and Limitations of Effects Research

Collectively, these results suggest that smoking portrayals in various media influence adolescent smoking behaviors. Media messages about smoking come in various forms. Many of these messages come in the form of paid advertising from tobacco companies. Others appear through promotions that offer accessories and clothing with cigarette brands emblazoned on them. Other communications about smoking appear in the context of movies and television programs and through sponsorships. All of these messages seem to influence adolescents' perceptions of tobacco use and may influence their eventual decisions about using tobacco.

Although persuasive, research findings nevertheless are marked by important limitations. For example, almost all R-rated movies contain smoking (Dalton et al., 2002). That makes it difficult to disentangle the effects of an R-rating and smoking content. Consequently, we cannot exclude the possibility that some other aspect of R-rated movies influences smoking initiation. Likewise, several of the studies do not reveal much about causality. The links between viewing smoking in movies and intentions to smoke tend to emerge from studies using cross-sectional designs which preclude conclusions about temporal relations. While correlation may suggest causality if confirmed over a wide variety of studies, a causal inference remains suspect if it fails to consider both the temporal ordering of the proposed relationship as well as the control of other possible causes. Thus, links between adolescents' exposure to media portrayals of smoking and their own smoking may be due to the manner in which smoking drives heightened attention to advertising, smoking portrayals in movies, and/or ownership of promotional products. Studies should also rule out other possible causes. Several viable possibilities exist; some of the most obvious would include income, peer influence, family smoking behavior, relationship with parents, and the local culture's influence on smoking behavior. Studies often fail to make a compelling case for either condition necessary for establishing causality.

Despite limitations, the effect of exposure to media images of smoking is important, both because the effect on smoking initiation is moderately strong and because the exposure is universal. For example, few adolescents are unexposed to movie smoking (Dalton et al., 2003). If the link between exposure to smoking in movies and smoking initiation proves to be causal, addressing adolescents' exposure to movie smoking could reduce smoking initiation, with some researchers finding that it could be reduced by half (Dalton et al., 2003). However, the equation might not be that simple, since many factors affect movie exposure and its effect on adolescent behavior. As we already have seen, for example, peers and families may play an important role that influences the manner in which media shapes adolescents' views of smoking and whether they do smoke. We now turn to research that seeks to explain the nature of the relationship between media exposure and adolescents' smoking.

Understanding the Media's Effects on Adolescents' Smoking

Evidence does suggest that the media may have an effect on adolescents' smoking. We already have seen that the media may be appealing to adolescents, even though many efforts seek to limit advertising that would directly aim to encourage adolescents to use tobacco products. Concluding that media may make tobacco use appealing to adolescents, however, does not necessarily offer a concrete understanding of why some adolescents choose to smoke while others do not. To understand variations, we briefly examine the leading theory that has driven research investigating variations in adolescents' responses. We also examine research that reveals actual variations in adolescents' responses to media images of tobacco.

Although numerous theoretical frameworks may help explain the process by which the media industry affects individuals' health-risk behaviors, one dominant framework highlights the media's potentially powerful role. Modeling theory pervasively drives research examining the impact of the media on adolescents' smoking. Recall that social-learning theories consider cognitive and social processes as they impact behavior acquisition; they assess the balance of current and past models of behavior and the behavior's associated rewards and punishments (Akers, 1998). The argument is that adolescents are more likely to learn and imitate behaviors performed by role models and behaviors they associate with positive outcomes, such as power, sex, romance, social status, and success (see Borzekowski, Flora, Feighery, & Schooler, 1999; Escamilla et al., 2000). The argument suggests that images of smoking in the media have the potential to play down the serious health consequences of smoking by portraying it in a way that youth interpret as a normal part of everyday life. These images also have the potential to desensitize adolescents to the negative health effects of smoking and to encourage a neutral or tolerant attitude towards smoking. The extent to which the media present favorable images (as defined by the particular viewer) influences whether adolescents are more likely to smoke and may even counter efforts to reduce smoking.

Research examining the above theory finds smoking imagery in popular media to be an important factor in adolescents' establishment or maintenance of prosmoking beliefs and intentions. Several important findings emerge from studies that explore links between smoking imagery in film and adolescent smoking behavior. As expected, preference for a smoking film star associates with favorable attitudes towards smoking (Tickle et al., 2001). Frequency of viewing smoking imagery in film strongly and directly associates with trying cigarettes (Sargent et al., 2002). And, the extent of film viewing associates with increased smoking initiation among adolescents (Dalton et al., 2003). These methodologically sound studies have attracted considerable attention.

In addition to shaping the attitudes toward smoking and the initiation of smoking, the media may help maintain adolescents' interest in continuing to smoke. Considerable evidence does support the claim that adolescents who view media images involving smoking rate those images positively. Adolescents view smoking as a normal part of their social environment, despite being aware of the negative health consequences (Watson et al., 2003). Adolescents predominantly perceive that smoking in films is normal and expected and that it provides an accurate representation of real life (McCool, Cameron, & Petrie, 2001, 2003). Studies reveal that images of tobacco use are perceived to be credible and salient if they reference a familiar or desired image, emotional state, or social context. Appraisals of smoking imagery in film reflect the viewer's experiences and expectations of the image and behavioral characteristics associated with smoking, within the cinematic and everyday context. These findings support film-industry research that reports how filmmakers value the use of smoking on-screen for its ability to communicate a range of moods, characteristics, and context (Shields, Balbach, & McGee, 1990). Filmmakers know, for example, that adolescents appreciate the familiar image of the stressed or sexy smoker as symbolic clues to the authenticity of an image, such as the actor's social status, lifestyle, and emotional state. This research complements studies indicating that the extent to which smoking in the media is portrayed as realistic and often incidental threatens to increase the likelihood that smoking is normalized and deemed socially acceptable (Hazan, Lipton, & Glantz, 1994). If anything, this research reveals well how films can play a powerful role in disseminating influential images of smokers and smoking.

An important line of research derives from tobacco companies' efforts to promote anti-youth-smoking messages through corporate image and responsibility campaigns. These campaigns, for example, include counter-marketing campaigns that use slogans such as "Just Say No." and "Think. Don't Smoke." Although these are viewed as antismoking educational programs geared for middle school students, these efforts may not reach their intended result. For example, these campaigns expose consumers, including children and adolescents, to images that portray tobacco companies as responsible and increase youth's familiarity with products. Adolescents' familiarity with cigarette manufacturers increases with exposure to the tobacco brands, which gains significance to the extent that familiarity and recognition are important antecedents of positive associations with brands, which in turn increase the likelihood of smoking (see R. G. Lee, Taylor, & McGetrick, 2004). Warnings, especially for those seeking social acceptance and thrilling experiences, can spark reactive conduct and actually encourage the warned against behavior. Not surprisingly, one study of the "Think. Don't Smoke" campaign found that it failed to increase anti-tobacco attitudes and beliefs among adolescents. And, more importantly, it found that adolescents exposed to these advertisements were more likely to express an intention to smoke during the next year (Farrelly et al., 2002). Even media efforts that aim to reduce adolescents' smoking run the risk, then, of reaching an unintended, opposite result.

As the above research suggests, not everyone similarly interprets media images. Adolescents are sensitive to the nuances of smoking portrayals in film, and studies have begun to distinguish differences in adolescents' appraisals of dominant smoker images in film. Demographic characteristics such as sex, age level, smoking status, and ethnicity thus may be important to decoding images of smoking in film and they provide important clues as to which groups may be more vulnerable to specific images and how best to manage this issue. Research has tried to tease out how different sociodemographic groups appraise dominant images of tobacco use and the types of smoker traits associate with susceptibility to smoking.

Although variable, smoking images in media tend to be perceived more positively during early adolescence. Younger adolescents attend to the stereotyped, glamorous image of smokers, whereas older teens appraise the images with a greater level of ambivalence and tend to associate film images of smoking with mood or situational factors (McCool et al., 2001, 2004). Age differences in stereotyping smokers in film also may reflect factors such as the perceived normalcy of smoking and expectations of smoking behavior derived from themselves or peers' smoking (McCool et al., 2003). However, that younger adolescents readily acknowledge the association between smokers in film and positive-image characteristics suggests that film offers a powerful means by which to register the social acceptability and desirability of smoking. Older adolescents are particularly attentive to the characters' negative emotional states. Specifically, older adolescents are more likely than younger adolescents to empathize with smoking and acknowledge the relaxant effect of smoking during emotionally distressing situations. Consistent with expectations, younger adolescents are more likely to appraise smokers in terms of their image (for example, sexy, stylish, intelligent, and healthy), whereas older teens are more likely to report empathetic interpretations (for example, stressed, depressed, bored; McCool et al., 2004).

These findings gain significance to the extent that other studies of smoking among adolescents report that smoking initiation and maintenance associates with stress and depression (Byrne, Byrne, & Reinhart, 1995). These emotional states seem related to adolescents' perceptions of the media and its influence on the extent to which they find smoking appealing. Even during adolescence, the perceived therapeutic qualities of nicotine appear to be readily understood and smoking is widely accepted as an important and appropriate coping strategy to manage stress during transitional periods. Moreover, as adolescents grow older they mature in their sensitivity to emotional experiences of others. Accordingly, older adolescents may be more attentive to smokers who display an emotionally based rationale for smoking. Younger adolescents, who may have had less direct experience with smoking, attend to the more stereotypical (or objectified) images and smokers' specific characteristics, such as the sexy woman or tough cop. To understand this difference, recall that older adolescents are more likely than younger adolescents to be smokers, socialize with smokers, and/or be affiliated with subcultural groups in which smoking is a normative behavior (Allbutt, Amos, & Cunningham-Burley, 1995; Nichter, Nichter, Vuckovic, Quintero, & Ritenbaugh, 1997; Michell, 1997). Older adolescents appear less likely to identify with image stereotypes of smokers in films, perhaps because of the greater heterogeneity in the kinds of people who smoke in the social worlds of older adolescents.

Sensitivity to media stereotypes of smokers also varies by sex. Smoking associates with weight control, self-image, self-esteem, and risk taking, all of which are sex-related predictors of smoking uptake among adolescents (Allbutt et al., 1995; Nichter et al., 1997). Boys and girls may, therefore, be differentially attracted to media images portraying related qualities (for example, sexy, healthy, stressed). These are expected findings. Males and females differ in sensitivity to emotional cues, with females exhibiting greater sensitivity to the emotional expressions and experiences of others (particularly negative emotions; Else-Quest, Hyde, Goldsmith, Van Hulle, 2006). Sex intensification emerges during adolescence, when adolescents increasingly start to conceptualize themselves in terms of masculine and feminine traits (Lobel, Nov-Krispin, Schiller, Lobel, & Feldman, 2004). As a result, adolescent girls may be more likely than boys to identify the emotional stereotypes of smokers in film, given that on-screen smokers are often portrayed as stressed, anxious, or angry (McCool et al., 2003). Studies have identified the importance of stress and depression as a factor in predicting smoking initiation and smoking maintenance, and young girls are especially aware of the association between smoking and relaxation, an image that is readily reinforced on-screen (Byrne & Mazanov, 1999; Lucas & Lloyd, 1999).

Adolescents' own susceptibility to smoking also predisposes them to hold different views of the media's tobacco images. Studies of smoking imagery in film have assessed adolescents' susceptibility to smoking as a predictor of subsequent tobacco use. Prospective studies reveal that adolescents who never smoked are more likely to smoke in the future if they report susceptibility in the form of expectations to smoke or holding prosmoking attitudes (Pierce et al., 1996; Tyas & Pederson, 1998; Dalton et al., 2003). Smoking susceptibility reflects a prosmoking attitude and is a highly significant predictor of future smoking (Pierce et al., 1996). Compared to nonsusceptible students, adolescents who were susceptible to smoking are significantly more likely to acknowledge tobacco image stereotypes. Adolescents who are more susceptible to smoking seem to be more sensitive to positive-image-focused stereotypes such as "sexy" and "stylish." For example, susceptible nonsmokers are more likely to appraise smokers in films in terms of positive-image stereotypes (McCool et al., 2003). One explanation may be that adolescents who contemplate smoking are highly responsive to accessible (stereotypical), positive images of tobacco use that support their interest in smoking behavior (Aloise-Young, Shenanigan, & Graham, 1996). Alternatively, frequency of viewing films with tobacco images, and viewing positive stereotype images on film, may promote susceptibility to smoking (Dalton et al., 2003). Although adolescents vary considerably in their appraisals of smokers in film, adolescents who are susceptible to smoking are more likely to identify with the image of on-screen smokers. These findings support the general proposition that the media may not influence adolescents in similar ways but still can play an important role in shaping and responding to adolescents' behaviors and attitudes.

As we can see, then, research reveals the immense complexity of media influences on adolescents. As with all other areas of media research we have examined, important theories suggest that the media industry highly influences adolescents, and that suggestion finds support from research that indicates how images often influence adolescents in counterintuitive ways. Importantly, the research reveals the need to consider adolescents' developmental needs and their social environments. For example, although the stereotyped "positive" image of tobacco (such as the sexy smoker) is attractive to younger adolescents, negative images of smoking (such as stressed, bored, and depressed) present an alternative "positive" image that may appeal to older adolescents or specific subcultures (McCool et al., 2003). Not surprisingly, advertisements seem to be able to capture adolescents' interests, with advertisements of "youth brands" viewed positively by adolescents (Arnett, 2001). Images portrayed in ways that appear realistic allow viewers to decipher meaning according to the viewer's experiences and expectations. Images also seem to have stronger influences on those susceptible to smoking.

The diverse ways that media images influence adolescents reveal the most important limitations of this area of research. The diversity of influence reveals the importance of placing the media in the context of a larger social system and attempting to understand the media's place in that system as it relates to adolescent development. We cannot fully understand media effects without understanding the media's role in adolescents' broader informational environments.

Placing the Media in the Context of Adolescent Development

Media influence exerted on adolescents' smoking interacts with a range of other individual, family, peer, and community-level factors. As with all other concerns that adolescents face, a look at the epidemiology of smoking identifies multiple and interrelated factors that seem to predict the strategies adolescents adopt. This section examines key factors identified by research and, where examined, the manner these factors relate to the relative power of various media in influencing adolescents' susceptibility to and eventual use of tobacco products.

Family and Peer Influences

Much remains speculative about the role that those close to adolescents—families and peers—play in impacting the media's influence on adolescents. However, it seems reasonable to conclude that families have a potentially powerful impact.

Given that families establish rules about media usage and help shape patterns of usage, families likely influence adolescents' responses to smoking in the media. By imposing limits, for example, families may reduce exposure to media that could influence adolescents. Similarly, siblings exposed to antismoking campaigns could be urged to not provide cigarettes to younger siblings. The media's impact could derive from the way the media interacts with family members to influence normative beliefs within families. Similarly, we know that peers greatly influence adolescent development and that the media can play an important role in shaping that development. Persuasive media images may, for example, elicit discussion, which may have an effect on the eventual appraisal of the message. Admittedly, much still remains hypothetical about the role of peers and families in impacting the media's influence on adolescents. Research, however, contributes some important findings.

A majority of the evidence from studies of adolescents' smoking initiation indicates that peer smoking, parental smoking, and siblings' smoking closely link to smoking initiation. For example, the role of families themselves, absent efforts to link that role to the media, appears quite strong in influencing adolescents' tobacco-use strategies. That is, the presence of an adult tobacco user in the home influences smoking among adolescents. For example, an important cross-sectional study of youth aged 12 to 14 years compared adolescents whose parents never smoked with those whose parents currently smoked and found that parental smoking nearly doubles the chance that adolescents will smoke (Bauman, Foshee, Linzer, & Koch, 1990). Some of the studies produced striking findings. For example, one study found that among children who have parents and best friends who smoke, 74% are frequent smokers and just 11% have never smoked (Lauer, Akers, Massey, & Clarke, 1982). Conversely, if both parents are nonsmokers and best friends do not smoke, 80% have never smoked and just 3% become regular smokers (Lauer, Akers, Massey, & Clarke, 1982). In addition to these important findings, we know that specific familial characteristics can serve as protective factors to decrease the vulnerability of adolescents to smoking. Adolescents are less likely to smoke when parents have intact marriages, monitor their children's activities, participate in activities with their children, use authoritative parenting, are supportive, and do not smoke themselves (for a review, see Kobus, 2003).

Although the role of parents may be important, research continues to highlight the importance of peers. Indeed, several studies have examined the varying roles of parents and peers in influencing adolescents' tobacco use. Some studies reveal a greater role of peers in adolescents' use of tobacco (Hu, Flay, Hedeker, & Siddiqui, 1995; Rose, Chassin, Presson, & Sherman, 1999). Other studies find a relatively equal influence (Chassin, Presson, & Sherman, 1995; Bauman, Carver, & Gleiter, 2001). Yet others find that parents have a greater role than peers, as they appropriately note that the influence varies at different stages in smoking behavior and adolescent development (Duncan et al., 1995; Flay, Hu, & Richardson, 1998). When focusing only on parents' own smoking behavior and the smoking behavior of peers, however, evidence does tend to support the view that peers more strongly influence adolescents (Avenevoli & Merikangas, 2003). Although this finding may be surprising to some, the finding actually fits well with other reports to the extent that adolescents initiate smoking in adolescence, a period known to be influenced by peers' behavior and attitudes and by the important place of peer selection.

Considerable research supports the conclusion that peers play a powerful role in adolescents' tobacco use. Peers continue to emerge as the best predictor of smoking behavior among a nationally representative sample of adolescents. The number of closest friends who smoke consistently remains the strongest predictor for ever having tried smoking, regularly smoking, number of days smoked in the last month, and the number of cigarettes smoked in the past month (Maney et al., 2004). Other research reveals that adolescents who report three or more friends who smoked had a smoking prevalence approximately ten times that of adolescents who reported that none of their friends smoked (Burns & Johnson, 2001). Having friends who smoke is one of the strongest correlates of adolescent smoking initiation (Jackson, 1997) and continued cigarette use (Tyas & Pederson, 1998). When closest friends smoke, adolescents are twice as likely to ever smoke and to become regular smokers. Those interacting among smoking peers also are significantly more inclined to "smoke more days" on average than those whose peers did not smoke (Burns & Johnson, 2001). These results comport with several national research reports (Burns & Johnson, 2001; United States Department of Health and Human Services, 2000, 2001a; Everett et al., 1999) and supports the premise that antisocial pathways, such as "friendship networks," contribute to tobacco initiation and continuation (Catalano & Hawkins, 1996). A substantial body of research suggests that smokers tend to befriend smokers, nonsmokers befriend nonsmokers, and that nonsmokers who affiliate with smokers are at greater risk for transitioning to tobacco use than youth without smoking friends (Kobus, 2003).

As with peer influences, school-based social norms regarding smoking may also influence adolescent smoking behavior. Schools remain important social contexts for youth that may impact adolescent behavior by establishing and maintaining social norms that provide positive and negative consequences for behavior. Several find that the school context creates an important developmental setting that warrants further study for its impact on adolescent tobacco use (Allison et al., 1999; Ennett, Flewelling Lindroth, & Norton, 1997). For example, one recent study conducted multilevel hierarchical analyses to model within-school and between-school variance in substance use as a function of school-level norms of disapproval of substance use on individual students' use. The study controlled for personal disapproval of substance use as well as school and individual demographic characteristics. Results suggest that school-level norms of disapproval of substance use negatively relate to students' use of these substances after controlling for personal disapproval of substance use as well as school and individual demographic characteristics (Kumar, O'Malley, Johnston, Schulenberg, & Bachman, 2002). These findings support the conclusion that school norms can play an important role in adolescents' tobacco use.

Importantly, adolescents tend to report that overt peer pressure is not a factor in their decision making regarding tobacco use (Lucas & Lloyd, 1999). Yet, researchers also note that the initial smoking experience takes place in the context of peers (Michell & West, 1996; Nichter et al., 1997). These findings suggest that pressures to smoke appear more normative, and not direct, overt, or coercive. This suggestion finds support from research indicating that teenagers feel internal self-pressure to smoke if others around them do and that their decision to try cigarettes links to their attempts to avoid potential exclusion by peers, to gain social approval, to facilitate social interactions, and to achieve a sense of autonomy or independence (see Nichter et al., 1997). This research links to findings that adolescents' perceptions of smoking prevalence contribute to their tobacco use: youth who perceive high prevalence rates of smoking are at an increased risk to initiate smoking (Sussman et al., 1988; Botvin, Botvin, Baker, Dusenbury, & Goldberg, 1992). Not surprisingly, then, adolescents who have never tried cigarettes report that they intentionally avoided smoking situations (Michell & West, 1996; Lucas & Lloyd, 1999). Adolescents who smoke essentially adapt their behavior to conform to that of other smokers, a point which leads us again to highlight the importance of the media's role in shaping adolescents' expectations.

As we already have seen above, research has tried to compare the relative importance of peers, families, and media influences. That research revealed that the media plays a potentially powerful role. Yet, it also is important to note that some report that peers and families exert stronger influences on adolescents' smoking patterns. For example, a recent study found that family smoking behavior, peer pressure, and prior beliefs about smoking were important predictors of smoking level of teens while advertising was not (Smith & Stutts, 1999). Predictor variables previously examined in separate studies (prior beliefs, peer pressure, family smoking, advertising, and antismoking information) were combined in a single study that surveyed 246 adolescents. Overall, family smoking behavior, peer pressure, and prior beliefs were more important in predicting smoking level than were advertising and antismoking information. Although advertising and antismoking information may not have an impact, that still leaves considerable room for incidental portrayals of tobacco use in the media. That research does reveal that the media can play an important role. Even though not much is known about the influence peers have on interpretations of media, peers do have a powerful impact. To the extent that an adolescent social system accepts media images and claims them as part of its culture, individuals in this system will, to a greater or lesser degree, choose to accept this image as their own and accordingly decide whether to smoke.

Psychological Influences

Researchers examine numerous theories to explain the initiation and maintenance of smoking behavior in both adolescents and adults. One of the most helpful theories suggests that adolescent smoking serves a number of purposes, often associated with specific developmental tasks (Perry, Murray, & Klepp, 1987). Smoking, for example, may be a coping mechanism for dealing with boredom and frustration. Smoking also may serve as a transition marker or a claim on a more mature, adult status. Smoking may be a way of gaining admission to a peer group. It also may provide a way to have fun, reduce stress, or maintain and increase one's personal energy. These factors most likely work together. For example, it has long been recognized that the desire for independence and individuality along with a concomitant disavowal of authority are characteristic of adolescence. This may mean that efforts that attempt to image tobacco products as problematic and "forbidden fruit" may create the undesired effect of reinforcing its appeal through its association with adulthood (see Willemsen & de Zwart, 1999). Although researchers often study factors in isolation, research does support many of these factors deemed to influence adolescents' smoking. Regrettably, researchers have yet to examine the interaction of these factors with the media's role in adolescents' smoking attitudes and behaviors. Even a cursory look at these factors, however, reveals a potential role for the media.

Research on the maintenance of smoking behavior has found that smokers experience their habit as having a calming effect (Leventhal & Avis, 1976), and pleasurable relaxation is the most frequently cited motive for smoking, particularly for adolescents (Klitzke, Irwin, Lombardo, & Christoff, 1990). Smoking can also be a quick and easy coping strategy for adolescents who have low self-image or who experience frequent dysphoric states (Semmer, Cleary, Dwyer, Fuchs, & Lippert, 1987). Personality factors, such as neuroticism, negative affect, hopelessness, and general psychological disarray also have been found to be integral in the maintenance of smoking (Breslau, Kilbey, & Andreski, 1993). Some children show a propensity for later, adolescent smoking as early as third grade by being cognitively susceptible or lacking a firm commitment toward not smoking (Jackson, 1998). For example, a study found that those with high-level attention deficit hyperactivity disorder (ADHD) were ten times more likely to smoke than those adolescents with low-level ADHD (Whalen, Jamner, Henker, & Delfino, 2001). Another study reported that early experimenters of tobacco and smokers were more likely to experience problem behaviors such as early pregnancy, dropping out of high school, stealing, and other illegal behaviors (Ellickson, Tucher, & Klein, 2001). Others have found that emotional distress reported in grade 10 associates with smoking in grade 12 for both boys and girls (Orlando, Ellickson, & Jinnett, 2001) and that cigarette smoking associates with sleep problems in youth aged 12–18 years (Patten, Choi, Gillin, & Pierce, 2000).

Of all the possible factors psychologically related to smoking, however, research highlights the place of depression in both the initiation (Kandel & Davies, 1986) and maintenance (Anda et al., 1990) of smoking (see Covey, Glassman, & Sterner, 1998, for a review). Depressive symptoms have also been found to predict continued smoking in adolescents (Zhu, Sun, Billings, Choi, & Malarcher, 1999). Despite the significant body of literature associating depression with smoking, the nature of this relationship remains unclear, and theories attempting to explain the observed correlation are sometimes contradictory.

Proposed theories tend to include both noncausal and causal relationships between depression and smoking. Several variables have been associated with both smoking and depression in adolescents. Smoking prevalence is highest among those with lower levels of education (Bartecchi, MacKenzie, & Schrier, 1995), and academic performance has been found to predict not only current smoking but also initiation of smoking and the intention to smoke in the future (Botvin, Epstein, Schinke, & Diaz, 1994). Family-related variables also have been associated with both smoking and depression. For example, we know that students who do not live with two parents are at increased risk of experimenting with cigarettes (Botvin et al., 1994). In addition, adolescents are at substantially higher risk of smoking if at least one of their parents smokes (Goddard, 1990; Patton et al., 1996). Parental smoking also predicts levels of major depression in their children (Chassin, Presson, Rose, & Sherman, 1998; Kendler et al., 1993). Although the exact nature of the relationship between parental and adolescent smoking and depression is unclear, research at least suggests that a predisposition of common factors, such as psychological vulnerabilities, contributes to the observed correlation between smoking and depression for adolescents (Koval, Pederson, Mills, McGrady, & Carvajal, 2000).

Previous research has examined smoking in relation to depression by focusing on depression as a one-dimensional variable. Although such studies suggest a strong link between smoking and depression for both adults (C. Brown, Madden, Palenchar, & Cooper-Patrick, 2000) and adolescents (Escobedo, Reddy, & Giovino, 1998), early studies did not examine independently specific aspects of depression. Recent research reveals that some of the classic indices of depression—low energy, sad mood, cognitive difficulty, low self-esteem, and learned helplessness—were not associated with adolescent smoking (Vogel, Hurford, Smith, & Cole, 2003). Instead, the more alienating aspects of depression—instrumental helplessness and social introversion—were associated with smoking. In fact, the latter two were significantly correlated (Vogel et al., 2003). It seems that the adolescents most likely to begin smoking are those least likely to seek help when their emotional needs are not being met. The experiences that lead to a sense of limited help and sympathy from others likely leave adolescents feeling vulnerable and isolated. They might smoke as a means of gaining social acceptance or to self-medicate depressive feelings.

To complicate matters, recent research has noted biological connections between smoking and depression (Balfour & Ridley, 2000). The early onset of regular tobacco use is highly predictive of depressive disorders, and a biological similarity between substance use and depressive disorders may exist (Hanna & Grant, 1999). Evidence has existed for many years regarding the genetic transmission of depression (e.g., Blumenthal & Pike, 1996) but only recently has a similar genetic vulnerability been proposed for smoking addiction. Yet, genetic subgroups of depressed individuals have been identified that are predisposed to self-medicate depressive symptoms by smoking (Lerman et al, 1998). More research in this area could serve to identify those adolescents who are most vulnerable to smoking initiation and maintenance, but the potential role of depression raises the possibility that the media may influence smoking, as we already have seen that the media industry serves as an important mechanism to deal with adolescents' normative transitional needs, including depressive thoughts and emotions.

Often ignored in research on adolescent smoking is the actual addictiveness of habits like tobacco use. For example, adolescent smokers generally believe that they would have less difficulty quitting smoking than other smokers and that they are less addicted than the average smoker (Weinstein, Slovic, & Gibson, 2004). In addition, adolescents tend to believe that they can quit when they are actually unlikely to do so; they (like adult smokers) greatly overestimate the likelihood that they will succeed in the coming year (Weinstein, Slovic, & Gibson, 2004). In addition, studies have shown that cigarette smokers are generally aware of increased health risks associated with smoking, but that smokers tend to underestimate their own susceptibility to disease and underestimate the health risks associated with short-term exposure to smoking (Murphy-Hoefer, Alder, & Higbee, 2004). Yet another consideration relates to the manner nicotine addiction generally develops within the first year of cigarette smoking (Burns & Johnson, 2001). We obviously are dealing with potentially powerful habits, some of which the media may play a significant role in fostering.

Racial/Ethnic Influences

Patterns of adolescent cigarette smoking differ substantially among racial and ethnic groups. The prevalence of cigarette smoking is higher among Whites than among Hispanics and Blacks, although these racial and ethnic differences may be disappearing among young adolescents (Kandel, Kiros, Schaffran, & Mei-Chen, 2004). White adolescents start smoking at an earlier age, are more likely to persist in smoking, and become more dependent on nicotine than minority youths (Griesler & Kandel, 1998; Kandel, Chen, Warner, Kessler, & Grant, 1997; Landrine, Richardson, Klonoff, & Flay,1994). Such disparities between smoking rates of ethnic groups highlight the importance of exploring ethnic group differences in appraisals of media images of smokers. Cultural norms and expectations of smoking behavior play an important role in registering and maintaining higher levels of tobacco use in some populations. There also may be cultural differences in consumption of different types of media.

Regrettably, the factors underlying these racial and ethnic differences are poorly understood. The surgeon general's report entitled Tobacco Use among Racial/Ethnic Minority Groups (United States Department of Health and Human Services, 1998) underscored the paucity and the methodological limitations of studies on racial and ethnic differences in the determinants of adolescent smoking. With few exceptions, most studies are cross-sectional and confound precursors and consequences of smoking. Reviews that are longitudinal are based on local samples (Landrine et al., 1994; O'Loughlin, Paradis, Renaud, & Gomez, 1998; Bauman, Carver & Gleiter, 2001) and report inconsistent results. Reviews reporting results from national longitudinal samples, such as the National Longitudinal Survey of Youth (Griesler, Kandel, & Davies, 2002), Add Health (Bauman et al., 2001), the National Education Longitudinal Study (R. A. Johnson & Hoffmann, 2000), and the Teenage Attitudes and Practices Survey (Flint, Yamada & Novotny, 1998), also report somewhat inconsistent findings. Overall, however, studies do point to few racial and ethnic differences in the predictors of various smoking behaviors. Studies using the National Longitudinal Study of Adolescent Health, for example, reveal that individual factors (adolescent, family, and peer) are more important predictors of smoking behaviors than are contextual factors (school). Other research reveals that predictors of smoking behaviors were mostly common across racial and ethnic groups (Kandel et al., 2004). Given the inability to identify adequate predictors and the apparent existence of important group differences, it seems clear that much remains to be investigated if we are to understand adolescents' smoking predispositions and habits.

Significance and Limitations of Influences Research

Many factors relate to adolescents' smoking strategies. A majority of the evidence from studies of adolescents' smoking initiation indicates that peer smoking, parental smoking, and siblings' smoking closely link to smoking initiation. In addition, we have seen how important psychological factors, such as perceptions of risk and optimistic biases, as well as even biological factors, influence whether adolescents will begin and continue smoking.

Despite an impressive number of studies, important links remain unknown and even misunderstood. For example, one of the most established findings is that peers influence adolescents' smoking habits. Yet, our understanding of how peers contribute to this behavior remains limited. The process by which teenagers are socialized to smoke, including both being influenced by and influencing their friends, remains unclear. The extent to which cigarette smoking, or variables related to smoking, are involved in adolescents' decisions to select into or select out of relationships with peers are as unknown as the complementary process of selection, where adolescents are selected by or excluded from relationships based on smoking. In addition to lacking in understanding of the bidirectionality and peer relationships is the lack of understanding of the potentially transient nature of such relations and the failure to assess changes in friendship patterns and the impact of those changes on adolescents' smoking. What constitutes "peers" also remains muddled, as research typically fails to consider the nature of the friendships, peer groups, and larger social system. The limitations are of considerable significance in that the reciprocal causal relationship between friend and adolescent behavior means that cross-sectional studies examining the correlation between peer and adolescent smoking risk producing spuriously inflated estimates of influence. The failure to understand the basic processes of the most key factors relating to adolescent smoking certainly challenges efforts to understand the place of the media in those relationships. Yet, given the significance of those factors, it seems that understanding the media's role in this aspect of adolescent development certainly requires a broader look at influences on adolescents' informational environments.

Modifying Media Influences
on Adolescents' Smoking Strategies

We have noted many factors that increase the likelihood that an adolescent nonsmoker will start using tobacco. Understanding the impact of the media, however, means understanding it in the context of efforts that simultaneously aim to control and limit the media's influence, such as through restricting access to tobacco products, providing health education, and even using targeted anti-smoking media efforts to limit the media's prosmoking influence on adolescents. Perhaps unexpectedly, antismoking public health campaigns typically report effectiveness. For example, campaigns typically inform children of the negative consequences of smoking. Young children express intentions not to smoke, hold negative attitudes regarding smoking, and are informed at levels much greater than before (Grandpre, Alvaro, Burgoon, Miller, & Hall, 2003). As a result, the adolescent population is among the groups most informed about the negative consequences of smoking. Yet, despite antismoking beliefs, attitudes, knowledge and intentions, a sizeable group of adolescents initiate smoking behaviors as early as middle school. Obviously, the many gains of successful substance abuse intervention programs dissipate as adolescents age. The surprising limits of media campaigns reveal the need to consider the nature of other prevention efforts, especially those deemed effective.

Smoking prevention programs primarily use school-based settings. Reviews reveal that nearly all studies from the past decade have a school-based component, if not a total focus on such programing (Backinger et al. 2003). Several studies have found school-based prevention programs to have short-term effects (that is, immediately following intervention) in delaying smoking initiation and enhancing attitudes against smoking, but little evidence suggests long-term prevention effectiveness (Elder et al., 1993; Noland et al., 1998; Eckhardt, Woodruff, & Elder, 1997). A meta-analysis of school-based prevention programs indicated limited efficacy (Rooney & Murray, 1996). More recently, however, reviews that emphasize social influences to deter adolescent smoking fare better than programs that simply focus on efforts to improve adolescents' self-esteem or increase knowledge of health risks (Lantz et al., 2000). These findings comport with well-established research that indicates a need to enhance adolescents' abilities to resist passive social pressure (Donaldson, 1995) and with research that finds programs ineffective when they group together deviant peers, or simply teach specific refusal skills to combat, for example, explicit drug use (Dishion, McCord, & Poulin, 1999). Generally, however, social-influences programming alone tends to be ineffective in the long term prevention of adolescents' tobacco use initiation (Backinger et al., 2003).

The limited efficacy of the most popular programs indicates a need to explore alternative settings for tobacco-use prevention. Although numerous tobacco-use prevention programs have been developed and delivered over the past 30 years, studies only recently have examined systematically the effects of such interventions in community settings. Some evidence supports multi-modal programming that combines school- and community-based components. One group of researchers developed and implemented such a randomized controlled trial of comprehensive community programming for tobacco-use prevention (Biglan, Ary, Smolkowski, Duncan, & Black, 2000). Targeting key social influences contributing to youth tobacco use, this intervention combined media advocacy, family communications, product sales deterrents, and anti-tobacco activities to reduce youth tobacco-use prevalence. Results indicate that a comprehensive community program targeting multiple determinants of youth tobacco use can enhance the effects of a school based program alone. The effects of the intervention were significant at 1 year into the intervention and 1 year post-implementation and were reported to have prevented an increase in prevalence in the community condition. Other research also finds positive effects. Five major statewide comprehensive tobacco-control programs that included media efforts have been found to reduce adult and youth smoking (Wakefield & Chaloupka, 1999). However, these efforts often override the aim of determining the impact of the overall program at the expense of more fine-grained research that might have focused on the media itself (Wakefield, Flay, Nichter, & Giovino, 2003). This type of research may reveal much about the extent to which comprehensive tobacco-control programs can reduce cigarette consumption and lower smoking prevalence among adolescents, but they do not tell us much about the media's potential role in such efforts.

Some efforts that have focused on the media in conjunction with other interventions have examined the comparative effectiveness of interventions. One longitudinal study, for example, specifically examined the impact of antismoking advertising on smoking behavior (Siegel & Biener, 2000). That study found that recall of antismoking advertising significantly associated with a lower rate of progression to established smoking at a 4-year follow-up, but the link was significant only for those exposed when they were young adolescents (12 to 13 years of age) and not older adolescents (14 to 15 years of age) at baseline. These results were consistent with other research that had conducted more comprehensive interventions and indicated that antismoking advertising may have a more demonstrable impact on younger than older adolescents (Wakefield & Chaloupka, 1999).

Mass media campaigns have been effective when linked with school interventions. At least four experimental studies support the conclusion that mass-media interventions significantly impact smoking prevalence when studies compare media and school interventions with school interventions without a media component (see Flynn et al, 1994; 1997; Worden, Flynn, Solomon, & Secker-Walker, 1996). For example, one study found that students in the media and school condition at a 4- and 6-year follow-up, compared with the school-only condition, reported significantly lower rates of smoking in the past week, self-reported smoking status, and daily smoking (Flynn et al., 1994). These impressive results suggest the durability of media- and school-based combined interventions. These results proved more effective when targeting higher risk youth—those who reported smoking at baseline or who had immediate social contacts, such as family and friends, who were smokers (Flynn et al, 1997). In addition, results revealed a greater relative benefit for high-risk girls than high-risk boys. Given the general challenges facing efforts to prove the significance of interventions, these are quite impressive results.

The above findings are impressive, but they exhibit important limitations that highlight the need to address often-ignored developmental considerations. Most notably, the failure to influence adolescents deemed at low risk reveals the need to ensure that campaigns continue so that they can impact adolescents at the point that they feel pressure to make decisions. It seems that campaigns protect those who have to make early decisions about smoking but not those who have to make decisions later, when the campaigns tend to stop. Despite these findings, the studies still support the claim that students exposed to a mass-media intervention in combination with a school-based tobacco-use prevention program may be at reduced risk for weekly smoking when compared with students exposed only to the school-based programming. Similarly, the results are encouraging to the extent that they highlight how characteristics of audiences matter, and campaigns reach their goals best when they consider timing, amount, and content of message exposure. Findings like these have led researchers to conclude that carefully addressing specific youth audiences through formative research and development of relevant media messages is crucial to the success of media-based interventions (Backinger et al., 2003).

The need to consider adolescents' developmental contexts finds support from research that reveals no link between media campaigns and school-based programs. One long-term, broad-based program, which included school-based programming in combination with mass-media and community grants, indicated that despite increased exposure to antismoking messages and information, weekly smoking rates were not significantly affected, suggesting a need for more intensive programming (Murray, Prokhorov, & Harty, 1994). Similarly, results from a field study of three media campaigns using two modalities (television and radio) combined with a peer involvement component showed only modest effects on expected consequences of smoking and friend approval of smoking (Bauman, LaPrelle, Brown, Koch, & Padgett, 1991). Neither modality proved more effective than the other, nor were effects on smoking detected. Importantly, the studies findings minimal effects have been criticized for having only superficial interventions that lack attempts to reinforce nonsmoking messages. It seems that anti-tobacco campaigns benefit from efforts that reinforce media messages.

Media- and school-based efforts cannot be addressed outside of major regulatory strategies for preventing adolescent tobacco use (Lantz et al., 2000). Until recently, adolescents in most states could readily purchase tobacco products. Because of this, efforts have increased to reduce the supply of cigarettes and other tobacco products in the hopes that it would reduce the number of adolescents who use them. Studies of statewide prevention programming indicate that legislative initiatives alone seem insufficient to produce significant impacts on tobacco-use prevalence. Tobacco control policies seek to reduce tobacco-use prevalence through smoking bans and enactment and enforcement of laws restricting youth access to tobacco products. Important federal initiatives, such as the Synar Amendment, now require states receiving federal funding for substance abuse and treatment to adopt and enforce tobacco age-of-sale laws and lower their rates of illegal sales of tobacco (see Dent & Biglan, 2004). Although a number of studies have found conflicting findings about the extent to which reducing illegal sales contributes to a reduction in smoking prevalence, recent reviews (Stead & Lancaster 2000) and a meta-analysis (Fichtenberg & Glantz, 2002) failed to find conclusive evidence of a relation between reductions in access and reductions in adolescent smoking prevalence. Studies on youth access show that young people continue to obtain cigarettes both from noncommercial sources, such as friends and family members, and from commercial sources, such as convenience stores, even though laws prohibit cigarette sales to individuals under the age of 18 years (Backinger et al., 2003). Most recently, for example, a large-scale study of several communities examined the relation between rates of merchant sales to minors and 13- to 17-year-old smoking rates (Dent & Biglan, 2004). The findings provided only limited support for the value of reducing young people's access to commercial sources of tobacco and indicated that social sources of tobacco (such as peers, siblings, and parents) are a significant factor in adolescent smoking. The results relating to tobacco source usage rates are consistent with other studies suggesting that the sources of tobacco for adolescents are largely social (DiFranza, Savageau, & Aisquith, 1996; Forster, Klepp, & Jeffery, 1998; DiFranza & Coleman, 2001). Importantly, to the extent that illegal sales in the community do relate to smoking rates, they matter most for those who are nearest the age limit. Adolescents adjust their tobacco sources depending on the level of commercial availability.

As expected, however, when communities adopt more comprehensive approaches and pass comprehensive youth access ordinances, communities can reduce the increase in daily smoking compared to other communities (Jason, Berk, Schnopp-Wyatt, & Talbot, 1999; Jason, Katz, Vavra, Schnopp-Wyatt, & Talbot, 1999). Data on the effect of cost show that youth are more responsive to cigarette price increases than adults, with a 10% increase in the price of cigarettes estimated to reduce youth smoking by approximately 5%, as compared to 1–2% among adults (Backinger et al., 2003). Economic estimates reveal that youth are up to three times more sensitive to price than adults, which suggests that raising cigarette prices will reduce smoking prevalence among youth, as well as reduce the amount that youth smoke (Evans & Farrelly, 1998; Lewit, Hyland, Kerrebrock, & Cummings, 1997). These are quite important studies that, at the very least, indicate that there are effective ways to address adolescents' smoking without directly addressing media images.

Whether comprehensive efforts can influence adolescents to quit smoking remains a largely uninvestigated issue. Although the vast majority of tobacco-cessation efforts have primarily focused on adult daily smokers, those that do include adolescents reveal important points. One review recently evaluated sixty-six studies of adolescent smoking-cessation studies (Sussman, 2002). The studies reported a mean quit rate of 12% at 3–12 months follow up, while the mean quit rate for the control groups was 7%. Length of follow up varied from 2 weeks to 64 months. Fourteen studies did not examine cessation past the end of the program, while the other fifty-two studies reported the following time lengths for follow up: ten studies at 1–2 months, sixteen studies at 3–5 months, eleven studies at 6–7 months, nine studies at 12 months, four studies at 1–2 years, and two studies at ≥3 years. Interventions using motivation enhancement or contingency-based reinforcement had higher quit rates, 19% and 17% respectively, than other intervention theories. When examining effect by type of program, classroom-based programs had the highest quit rate at 19% and computer-based and school-based clinics showed promise with 13% and 12% quit rates, respectively. These quit rates were derived from averaging all quit rates from each study category. The study concluded that overall data suggest that quit rates double with tobacco-cessation interventions. Despite these encouraging findings, it is remarkable that efforts did not include media interventions, an exclusion that again highlights the need to not simply focus on media efforts.

The significance and limitations of existing research are worth emphasizing. Important gains have been made with regard to new knowledge in the areas of adolescent tobacco-use prevention. Yet, continued work needs to focus on several areas of inquiry. Despite the promise held by the multi-modal tobacco prevention approaches, it is clear that the full trajectory of smoking does not occur in a vacuum. Multiple social, psychological, biologic, and environmental influences contribute to adolescents' smoking. Media efforts that seek to influence adolescent tobacco use must consider the media's place in these contextual forces.

Many of the studies present methodological limitations but still point us toward promising directions. Interventions often have at least one major limitation, such as a failure to use nonrandomized designs, a weak dose of intervention, lack of follow-up, or inability to control factors from the context of other tobacco-control strategies, which themselves have potential to influence adolescents' smoking behavior. Yet, existing studies support the notion that the media can play an active role in efforts to prevent and even stop adolescents' tobacco use. These studies suggest that antismoking efforts can have an effect on smoking uptake, and that media efforts work best when strengthened by concomitant exposure to school-based smoking prevention programs. Studies examining community-based and policy initiatives to prevent tobacco use suggest that utilizing approaches such as mass-media and smoking bans, in addition to school-based programs, can be effective in preventing tobacco use among adolescents. These comprehensive tobacco programs address the range of influences on youth tobacco use, such as tobacco-free policies, active parent and community involvement, school-based programs, cessation services, and media to counter tobacco advertising. In addition, research reveals important age effects and the need to address developmental considerations; the effects seem more robust when exposure occurs early among youth in pre-adolescence or early adolescence than later in adolescence. These findings highlight the important point that social-group interactions through family, peer, and social contexts can either neutralize or reinforce potential media effects. Effective efforts use developmentally appropriate school- and community-based prevention messages to support media efforts. Again, adolescents' broader informational environments cannot be ignored by efforts aiming to shape adolescents' responses to media portrayals.

Conclusions

It would be difficult to underestimate the significance of any of the social problems we have examined. Yet, even though the other areas we have examined receive the most attention, they actually may not be the most problematic, and they certainly are not the most lethal. Adolescence certainly constitutes a sensitive time period in the onset and eventual maintenance of tobacco use. During adolescence, nonsmokers may be initiating smoking, smokers may be transitioning from experimentation to regular smoking, and they may be transitioning from nondependent smokers to dependent smokers. Despite the significance of smoking as a public health issue for adolescents and broader society, media research pervasively fails to pay as close attention to adolescents' tobacco-use strategies as it does to other issues adolescents face.

Although this aspect of adolescent development remains one of the least understood in media research, emerging research reveals the media's potentially powerful role. A strong case, from cross-sectional and experimental studies, already indicates that smoking images in the media increase adolescents' smoking uptake. Media provide models that adolescents seek to emulate. Advertising continues to alert consumers to new brands. Movies and television programs portray particular life styles and issues, so that product placements, or even incidental use, of tobacco may be highly appealing and even more influential than direct advertising campaigns. In addition, the media also now figures prominently in antismoking campaigns. These campaigns have emerged because governments believe that the public requires adequate information, additional motivation, and accessible assistance to quit smoking or not start smoking. Researchers have yet to address systematically the many complexities of the media's role in fostering adolescents' tobacco use strategies, but few doubt that the media both shapes and reflects social values about smoking.

As we have seen, the literature reveals that numerous physiological, psychological, social, economic, political, and cultural factors influence adolescent smoking. No single factor working alone causes underage smoking. Research suggests a veritable laundry list of factors that positively associate in some cases with smoking among adolescents. Most notable, the social influence of peers and others on adolescent smoking, such as perception of smoking prevalence among peers, smoking prevalence among peers, smoking prevalence among desired peers, peer pressure and perception of peer approval. In addition, family issues arise, such as perception of parental approval, parental smoking, smoking by an older sibling, and socio-economic status. Levels of exposure to cigarette advertising and marketing also now figure prominently in research; how they work with other factors remains to be seen, but we already know that the media play an important role in modeling behaviors, exerting indirect pressure, and fostering normative beliefs that shape adolescents' perceptions, needs, and social interactions. As the media infiltrate adolescents' environments, they influence adolescents' responses to tobacco products.

The focus on adolescents' environments highlights the need to engage adolescents in their relationships. It reveals a need to consider basic psychological needs like depression and deviance, as well as normative factors like peer pressure and commitment to schooling. How the media influence those factors remains a largely unchartered research area, but the media and mass information need to be considered in a much broader focus than does current research examining the media's role in adolescents' smoking behaviors. Effective responses to adolescents' smoking and other tobacco use require addressing adolescents' instrumental and social effectiveness as they navigate their informational environments.

5

Adolescent Sexuality and the Media

Like any other socialization, sexual socialization involves the process by which adolescents acquire knowledge, attitudes, and values. This multidimensional process coordinates messages from a wide variety of sources that cover a broad range of topics, including information about physical appearance and biological reproduction to values and attitudes about dating, sex, and romantic relationships, to perceptions of marriage, parenthood, family life, and work. As expected, the media provide a potentially powerful source for this wide variety of messages. The media transmit these messages both verbally and nonverbally and often in subtle, ambiguous, and inconsistent ways. This complexity poses considerable challenges for research. Such complex messages are, by their nature, difficult to identify, evaluate, and place in the broader context of adolescents' informational environments. In addition, the potential pervasiveness of sexual messages challenges efforts to evaluate the sources of messages. Arguably more so than we have concluded in prior chapters, these realities lead us to conclude that media effects must be considered in light of their influence on adolescents' entire informational environments.

The place of the media in adolescents' informational environments relating to sexual knowledge and attitudes seems particularly important to consider given that adolescents and parents themselves, albeit for different reasons, attach great significance to the media's role. Our society generally views parents as the most influential sexuality educators of their children (Levesque, 2000). Yet, in terms of concrete information about sex, adolescents typically report learning more from their same-sex peers and the media than from any other source (see, e.g., Ballard & Morris, 1998). The media industry (especially television and magazines) generally ranks among adolescents' top three sexual informants, often following either peers or schools in importance. Recent research interviewing young teens now even ranks entertainment media as *the* top source of information about sexuality and sexual health (Kaiser Family Foundation and Children Now, 1997). Early adolescents, those 12 to 15 years of age, may have few options other than to use the media to shape their own conceptions of sex and intimacy (Connolly & Goldberg, 1999), especially given that direct observations of sexuality seldom occur, that sexual relationships are difficult subjects to discuss, especially with parents (Gordon & Gilgun, 1987), and that educational programs usually focus on purely biological aspects of sexuality (Levesque, 2003). Not surprisingly, leading researchers now view the media as acting as a "super peer" that influences adolescents' sexual attitudes and behaviors (J. D. Brown, Halpern, & L'Engle, 2005). The media undoubtedly provide important sources of information, but it may not necessarily present information that actually would influence behavior. The significance of this distinction arises from the extent to which parents may no longer provide the most information yet still remain highly influential (Levesque, 2000). Adolescents actually seem to agree as they note their indifference to the media's influence, even when parents and adults express significant concern about the impact of the media on youth (Werner-Wilson, Fitzharris, & Morrissey, 2004). This third-person effect—the belief that something influences others but not oneself—afflicts adolescents and adults alike and reveals the need to convince adolescents of the validity of concerns and the need to determine the actual validity of the concerns themselves.

On its face, media portrayals that cause concern certainly seem to reflect adolescents' sexual behavior. As we will see below, media experts generally agree that the media encourage sexual activity by shaping and fostering irresponsible attitudes. Ample evidence supports the claim that adolescents feel encouraged to engage in sexual activity, with much of it posing risks to their well-being. Well known, for example, are findings indicating that nearly two thirds of students graduating from high school (typically just turning 18) will have had sexual intercourse (Centers for Disease Control & Prevention, 2002). These are impressive statistics, but even they underestimate a wide range of potential sexual behavior outside of intercourse. No valid statistics reveal the frequency of adolescents' other types of sexual behavior, but those behaviors also hold considerable significance to the development of "sexual cognitions" that influence sexual behavior (e.g., arousability, sexual agency, abstinence attitudes, perceived parental and peer approval, and sexual self-esteem). Research increasingly identifies sexual experiences that occur before adolescents begin to engage in intercourse (e.g., breast fondling) as central to sexual development and, compared to intercourse, as related to greater changes in sexual cognitions (O'Sullivan & Brooks-Gunn, 2005). The focus on the broad range of sexual activity also gains significance to the extent that groups of adolescents experience sexual debut differently. Adolescents' sexual activity, including the type of activity they engage in before their first sexual intercourse, relates to age, physical development, cultural background, and numerous other factors (Blum et al., 2000; Levesque,

2000). Sexual activity, then, clearly increases during adolescence, a time when adolescents pay close attention to information around them to form attitudes about their sexuality and behavior.

A similar parallel emerges between beliefs that the media encourage irresponsible behavior and the belief that adolescents do place themselves at risk of harm when they do engage in sexual activity. A large number of adolescents may well engage in sexual activity and not incur negative consequences, but engaging in sexual activity clearly increases the risk of negative outcomes. For example, research rather extensively documents the physical, emotional, and social consequences of teen sexual activity resulting in high rates of teen pregnancy. Each year in the United States, 800,000 to 900,000 adolescents 19 years of age or younger become pregnant; about 425,000 give birth, with nearly half of those births from those 17 years of age and younger (Martin et al., 2003). In addition, ample evidence reveals early childbearing's profound consequences for the adolescents and their children. For example, teenaged mothers more often head single-parent households, live in poverty, and have lower educational attainment than mothers who begin childbearing later in life (Levesque, 2000). A substantial literature also documents the adversities suffered by children born from women who begin childbearing at young ages. Children born to mothers who began childbearing at a young age, for example, are more prone to general delinquency, violence, and arrest than are children born to mothers who began childbearing when they were older (e.g., Corrado et al., 2002; Pogarsky, Lizotte, & Thornberry, 2003). No evidence supports the claim that engaging in sexual activity does not involve risk.

Risks of pregnancies and their consequences, traditionally the major concern arising from sexual activity, increasingly pale in comparison to the negative outcomes that arise from the increased risk of contacting a sexually transmitted disease (STD). A recent study found that at least one third of a sample of 921 adolescents, for example, experienced condom failure over the past 90 days, regardless of gender. Given that it may be assumed that not all of them were sexually active and actually used condoms, these are striking findings. More important, however, the study also found that the frequency of condom failure positively associated with diagnosis STD, with the odds of testing positive increasing 22% for each added event of failure (Crosby et al., 2005). These findings concur with the view that, compared with those who postpone sexual activity until later, individuals who initiate sexual activity in adolescence have an increased risk of acquiring an STD, not just a pregnancy. Of the more than 15 million sexually transmitted infections that occur annually in the United States, nearly four million are among teens and over six million are among youth ages 20 to 24 (Cates, 1999; Weinstock, Berman, & Cates, 2004). The high rates of transmission of STDs during the adolescent period has led to concern about HIV infections, but increasing concern now moves to other STDs. Most notably, human papillomavirus (HPV) constitutes a significant source of morbidity and mortality worldwide, and the primary risk factors for acquiring HPV generally associate with sexual activity among adolescents. Cumulative prevalence rates reach as high as 82% among adolescent women in select populations; nearly all sexually active adolescents are at high risk for acquiring HPV (Moscicki, 2005). These types of findings certainly lend support to efforts that tout the need for adolescents to resist sexual activity.

Sexual activity plays other important roles in placing adolescents' healthy development at risk. Sexual activity relates to experiences of significant victimization, which increases adolescents' risk of negative outcomes during and after adolescence (Kaukinen & DeMaris, 2005). For example, the younger a female is when she first engages in sexual activity, the more likely she will have suffered involuntary or forced sex. Data from the National Longitudinal Study of Adolescent Health reveals that 7% of adolescent girls have experienced forced sexual intercourse (Raghavan, Bogart, Elliot, Vestal, & Schuster, 2004). These figures are slightly lower than those from the national Youth Risk Behavior Survey, which respectively revealed 10.2% and 5.1% lifetime prevalence of forced sex for high school females and males (Howard & Wang, 2005). Although of significance in and of itself, having a history of forced sex relates to numerous other past and potential harm; sexual victimization during adolescence increases both males and females' risk of feeling sad or hopeless, having considered or attempted suicide, being a victim of physical dating violence, engaging in binge drinking, having multiple sex partners, and having unprotected sex (Howard & Wang, 2005). In addition, history of victimization relates to multiple forms of drug use, drug-related problems and STDs like HIV (Ellickson, Collins, Bogart, Klein & Taylor, 2005). Likewise and returning to STDs and infections, a report of a prior coercive sexual experience associates with a higher lifetime number of sexual partners, which in turn associates with subsequent HPV and other sexually transmitted infections (Kahn, Huang, Rosenthal, Tissot, & Burk, 2005). These recent findings certainly present impressive results indicating that adolescents who engage in sexual activity most likely already have suffered significant harms and are engaging in a wide variety of related harms.

Adolescents certainly encounter considerable harms resulting from their sexual activities, but it remains to be determined how the media contribute to those harms. Clearly, however, adolescents seem interested in sexually embedded media and the media reinforce that intrigue. This reinforcement quickly becomes problematic to the extent that parents, schools, and policy makers continue to argue about what adolescents should know and be taught, and the mass media increasingly portrays sexuality and relationships in ways that parents, schools, and policy makers claim to find problematic and often offensive. To complicate matters even more, the media are often forthcoming and explicit about sexuality, and other socializing institutions muffle their responses to adolescent sexual development. In comparison to other sources, the media actively support sexual activity as it typically focuses on the positive possibilities of sex rather than its problems and negative consequences (J. D. Brown & Keller, 2000), and other sources appear much more hesitant than the media to address such taboo topics as passion and sexual pleasure. While traditional socializing agents, such as churches and schools, increasingly invest themselves in socializing adolescents to accept restrictive attitudes, values, and beliefs, the media actively blaze different paths that appeal to and compel adolescents into sexual activity (Levesque, 2003). As a result, informational environments provide conflicting and confusing messages about sexuality and relationships, all as the media seem to play an increasingly powerful role in shaping the types of relationships society finds deviant, unhealthy, and distressing. The polarization of attitudes and information—the lack of alternative sources of information coupled with the enticing, sexualized nature of the media—ensures that the media will play a dominant role in sexual socialization.

The wide attention paid to the place of sexuality in diverse media, coupled by the significance of sexuality in adolescents' lives, makes this area of research essential to understanding the media's role in adolescent development and its consequences. Understanding how to respond to sexualized media and its effects requires a close look at the strengths and weaknesses of the empirical literature and an effort to integrate that literature with possible responses to address problematic media effects. To do so, this chapter explores the nature of the media's portrayals of sexuality and its particular influence on adolescents and their sexual development. Although researchers have not embraced this area of research as much as the others we have examined, it seems increasingly clear that the media potentially play an important role in adolescents' sexual development, including a role in shaping sexual dispositions, attitudes, behaviors and relationships. To understand the media's socializing force, this chapter pays attention to factors that moderate and mediate media effects, although research only recently has turned to these considerations. And, like previous chapters, this one focuses on the potential role the media can play in fostering healthier development and relationships. Together, findings reveal the need to reconsider how best to prepare adolescents to respond more effectively to sexualized media as well as to adolescents' broader informational environments.

Sexuality in the Media and Its Effects

Several theoretical approaches and practical circumstances help explain the media's potential role in educating adolescents about sexuality. Sexual content pervades the media. From prime-time situation comedies (sitcoms) and dramas to feature films, the media present adolescents with countless verbal and visual examples of how to approach intimacy, sex, and dating relationships. Estimates reveal that adolescents typically encounter approximately 10,000–15,000 sexual messages, jokes, and innuendoes from the media each year (Strasburger & Donnerstein, 1999). Adolescents easily access and widely consume the media. As we have seen, adolescents watch 16–17 hours of television weekly and spend 38 hours each week using some kind of media (Roberts, Foehr, Rideout, & Brodie, 1999). This commitment actually exceeds the time adolescents spend in school or directly interacting with their parents (Hofferth & Sandberg, 2001). Simply noting that adolescents encounter sexual messages, however, does not reveal much about the nature of those references and their meaning for adolescents.

This section examines the nature of sexuality in the media and then examines what existing research reveals about its effects.

The Media's Sexual Content

Research in this area typically focuses on content presented on prime-time comedies and dramas, music videos, and daytime soap operas. In assessing the nature of television programs' sexual content, researchers tend to focus on blocks of programming and analyze their characters' dialogues and actions for sexual acts or references to sexual acts. This approach counts the number of times the programs visually or verbally display certain physical and intimate behaviors, such as kissing, affectionate touching, and intercourse. In addition to focusing on the sexual acts themselves, these studies tend to document the gender and marital status of the participants, the genre of the program, and the participants' attitudes toward the actions (i.e., positive or negative). Together, these analyses allow researchers to identify the frequency of sexual depictions and evaluate their nature.

Data gathered across several different media reveal quite consistent themes in analyses of the media's portrayals of sexuality. Sexual references and imagery are quite prevalent and have been increasing in number and explicitness since the 1970s. Analyses of the content of prime-time television, soap operas, movies and music television have long found, by most standards, large amounts of implicit sexual activity (see Donnerstein & Smith, 2001). Given the popularity of sexually embedded content with adolescents, adolescents are likely to be exposed to various types of embedded sexual content. The pervasiveness of sexualized media is highlighted by adolescents' exposure to sexually explicit media rated as inappropriate for them. The vast majority, over 85%, of young adolescents have read adult pornography; and over 90% of 13- to 15-year olds have seen X-rated films (Greenfield, 2004). Nearly half of adolescents have visited Internet sites with various types of "adult" content by the time they have reached the eighth grade (Malamuth & Impett, 2001). Adolescents seem to exhibit a rather uncanny ability to obtain media deemed problematic for them and even out of their reach, and even those who do not try cannot avoid the remarkable extent to which the media saturates their environments.

Although adolescents may have access to materials presumably deemed beyond their legal reach, it is important to note that the materials within their everyday reach may actually be the most troublesome. The standard fare of adolescents' movies, those R-rated, contains considerable sexual content. Adolescents 13 to 14 years old regularly have access to R-rated movies and those who desire access generally are able to view whatever rental videos they wish (Greenberg, Linsangan, et al., 1993). Adolescents comprise the largest demographic segment of moviegoers (Strasburger, 1995), and increasing numbers of movies with sexual themes actually target adolescents (Federal Trade Commission, 2004). The sexual content of feature films appears quite substantial. For example, 60% of the 50 top-grossing films of 1996 contained at least one sex scene (Bufkin

& Eschholz, 2000). Considering that only half of these films were rated R and the others were rated PG or PG-13, this percentage is quite large. The content of these movies seems most problematic in that it tends to be much more coercive, violent, aggressive, and antisocial than other movies. For example, R-rated movies contain at least five times more violent behavior than movies rated X or even XXX (Yang & Linz, 1990). This is not to say that sexually explicit materials are not problematic, but it is to say that the less explicit materials may well be. The lower the rating for mature audiences, the higher the rate of aggression and violent sexual encounters, and the more available the movies are to adolescents.

Of course, even though adolescents have access to certain media, it does not mean that they seek it out or actually listen or regularly view it. It does seem, however, that even adolescents' everyday media consists of sexual talk and displays, and the nature and prevalence of this sexual content significantly vary across genres. For example, while soap operas make more sexual references than prime-time programming, prime-time programs typically contain more varied sexual activity, more premarital sex, and greater explicitness (e.g., Greenberg, Siemicki et al., 1993). One important content analysis indicated that sexual content that ranged from flirting to sexual intercourse had jumped from slightly more than half of television programs in 1997–1998 to more than two thirds of the programs in the 1999–2000 season (Kunkel et al., 2001).

Considerable research reporting content analyses of these programs reveal much about the nature of those depictions. It is commonly reported that television's sexual content is not typically visually graphic, but is instead dominated by either verbal innuendo or less explicit physical acts of flirting, kissing, hugging, and erotic touching (e.g., Kunkel, Cope, & Biely, 1999). Explicit visual indications of sexual intercourse are rare. Suggestive or explicit depictions of intercourse occurred in one of every ten programs (Kunkel et al., 2001). The most common type of sexual content on prime-time programs, and on sitcoms, especially, is often verbal suggestiveness or innuendo (Shidler & Lowry, 1995); the dominant modes of sexual expression on daytime soap operas and prime-time dramas are passionate kissing and erotic touching and verbal references to sexual intercourse such as "having an affair" and "going to bed" (Greenberg & Busselle, 1996). But, the number of portrayals of sexual behaviors, including sexual intercourse, on television clearly rises as the number of programs that simply talk about sex declines (Kunkel, Biely, Eyal, Cope-Farrar, & Donnerstein, 2003). Overall, television's sexual content is often verbal, and when visual, the behaviors depicted are mostly precursory (e.g., flirting or kissing).

Significance attaches to this research to the extent that the bulk of sexual action and language occurs outside of committed relationships and does not consider risks. Analyses of television programs reveal that verbal and visual references to sexuality originate more frequently from unmarried than married people. Sexual depictions among unmarried partners always are more common (Greenberg, Brown, & Buerkel-Rothfuss, 1993). In addition, programs portray a lack of discussion and depiction of sexual planning and consequences, with few references to STDs, contraception, pregnancy prevention, and abortion. Of the hundreds of sexual acts and statements uncovered, references to STDs and pregnancy prevention typically make up 0–6% of the total (Kunkel et al., 2003; Shidler & Lowry, 1995). Importantly, however, the increase in percentage of prime-time programs with sexual content has brought with it an increase in references to risk and responsibilities, now with 15% of all prime-time shows with sexual content making references to risk (such as sexual patience, sexual precaution, depictions of negative consequence), meaning one of every seven television shows that include sexual content now includes safe-sex messages (Kunkel et al., 2003). Even this encouraging statistic, however, is somewhat disheartening to the extent that these messages do not happen frequently and that nearly two thirds of these instances (63%) are minor or inconsequential in their degree of emphasis within scenes (Kunkel et al., 2003). These important findings highlight the point that what is shown on television appears more important than how much is shown.

Research examining the content of movies also reveals sexual activity marked by risk. Most notably, this area of research seeks to tap into the extent to which individuals engage in sexual activity within committed relationships. This research generally focuses on the existence of marital relationships and finds considerable nonmarital sexual activity. For example, analyses of the top twenty-five movie video rentals of 1998 revealed that sexual behavior was not only exhibited more frequently among unmarried versus married partners (85% of total behaviors versus 15%) but also involved more explicit behaviors among unmarried partners (Dempsey & Reichert, 2000). A similar disparity was reported in an analysis of sixteen popular R-rated films. In those films, references to sexual intercourse between unmarried partners accounted for 45% of all sexual activity coded and outnumbered references to married sex in a 32:1 ratio (Greenberg, Siemicki, et al., 1993). Similar findings are reported by research examining the content of the movies that early adolescents themselves note are their favorites (Pardun, L'Engle, & Brown, 2005).

Although R-rated movies have been seen as problematic, music videos contain even more sexual images and have the added impact of blending the content of songs with images. As a result, music videos have been viewed as illustrating the media's increasingly frequent, explicit, and irresponsible portrayals of sexual behavior. For example, even when they were only starting to be so popular among teenagers, music videos presented adolescents with provocative clothing and sexually suggestive dance movements, including sadomasochism and sexual bondage. Music videos simply incorporated the sexual content of explicit popular music, with all that it entailed. Even nearly two decades ago, Music Television (MTV) aired concept videos that were deemed problematic: 75% of their videos told stories involving sexual imagery, with over half involving violence, and 80% combined violence and sexuality to portray violence against women (Sherman & Dominick, 1986). Because of their distinct format, music videos have been examined using an analytic approach that emphasizes imagery over dialogue or lyrics, with reports indicating that over half of all videos contain sexual imagery characterized by innuendo and suggestiveness (Baxter, De Riemer, Landini, Leslie & Singletary, 1985). One analysis of 40 videos from 1990 found that 90% of the 30-second intervals coded contained implicit images of sex (Sommers-Flanagan, Sommers-Flanagan, & Davis, 1993). In keeping with prior research, both males and female acted in sexually explicit ways in a very small percentage (1.6%), of sexual occurrences. And, although women were more likely to act in implicitly sexual ways, in 45% of sexual occurrences, men also behaved implicitly sexual at a high rate, at 33% (Sommers-Flanagan et al., 1993). Likewise, the small fraction of direct-sex appeals and various states of undress found in network television commercials pale in comparison from MTV's ads explicitly geared toward youth (Signorielli, McLeod, & Healy, 1994). The sexed nature of music videos and advertisements has yet to wane. Despite MTV's status as cutting edge, MTV's videos and advertisements continue to offer stereotypic and sexualized images that provide adolescents with rather restricted views of gender and sexuality; males continue to be portrayed as more adventuresome and violent while females are portrayed as being more affectionate, nurturing, sexually pursued, and wearing revealing clothing (Seidman, 1999).

Sexual images and messages in mainstream magazines appear more graphic than and equally abundant to their portrayals in television. Magazines aimed to adolescent audiences actually are one of the most accessible media for information about sexuality. Magazines are explicit and direct, exposing readers to nude and provocatively posed models, frank discussions of sexual techniques, and specific suggestions on how to improve sexual relationships (Duffy & Gotcher, 1996; Duran & Prusank, 1997). When compared to other media, it seems that magazine content presents conflicting and contradictory pictures of female sexuality and are actually not that responsible either. Magazines devote minimal space to discussions concerning the danger of AIDS and other STDs and methods of prevention. Teen magazines encourage adolescents to be sex objects and teachers of interpersonal communication; they provide little encouragement for young women to discuss issues of pregnancy, birth control, or AIDS with their male partners (Garner, Sterk, & Adams, 1998). Analyses of teen and women's magazines reveal that readers are increasingly likely to have learned that they need to be more concerned about sex per se rather than sexual health (Walsh-Childers, Gotthoffer, & Lepre, 2002).

Much evidence supports the claim that the media provide adolescents with high levels of sexually charged materials, but it is important to note that popular media also embeds products and portrayals that may not appear to impact adolescents' sexual development and behavior but which undoubtedly do so on closer examination. Most notably, alcohol appears in more than 70% of prime-time television shows and in 90% of movies; beer and wine are among the most heavily advertised products on television and radio (J. D. Brown & Witherspoon, 2002). Likewise, despite the stated commitment of the media to reduce the frequency and glamorization of violence, the effects of efforts to reduce violence have yet to be documented. In the most comprehensive content analyses of U.S. television non-news programming, for example, only a minority of programs were characterized as having an overall nonviolent theme (Wilson et al., 2002).

Taken together, the content of media does not bode well for societal efforts to instill restrictive values and responsible skills.

Effects of Sexualized Media Portrayals

Compared to other areas of media-effects research we have examined, strikingly little research seeks to understand the sexual media content's effects on adolescents. Despite the paucity of research in this area, studies increasingly reveal important links between media use and sexual attitudes and behaviors. Although largely correlational until quite recently, research does illustrate the media's power in shaping adolescents' development of sexual attitudes and activities. This new research, examined briefly in this section, reveals important experimental and longitudinal components.

The vast majority of research that examines the effects of exposure to sexual media content uses cross-sectional methods. Research tends to address three major issues. The first area of study examines the extent to which media exposure shapes viewers' sense of social reality, such as views of sexual actions or outcomes. Research reveals strong and consistent associations between exposure levels and viewers' perceptions. Adolescents who spent more time viewing television make higher estimations of their peers' average sexual activity level (Eggermont, 2005). Greater exposure to sexually oriented genres (e.g., soaps, music videos) links to viewers' assumptions and expectations about the prevalence of sex and of certain sexual behaviors. For example, frequent viewers of talk shows overestimate the numbers of sexually active youth and the number of teen pregnancies (Davis & Mares, 1998). Presumably because action or adventure programs pay less attention to sexual relationships, frequent viewers of this genre offer lower estimates of divorces and affairs (Potter & Chang, 1990). As expected, regardless of their viewing amounts, young women who identify more strongly with popular television characters assume that greater percentages of their peers are sexually active (Ward & Rivadeneyra, 1999). Several studies have indeed supported the idea that television's recurrent portrayal of certain sexual acts makes them seem more widespread (Aubrey, Harrison, Kramer, & Yellin, 2003; Buerkel-Rothfuss & Strouse, 1993; Ward, 2002). A sample of 259 undergraduates revealed, for example, that heavy viewers (of soap operas) tend to overestimate the prevalence of sexual activity in real life, and that more frequent television exposure is related to greater expectations of peer sexual experience (Buerkel-Rothfuss & Strouse, 1993). It appears, then, that frequent and more involved viewers are likely to cultivate expectations that sex is prevalent and that sexual relationships are often fleeting (see Buerkel-Rothfuss & Strouse, 1993; Larson, 1996; Ward, 2002).

Second, research finds links between exposure to media genres and adolescents' attitudes about sexuality and sexual relationships. Survey research indicates that greater regular exposure to or involvement with sexually oriented genres links to more liberal and more stereotypical sexual attitudes, especially among young women (Strouse & Buerkel-Rothfuss, 1987; Strouse,

Buerkel-Rothfus, & Long, 1995; Walsh-Childers & Brown, 1993). In this regard, young women who view more sexually oriented television more strongly endorse certain dysfunctional beliefs about relationships (Haferkamp, 1999). Being a frequent television viewer and perceiving media characters as sexually more competent and as experiencing more pleasure than oneself also associates with holding negative attitudes towards remaining a virgin and holding more negative attitudes about one's sexual experiences (Courtright & Baran, 1980). Adolescents who view more television with a high level of sexual content view casual sexual encounters less negatively (Bryant & Rockwell, 1994). The dominant trends across the literature indicate that frequent exposure to certain television genres links to attitudes that elicit displeasure with virginity and support nonrelational sex and stereotypes about relationships. Teens with a heavier diet of music videos tend to endorse more permissive sexual attitudes (Strouse et al., 1995). Teens who view more soap operas tend to view single motherhood as more manageable and as supported by men who play important roles in their children's lives (Larson, 1996). Earlier maturing girls, regardless of race, are more likely to be listening to music and reading magazines with sexual content, to see R-rated movies, and to interpret the messages they saw in the media as approving of teens having sexual intercourse (J. D. Brown et al., 2005). Although there may be ethnic differences, adolescents who frequently watch people talking about sex and behaving sexually on television are more confident (arguably delusionally) that they could enact safe sexual behaviors (e.g., obtaining condoms, communicating with a potential partner) than are adolescents with less exposure to sexual content on television (Martino, Collins, Kanouse, Elliott, & Berry, 2005). Moreover, these findings appear to be stronger, broader, and more consistent among women than among men (Walsh-Childers & Brown, 1993; Ward & Rivadeneyra, 1999).

Third, tentative evidence also reveals that greater television exposure actually does link to viewers' sexual behavior. Two groundbreaking articles published in the early 1990s examined the question of whether exposure to sex on television influences adolescent sexual behavior (J. D. Brown & Newcomer, 1991). The studies found positive associations between any lifetime intercourse and television viewing among adolescents, but methodological limitations rendered the results inconclusive. Higher levels of exposure to sex on television might have led to sexual initiation in that research, but a plausible alternative interpretation was that, because sexual content more closely reflects their identities and interests, sexually active adolescents choose to watch more of it than their inactive peers. This possibility could not be excluded, because the studies failed to account for the relative timing of these events. These two studies also were unable to attribute the sexual behavior of youths to differences in television exposure to sex, rather than to other closely related factors. For example, youths who receive little supervision may be free to watch more television and to choose programs with sexual content and may also have more opportunities to engage in sexual activity. Finally, previous work mainly relied on imprecise measures of content, making it difficult to determine whether exposure to sexual content per se was the source of the observed associations, but those investigations are quite recent.

It was only a few years ago that longitudinal research sought to examine causality. A national longitudinal survey of adolescents demonstrated that adolescents who viewed more sexual content at baseline were more likely to initiate intercourse and progress to higher levels of noncoital sexual activity over the subsequent year, even after controlling for a broad set of respondent characteristics that might otherwise explain these relationships (Collins et al., 2004). The effects found were not insubstantial. For example, 12-year-olds who watched the highest levels of sexual content among youths their age appeared much like youths 2 to 3 years older who watched the lowest levels of sexual content among their peers. The magnitude of these results is such that a moderate shift in the average sexual content of adolescent television viewing could produce substantial effects on sexual behavior at the population level. A similar longitudinal survey, drawing from fourteen middle schools in North Carolina, recently found comparable effects (J. D. Brown et al., 2006). These longitudinal studies all point in the same direction.

The above research gains significance in that it also comports with other long-established findings. Research has long revealed that the amount of total television viewing typically has not been related to viewers' level of sexual activity (J. D. Brown & Newcomer, 1991; Strouse & Buerkel-Rothfuss, 1987) and that stronger results emerge when researchers examine exposure to more specific genres of programming. Among young women, frequent viewing of music videos has been linked both with a greater number of sexual partners (Strouse & Buerkel-Rothfuss, 1987) and with more sexual experience, especially for women from low-quality family environments (Strouse et al., 1995). Yet, for both sexes, adolescents whose television viewing diets include higher proportions of sexual content are more likely to become sexually active earlier than are adolescents whose diets included lower proportions of sexual content (J. D. Brown & Newcomer, 1991). Content analyses of 12- and 14-year-old's top television programs, movies, music, newspapers and Internet sites reveal that greater exposure to sexual content in their favored programs links to their future sexual intentions and current sexual activity, with measures of movie and music exposure showing the strongest associations (Pardun, L'Engle, & Brown, 2005).

Not all studies report consistent results and not all studies neatly fit together. Important studies have examined associations between levels of viewer involvement and students' sexual behaviors and experiences, but they also provide mixed results. For example, college students who perceive television's typical sexual situations as likely to happen in their own lives report greater levels of experience with sexual relationships (Ward & Rivadeneyra, 1999); yet, the same study found other dimensions of viewer involvement inconsequential, such as level of active viewing and identification with characters. Evidence also indicates that selecting a media figure or peer as a model of sexual behavior relates to more frequent sexual intercourse, but neither relates to the number of sexual partners nor to the frequency of birth control use (Fabes & Strouse, 1987).

Studies failing to consider age and developmental differences also report inconsistent findings. Twelve-year-olds experience more difficulty understanding sexual innuendo in television shows than 15-year-olds (Silverman-Watkins & Sprafkin, 1983). Preadolescent girls react uninterestedly or disgustedly to sexual media content, whereas older girls often are intrigued (Eggermont, 2005). Early adolescents (e.g., eighth graders) often miss the sexual meaning of lyrics and videos (see Christenson & Roberts, 1998); high school aged males respond to sexually explicit videos more favorably than other age groups (Greeson, 1991). Yet, 12-year-old girls who display a higher level of pubertal development and generally spend much time with television viewing are not distinguishable from older girls in terms of the impact of television on indicators of sexual health outcomes (Eggermont, 2005); early-maturing girls report and actually view or listen to more sexualized content, and it effects them more regardless of age and race (J. D. Brown et al., 2005). Equally interesting research notes wide disparities according to race, such as an interesting study that found how white females viewed a song about a teen girl singing about keeping her baby as referring to keeping an unwanted baby while black males viewed it as referring to the girl's desire to keep a wanted boyfriend (J. D. Brown & Schulze, 1990).

Although studies generally focus on prime-time television, it appears that other media may actually be more determinative. Adolescent girls who report exposure to X-rated movies are more likely to have attitudes nonsupportive of STD/HIV prevention, to engage in STD/HIV sexual risk behaviors, and to engage in contraceptive risk practices; they also are more than twice as likely to have a strong desire to conceive and are more than one and a half times as likely to test positive for chlamydia (Wingood et al., 2001). Adolescent males and men who view sexually aggressive media, especially pornography, are more likely to accept cultural stereotypes relating to violence against women (such that women deserve or desire rape; Allen, D'Alessio, & Brezgel, 1995; Allen, Emmers, Gebhardt, & Giery, 1995; Weisz & Earls, 1995). These findings help highlight the challenges facing researchers. Sexuality behavior is complex and much of the potential impact of media exposure on sexual behavior is likely to be both direct and indirect, working through the media's effects on viewers' attitudes, schemas, and belief systems as well as their social environments that permit or foster exposure to vastly different media.

The nature of sexuality and its typical presentations in the media challenge efforts to conduct experimental studies. Not surprisingly, only a few have been attempted. These studies typically expose one group of students to sexual content, another group to nonsexual content, and then compare the sexual attitudes of the two groups on measures administered immediately after the exposure. This may be the appropriate way to conduct experimental research, but it is difficult to expect significant differences. Yet, some interesting findings do emerge.

The information-processing model of media effects, the most dominant theoretical model used in this type of research, proposes that the messages embodied in sexual content, the degree to which viewers perceive television content as realistic, and whether sexual content is conveyed using visual or verbal symbols may influence the nature or degree of media effects. A recent study exposed 182 college undergraduates to visual or verbal sexual television content, neutral television content, or no television at all prior to completing measures of sexual attitudes and beliefs (Taylor, 2005). Although exposure to sexual content generally did not produce significant main effects, it did influence the attitudes of those who perceive television to be relatively realistic. Verbal sexual content was found to influence beliefs about women's sexual activity among the same group. Laboratory exposure to sexual scenes drawn from prime-time soaps and dramas was found to increase teens' acceptance of sexual improprieties in one study (Bryant & Rockwell, 1994). A multiethnic sample of 259 undergraduates aged 18–22 was assigned to view a set of clips depicting either one of three sexual stereotypes or neutral, nonsexual content (Ward, 2002). The study reported that regardless of their regular viewing levels and sexual experiences, young women (but not men) exposed to prime-time television images depicting men as sex-driven, women as sexual objects, or dating as a game offered stronger support of each of these stereotypes than did women in control groups. Women exposed to clips representing a particular sexual stereotype were more likely to endorse that notion than were women exposed to nonsexual content; experimental exposure also predicted students' sexual attitudes and assumptions, even with demographics and previous sexual experiences controlled. Additionally, experimental exposure to magazine ads featuring women as sexual objects produced a stronger acceptance of sex role stereotyping and of rape myths among male undergraduates but these studies reported mixed results among females, who offered both stronger (MacKay & Covell, 1997) and weaker endorsement of these constructs than did women in control groups (Lanis & Covell, 1995).

Evidence does suggest that students exposed to the sexual and sexist content of music videos offer stronger endorsement of casual and stereotypical attitudes about sex than do students exposed to nonsexual content (e.g., Greeson & Williams, 1986), and that female viewers are more affected than are male viewers (e.g., Calfin, Carroll, & Shmidt, 1993). For example, a study that exposed girls to eight sexist, nonviolent rap videos found them more accepting of teen dating violence than girls without such exposure; boys' attitudes were not affected (J. D. Johnson, et al., 1995). Despite the occasional null and conditional findings, the dominant trend produced by the experimental studies indicates that students exposed to sexual content are more likely than those exposed to neutral or to no content to offer a stronger postexposure endorsement of casual, sexist, and stereotypical notions about sexual relationships.

Essentially no experimental research examines the effects of media on sexual behavior. The leading study in this area exposed male undergraduates to sixteen commercials that depicted women as sexual objects and then asked them to interview and evaluate a female confederate (Rudman & Borgida, 1995). In comparison to young men in the control condition, men exposed to the sexist images asked more sexist questions during the interview, recalled more about the woman's appearance and less about her personal background, and rated her as friendlier, more hirable, but less competent. Moreover, the interview behavior of these primed men was perceived to be more sexualized by both the female confederates and independent observers. Studies have examined, for example, whether experimental exposure to sexual content affects students' perceptions of women encountered in the real world. Here, it seems that neutral women encountered after sexual content has been viewed take on attributes of that content and appear more sexual. For example, exposure to sexually suggestive hip-hop videos featuring black female performers lead white students to attribute fewer positive traits and more negative traits to subsequently encountered black women (Gan, Zillman, & Mitrook, 1997). Another study asked undergraduates to watch three music videos and then to evaluate the taped interactions of a male and female job applicant (Hansen & Hansen, 1988). While students who had watched the neutral music videos later perceived the man's sexual advances toward the female applicant to be akin to sexual harassment, students who had viewed the stereotypic music videos perceived his sexual advances as appropriate, and thought less favorably of her if she rejected him. Hence, by means of contrast and comparison, viewers appear to draw from fictional content in developing expectations about real-world sexual interactions.

Viewers' impressions of flirtatious or sexy women and men are affected by the nature of the media content just viewed. Experimental studies have demonstrated that, compared with individuals not exposed to X-rated films, individuals exposed to X-rated films are more accepting of premarital sex, more likely to overestimate the prevalence of sexual activity, more likely to regard sex without emotional commitment as important, and less likely to value the concepts of marriage and monogamy (Zillman & Bryant, 1988a, 1988b). Together, these findings offer tentative support for a link between exposure to sexual content and a variety of sexual behaviors. However, with little longitudinal or experimental evidence, the meaning of these associations remains unclear, indicating that media exposure shapes viewers' sexual attitudes and behaviors, and that viewers with liberal sexual attitudes and behaviors are drawn to programming that confirms their beliefs.

Significance and Limitations of Effects Research

As we have seen in previous chapters, determining the effects of sexual media content would involve either randomized assignment to different sexual media diets or longitudinal surveys. Such studies would establish whether media exposure or behavior came first and would allow for generalizations about what kinds of media content cause what kinds of behaviors. The vast majority of research in this area, however, does not meet those standards. Yet, the available evidence still is quite illustrative.

The relatively few correlational and still fewer experimental studies of the relationship between exposure to sexual media content and effects suggest that the media do have an impact in at least three ways. Effects emerge from the manner in which the media keep sexual behavior on public and personal agendas, reinforce a relatively consistent set of sexual and relationship norms, and ignore sexually responsible models. While current research reports only conditional results, with outcomes varying by the genre and by the dependent variable investigated, the overall trend reveals that media exposure and involvement are likely to play prominent roles in shaping adolescents' sexual attitudes and expectations. Frequent and involved exposure to sexually oriented genres associates with greater acceptance of stereotypical and casual attitudes about sex, with higher expectations about the prevalence of sexual activity and of certain sexual outcomes, and even occasionally with greater levels of sexual experience. Experimental exposure to sexual content has been found to prime these attitudes and expectations in the laboratory, enhancing the strength of the correlational findings.

Research remains limited in breadth and depth. Most notably, research tends to count sexual acts, like violence research has done. Yet, acts of violence and sexuality differ in critical ways. Most notable, violence tends to be negative, while relationships and sexuality may be as positive as negative. Research has yet to examine the prevalence of positive portrayals of sexuality and of sexual health. In addition, research has focused mainly on prime-time comedies and dramas, daytime soap operas, music videos, and magazines. Research has yet to expand much to the media adolescents increasingly spend their time with: feature films, popular music, men's magazines, and the Internet, as well as other formats of television programming, such as talk shows, reality programming, and cable networks.

Research has yet to examine how sexual messages from the media interact with messages from other sources to shape sexual views. Because the media are but one of many sources contributing to sexual socialization, it appears necessary to examine how their input works with that of other socializing agents. Only by doing so would we be able to determine whose messages are most influential. We do not know, for example, whether a strong foundation of sexual input from other agents (e.g., parents) results in giving less weight to media claims. We may well expect that it would, but it has yet to be investigated satisfactorily. Because few have assessed contributions of the media and other agents in the same study, minimal evidence exists on which to make such comparisons. Recent studies that have examined different influences reveal that other sources of influence, especially peers but also parenting, religiosity, and school connectedness, can play even stronger roles than the media (J. D. Brown et al., 2006). In addition to examining what each source contributes, it is also necessary to consider the strength of participants' attachment to each source. Current summaries of the field indicate that sexual topics communicated by parents may be less influential to adolescent sexual risk-taking than the general warm and communicative nature of the parent–child relationship (Miller, Benson, & Galbraith, 2001). Our understanding of adolescent development suggests that it is no accident that the media industry is so sexually saturated. The media play a peculiar and dominant role in the adolescent period because its contents relate to the central tasks and concerns of adolescent development.

Differences in understanding are central to deciphering how the media influence adolescent development. As teens attend to and interpret sexual media content, they also evaluate it in ways that will influence the extent to which they will incorporate it into their own developing sense of sexuality and identity. Adolescents carry with them their life histories, and their perceptions of media are filtered through these experiences, which encompass neighborhood experiences, family life, friendships, peer culture, religious beliefs, and the multitude of conditions in which adolescents find themselves. This line of investigation supports the important conclusion that you hear what you are, rather than the popular belief that you are what you hear. But it certainly does seem that the media's impact may be recursive. If there is any conclusion that seems reasonable to infer from current research, it is that links between sexualized media and adolescent sexual behavior are far from linear. The levels of viewing change throughout adolescence and the associations between viewing and sexual activity changes. And these changes depend as much on who the adolescents are as they do with the nature of the media.

Understanding the Media's Effects on Adolescents' Sexuality

Although it continues to be argued that portrayals in the media provide adolescents with powerful messages concerning the appropriateness of sexual activities and attitudes, no currently well-developed theoretical perspective guides this area of research, especially in the context of adolescent development. Unlike research we have examined in previous chapters, research examining the media's role in the development of adolescent sexuality remains rather atheoretical. Despite this lack of theory, we actually can discern theoretical orientations that mirror those in other contexts. These orientations help make the important point that viewers construct meaning from the media based on their existing worldviews, schemas, and personal experiences. These theories help us understand how adolescents individualize content as they integrate their existing perspectives and input from other sources (e.g., peers, family) into their experiences.

Research mostly draws from three general theoretical models that emphasize that adolescents actively engage in their media environments. Cultivation theory figures prominently in research examining media effects on adolescents' sexual attitudes and behaviors, especially large-scale survey research (Gerbner, Gross, Morgan, & Signorielli, 1994). Cultivation theory proposes that the media's consistent yet restricted images construct a specific image of reality; as viewers are exposed to that media, they cultivate or adopt beliefs about the world that coincide with its images. In a real sense, cultivation theory predicts that consumers differently "cultivate" certain media in a manner that shapes their worldviews. That theory suggests, for example, that adolescents who watch a lot of television will come to perceive the world portrayed by television as an accurate reflection of reality (see Davis & Mares, 1998; Gerbner et al., 1994). This perspective leads researchers to focus on adolescents' regular exposure levels and on the differing perceptions of "heavy" versus "light" viewers. For example, we have seen that content analyses of television portrayals of sexuality present sex as glamorous, prevalent, and relatively risk free. Cultivation theory predicts that those who view television more frequently, especially its sexualized content, will be more inclined than sporadic viewers to endorse and accept this image of sexuality.

Priming theory provides another theoretical perspective supporting research in this area. This theory, mainly used to examine short-term experimental effects, draws from several cognitive theories focusing on schema activation and accessibility (Jo & Berkowitz, 1994). This perspective suggests that the presentation and processing of a stimulus with a particular meaning activates related concepts and calls them to mind. By making schema-related information temporarily highly accessible, priming increases the likelihood that subsequently encountered persons, stimuli, or events will be appraised in the context of the primed and accessible schema. The priming process renders conceptually related material viewed or experienced after the exposure seem more acceptable or appropriate. The belief is that frequently activated schemas eventually become readily accessible and influence judgments even regardless of priming manipulations or situational influences. For our purposes, this means that the theory proposes that frequently encountered and related schemas eventually lead to sexual stereotypes and shape sexual behaviors and attitudes.

Bandura's cognitive social-learning model provides the third relevant theoretical perspective (Bandura, 1994). This perspective proposes that the media allow viewers to learn the appropriateness of certain behaviors, which then shapes the viewers' own behaviors and attitudes. Viewers store the observations as behavioral scripts to be retrieved and applied when individual circumstances elicit them. This theory emphasizes the relevance of models and the salience of the images. It contends that people observe important role models, make inferences and attributions, and acquire scripts, schemas, and normative beliefs that then guide their subsequent behavior. This theoretical perspective predicts, for example, that adolescents learn sexual behaviors and their likely consequences by engaging with the media and are more likely to be influenced by relevant models. According to this perspective, adolescents will seek to emulate the behavior of others when those models are valued to the observer and when the models are rewarded for their behavior.

Models highlight the ongoing reciprocal nature of media uses and effects; they assume that these processes interact with each other and with the viewer's current and emerging sense of identity. These theories place emphasis on the interactive influences of environmental factors and other mediating and moderating influences (Hogben & Byrne, 1998). They posit, for example, bidirectional influences by which individuals' characteristics (age and personality characteristics) affect how they attend to certain content in the media and the extent to which such experiences are influential. Importantly, these approaches suggest that the impact of particular information will depend on the extent to which it is distinctive, functional, and salient while not being contradicted by other influences (such as peer groups and family members). This perspective is particularly relevant to adolescent development given that it is generally expected that age correlates with susceptibility to media influences, an expectation based on the theory that younger adolescents are less skillful in analyzing the degree of realism of mediated information (Markham, Howie, & Hlvaacek, 1999) and may be less confident about their own values and views. Perceptions and influences of media vary from adolescent to adolescent, and from the wide variety of other influencing factors.

The theoretical approaches to understanding the media's role in adolescent sexuality highlight the need to understand media effects through its larger contexts. Many factors influence adolescents' selections, interpretations, and uses of the media, such as age, gender, and race, as well as adolescents' developing identities and the multitude of conditions in their lives, what media researchers now label as "lived experience," which encompass neighborhood influences, family life, friendships, peer culture experiences, and religious backgrounds and beliefs (Steele & Brown, 1995). The notion is that adolescents carry their particular life histories with them, and that their perceptions of media content are filtered through these experiences (J. D. Brown, 2000). The individualized effects of media certainly complicate efforts to find broad trends and actually make it unlikely that broad trends would emerge, but research increasingly reveals important trends even as the research becomes even more specific and methodologically exacting.

Modifying Media Influences on Adolescents' Sexuality and Development

Concerns about the impact of the media on adolescents has led educators, researchers, and policy makers to respond and support a wide range of media-education curricula for students from grade school to university levels. Although existing programs are not as common as may have been expected, they range widely in perspectives. Several basic strategies now address media consumption and its potential influence on adolescents' sexual attitudes and behaviors. These strategies can be grouped in three key responses that seek to address the influence of the media on adolescent sexuality. The first approach involves media-literacy programs that aim to educate adolescents about the media industry itself, rather than focus on sexual images. The second group of responses seeks to involve the media industry itself in shaping adolescent sexuality. Unlike media-literacy efforts, which do not seek to change or harness the media, these efforts intentionally use the media as an educational resource. The third involves media advocacy, which is the use of the media to influence policy makers and media producers themselves. Each strategy does seem to have its strengths and weaknesses, but, as we will soon see, we have surprisingly little empirical research addressing their effectiveness. This has not stopped commentators from suggesting that a media-literacy curriculum and media programs may help inoculate adolescents against the problematic media messages they encounter (J. D. Brown & Witherspoon, 2002; Heins, 2001). This section examines the reasonableness of existing efforts and whether room exists for optimism.

Media Literacy's Ranging Perspectives and Outcomes

Just as different contexts use the term *literacy* differently, so too is *media literacy* defined in many ways. The term media literacy may be characterized as the ability to produce one's own multimedia texts, the ability to reflect on the pleasures and harms derived from mass media, or the ability to choose selectively among icons in popular culture (see Luke, 1999). Each of these approaches offers very different starting points for developing programs that respond to adolescents' needs, including their sexuality.

Early efforts tended to adopt a protectionist stance aimed to equip viewers to defend themselves from the negative impact of problematic values disseminated by the mass media (Kubey, 1998). This approach, which still dominates, typically interprets media literacy as a strategy to inoculate adolescents from the media's harmful effects. Media educators who adopt this approach believe that understanding the mass media's construction of "reality" means understanding the production process (including technological, economic, bureaucratic, and legal constraints); the text; and the audience, receiver, and end user. Basic precepts of this form of media literacy include the beliefs that media are constructed and construct reality; that media have commercial, ideological, and political implications; that receivers negotiate meaning from the media; and that teaching media literacy requires hands-on and participatory approaches (Hobbs, 1998). As it seeks to minimize the media's influence on individuals, this approach tends to focus on negative issues pertaining to the media, such as violence, manipulation, and sex-role stereotyping.

In terms of the manner this view of media literacy relates to efforts to address adolescent sexuality, expectations run high. Commentators suggest that media literacy does much more than lead adolescents to a greater understanding of the media images and narratives (including sexual scripts) and the sources they use. Those who hold this view of media literacy believe that it fosters personal changes, such as improving self-esteem (e.g., the ability to say "no" to sex), taking responsibility for one's life (e.g., practicing safe sex), sharing experiences with others (e.g., negotiating condom use), and learning the ability to express oneself (Kawaja, 1994).

More recent efforts have focused on presenting the complexity of the media's place in society. Rather than taking a media studies perspective, this approach takes a cultural studies approach. From a cultural studies perspective, critical media literacy is concerned with how society and politics are structured and work to one's advantage or disadvantage (Kellner, 1995) and how issues of ideology, bodies, power, and gender produce various cultural artifacts (McRobbie, 1997). Attention is placed on how the meanings that audiences make of various media texts are negotiated in relation to one's different situations and positioning (e.g., adult, child, teenager, male, female, race, ethnicity, socioeconomic class) and cultural contexts (Luke, 1999).

The cultural studies approach abandons attempts to have students critique the very texts and images they find appealing in favor of engaging students in critical analyses of the politics of pleasure and their own location in that politics (see Alvermann & Hagood, 2000). The approach seeks to have students analyze how they use or resist particular media messages on the basis of their sociocultural locations and from different media users' positions (Luke, 1997). Proponents of cultural studies view approaches to critical media literacy that focus on visual or critical viewing literacy as limited by their reliance on the outdated notion of audiences' passivity. Cultural studies seek to move beyond early versions of media literacy, which were constructed on a model of the media acting as a creator of messages that imposed meaning on the audience. This approach views adolescents as active in relation to media messages. The approach seeks to ask, To whom are texts addressed through their words, images, and sounds? Who is absent in these texts, and what might explain their absence? Whose interests are served in texts? How are we positioned by them? This approach places emphasis on students' own experiences with the media and rejects predetermined sets of learning outcomes on the grounds of paternalism and protectionism (Buckingham, 1998). The field of cultural studies reminds us that the same text often evokes different responses from people thought to share similar cultural understandings. Further unlike more traditional approaches, cultural studies seeks to address technological advances that have spawned new forms of youth cultures that are proliferated (such as chat rooms or e-mail) and require multiple literacies. These efforts seek to address adolescents' shifting formation of culture and literacy practices to develop their critical understanding of these new developments in youth culture.

Although the cultural studies approach has much to commend it, how it may address adolescents' responses to sexually embedded media remains to be explored. This view of media literacy has fostered considerably high hopes given that it may serve many functions. Like other aspects of education, it contributes to the formation of thoughts, opinions, and attitudes. If students can develop the ability to critically view their surroundings, they can better make use of the media. There is no reason not to believe that knowledge, awareness, attitudes and opinions may be shaped in a manner that reinforces future behavior; but it is unclear how to document that influence.

Media Literacy's Outcomes

Few analyses evaluate the goals or outcomes associated with media-literacy programs. Studies even generally do not explicitly define or measure the results of curricula. Currently no national standards exist to guide the development of media literacy and its assessment, nor is there agreement on whether the outcomes generated from it should consist of knowledge, skills, behaviors, attitudes, or values (see Christ & Potter, 1998). Recent efforts have articulated general notions of desired outcomes (Scharrer, 2003). As expected, those outcomes follow the general approaches to media literacy we have outlined above. One of the most popular approaches focuses on the extent to which participants engage in ongoing critical inquiry and the development of critical viewers (J. A. Brown,

1998; Singer & Singer, 1998). Relatedly, other approaches focus on the need to develop an awareness of media messages and the effects they can have on attitudes and behavior (Silverblatt, 1995).

Little research has defined or tested these or other anticipated outcomes from a social science research perspective (Singer & Singer, 1998). Few media-literacy efforts and no sexually relevant curricula have been evaluated empirically. Even critical media literacy, without a focus on sexuality, has not been the subject of much research. A few early studies of other kinds of media-literacy curricula suggest that such efforts have value. Singer and Singer (1998) used a case-control design to study a general media-literacy curriculum involving eight lessons and 10-minute videotapes. Elementary school students exposed to the lessons made significant progress in television literacy, compared to students in a control group. In another experimental study, researchers found that media-literacy training on alcohol advertising increased third-graders' understanding of the persuasive intent in alcohol advertising and social norms for alcohol use (Austin & Johnson, 1997). Likewise, another group of researchers found that even a very simplified media intervention program resulted in demonstrable decreases in aggressive behavior (Robinson et al., 2001). Although these findings report important trends, more effort is needed to discover whether critical thinking has increased and whether critical thinking has been encouraged, whether students are asking questions about the media, and what outcomes are appropriate in determining the effects of participation in media literacy.

The need for more research is obvious. Efforts run the danger of failing to take seriously how adolescents make choices about the media they consume, based on their own preferences. A most fundamental reason is that media literacy may be focusing on media that has decreasing relevance to adolescents. Media-literacy efforts pervasively focus on television, most likely because it is the media that has received the most research (Strasburger, 1995). Yet, adolescents spend more time listening to music than watching television and they watch less television than persons in any other stage of life (Arnett, 1995). These findings reveal that the media that are used in literacy programs are not necessarily appealing to adolescents. A second fundamental reason is that, even if the selected media resonated more with realities of adolescents' media use, the efforts still would remain limited. Even examining the forms of media that are sexually explicit and examining their impact on adolescents' attitudes remains problematic when, in reality, adolescents would not necessarily watch those videos on their own volition nor be exposed to them in their everyday lives.

The dearth of research exploring how media literacy could affect adolescents' responses to sexually embedded media does not mean that we should not look to move media-literacy efforts forward. As we wait for research, however, it is important to remind ourselves of the need to remain realistic about the potential role of such efforts. Given the multidetermined nature of human behavior, it seems unrealistic to expect media-literacy programs to help individuals resist the media's effects. The literacy curriculum may be insufficient to change such a complex phenomenon as an individual's unique responses to media messages. It also seems theoretically unsound to expect that even a critical understanding of the media will influence the media's impact. Critical thinking does not necessarily lead to resisting the media's negative effects.

For example, understanding that media portrayals of violence and sexual activity are fictional may not do much for those interested in sexual activity and excited by violence. Participating in literacy curriculum would be simply one factor to weigh against numerous others in determining a person's susceptibility to media effects; the media is simply one of many factors that shape our ideas, views, and actions. Indeed, it would seem quite unreasonable to expect that participation in a topically limited and short curriculum to make much of a profound difference in how we respond to media. Despite skills in critical thinking, it remains a challenge to address the many forms of media reaching adolescents. We already have seen that media impact different and differently situated people differently. Literacy programs would be expected to influence differently audience members with different personality traits and differently impacted by their friends, families, and broad environment.

Even though we could expect an impact from participating in media-literacy efforts, it remains difficult to envision what and when the impact would be. The impact may be immediate, long-term, neither, or both. Likewise, it is difficult to envision what media messages are at work. Just as the media presumably do not impact all audiences in a similar way, it would be unwise to expect similar results from media-literacy efforts.

Mass-Media Campaigns, Advocacy, Embedded Interventions, and the Internet

Rather than focus on traditional educational efforts in schools, other efforts involve social marketing and entertainment education. Public information campaigns are the most common form of intentional use of the mass media for public health purposes. Effective health-oriented campaigns typically are similar to campaigns for commercial products in that they use a number of media channels and are designed to generate specific effects in a relatively large number of people within a specified time period (Singhal & Rogers, 1999).

Although public announcement campaigns relating to adolescent's sexuality may be common, their effectiveness remains to be documented with the type of systematic empirical rigor typically associated with peer reviewed research. Practical concerns also arise. Because of the complexities and costs of conducting scientific evaluations of mass-media campaigns, most large-scale health communication programs rely on self-report data to track their effects. Public health experts question the methods employed, pointing to at least two major flaws in the evaluation of impact: the lack of random sampling and the lack of long-term studies. The large-scale nature of mass-media interventions makes them difficult to assess in isolation from other societal variables (Atkin & Marshall, 1996). Equally important, it is difficult and expensive to conduct studies that will track participants long enough to be able to detect changes in behavior which typically occur gradually.

Numerous campaigns have experimented with key strategies to overcome the obstacles to providing reproductive health services to targeted populations, and especially to reach youth. Community mobilization can diminish social disapproval and intimidation (AIDS Alert, 2000; Alstead et al., 1999). Gearing reproductive health messages to specific subgroups of the population, through audience segmentation and message tailoring, has been known to increase access to health services and overcome reluctance (Backer, Rogers, & Sopory, 1992). Motivational media campaigns using clear messages, multiple media channels, and positive images can increase awareness about the risks of being sexually active and teach people how to take preventive measures (Kirby et al., 1999).

Campaigns also will be most effective when the media are complemented by other activities at the individual, community, and policy levels, and when the campaign can be sustained over the long term (McGuire, 1960). Most notably, lack of links to health services—such as a hotline number—render a media campaign's success unlikely. Youth have many obstacles to health services, not the least of which is their limited availability (Heath & McLaughlin, 1993). Illustrative of the approach is project ACTION, a recent effort credited to have increased teen condom use with casual partners from 72% to 90% and to have reduced the number of teenagers reporting sexual activity from 82% to 75% in Portland, Oregon. The campaign made use of public service announcements, teen talk shows about AIDS, and condom vending machines. To the extent that the project did reach significance, it is important to note that the use of distribution machines moved beyond traditional media campaigns; this highlights the need to move toward more comprehensive efforts (AIDS Alert, 2000).

Media campaign messages will get lost in the sea of competing messages unless they are repeated extensively and reinforced by service providers and public policy. Mass-media influences seem to occur through indirect mediating processes. Research on health promotion, such as campaigns designed to change diet, exercise, and smoking, primarily induce change not by influencing behaviors directly but by changing processes that ultimately change behaviors, such as information seeking and interpersonal communication skills (Rimal, Flora, & Schooler, 1999). As a result, media campaigns may influence discussion with peers but they will have the most positive impact if adolescents are allowed access to information and services. Indeed, this may be an area where sex education may increase effectiveness. Some studies report that some forms of sex education, especially regarding HIV and contraception, lead to an increase in adolescents' abilities to discuss sexual issues with parents (Barth, Fetro, Leland, & Volkan, 1992; Levy et al., 1995). It is important to note, however, that even discussions with parents, who themselves hold widely variant views of sexuality, do not necessarily evoke desired responses (Levesque, 2000). These efforts highlight the significance of public policy reforms beyond media efforts.

An often-ignored approach involves cooperation between advocacy groups and commercial media to incorporate subtle health messages into existing entertainment programs. The National Campaign to Prevent Teen Pregnancy, for example, assists writers for popular teen-targeted shows to develop episodes dealing with a wide range of sexual issues, from teen sexual health, contraception, date rape, and AIDS (Brodie & Foehr, 2001). These partnerships help address the general and practical inability of government and nonprofit agencies to produce and disseminate long-running prosocial messages. It also counters First Amendment concerns as well as problems arising from private ownership of the media: the government must respect the right to expression.

Although potentially influential, these efforts still remain controversial and even problematic. They remain controversial to the extent that subtle messages are produced by government agencies and advocacy groups with agendas. Although these agendas seek to counter what has been perceived as negative media messages from commercial industries, the agendas of advocacy groups do not necessarily reflect the needs of adolescents or their parents. This reality relates to a primary drawback. Some media are unlikely to publicize controversial messages or content that may alienate advertisers (Wallack, Dorfman, Jernigan, & Themba, 1993), which could lead to the false impression that existing media are producing appropriate messages when they in fact are not. Even the news media may portray research in misleading ways, including studies about media effects (Bushman & Anderson, 2001), and may act opportunistically, in concert with politicians and advocacy groups, to amplify events which may not reflect reality. The efforts also remain problematic to the extent that their effectiveness has not been systematically evaluated. Some research does reveal that these campaigns may result in immediate increases in awareness and knowledge (Brodie & Foehr, 2001; DeJong & Winsten, 1999), but that same research reveals that the awareness seems short term (Brodie & Foehr, 2001), and that awareness and knowledge may not transfer to practice. Much remains to be determined, but it does seem clear that these efforts may not achieve broad goals set for themselves without considering how else to influence adolescents' use of media and how adolescents can respond to harms associated with media.

If changing interactions between adolescents and the media and transforming the nature of media itself remain key goals in fostering environments more conducive to healthy adolescent development, it is clear that recent technological changes provide unique opportunities. Most notable, the Internet may provide adolescents (and their peers and families) with many ways to obtain sexual information. Potential access to information is quite free ranging. The Internet remains largely unregulated, and broad efforts to limit contents that would be inappropriate for adolescents and children have been found unconstitutional (Levesque, 2000). The nature of the Internet obviously provides many opportunities, but those opportunities may be both positive and negative.

The Internet provides a communication medium especially suited to address adolescents' peculiar circumstances and place in society. Unlike other media, the Internet has the advantage of being able to relay information on demand and to allow for meeting immediate needs. This feature makes the Internet an especially important service for issuing reproductive health information to adolescents who may not be connected to health care services and who may lack transportation or resources to contact providers. The Internet also can facilitate personal decision making—an important factor in addressing sexual risks—through personal risk assessment and can help individuals evaluate potential outcomes in combination with personal circumstances. The Internet is unique in its ability to provide online peer support and informational exchange through message boards, chat rooms, and e-mail. The Internet also can help adolescents manage some health problems on their own, a preventive feature especially important for teenagers who often lack access to health facilities. Finally, the Internet can promote self-efficacy and model communication skills, key components of healthy adolescent development and prerequisites to safe-sex practice and STD prevention.

Recognizing the utility of the Internet seems especially important in light of efforts to limit sexuality education in schools. For example, this utility becomes important given mandates that require educators to teach abstinence programs, which may lead to ignoring more taboo issues of sexuality and health. The significance of attempts to limit educational efforts is important given that, even with mandates, programs tend to shy away from controversy, which may curb access to information that even parents would assume adolescents have learned. Also important to consider is how the Internet can be used to reach large audiences with individualized messages. That it occupies a uniquely intermediate status between a mass medium and interpersonal communication also makes the Internet an ideal venue for communicating sensitive information.

Despite its advantages, the Internet is not without its limitations. First, no solid empirical research exists to support the claim that the Internet can be harnessed for sustained, positive effects. Likewise, and as we have seen, providing information is far from enough in that knowledge does not necessarily relate to practice. Adolescents seeking information also run the risk of having their privacy violated as they share personal information. The Internet also may provide inaccurate or inappropriate information. The provision of adequate information may be limited as parents and libraries may use software to block out sexually explicit information. Because pornography-blocking software cannot perfectly discriminate between pornographic and nonpornographic materials, the software also blocks access to health information sites, particularly those related to sexuality. When using these programs' restrictive settings, for example, one study found that pornography blocking increased (91%) but that health information blocking also increased substantially (24%; Richardson, Resnick, Hansen, Derry, & Rideout, 2002). Relatedly, different adolescents will have different access, and those arguably with the greatest need and most limited access to health information (i.e., those deemed "at risk," such as homeless and runaway youth and some low-income youth) are the least likely to have access to the Internet. Last, the Internet increasingly provides avenues for groups to reach adolescents in ways that broader society may find harmful, such as the manner in which hate groups now use the Internet to express their viewpoints, sell their paraphernalia, and recruit new members (Lee & Leets, 2002). Even technological advances that provide considerable hope to efforts aiming to address the media's potential harm, then, bring with them important limitations and risks.

Media Advocacy

Some health activists also have begun to use the mass media as tools for bringing health issues to the attention of the public and policy makers. Rather than waiting for the media to cover an issue, health activists generate news that attracts the attention of the news media (Wallack et al., 1993). Research has long uncovered how mass media can do more than tell people what issues to think about; they also can be agenda setters in that they help conceptualize issues. This approach typically focuses on public policies relating to health rather than on individual health behaviors. The underlying rationale is that individuals will not be able to change unhealthy behavior unless policy and systematic changes support the desired behaviors. Thus, for example, public policies that affect access to and affordability of sexuality education and health services could be important topics for media advocacy. Media campaigns could help foster the political will needed to ensure the development of media-literacy efforts. These efforts are necessary to ensure, for example, that teachers will be trained, curricula will be developed, and school systems will be persuaded of the need to address the media's role in adolescent development. Although adults may know of the negative impact of some media, they still need to learn how to ensure that they can better respond to the media's influence in their children's lives and recognize how the media can become a positive force.

By far the most common media advocacy has been efforts to limit access to sexually charged media. The use of content ratings and screening devices has been the most popular. Yet, the value of these tools remains debatable, which highlights the need to proceed with caution and the need to integrate media advocacy with other efforts. Although these efforts allow viewers (parents) to screen programs of content and age appropriateness, they remain problematic to the extent that parents still do not use them, a stumbling block made more challenging by the manner screening tools do not allow for meaningful decision making about the content of shows, books, or Internet media (Kunkel & Wilcox, 2001); the reticence by industry to label programming as inappropriate for some audiences (Hamilton, 1998); the manner some teenagers would be drawn to content that is not age appropriate (Cantor, 2000); and the general finding that adolescents (much like their parents) seldom use the ratings and that parents' understanding of the ratings are close to chance (Greenberg & Rampoldi-Hnilo, 2001).

Conclusions

We are educated by the entertainment media, even if unintended by the source and unnoticed by the audience. By default or by design, various media have assumed a prominent role in adolescents' sexual socialization. Their sexual messages are prevalent, exciting, glamorous, and perceived as realistic by adolescents. These are all qualities of a powerful role model. Whereas it is assumed by parents, teachers, and youth themselves that the media play such a role, empirical research has been slow to investigate it. Yet, we recently have learned a fair amount about the role of the media in the sexual socialization of adolescents. The evidence so far suggests that media sexual content hastens the initiation of various adolescent sexual behaviors and that media exposure links to sexual outcomes. We know very little beyond that.

We know surprisingly little about the manner in which the media influence adolescents' sexual activity and attitudes. These factors include both characteristics of the media content, such as the genre, complexity of the messages, and attractiveness of the protagonists, as well as several features of the viewer, such as age, developmental level, sex, and cognitive capacities. But, as with other areas of research we have examined, we know that the media influence adolescents' sexuality through their social environment. Studies consistently have demonstrated that adolescents' perceptions about their friends' sex-related beliefs and behaviors predict their own future sexual behaviors (Kinsman, Romer, Furstenberg, & Schwarz, 1998; Santelli et al., 2004). But, the role of the media in influencing much of these factors remains a subject in need of rigorous empirical enquiry. The best we can conclude is that adolescent sexual behavior and attitudes are diverse, complicated, and driven by many forces—internal, interpersonal, and environmental. These forces are likely to play important roles in determining the influence of media exposure on adolescent sexual behavior.

The lack of understanding of the media's influence on adolescents' sexual attitudes and behaviors is reflected in an equally surprising lack of understanding and research aimed at modifying the media's effect on adolescents' sexual development. Given society's keen interest in the extent to which sexuality pervades dominant media, not to mention those directly aimed at adolescents, the failure to investigate how to address the media's influence on adolescent sexuality remains quite perplexing. Again, however, we are left with the conclusion that efforts to address the media's influence must move beyond the media itself and focus on adolescents' relative place in families and society, especially including adolescents' abilities to access and benefit from their informational environments.

Part II

SPEECH IN FIRST AMENDMENT LAW:
LEGAL FOUNDATIONS

6

Regulating Speech

The extent and manner to which society may regulate the media and, indeed, any expression falls squarely into the highly technical area of "free speech" jurisprudence grounded in First Amendment law. On its face, the language of the First Amendment and its free speech clause appears quite forceful and strikingly clear. By providing that "Congress shall make no law . . . abridging the freedom of speech," the Amendment states in plain and simple language that government shall make no law abridging free speech. This straightforward guarantee of freedom of speech contains no qualifications and reasonably yields an absolutist orientation. Yet, despite the clarity of its language, the First Amendment has been, and still is, the source of much controversy. Controversies abound despite considerable judicial activity analyzing this area of law and despite the belief that the First Amendment harbors the preferred values of the American constitutional order. As a result, our legal system may herald the fundamental and preferred nature of the freedom of expression, but such pronouncements do not easily translate into effective laws protecting the freedom to express and the freedom to be protected from certain expressions.

The place of the media in adolescent development and broader society fundamentally serves as a testament to the potential significance, power, and limitations of First Amendment jurisprudence. Most notably, we have observed how various forms of media actually do affect adolescents. Although the accumulating findings reveal important trends and consistencies, their legal implications are far from obvious. Currently, the findings form the basis for an increasingly dominant response that champions tighter restrictions on the amount or type of media available to minors. For example, scholars continue in their effort to expand existing prohibitions that limit media exposure to youth. Some propose that the long-established obscenity exception to First Amendment protections—the First Amendment permits limiting expressions deemed obscene, without social value—should be expanded to include media violence (see Saunders, 2003). In addition and as we already have seen throughout the preceding chapters, leading medical and mental health professional organizations similarly charge that popular media contribute to many unnecessary and preventable harms. They, too, champion the need to regulate and the need to limit access to media.

Although popular and often roundly accepted by scientific communities, proposals to limit adolescents' exposure to the media and other potentially disruptive expressive environments have yet to gain much legal currency. Proposals to limit media access have yet to sway courts and the broader legal system. Indeed and as we will soon see, appellate courts have moved toward an opposite direction as they stifle important efforts to restrict access to media and control its content. The reluctance to curb expression rests on the belief that numerous valid reasons, including concerns over media effects on children, do not necessarily justify First Amendment exceptions to protections. Even though many proffered restrictions may appear reasonable, and no matter how compelling the scientific evidence detailing various media's potential harm, our system of government makes it difficult to justify censorship. The current constitutional mandates do not even require some ubiquitous forms of media to curb materials deemed obscene as to children, as revealed by numerous failed efforts to control exposure to pornography transmitted over the Internet.

That the legal system restrains efforts to limit media expressions does not mean that the legal system fails to place important limits on adolescents' media environments. In fact, adolescents' media environments and adolescents' own expressions are, in many ways, highly restricted, regulated, and controlled. Most notably, adolescents' access to information finds limits to the extent that the legal system bestows control over adolescents' expressive and media rights onto parents, teachers, social service personnel, and the state itself. For example, the law allows school officials to curb adolescents' political, sexual, and religious expressions as well as the environments that would contain such expressions (Levesque, 2002b). The law also permits parents to determine whether their children have access to all forms of media readily available to adults, and parents continue to retain the right to control their children's expressions as well as their exposure to expressive environments (Levesque, 2000). The law further limits what social service providers can discuss with adolescents who seek certain types of services, just as the law controls whether adolescents have the right to certain services in the first instance (Levesque, 2002c). It is difficult to argue that the law recognizes that adolescents have a general, compelling, and individual right to express themselves and access information, let alone a right to access media and to be protected from the media's many potential harms.

In addition to the general failure to recognize and envision ways to respect adolescents' own expressive rights as they relate to the media, it important to note that the law's limits do not mean that legislatures have not responded and sought to influence the content of media reaching adolescents. Congress continues to exert pressure on the content and form of entertainment media and popular culture, particularly programs and products directed toward youth. Over the past century, for example, Congress and other governmental bodies have used hearings, the threat of legislation, and political pressure to accomplish what government is unable to do directly: suppress or discourage unpopular or unpalatable speech. This has led to self-regulation that shapes the content of films, comic books, popular music, and television (see Paulson, 2004). While legislators are often heavy-handed and coercive in addressing media content, few doubt that entertainment media furnishes law makers ammunition and consistently pushes content boundaries across the bounds of propriety. Like other institutions (families, schools, and social services), then, the media industry itself cannot be said to insulate and protect adolescents from media harms.

This cursory glance at regulations of expression and of adolescents' expressive environments reveals how efforts to understand and shape adolescents' media environments require understanding well established constitutional mandates. Unfortunately, sifting through the great body of First Amendment law reveals a vast array of complexities. The complexities have to do with much more than the peculiar place of adolescents in our legal system. Complexities also take the form of overarching jurisprudential principles as well as standards used to determine how to apply them. These overarching principles and standards are further complicated by the sheer vastness of the substantive areas of law that fall under the First Amendment's umbrella. As a result, free speech jurisprudence addresses wide ranges of speech and conduct, ranging from cursing, body piercing, enacting dress codes, tattooing, nude dancing, proselytizing, dating, watching pornography, and entering video arcades, to burning flags, challenging school speech codes, spewing racial epithets, accessing the Internet, and making verbal threats, to protesting in schools and shopping malls. It is difficult to conceive of any areas of our lives and development that do not hold First Amendment implications.

The sheer vastness of laws and their potential applications makes it unrealistic for us to examine fully this complex body of cases and academic debates surrounding those cases. This examination is further complicated by the Supreme Court's inability to offer a clear jurisprudence to guide evaluations of efforts to restrict or enhance speech. As we soon will see, the Court's cases actually have not developed a comprehensive theory of the First Amendment that would provide satisfactory tools to deal with many new developments. Efforts to provide unifying first principles have yet to mold the developing judicial canon. Not surprisingly, this area offers a hodgepodge of jurisprudence that finds certain types of speech either protected or unprotected by the First Amendment, and the hodgepodge of jurisprudence means that reasons for either protecting or not protecting speech often remain unexplored, obscure, or simply presumed. To understand why this remains the case after even hundreds of Supreme Court cases, this chapter provides a brief overview that highlights rules and findings from some of the Supreme Court's important "freedom of speech" cases. The analysis also highlights key jurisprudential concerns and insights offered by academic commentators who continue to set the broad parameters for discussion. It also highlights the Court's historical effort to dichotomize speech to determine which gains First Amendment protections. We end with a close delineation of trends in the manner the legal system approaches efforts to protect expression. This chapter, then, maps the main lines of doctrinal development and the general contours of First Amendment protection. Our review necessarily limits itself to cases most relevant to our eventual analyses, a limitation important to bear in mind given the vast number of cases and the manner commentators often differently lump together or differentiate forms of expression. This mapping serves as a necessary prelude for the next chapter, which turns our discussion to the rights of adolescents to express, receive, and control various sources of information and media environments.

Justifying and Expanding the Protection of Speech

The American legal system attributes great significance to the need to ensure individual freedom and respect individual autonomy. This vision of freedom and autonomy undergirds our entire legal system's views of individuals and what the legal system can assume in its response to individuals' actions. Most notably, for example, the law assumes that individuals are rational actors, that they make free choices and, when they make wrong decisions, that they can be held accountable for those actions because they acted freely. The assumption runs deep. Even despite evidence that we are far from truly autonomous thinkers and actors (see Levesque, 2006), the assumption of autonomy serves as the foundation for the Constitution's premises about individuals and their place in society.

Recognizing the significance of autonomy in the law's assumptions helps us understand why the First Amendment rests on the need to ensure individual freedom from the control and coercive thinking of censorial authorities. To protect this freedom, the Framers crafted the free speech clause in absolute terms that serve twin, core purposes. The free speech clause seeks to preserve individuals' abilities to (1) control their own thought process and (2) engage in expression according to their own motivations. The integrity of thought, conscience, and expression lies at the root of ideals of the ability to act freely and autonomously. Free human beings require the freedom to think and speak as they wish, or not speak or not listen as they like. The belief that people must control their own thoughts and the nature of discussions in which they take part inevitably reveals something fundamental about the nature of governments that would support such visions of freedom. Given the belief that free speech is an essence on which the social order is founded, our system of government assumes that the best way to support this vision is to limit its own efforts to control speech and expression. In a very fundamental way, then, the First Amendment concerns itself with furthering individual human development and furthering a more prefect union of individuals to foster that development.

The twin goals carry much significance for efforts to regulate media and expressive environments. The goals support the well-established and accepted principle that entertainment media must receive robust First Amendment protection. Most notably, the underlying activity that is the focus of the entertainment industry's marketing efforts—the actual movie, or music, or video game, and so forth—receives full First Amendment protection. The legal system generally treats movies, music, video games, and other entertainment generally as "speech" deserving the full protection of the First Amendment, just as any work of art is fully protected under the First Amendment. As the Supreme Court advised over a half century ago:

> Under our system of government there is an accommodation for the widest varieties of tastes and ideas. What is good literature, what has educational value, what is refined public information, what is good art, varies with individuals as it does from one generation to another. . . . [A] requirement that literature or art conform to some norm prescribed by an official smacks of an ideology foreign to our system. (*Hannegan v. Esquire*, 1946, pp. 157–58)

In keeping with that principle, the Court would later deem the First Amendment to bar government officials from censoring works said to be "offensive," (*Texas v. Johnson*, 1989, p. 414), "sacrilegious," (*Joseph Burstyn, Inc. v. Wilson*, 1952, p. 506), "morally improper," (*Hannegan v. Esquire*, 1946, p. 149), or even "dangerous" (*Regan v. Taxation with Representation of Washington*, 1983, p. 548); the First Amendment would even protect expressions that challenge values that "touch the heart of the existing order" (*West Virginia State Board of Education v. Barnette*, 1943, p. 642). The Court's expansive proclamations would later be somewhat tempered, refined, and even somewhat retracted. Yet, it remains difficult to deny the rigorous protection our legal system bestows on materials that fall within the broad ambit of "public information."

The twin concerns of fostering individual fulfillment and a robust society through strong free speech protections persist even in the face of intense criticism and incendiary cases that, somewhat surprisingly and often ignored, actually involve adolescents. The landmark flag-salute case, *West Virginia State Board of Education v. Barnette* (1943), likely remains the Court's best-known and most eloquent expression of the First Amendment's prohibition on viewpoint discrimination (the notion that the government may not censor certain views and thereby skew public debate). In *Barnette*, the Court invalidated West Virginia's compulsory flag-salute requirement, even though the Supreme Court had just upheld a similar school regulation requiring children to salute the flag and recite the Pledge of Allegiance. In its new opinion, the slim Supreme Court majority wrote that forcing schoolchildren to salute the flag was different only in degree from the Roman persecution of Christians or from other totalitarian efforts to eliminate dissent and, ultimately, dissenters: "Those who begin coercive elimination of dissent soon find themselves exterminating dissenters. Compulsory unification of opinion achieves only the unanimity of the graveyard" (*West Virginia State Board of Education v. Barnette*, 1943, p. 641). The Court continued and assured lawmakers that democracies need not fear contrary views. Only by respectfully tolerating diversity and dissent, the Court said, do we possess the true freedom of thought and belief that allows us to thrive individually and collectively as a nation. For these reasons, the Court concluded: "If there is any fixed star in our constitutional constellation, it is that no official, high or petty, can prescribe what shall be orthodox in politics, nationalism, religion, or other matters of opinion or force citizens to confess by word or act their faith therein" (p. 642). These are strikingly uplifting words, words that the Supreme Court still aims to take very seriously.

A more recent but equally compelling landmark case, *R.A.V. v. City of St. Paul* (1992), provides another illustration of the remarkable extent to which the legal system seeks to protect expressions, even undoubtedly harmful expressions. In *R.A.V.*, a group of white adolescents fashioned a cross from broken chair legs and burned it on the lawn of a black family. The youth were convicted for violating a hate crime ordinance that specifically banned the burning of crosses as well as other expressions of extreme racist speech. The Supreme Court *unanimously* reversed the conviction and did so in a sweeping opinion. The Court observed that the government had singled out racist ideas for special regulation. The Court invoked the principle that the government may not regulate speech based on hostility—or favoritism—toward the underlying message expressed. *R.A.V.*, and numerous cases like it, stands for the fundamental proposition that the government must stay out of the business of repressing even hateful and dangerous ideas. The Court would later revisit cross-burning and eventually permit its proscription under a very narrow set of circumstances (see, e.g., *Virginia v. Black*, 2003), but *R.A.V.'s* general thrust and decisions like it stand very firmly in constitutional jurisprudence. Our legal system clings to the ideal that even problematic expressions deserve careful consideration, including those expressions that emanate from adolescents.

Extreme cases may seem of little consequence for efforts to understand the regulation of adolescents' media environments. Yet, these cases actually provide us with the necessary contours of regulations and possible rationales for supporting legal developments and reform efforts. Rationales and justifications that have strong roots in our nation's history and legal precedents are important for us to consider as we seek to understand the foundation of rights that eventually must support efforts that respond to adolescents' media environments. Leading constitutional law scholars and the Supreme Court itself present important justifications for placing a high value on freedom of speech in our constitutional scheme of governance. That high value is best understood by taking a close look at jurisprudential developments that expanded the First Amendment's reach.

Jurisprudential Developments Expanding
the First Amendment's Reach

Despite its deep intellectual links to Enlightenment thought, the significance of the First Amendment to society and individuals' fulfillment essentially went unexamined until the twentieth century. When First Amendment cases initially arose, they tended to focus predominantly on very narrow concerns and did not offer much protection to speech. As a result, the opinions and rulings from those cases were hardly inspired explorations into the meaning of free speech for either society or human development. Most notably, for example, *Abrams v. United States* (1919) upheld a conviction of activists accused of publishing pamphlets critical of President Woodrow Wilson's sending of troops to help counter the Russian revolution. A majority of the Court ruled that the First Amendment did not protect those who published such pamphlets during wartime. Under early First Amendment jurisprudence, then, the Constitution would not even protect critics who challenged government actions when those actions presumably mattered most. Early opinions were not only narrow for what they dealt with, they were narrow for lack of a need to confront the changing role of government and speech in modern society. Thus, even half a century ago, the legal system did not need to concern itself with the multimedia environment in which we live, the commercialization of society, and the expansive reach of federal and state governments. How the legal system would poise itself to address these issues would fundamentally transform First Amendment jurisprudence.

Protecting Political and Social Criticism

Although the full richness, power, and reach of the First Amendment went long ignored by the majority of Supreme Court justices who would number enough to establish legal precedents, some justices provided vigorous dissents. *Abrams v. United States* (1919) is again illustrative. *Abrams* would become a classic case cited not for what it ruled but for what it ignored and for the dissent's rhetorical power that was commanding enough to launch efforts to reshape the very meaning of the First Amendment. In dissent, Justice Oliver Wendell Holmes wrote:

> But when men have realized that time has upset many fighting faiths, they may come to believe even more than they believe the very foundations of their own conduct that the ultimate good desired is better reached by free trade in ideas—that the best test of truth is the power of the thought to get itself accepted in the competition of the market, and that truth is the only ground upon which their wishes safely can be carried out. That at any rate is the theory of our constitution. (*Abrams v. United States* , 1919, p. 630)

Holmes vigorously championed the need to embrace the First Amendment to promote speech in the marketplace of ideas. That position advises that people are better able to function as citizens if they are knowledgeable and exposed to different points of view. As a result, courts should fashion the protection given speech so as to assure an unfettered interchange of ideas for fostering political and social changes desired by the people. That presidents and other government officials continue to be criticized, especially in wartime, serves as a testament to the force of Holmes' prescient articulations. Few now question the rights of citizens to criticize their governments, yet the right had long gone unrecognized and unprotected.

The marketplace approach accords constitutional protection to the freedom of speech and of the press not on the naive belief that speech can do no harm. Rather, the approach rests on the confidence that the benefits society reaps from the free flow and exchange of ideas outweigh the costs society endures by receiving reprehensible or dangerous ideas. Instead of censorship, a possible "proper response to offensive speech is not to prohibit it, but to combat it with counter-speech" (*Abrams v. United States*, 1919, p. 630). The costs in allowing censorship to persist in response to society's concerns range widely. Costs derive, for example, from the problems that emerge when a privileged minority controls much of the nation's communication system. Costs also arise when censorship mentalities seek to solve societal concerns by suppressing speech. Instead, according to Holmes and this jurisprudential position, only by staunchly defending every person's right to public speech does our society guarantee that the best ideas will continue to enter and prevail in the public arena. This "marketplace of ideas" concept recognizes that truth ultimately prevails in a truly open marketplace of ideas and urges the government to remain neutral and only intervene to control the content of speech in a narrow, compelling set of circumstances.

A Supreme Court's dissenting opinion that recognizes the need to protect speech to ensure the flow of ideas typically does not constitute firm grounds to guide jurisprudence. But, as the view itself suggests, ideas can be powerful and, if well grounded, can prevail and deeply influence society and its laws. Fifty years after *Abrams*, the full Court recognized and accepted its dissenting opinion's market-based rationale. The Court did so in the landmark case *New York Times Co. v. Sullivan* (1964). *Sullivan* receives credit for revolutionizing the common law tort of defamation and, in doing so, energizing once again the First Amendment's rhetorical power and moving it in new directions. In *Sullivan*, the *New York Times* newspaper carried an advertisement based on a statement of facts, some of which were conceded to be false. On the libel suit of a city police commissioner in Alabama, a unanimous Court held that public officials could sue in defamation only upon providing proof that defendants made the statement about their official conduct with "actual malice," that is, with "knowledge that it was false or with reckless disregard of whether it was false or not" (*New York Times Co. v. Sullivan*, 1964, p. 280). The Court reasoned that its standard was necessary to counter the potential threat that already powerful public officials could wield if they were granted more sweeping authority to use the courts to punish their critics. The Court articulated that rationale expansively throughout *Sullivan* in terms of the great need to maintain the people's speech rights against encroachment by more powerful influences. This rationale would mean that *Sullivan* would confirm the need for an important element in First Amendment jurisprudence—robust debate, even debate fueled by falsities. As the Court noted:

> We consider this case against the background of a profound national commitment to the principle that debate on public issues should be

uninhibited, robust, and wide-open, and that it may well include vehement, caustic, and sometimes unpleasantly sharp attacks on government and public officials. (p. 270)

The decision considerably diluted the common-law distinction between "fact" and "opinion." Now there could be no recovery even for a false statement of fact unless made with actual malice. This approach would allow the necessary "breathing room" for free speech. The case highlights why neither falsity, defamatory nature, nor the combination of those two traits may suffice to justify suppressing free speech and chilling criticisms of official conduct. By emphasizing that even utterly false statements targeting the government enjoy constitutional protection, the case offered full doctrinal support to the importance of free speech that Holmes had dictated in his analysis of the significance of an unfettered market of ideas. The Court found that

The general proposition that freedom of expression upon public questions is secured by the First Amendment has long been settled by our decisions. The constitutional safeguard, we have said, was fashioned to assure unfettered interchange of ideas for the bringing about of political and social changes desired by the people. (*New York Times Co. v. Sullivan*, 1964, p. 269)

The threat addressed specifically in *Sullivan* was excessive power of government to punish criticism of government officials by citizens. Although *Sullivan's* rule may seem narrow, the impact of this approach was rather profound. The case confirms the societal value in protecting some false speech in discussions of public issues when doing so serves a greater good. As a result, demands that seek to restrict speech must survive the most rigorous level of constitutional scrutiny grounded in the manner the Court articulated its ruling in *Sullivan*—declaring the fullest protection for speech involving "debate on public issues" (p. 270).

Protecting Commercial Speech

The *Abrams* and *Sullivan* cases do much more than champion a place for free exchanges of ideas; the cases themselves reveal the power of ideas to reshape entire areas of law. The cases demonstrate how the give and take of free discussion introduces and then sharpens ideas, and how these ideas are ultimately sifted through debate and either discarded or accepted as policies or objectives. Not long after *Sullivan*, yet another entire area of law would begin to change and greatly impact the dissemination of ideas—laws dealing with commercial transactions, namely advertisements. As with defamation, the Supreme Court had earlier treated the entire category of commercial advertisements as not falling under the First Amendment's protection. Starting in 1976, however, the category of utterances that do no more than propose a commercial transaction became subject to regulation only when the regulation satisfied a test molded by First Amendment jurisprudence.

Proposing and then actually finding that the First Amendment protected commercial speech constituted a remarkable development. Commercial speech historically had not been viewed as necessary for debate on public issues and thus had gone unprotected by the First Amendment. This was the position the Court noted in *Virginia State Board of Pharmacy v. Virginia Citizens Consumer Council, Inc.* (1976). In that case, the Court defined commercial speech to include "speech which does 'no more than propose a commercial transaction'" (p. 762). Courts historically had reasoned that commercial speech was more hardy and verifiable and, as a result, less dependant on judicial protection—an assumption based on the belief that, since commercial enterprises rest on speech, commerce would provide enough power to support circulation in the marketplace of ideas. But, this case would challenge that reasoning and begin the dramatic transformation of this area of law.

Virginia Citizens Consumer Council invalidated a statute that prohibited Virginia pharmacists from advertising the prices of prescription drugs. For our purposes, that case gains considerable significance for holding that the government may not "completely suppress the dissemination of concededly truthful information about entirely lawful activity, fearful of that information's effect upon its disseminators and its recipients" (p. 773). Although the Court expressly held that the First Amendment provides some protection for commercial speech, the Court understood the hybrid nature of commercial speech, and noted that although it "is protected, we of course do not hold that it can never be regulated in any way" (p. 770). In particular, the Court observed that "false or misleading" commercial speech could be proscribed and it disclaimed any suggestion that its holding prevented states from outlawing advertisements for illegal transactions. The government, then, could still regulate speech that historically was unprotected, but the government could not fetter the exchange of truthful ideas. As a result, then, ideas traditionally deemed unworthy of First Amendment protection were corralled within it and provided protection because the government could not suppress truthful ideas, even those not necessarily dealing with political or cultural ideas central to public and democratic discourse.

The *Virginia Citizens Consumer Council*'s approach was firmly endorsed by a landmark decision that would set the standard for evaluating the extent to which commercial speech would receive constitutional protection: *Central Hudson Gas & Electric Corp. v. Public Service Commission of New York* (1980). That case involved a ban, intended to prevent an increase in demand for electricity, on certain promotional advertising by electric utilities. In that case, the Court again acknowledged that the Constitution granted lower constitutional status to commercial speech and accorded it less protection. Yet, the Court found the advertising ban unconstitutional. Under the *Central Hudson* test, truthful speech may be regulated if the government interest is substantial, the regulation directly advances the government interest, and the regulation is no more extensive than is necessary to serve that interest (p. 566). In this case, the government did have an interest in banning the speech but the regulation was deemed more extensive than was necessary to serve that interest (pp. 569–72). The case, then, revealed the emergence of the Court's move toward protecting yet another area of previously unprotected speech, one quite important to understanding the regulation of media and exchange of information.

Central Hudson retains its vitality as the Court increases the rule's potency, and two cases relevant to our analyses reveal the significance of the development. In *44 Liquormart, Inc. v. Rhode Island* (1996), the Court struck down a statute that prohibited any advertising of prices of alcoholic beverages except "for price tags or signs displayed with the merchandise within licensed premises and not visible from the street" (*44 Liquormart, Inc. v. Rhode Island,* 1996, p. 489). The Court noted that "when a State entirely prohibits the dissemination of truthful, nonmisleading commercial messages for reasons unrelated to the preservation of a fair bargaining process, there is far less reason to depart from the rigorous review that the First Amendment generally demands" (p. 501). As the Court observed, "[t]he First Amendment directs us to be especially skeptical of regulations that seek to keep people in the dark for what the government perceives to be their own good. That teaching applies equally to state attempts to deprive consumers of accurate information about their chosen products" (p. 503). Indeed, the government has no legitimate interest in keeping legal users of a product or service ignorant in order to manipulate their choices in the marketplace. Not surprisingly, the Court has proceeded to protect tobacco retailers and manufacturers as it recently invalidated Massachusetts's outdoor advertising restrictions on smokeless tobacco and cigars, in *Lorillard Tobacco Co. v. Reilly* (2001). The Court found that the retailers and manufacturers had an "interest in conveying truthful information about their products" and, perhaps even more significant for our purposes, noted that consumers "have a corresponding interest in receiving truthful information about tobacco products" (*Lorillard Tobacco Co. v. Reilly,* 2001, p. 564).

This line of cases' developments is impressive for three reasons. First, they are significant given that the Court invalidates laws regulating commercial speech, including even provisions pertaining to traditionally highly regulated activities such as food and drug law. Thus, commercial advertising now falls within the scope of the First Amendment and there seems to be a move toward a stronger commercial speech doctrine, with a possible shift toward fuller First Amendment protection. Second, the underlying activity that is the focus of an industry's marketing efforts potentially still retains First Amendment protection. This remains the case for entertainment media, where the actual movie, or music, or video game is subject to full First Amendment protection. By having the marketing of entertainment protected, the media gain considerable power to infiltrate the lives of adolescents. Lastly, given that the cases involved groups litigating for a right to information, these cases shed light on the extent to which individuals have rights to access ideas. Of course, to say that people have a right to express noxious and offensive ideas is not the same as saying that people have a right to access those ideas, but the former has generally implied the latter. First Amendment cases usually discuss speakers' rights because laws typically punish speakers. But this line of cases recognized a corollary right of listeners to receive information. Most notably, in *Virginia State Board of Pharmacy v. Virginia Citizens Consumer Council, Inc.* (1976), where the Court upheld the right of a consumers' group to challenge a law regulating advertising by pharmacists, the Court concluded that "[if] there is a right to advertise, there is a reciprocal right to receive the advertising" (p. 757). We will return to the nature of that right in the next chapter, but for now it is important to emphasize that the Court endorses the right of citizens to receive information without governmental interference, even information that traditionally has gone unprotected. That individuals retain the right to receive information gains significance to the extent that governments can be involved in supporting speech. To understand the extent to which the state can actively support speech, we must turn to another important series of landmark cases.

Supporting and Subsidizing Speech

Government at all levels has expanded dramatically since the nation's founding. The influence of government spending on most Americans, both rich and poor, is inescapable. As a consequence, much citizen speech occurs either in forums provided by the government or in connection with enterprises partly financed by governmental largesse. The government's expansion creates a First Amendment dilemma. On one hand, the government naturally uses the power of the purse to discourage policies or behaviors with which it disagrees. On the other hand, the state sometimes chooses not to discontinue a controversial initiative, but rather imposes conditions on the use of public funds to coax the program toward particular governmental objectives. The First Amendment becomes implicated when the government attempts to restrict speech as part of its benefit package.

Addressing the governmental support-restraint dilemma hinges on the venerable First Amendment concept of viewpoint discrimination. In the span of five years around 1940, the Supreme Court decided several landmark cases that advanced First Amendment interests in this area. The first case, *Hague v. Committee for Industrial Organization* (1939), gave rise to the public forum doctrine, which holds that the government, as landowner, could not completely forbid citizens from using public streets and parks for expressive purposes. The Court described the need for protection as arising from the historical use of public streets and parks as public forums where citizens congregated to express their opinions. While these traditional forums might literally belong to the government, the public had accrued a guaranteed right of access to them that could be regulated, but not arbitrarily denied. In quintessential public forums, such as streets and parks, government may regulate on the basis of content only if it can show a compelling state interest and a narrowly drawn regulation to achieve that end. The state may also impose reasonable content-neutral time, place, and manner regulations. The law must serve significant governmental interests and must leave open alternative channels of communication. The Court articulated other types of forums which may be public but not necessarily protected much from regulations. If the state has opened up or designated public property as a place for expressive activity, it has created a limited public forum. In such instances, the same First Amendment principles apply as in a traditional public forum. On the other hand, if public property is not by tradition or designation a forum for public communication, it is a nonpublic forum. Regulation in a nonpublic forum need only be viewpoint-neutral and rational. These widely accepted formalities owe much to the *Hague* decision.

On its facts, *Hague* involved viewpoint discrimination to such an extent that it amounted to an arbitrary denial of access to a public forum. In *Hague*, a Jersey City mayor had used a permit requirement to prevent labor organizers from meeting, speaking, or distributing literature within the city on the grounds that they were Communists or were affiliated with Communist organizations. The mayor had literally evicted union speakers by having them arrested and forced aboard ferry boats headed for New York City. Because the permit ordinance gave municipal authorities unlimited discretion to control public communication within the city, the Court invalidated it as an "instrument of arbitrary suppression of free expression of views on national affairs" (*Hague v. Committee for Industrial Organization,* 1939, p. 516). The need to respond to such dramatic facts may have led some to view the case as an anomaly. Not surprisingly, subsequent decisions clarified that the state could regulate public access to traditional forums, but the Court would firmly hold that it could regulate those forums only as long as it did so pursuant to reasonable and content-neutral time, place, and manner restrictions.

Hague was complemented well by the second landmark decision in this public forum series of cases, *West Virginia State Board of Education v. Barnette* (1943). It was in *Barnette,* as we have seen above, that the Court opined that lawmakers in a democracy need not fear contrary views, even those that "touch the heart of the existing order" (*West Virginia State Board of Education v. Barnette,* 1943, p. 642). Only by respectfully tolerating diversity and dissent, the Court found, do we possess the true freedom of thought and belief that allows us to thrive individually and collectively as a nation. Thus, *Barnette* recognized the dual function of the public schools: they must inculcate basic information, but they also must serve as the training grounds of democratic self-government. Significantly, the *Barnette* Court expressly found judicial review of the school administrator's action important because school officials in small, local jurisdictions might not fulfill their constitutional responsibilities as a result of local political pressure. Together, these considerably expansive cases revealed how speech on public grounds receives full First Amendment protection against the government's urge to engage in viewpoints discrimination, which suppresses one side of arguments or views.

The 1940s also witnessed an extension of the rationale used to support the claim that the government could not engage in viewpoint discrimination in its subsidizing of private and publicly supported press entities. For example, the Court, in *Hannegan v. Esquire, Inc.* (1946), held that the Postmaster General could not revoke *Esquire*'s second-class mail status because of the magazine's sexual content. Recognizing that second-class mailing privileges were a "form of subsidy," the Court opined that the government could not withhold the subsidy in an attempt to censor speech even though it need not provide that benefit to all publications. The Court explicitly rejected the argument that use of the mail system is a privilege that can be conditioned in whatever manner the government chooses. The Court saw revocation of *Esquire*'s mailing privileges as a penalty and not just as a governmental decision to deny a benefit.

The *Esquire* principle finds clear expression in more recent cases that have struck down selective tax exemptions for the press in instances where the Court feared that exemptions might be used to punish disfavored media outlets. For example, in *Minneapolis Star & Tribune Co. v. Minnesota Commissioner of Revenue* (1983), the Court invalidated a state law that exempted from the state's use tax the first $100,000 spent by publications on paper and ink. As a result of the exemption, only a few newspaper publishers paid any tax. Noting that the threat of burdensome taxes can act to censor critical commentary, the Court concluded that the law's differential treatment of news publications suggests that the goal of the regulation is not unrelated to suppression of expression, and such a goal is presumptively unconstitutional. This deference to the press as an independent actor flows logically from the crucial role of the press as government watchdog. The Court specifically recognized this role in *Minneapolis Star*, stating "the basic assumption of our political system [is] that the press will often serve as an important restraint on government" (*Minneapolis Star & Tribune Co. v. Minnesota Commissioner of Revenue*, 1983, p. 585). The Court has been unwilling to let the government compromise—or even appear to compromise—this checking function of the press by attaching conditions to state benefit programs or engaging in viewpoint discrimination. The Court has been sensitive to the danger of viewpoint discrimination that selective subsidization of the press can present.

In subsidy situations that involve nonmedia grantees, the Court has taken a far different approach. Two of the most controversial cases decided by the Court in the last decade, *Rust v. Sullivan* (1991) and *National Endowment for the Arts v. Finley* (1998), involved the uncertain constitutional relationship between government-subsidized speech and viewpoint discrimination. Both cases questioned whether the First Amendment places any limits on the government's ability to use its spending power to influence private speech. *Rust* involved a challenge to the constitutionality of Title X regulations specifying that federally funded family planning clinics could not provide abortion counseling or referrals, but were required to refer pregnant clients for prenatal care. The regulations also prevented Title X grantees from acting in any way to "encourage, promote or advocate abortion" as a family planning method, while imposing no restrictions on grantees' ability to speak against abortion as an alternative. The Court's majority rejected the Title X grantees' argument that the regulations unconstitutionally discriminated on the basis of viewpoint by prohibiting them from disseminating factual information about abortion as a lawful choice, while compelling them to provide information about carrying a pregnancy to term. The majority argued that

The Government can, without violating the Constitution, selectively fund a program to encourage certain activities it believes to be in the public interest, without at the same time funding an alternative program which seeks to deal with the problem in another way. In so doing, the Government has not discriminated on the basis of viewpoint; it has merely chosen to fund one activity to the exclusion of the other. (*Rust v. Sullivan*, 1991, p. 193)

A few paragraphs later, the majority conceded that the forbidden activities in *Rust* included speech, but it made no difference to the rationale and conclusion. The government was not "'suppressing a dangerous idea'" (which the Court still believed would be unconstitutional), but was imposing boundaries on the scope of a federally funded project: "When the Government appropriates public funds to establish a program," the Court wrote, "it is entitled to define the limits of that program" (p. 194).

That *Rust* was not an aberration was demonstrated in the next major subsidized speech case to reach the Court, *National Endowment for the Arts v. Finley* (1998). In *Finley*, the Court voted eight to one to uphold federal regulations requiring the National Endowment for the Arts (NEA) to consider "general standards of decency and respect for the diverse beliefs and values of the American public" in awarding artistic grants (pp., 572–73). Four individual artists and an artists' organization had filed a facial challenge to the law as unconstitutional viewpoint discrimination, arguing that, on its face, the law inappropriately denied funding to nonobscene art, deemed by the state to be offensive or outside mainstream values. The majority relied on three main arguments to deny that the law violated the First Amendment's neutrality principle. First, the decency clause as interpreted by the NEA was merely advisory, which technically did not disallow any viewpoints. Second, it claimed that the decency clause did not discriminate by viewpoint because Congress enacted it with what the Court considered to be speech-protective motives. Finally, it argued that the decency clause did not amount to viewpoint discrimination because it was inconceivable that the government could administer its competitive grant programs in a neutral way; awarding grants only on the basis of artistic excellence or on the requested decency standard still requires the NEA to allocate its limited resources in some content-based manner. Citing *Rust* for support, the majority concluded that "the Government may allocate competitive funding according to criteria that would be impermissible were direct regulation of speech or a criminal penalty at stake," and that "Congress has wide latitude to set spending priorities" (*National Endowment for the Arts v. Finley*, 1998, pp. 587–88).

More recently, the U.S. Supreme Court decided *United States v. American Library Association, Inc.* (2003). That case provided the Court with an opportunity to examine the constitutionality of the Children's Internet Protection Act, which provides that public libraries must install Internet filters on library computers to receive federal funding. Writing for the plurality, Chief Justice Rehnquist stated that Congress has broad discretion in attaching conditions to the receipt of federal funds. He also noted that Congress may not impose conditions on the receipt of federal funds that would require the recipient "to engage in activities that would themselves be unconstitutional" (*United States v. American Library Association, Inc.*, 2003, p. 203). The plurality then considered the role of libraries in modern society to determine whether filter requirements violated the First Amendment. Libraries, the Court pointed out, strive to provide a vast amount of information and acquire materials that will directly benefit the community. As such, libraries provide a wealth of information tailored to meet the public's needs. The Court relied on *National Endowment for the Arts v. Finley*, reasoning that, like art-funding program employees, library employees consider content and are entitled to broad discretion when selecting material. The Court also relied on *Rust* as it stated that the government is entitled "broad limits" when it creates a program and determines how public funds are appropriated to that program (*United States v. American Library Association, Inc.*, 2003, p. 211). The plurality held that "Congress may certainly insist that these 'public funds be spent for the purposes for which they were authorized'" (p. 211–12). The plurality further justified its reasoning by stating Congress acts entirely within its limits when it excludes funding for electronic versions of pornographic material since libraries have excluded such materials from their other collections. Additionally, the Court reasoned that libraries still are allowed to offer unfiltered Internet access, but if they do so, they will not receive federal funding.

The above cases reveal the complexity of cases and the importance of considering exemptions. Several cases have suggested that the government would be unable to limit speech based on viewpoint. As we have seen in *R.A.V.*, the Court used a broad understanding of viewpoint discrimination to hold that the First Amendment prohibits official attempts to drive unpopular or offensive messages from the marketplace of ideas, even when done in an arguably impartial way. *R.A.V.* and its lineage overturned speech-restrictive precedents and struck blows against the government's ability to restrict speech based on viewpoint. The Court has been vigilant in the traditional public forum and general speech domains to invalidate government regulation of speech that expresses a disfavored viewpoint or, alternatively, that eliminates a particular perspective. The Court continues to recite that the government may determine what to subsidize and what not to subsidize as long as it does so in a viewpoint-neutral manner. Yet, while ostensibly acknowledging that the government may not discriminate against disfavored views in allocating subsidies, the Court nevertheless grants the government considerable leeway to delineate the scope of its generosity. As we will see in the next chapter, these developments would eventually parallel much of First Amendment law affecting adolescents, particularly in terms of their educational, medical, and other service-providing environments.

Conceptual Developments Championed by Commentators

Judicial doctrines do not develop in the absence of broader intellectual discourse. Although judges and justices cite commentators, and vice versa, it often is unclear who influences whom. Commentators, however, help us further understand First Amendment jurisprudence; they reveal how the legal system struggles with pressing social concerns and efforts to shape the law's proper place in society. As with judicial developments, we see analyses that move First Amendment jurisprudence beyond political concerns to concerns about self-development and one's proper place in a modern civil society fraught with governmental support and potential intrusions. These are impressive developments worth highlighting for they serve as the intellectual foundation for our next chapters' analyses and, as we will see, they seem to reflect and inform the development of actual doctrine.

The rhetorical power of Holmes' writings on the marketplace of ideas exemplifies reliance on commentators. The market place orientation was informed deeply by political philosopher John Stuart Mill's work *On Liberty* (1859/1985). It was in that nineteenth-century essay that Mill had examined the relationship between free speech and "truth." In his understanding of political and social liberties, Mill had called for an almost absolutist approach to free speech and complete protection of political speech. Key to Mill's views was that truth could be discovered only through open discussion. Mill argued that allowing the government to restrict speech based on the falsity of an idea was impractical for three reasons: the suppressed opinion might be true, all false ideas contain some element of truth, and false opinions are needed to keep the truth from becoming dead dogma. Although the Court has never adopted Mill's absolutist views, the Court does continue to rely on similar justifications to protect speech from governmental censorship and regulation.

Conceptual developments in First Amendment jurisprudence also have been predated by the work of other influential commentators. Jurisprudential developments in the 1920s to the 1940s were predated by the works of Zechariah Chafee (1920, 1941) and in the late 1940s through the early 1960s by political theorist Alexander Meiklejohn (1965). Chafee's work is considered the seminal legal scholarship on the First Amendment during the early part of the twentieth century. His writings focused specifically on sedition and the cases concerning the Espionage Act of 1917. More generally, Chafee focused on the protection of speech as a means to the spread of truth. He wrote: "The true meaning of freedom of speech seems to be this. One of the most important purposes of society and government is the discovery and spread of truth on subjects of general concern" (Chafee, 1920, p. 34). Chafee criticized *Schenck* and other Espionage Act decisions for treating free speech "as merely an individual interest, which must readily give way like other personal desires the moment it interferes with the social interest in national security" (p. 37). Instead, Chafee argued that the most important purpose served by free speech was the social interest in the discovery and spread of truth on subjects of general concern. Although he regarded the social interest in truth as extending to all "subjects of general concern," he believed that free speech had special importance in the political realm, "so that the country may not only adopt the wisest course of action, but carry it out in the wisest way" (pp. 34, 36). Despite this strong sentiment towards protecting speech, Chafee was not an absolutist. He argued for a preferred balancing of free speech against other social necessities, such as maintaining order. In doing so, he highlighted the significance of the First Amendment's role in protecting not only the social interest in truth, but also the need of many individuals to "express their opinions on matters vital to them if life is to be worth living" (p. 36).

Meiklejohn (1965) pinpointed and initiated a more specific value in freedom of speech—its necessity for ensuring self-government. Meiklejohn is regarded as the foremost proponent of the theory that freedom of speech must link to democratic politics. Under this view, the central aim of the First Amendment is to protect the power of the people to collectively govern themselves, a view of self-government focusing on the group rather than on the individual. His reasoning would still incorporate the ideas about truth found in Mill's philosophy with those found in Holmes' dicta about maintaining free speech in the marketplace of ideas. He wrote: "To be afraid of ideas, any ideas, is to be unfit for self-government. Any such suppression of ideas about the common good, the First Amendment condemns with its absolute disapproval" (p. 20). He claimed that freedom of speech principles spring from the necessities of self-government, because a citizen must be well informed in order to make intelligent policy decisions. Although this may be interpreted very expansively, Meiklejohn's theory argued that only speech serving democratic or political functions deserved the fullest protection. Eventually, this approach, and other theories which called for only protecting political speech, proved problematic because of the challenge of determining just what speech is necessary for effective self-government. Importantly and despite these and other problems, some theorists, such as jurist Robert Bork (1971), continue to argue for the protection of only purely political speech. Although Meiklejohn (1948) originally had argued that only political speech relevant to self-government was protected by the First Amendment, even absolutely protected, he later came to include more speech as potentially political speech relating to self-government. But by admitting that almost all kinds of speech can involve self-government, Meiklejohn reopened the jurisprudential problem of how one distinguishes political from nonpolitical speech.

Other theorists, although not adhering to Meiklejohn's apparent absolutism, have focused on the importance of the First Amendment to the protection of political speech to foster and maintain participation in our democratic system of government. Blasi (1977, 1985) for example, sought to expand the conception of free speech to argue that speech gains protection mainly because of the checking balance it offers against government control. Even nearly three decades later, Blasi (2004) argues that free speech is necessary in constitutional regimes fearful of political entrenchment and dedicated to continual adaptation. Embracing the free marketplace ideal, he views free speech protections as needed to offer counterweight, both conceptual and rhetorical, to illiberal attitudes about authority and change on which censorial mentality thrives. Free speech serves a checking function, as a cultural force that contributes to the control of abuses of power and the promotion of adaptive character traits needed for civic adaptation.

Despite the strong focus on political, especially democratic, government, some important commentators sought to expand the First Amendment's reach into other social domains. Thomas Emerson is perhaps one of the most influential theorists who envisioned a more expansive First Amendment jurisprudence. Emerson added breadth to earlier free speech theory by arguing that, in addition to the importance of speech in politics, speech also carries with it some intrinsic "human" value. His groundbreaking work, *Toward a General Theory of the First Amendment* (1963), began a movement in First Amendment scholarship that views speech as responsible for creating fully realized individuals, not just enabling them to participate in the democratic form of government but also allowing them to enjoy complete social lives. Emerson posited that the value of free speech rights in our democratic society could be grouped into four categories: (1) as a means of assuring individual self-fulfillment, (2) as means of attaining the truth, (3) as a method for securing citizens' participation in the political and social process, and (4) as a means of maintaining the balance between stability and change in society. Emerson felt so strongly about the need for complete freedom of speech that he argued that the "suppression of belief, opinion and expression" was "an affront to the dignity of man, a negation of man's essential nature" (p. 5).

Building on Emerson's frame of analysis, other important constitutional scholars have restructured discussions of speech protections to include its centrality to self-fulfillment and self-realization. For example, Baker (1989) has argued that the First Amendment protects not a marketplace but rather an arena of individual liberty as he collapsed Emerson's four categories into two—protection of speech as means of ensuring individual self-fulfillment and as a means of maintaining the balance between stability and change in society. Baker (1997) defends the notion of autonomy as uninhibited self-expression, maintaining that speech should be protected when it is an expression of the speakers' individual autonomy. He describes even the listener's constitutional interest as one of self-expression. He espoused the view that outlawing speech fails to treat the listener as an agent presumptively capable of responsible choice. Restricting access to speech, he argued, paternalistically denies individuals the opportunity to obtain perspectives relating to how she will define herself, even in dissent from the law.

Redish (1982) went so far as to contend that the First Amendment protection of speech serves only one purpose—to promote "individual self-realization" (p. 591). His view stresses that jurisprudential underpinnings of the First Amendment emphasize the value of free expression, as with democracy itself, to individual development. Thus, freedom of expression and the right to receive ideas is valued because it enriches one's life and supports personal fulfillment, not just because of the social values it promotes. In this regard, the right to free expression derives solely from one's capacity as an individual. It rests on the widely accepted premise that the proper end of human development is the realization of one's character and potentialities as a human being. This model views expression as a route to individual development and fulfillment. Thus, it expresses the sort of society we wish to become and the sort of persons we wish to be. Lack of access to a wide range of ideas prevents individuals from imagining the full range of possibilities in their lives. Free speech aids all life-affecting decision-making, no matter how personally limited, in much the same manner in which it aids the political process.

Other commentators also emphasize autonomy but highlight different dangers of regulation. Most notably, Raz (1991) emphasizes the effects of speech regulation on individuals' realization of autonomy. He locates the harm of government regulation of speech in the attitude it expresses toward individuals, but is concerned only with the government's attitude toward individual conceptions of the good—not the government's attitude toward individuals' underlying capacity to endorse one conception of the good over others. Because a ban on speech condemns a way of life associated with that speech, and because we have a fundamental need for public validation of our way of life, Raz identifies the harm from regulation as the actual effect that denial of recognition has on individuals. Individuals whose lives are condemned through speech regulation will feel alienated from society and "it is normally vital for personal prosperity that one will be able to identify with one's society" (p. 31). According to Raz, the government should respect ways of life so as to maximize the possibilities available to all persons. Such an operative principle would enhance the achievement of autonomy as an ideal and provide a firm rationale for robust free speech protections.

Other contemporary legal scholars ask different questions about the value of speech and what the First Amendment should and does mean. For example, Bollinger (1986) suggests that the First Amendment promotes the democratic virtue of tolerance and that the very purpose of freedom of speech is to curb intolerance. He claims that free speech teaches us skills of self-restraint because it confronts us with views with which we disagree:

> A central function of free speech . . . is to provide a social context in which we collectively speak, in a public and official setting, to an important aspect of what we might think of as the intellectual character of the society. Taking this approach . . . the purposes of the free speech enterprise may reasonably include not only the "protection" of a category of especially worthy human activity but also the choice to exercise extraordinary self-restraint toward behavior acknowledged to be bad but that can evoke feelings that lead us to behave in ways we must learn to temper and control. (p. 120)

Thus, he makes an instrumental point: protecting extremist speech is helpful because egregious cases teach by example. This account of the First Amendment emphasizes the benefits of free speech to the development of individual character, which also benefits society. This view that free speech cultivates a characteristic of tolerance among social actors rests on the twin premises that persons have a capacity for profound intolerance that can manifest itself through majority rule, and that speech represents an area in which enforced tolerance can maximize human tendencies toward reasoned understanding.

What is notable about these conceptual developments is that each makes strong assumptions. They assume power is governmental and individual autonomy is a given. This traditional liberal position, as well as the past century or more of free speech cases, seems to point to one main objective: speech must be valued as one of the most important elements of a democratic society. Scholars tend to see speech as a fundamental tool for self-realization and social growth and find that the remedy for troublesome speech is more speech, not more government regulation of speech.

Despite the strong focus on the need to support individuals' ideas in the marketplace of ideas, a new stream of scholarship proposes alternative views of speech. Among the most noteworthy are those that champion the need for governmental restrictions of speech. For example, Matsuda (1989) questions relying on a system that assumes that no ideas are absolutely false and that all ideas deserve a public forum. Instead, she would allow for censoring racist speech and ones where the message is persecutorial, hateful, and degrading. Such an exception would be analogous to the fighting words doctrine that permits the government to regulate messages that have such slight social value as a step to truth that any benefit that may be derived from them is clearly outweighed by the social interest in order and morality. Similarly, Delgado (1982) and his colleagues (Delgado & Stefancic, 2004) have called for the regulation of racist speech. In effect, they view racist and other forms of hate speech as antidemocratic and as reinforcing inequalities. These recent developments significantly highlight the place of ideas in shaping the very definitions of democracy, autonomy, individuality, and civil society. These developments also highlight the real need to place some limits on free speech protections. Given our system's apparent attachment to freedom, these proposals are not without controversy. Yet, as we see in the next section, our legal system actually has a long and strong history of regulating speech.

Permitting Exceptions to Expansive Free Speech Protections

As we have seen, the prioritization of free expression in the constitutional order has led the Supreme Court to restrict the government's ability to regulate speech. Despite this expansive protection, the freedom of speech still potentially faces firm limits. Indeed, despite the Supreme Court's passionate language about the evils of government censorship, the Court always has accepted that the First Amendment does not protect some contents of speech. The Court has carved out important exceptions to free speech protections, and these exceptions are increasingly nuanced. Early cases had announced entire types of speech as outside of protection, but the ensuing jurisprudence renders it a gross oversimplification to claim that any category of speech is without First Amendment protection. This section takes a brief look at the types of speech traditionally deemed *less* worthy of protection through First Amendment jurisprudence. As we have seen and will see below, even these categories are in a state of flux. The Supreme

Court's free speech cases generally have become more protective of speech over time, making it more challenging for the government to regulate speech. Those limits tend to be understandable in terms of the justifications for the vigorous protection of speech we have examined above. In our examination, we consider the extent to which the Court allows exceptions to vigorous speech protections in order to protect our liberties—those related to political, cultural, and individual development.

Incitement of Imminent Illegal Conduct

The First Amendment tends not to protect speech that incites imminent lawless activity. In *Schenck v. United States* (1919) the Supreme Court articulated the clear and present danger test to determine whether speech should be protected from attempts to censure. Schenck was convicted under the Espionage Act of 1917 for distributing leaflets that the Court believed encouraged draft resistance. The Court held that the First Amendment did not insulate the defendants from prosecution because the speech enjoyed no constitutional protection. In reaching this conclusion, the Court noted that the clear and present danger standard is met when "the words used are used in such circumstances and are of such a nature as to create a clear and present danger that they will bring about the substantive evils Congress has a right to prevent" (*Schenck v. United States*, 1919, p. 52). Importantly, in upholding the conviction, the Court took heavily into consideration that the leaflets were distributed during a time when the country was at war. Given the facts of the case and the Court's own words limiting its reach, it is no surprise to find that the case actually became famous for a situation that its facts did not even present. It was in that case that Justice Holmes famously offered his example of a person falsely shouting "Fire!" in a theater. Under those circumstances, the speech's perceived threat ensures that it will gain no protection under the First Amendment.

The Supreme Court has proceeded to reshape the incitement test through numerous cases. Most notably, *Brandenburg v. Ohio* (1969) has emerged as the seminal First Amendment incitement case that continues to serve as the gold standard. In *Brandenburg*, the Court held that speech qualifies as "unprotected speech" when it is "directed to inciting or producing imminent lawless action and is likely to incite or produce such action" (p. 447). In that case, a Ku Klux Klan speaker was convicted of promoting violence in a speech he made at a rally where there was also a cross burning. His speech included a statement against the U.S. government and minorities, saying that "it's possible that there might have to be some revengence taken" (pp. 446, 448). The Court reversed the conviction. No one was present at the Klan rally except the Klan members themselves, the television reporter, and his cameraman. Nothing in the record indicated that the racist messages of the Klansman at the rally posed any immediate physical threat to anyone. In these circumstances, the Court said the Klan was guilty only of the "abstract teaching" of the "moral propriety" of racist violence, which was not the same as preparing a group for violent action and steeling it to such action (p. 448). According to the Court:

> The constitutional guarantees of free speech and free press do not permit a State to forbid or proscribe advocacy of the use of force or of law violation except where such advocacy is directed to inciting or producing imminent lawless action and is likely to incite or produce such action. (p. 447)

This quotation—this one sentence upon which so much First Amendment litigation is focused—is limited by its own language to situations in which government seeks to "forbid or proscribe advocacy of the use of force or of law violation" (p. 447). Moreover, the discussion of advocacy of the use of force makes obvious that such advocacy was the sole context within which the Court decided *Brandenburg*. The Court's application of the test to the facts before it reveals that the context of violent protest was the nucleus of the Court's analysis. "[W]e are here confronted," the Court observed, "with a statute which, by its own words and as applied, purports to punish mere advocacy and to forbid, on pain of criminal punishment, assembly with others merely to advocate the described type of action" (p. 449). The Court in *Brandenburg* understood the Klan's actions in the case as evil, but not inciting. As reprehensible as the racist and anti-Semitic speech was in *Brandenburg*, the Court understood the Klan members' speech as posing no palpable danger to anyone. The Court made it clear that the Constitution protected the mere act of assembling and expressing hate.

The imminence requirement has become the focal point of the *Brandenburg* test, and in a subsequent case, the Court suggested that imminent lawless action amounted to a matter of hours—or, at most, several days; it did not open the door to indefinite action. The Court did so in *Hess v. Indiana* (1973). *Hess* dealt with statements made during antiwar protests. The case involved the disorderly conduct conviction of a student who faced a crowd of antiwar demonstrators and shouted: "We'll take the fucking street later" (*Hess v. Indiana*, 1973, p. 107). The Court overturned the conviction on First Amendment grounds, finding that language was "not directed to any person or group of persons, it cannot be said [to be] advocating . . . any action" and it did not have a "tendency to lead to violence" (pp. 108–09). As these cases illustrate, the evolution of the exception to free speech protection reveals an effort to reign in attempts to limit its reach.

True Threats and Fighting Words

The "true threat" provides a second important exception to the general invalidity of regulations that prohibit the content of speech. Rather than mere advocacy of illicit action, a true threat involves the actual threat of impending violence. The Supreme Court's decision in *Milk Wagon Drivers Union v. Meadowmoor Dairies* (1941) presents a dramatic illustration of the place of threats and impending violence in First Amendment analysis. In *Milk Wagon*, the Court reviewed an order enjoining (i.e., stopping) protesters from picketing a dairy. While the Court acknowledged that the First Amendment ordinarily protects protesting, it upheld the injunction based on the defendants' prior conduct. The record revealed that multiple incidents of violence had accompanied the defendants' prior protests, including beatings, window smashing, and looting. Because of the violent background of the protesting, the Court found that even peaceful protesting had acquired a coercive taint. The Court concluded that "acts which in isolation are peaceful may be part of a coercive thrust when entangled with acts of violence" (*Milk Wagon Drivers Union v. Meadowmoor Dairies*, 1941, p. 294). The Court held that the First Amendment would not protect such expression simply because protesting constituted speech. Instead, the Court stressed the importance of a more nuanced consideration of context to assess the value of speech: "Utterance in a context of violence can lose its significance as an appeal to reason and become part of an instrument of force" (p. 293). Because they lose that appeal, the Constitution no longer shelters such utterances.

The Court has subsequently affirmed, in various contexts, the general rule that a threat of violence is not protected expression. In *Watts v. United States* (1969, p. 705) the Court upheld the constitutionality of a statute prohibiting a person from knowingly threatening violence upon the president of the United States. Although the Court reversed a conviction that had been erroneously based on the statute at issue, the Court maintained that the statute itself was "certainly" constitutional on its face because such a threat of violence "must be distinguished from what is constitutionally protected speech" (p. 707). In 1992, writing for the majority in *R.A.V. v. City of St. Paul*, Justice Scalia stated that "threats of violence are outside of the First Amendment" because the government has an interest in "protecting individuals from the fear of violence, from the disruption that fear engenders, and from the possibility that the threatened violence will occur" (p. 338). A few years later, the Court reaffirmed the exclusion of true threats from First Amendment protection in the context of abortion clinic protests. In *Madsen v. Women's Health Center* (1994) the Court considered the constitutionality of an injunction creating a "buffer zone" around abortion clinic entrances and driveways. The Court found that, if a protestor's expression was "so infused with violence as to be indistinguishable from a threat of physical harm," the expression was proscribable consistent with the First Amendment (*Madsen v. Women's Health Center*, 1994, p. 774).

This exception covers some forms of what is often referred to as hate speech. More specifically, the First Amendment does not protect face-to-face epithets intended to cause a violent reaction. The words under this exception will tend to incite an immediate assault. The leading case in this area is *Chaplinsky v. New Hampshire* (1942, p. 571). Chaplinsky, a Jehovah's Witness, was proselytizing and distributing religious literature to pedestrians in Rochester, New Hampshire. Although he was engaged in a lawful activity, the crowd disapproved of his message and complained to the city marshal, who in turn warned Chaplinsky. Later that day, Chaplinsky had an altercation with a police officer and was arrested. While being escorted to jail, Chaplinsky encountered the marshal and uttered offen-

sive words against the city and city marshal: "You are a God damned racketeer
. . . the whole government of Rochester are Fascists" (*Chaplinsky v. New Hampshire*, 1942, p. 571). Those words lead to his conviction, which the Supreme Court
would subsequently uphold. In reviewing the case, the Court observed that "it is
well understood that the right of free speech is not absolute at all times and under
all circumstances" (p. 571). Accordingly, the opinion stipulated the existence of

> certain well-defined and narrowly limited classes of speech, the pre-
> vention and punishment of which has never been thought to raise any
> Constitutional problem. These include the lewd and obscene, the pro-
> fane, the libelous, and the insulting or "fighting" words—those which
> by their very utterance inflict injury or tend to incite an immediate
> breach of the peace. (pp. 571–72)

The specified categories did not warrant First Amendment protection, the Court
ruled, because such utterances are no essential part of any exposition of ideas,
and are of such slight social value as a step to truth that any benefit that may be
derived from them is clearly outweighed by the social interest in order and morality. The fighting words referenced by the opinion usually involved face-to-face
encounters and, unlike the clear and present danger test, concerned the specific words of the speaker and not the danger presented by the specific factual
circumstance. The test, according to the *Chaplinsky* opinion, "is what men of
common intelligence would understand would be words likely to cause an average addressee to fight" (Id., p. 573). Because the epithets uttered by defendant
Chaplinsky were "likely to provoke the average person to retaliation," they were
fighting words and, according to the Court, outside of the First Amendment's
protection (*Chaplinsky v. New Hampshire*, 1942, p. 574).

Society's interest in order may supersede the need to protect expression of
a rather broad category of ideas, but the Court has narrowed the fighting words
doctrine, most obviously in *Gooding v. Wilson* (1972). Wilson and a group of
people opposing the Vietnam War were arrested when they blocked the door
so that recruits could not enter the U.S. Army headquarters in Fulton County,
Georgia. Wilson was arrested after he said to one of the officers removing the
protesters, "White son of a bitch, I'll kill you. You son of a bitch, I'll choke you
to death" (*Gooding v. Wilson*, 1972, p. 519 n.1). Wilson was convicted under
a Georgia statute which forbids the use of "opprobrious words or abusive language, tending to cause a breach of the peace" (p. 519). The Supreme Court reversed the conviction. In doing so, the Court only briefly mentioned fighting
words, stating that the holding in *Chaplinsky* was narrow and only prohibited
words which "have a direct tendency to cause acts of violence by the person to
whom, individually, the remark is addressed" (p. 524). The Court's main reason
for overturning the conviction, however, was that the state statute was vague and
overbroad because the definitions of "opprobrious" and "abusive" were broader
than the fighting words definition.

Half a century and many cases after *Chaplinsky*, the Court affirmed that
speech or an act is punishable when it is done with the intent to intimidate. In

that case, *Virginia v. Black* (2003, pp. 347, 361), the Court analyzed the constitutionality of a Virginia law specifically banning cross burning as a threat, which read in part: "It shall be unlawful for any person or persons, with the intent of intimidating any person or group of persons, to burn, or cause to be burned, a cross on the property of another, a highway or other public place" (pp. 348–349). The Court upheld the ban on cross burning with the intent to intimidate. However, the Court also struck down, in a plurality portion of the decision, a provision of the statute that provided that the public burning of a cross was itself *prima facie* evidence of intent to intimidate. The ban on one specific type of threat was justified, the Court found, because the particular type of threat singled out in the statute was an especially intimidating one. However, the plurality refused to accept cross burning itself as *prima facie* evidence of intent to intimidate. The Court rejected the notion that the symbol could in effect be banned entirely by presuming intent to threaten from every burning of a cross and thereby chilling the symbol's use. Cross burning is not per se illegal. Because a burning cross can be banned as a threat when used to intimidate but is otherwise constitutionally protected (symbolic) speech, the First Amendment demands a contextual, individualized analysis before a particular cross burning is punished. The provision permits the Commonwealth to arrest, prosecute, and convict a person based solely on the fact of cross burning itself. It is apparent that the provision as so interpreted "would create an unacceptable risk of the suppression of ideas" (*Virginia v. Black,* 2003, p. 366). The majority of the Court found that the law forbidding cross burning as a form of intimidation was a permissible content based distinction within a category of unprotected speech and upheld the law. The dissenting justices found that the law was an impermissible viewpoint based law. The difference was that the majority considered the law as aimed at the harms of cross burning (threats and intimidation), while the dissenting justices found that the reason for the content discrimination was disapproval of the Ku Klux Klan and its racist message. Despite disagreements when applying the rule that prohibits incitement to violence, no one disputes the validity of the rule itself.

Obscenity

The Supreme Court had remarked in *Chaplinsky v. New Hampshire* (1942, pp. 571–72) that the right of free speech is not absolute; the Court had included lewd, obscene, and profane speech in its short list of categories of speech undeserving of First Amendment protection. The Court offered this conclusion on the rationale that these utterances are no essential part of any exposition of ideas. As a result, these utterances are of such slight social value as a step to truth that the social interest in order and morality clearly outweighs any benefit that may be derived from these expressions.

The Supreme Court did not revisit the constitutionality of obscenity regulations until 15 years later, in *Roth v. United States* (1957). In *Roth,* the Court went beyond mere dicta, and for the first time reached a decision on the issue of obscenity. *Roth* actually involved two different convictions, one from New York dealing with the mailing of obscene advertising and an obscene book and another from California involving lewdly keeping for sale obscene and indecent books and publishing an obscene advertisement in them. The Court began by noting that the obscenity of the material involved in the case was not at issue; rather, the issue was "whether obscenity is utterance within the area of protected speech and press" (p. 481). Acknowledging that "this is the first time the question has been squarely presented to this Court," the Court noted that "expressions found in numerous opinions indicate that this Court has always assumed that obscenity is not protected by the freedoms of speech and press" (p. 481). Circumstances surrounding the ratification of the Constitution, the Court noted, made it apparent that the unconditional phrasing of the First Amendment was not intended to protect every utterance. The Court reasoned as follows:

> All ideas having even the slightest redeeming social importance—unorthodox ideas, controversial ideas, even ideas hateful to the prevailing climate of opinion—have the full protection of the guaranties, unless excludable because they encroach upon the limited area of more important interests. But implicit in the history of the First Amendment is the rejection of obscenity as utterly without redeeming social importance. (p. 484)

The Court proceeded to hold that "obscenity is not within the area of constitutionally protected speech or press" (p. 485).

Importantly, the *Roth* majority narrowed the definition of obscenity as it explained that "sex and obscenity are not synonymous" (p. 487). The Court defined obscene material as "material which deals with sex in a manner appealing to prurient interest" (p. 487). Mere portrayal of sex was not seen as a "sufficient reason to deny material the constitutional protection of freedom of speech and press," because sex "is one of the vital problems of human interest and public concern," meriting freedom of discussion (p. 487). "Prurient" was defined as "material having a tendency to excite lustful thoughts" (p. 487). The Court also provided a standard for distinguishing sex from obscenity: material was obscene if "to the average person, applying contemporary community standards, the dominant theme of the material taken as a whole appeals to prurient interests" (p. 489). Thus, *Roth* upheld the *Chaplinsky* categorization of obscenity, which focuses on catering to prurient interests.

In the years following *Roth*, the Supreme Court struggled to define obscenity, vacillating between often conflicting definitions. In an attempt to extricate itself from a case-by-case obscenity review, the Court undertook to formulate an acceptable definition of obscenity in *Miller v. California* (1973, pp. 23–24). After declaring that the First Amendment does not protect obscene works, the Court proceeded to provide a definition more restrictive than *Roth*'s. The Court stated, in relevant part:

We now confine the permissible scope of such regulation to works which depict or describe sexual conduct. That conduct must be specifically defined by the applicable state law, as written or authoritatively construed. A state offense must also be limited to works which, taken as a whole, appeal to the prurient interest in sex, which portray sexual conduct in a patently offensive way, and which, taken as a whole, do not have serious literary, artistic, political, or scientific value. (p. 24)

As the highly cited but often misunderstood excerpt reveals, the touchstone in obscenity cases is, of course, "sex." As a result, the Supreme Court has retained the *Chaplinsky* categorization of obscenity as being outside of First Amendment protection, but the actual definition of obscenity has been significantly narrowed to sexual conduct.

Since 1973, the Court has embarked on only one significant departure from the *Miller* approach to defining materials obscene enough to warrant prohibition. That prohibition began in 1982, in *New York v. Ferber* (1982, p. 763). In that case, the Supreme Court unanimously upheld a New York law banning child pornography and in the process declared child pornography to be "a category of material outside the protection of the First Amendment" (p. 763). The Court upheld a statute making unlawful "the use of a child in a sexual performance" if the person knows "the character and content thereof he employs, [and] authorizes or induces a child less than sixteen years of age to engage in a sexual performance" (pp. 750–51). The majority contended that the distribution of photographs and films depicting sexual activity by juveniles is intrinsically related to the sexual abuse of children. Because the "prevention of sexual exploitation and abuse of children constitutes a government objective of surpassing importance," the Court maintained that, even if child pornography does not fall within the *Miller* definition of obscenity, states still are entitled to regulate it (*New York v. Ferber*, 1982, p. 757). States are entitled to greater leeway in the regulation of pornographic depictions of children because it is "harmful to the physiological, emotional and mental health of the child" (p. 758).

The Court made clear that the exception for child pornography is separate from the obscenity standard set out in *Miller*. The difference is that the standard set forth in *Miller* "does not reflect the State's particular and more compelling interest in prosecuting those who promote the sexual exploitation of children" (*New York v. Ferber*, 1982, p. 761). As a result, the *Ferber* exception differs from *Miller*'s exception in that it does not require prurient interest, patently offensive material, "and the material at issue need not be considered as a whole" (p. 764). The Court ruled that child pornography is unprotected speech because "the evil to be restricted so overwhelmingly outweighs the expressive interests" (pp. 763–64). The overall goal set out in *Ferber*, then, is to protect minors without attempting to restrict the expression of ideas. Importantly, the Court emphasized that "whatever overbreadth may exist should be cured through case-by-case analysis of the fact situations" (pp. 773–74). The Court would later add more rationales for the child pornography exception, such as "the materials produced by child pornographers permanently record the victim's abuse" (*Osborne v. Ohio*, 1990, p. 110). These other cases, like *Ferber* itself, make clear that the Court has added child pornography to the *Chaplinsky* list of speech that may be regulated, but that regulation may be closely scrutinized on a case-by-case basis.

Ferber's apparent extension of *Miller* and *Chaplinsky* may appear expansive but, in practice, it remains a limited exception. The Court consistently has resisted efforts to expand the category of child pornography. Recently, in *Ashcroft v. Free Speech Coalition* (2002, p. 249), the Court granted First Amendment protection to virtual child pornography—pornography in which adult actors portray juveniles or in which computers modify images to make them appear like real children. The images at issue in the case did "not involve, let alone harm, any children in the production process" (p. 241). The Court made the important distinction that minors must actually be at risk of being harmed in the production of the pornography in order for the speech to be unprotected; "the creation of the speech is itself the crime of child abuse" (p. 254). *Ferber's* judgment about child pornography was based on how it was made, not on what it communicated. Using virtual minors certainly does not involve the use of real children, and therefore minors cannot be harmed (e.g., sexually abused) in the production. The Court observed that the "prospect of crime, however, by itself does not justify laws suppressing protected speech" (*Ashcroft v. Free Speech Coalition*, 2002, p. 245). The Court reiterated the important principle that "speech may not be prohibited because it concerns subjects offending our sensibilities" (p. 245). Notably, this case restricts the child pornography exception to a very narrow class of cases. More relevant to our analysis below and in the next chapter, the Court notes that the objective of shielding children does not suffice to support a blanket ban if the protection can be accomplished by a less restrictive alternative.

Indecent Speech

Obscenity cases relate quite closely to the Court's responses to indecent materials. Although the cases in this area are quite numerous, two lines of cases illustrate this exception's significance. The first line of cases involves child protection. In *Ginsberg v. New York* (1968), the Supreme Court held that the State may prohibit the sale to minors of speech that is obscene as to minors, even if the speech would be protected as to adults. The Court held that "even where there is an invasion of protected freedoms 'the power of the State to control the conduct of children reaches beyond the scope of its authority over adults'" (p. 638). This control is of determinative significance in cases involving minor's speech. Under *Ginsberg*, child pornography is unprotected speech and the State is not required to provide "empirical" evidence that exposure to sexually explicit materials may harm children, because legislators are permitted to assume such harm based on common cultural understandings. This exception, therefore, makes the regulation of child pornography a relatively easy task. This test has been the subject of intense controversy and sometimes even ridicule. But, the general rule remains that indecent speech that becomes obscene for a group may be restricted and controlled for the benefit of that group.

The indecency exception was somewhat expanded when the Court considered the emergence of broadcast media. That consideration led to the rule that the government can regulate indecency on broadcast television and radio stations without violating broadcasters' First Amendment rights. Most notably, the Court in *FCC v. Pacifica Foundation* (1978, p. 750) held that the unique qualities of the broadcast media justified the "special treatment of indecent broadcasting." The Court ruled that the Federal Communications Commission (FCC) had the power to regulate broadcast material that was indecent but not obscene, despite the fact that the First Amendment protects non-obscene speech. Specifically, the Court upheld FCC action against a radio station that had broadcast a monologue by comedian George Carlin entitled "Filthy Words" which, while indecent and profane, was not obscene. The Court justified its holding on two principal grounds. First, the broadcast media are "uniquely pervasive" in the lives of all Americans, present not only in public but in the privacy of the home (p. 748). Second, "broadcasting is uniquely accessible to children" (p. 749). Because certain forms of protected speech may nonetheless be withheld from children, special restrictions on indecent broadcasting were justified in light of this unique accessibility.

The holding in *Ginsberg* that protected speech may be restricted to make it inaccessible to children was the principal support for the unique accessibility justification. In explaining this justification, the *Pacifica* Court characterized *Ginsberg* as holding that "the government's interest in the 'well-being of its youth' and in supporting 'parents' claim to authority in their own household' justified the regulation of otherwise protected expression" (*FCC v. Pacifica Foundation*,1978, pp. 749–50). In addition to making use of the *Ginsberg* rationale, the Court noted that broadcasting, as a medium, traditionally has received the most limited First Amendment protection, for four primary reasons related to the technological characteristics of the medium itself. First, the scarcity of the broadcast spectrum requires that those allowed to make use of this resource do so in a way that serves the public interest. Second, broadcasting is pervasive. Third, the practicalities of a continuous broadcast make prior warnings about forthcoming content ineffective, thus increasing the invasive nature of a potentially offensive broadcast. Lastly, broadcasting is uniquely accessible to children who in many cases are unsupervised by parents. Thus, sanctions against a radio broadcaster for a broadcast that was not obscene did not violate the First Amendment. The *Pacifica* decision thus enabled the FCC to regulate indecent and profane broadcasts despite Supreme Court precedent holding these forms of speech to be constitutionally protected.

The Supreme Court has used a medium-specific approach as a basis to analyze the rights and interests at stake in other efforts to censure indecent materials. This approach recognizes that each method of expression tends to present its own peculiar problems. Given differences in medium, for example, the Court has been unwilling to extend the *Pacifica* limitations beyond broadcast media.

In other contexts, efforts to limit often are deemed unconstitutional in that they run the risk of sweeping too broadly. For example, the Court struck down another indecency-based FCC regulation in *Sable Communications of California, Inc., v. FCC* (1989), which involved a criminal ban on pornographic telephone services. The Court found that Congress's conclusory consideration of the failures of less restrictive regulations to protect minors from pornographic phone messages was insufficient to justify an outright criminal ban. The Court's ruling was not surprising. The Court had long established this principle in *Butler v. Michigan* (1957). *Butler* had invalidated a Michigan statute that had made it a crime to sell to the general public literature that was inappropriate for minors. The *Butler* Court had noted that the "incidence of this enactment is to reduce the adult population of Michigan to reading only what is fit for children" (*Butler v. Michigan*, 1957, p. 383). The Court would routinely return to this language to invalidate many child-protection censorship laws on the ground that the laws unduly burden adult's access to speech (see, e.g., *Denver Area Educational Telecommunications Consortium v. FCC*, 1996; *Bolger v. Youngs Drug Products Corporation*, 1983).

The significance of the medium continues. Cases involving the cable industry are illustrative. In *United States v. Playboy Entertainment Group* (2000, p. 813), for example, the Court took special notice of the characteristics of the medium of cable television to "inform [the] assessment of the interests at stake." Interestingly, the Court pointed out that the nature of a particular medium can justify restrictions that might be unacceptable when applied to other media, but in this case the medium-specific approach led it to strike down restrictions similar to those approved in other contexts. The Court distinguished *Pacifica*, and found dispositive a crucial technological difference between cable television and broadcasting—the ability to block specific programs at the request of the user. More specifically, this feature of cable television made possible a plausible, less restrictive alternative to the regulation at issue, which required cable operators to fully scramble channels displaying adult content or limit the display of such content to certain hours.

Also illustrative are cases involving the Internet, most notably *Reno v. American Civil Liberties Union* (1997). Immediately after the Communications Decency Act (CDA) of 1996 became law, plaintiffs challenged the constitutionality of two of its provisions. The first challenged provision prohibited the "knowing transmission of obscene or indecent messages to any recipient under 18 years of age" (*Reno v. American Civil Liberties Union*, 1997, p. 859). The second provision prohibited the "knowing, sending, or displaying of patently offensive messages in a manner that is available to a person that is under 18 years of age" (p. 859). The Court analyzed the particular qualities of the Internet as a medium and distinguished it from broadcast media. Among other differences, the Court noted the absence of a tradition of government supervision over the Internet, and the fact that the medium was not as invasive or subject to accidental exposure to unwanted material as is broadcast. The Court then determined that the ambiguities in the statute's language, which went beyond the inherent "vagueness" of the *Miller* obscenity standard, would provoke uncertainty among speakers and the imposed criminal penalties would further exacerbate the chilling effect. The Court found the potential burdens on adult speech unjustified because "less restrictive alternatives would be at least as effective in achieving the legitimate purposes the statute was enacted to serve" (p. 874). The Court then held that the CDA placed too heavy a burden on lawful adult speech (including sexually explicit indecent speech), which made its provisions overbroad.

Offensive Speech

Pursuant to *Chaplinsky*, profanity remained outside First Amendment protection until the 1971 Supreme Court decision of *Cohen v. California* (1971). Cohen had been convicted of disturbing the peace for wearing a jacket that displayed the phrase "Fuck the Draft" (p. 16). Justice Harlan, writing for the majority, assumed Cohen's conviction was predicated on the "asserted offensiveness of the words Cohen used to convey his message" and not on Cohen's conduct (p. 18). In fact, other than the content and expression of his message, Cohen was quite respectful. When he entered the courtroom, Cohen stood in the back with his jacket removed and folded over his arm. A judge, alerted by a policeman to the jacket, declined to follow the officer's request to hold Cohen in contempt. Cohen was not arrested until he had left the courtroom. The police officer seemed to be the only one who had a problem with the jacket. Given that the language did not fall into the *Chaplinsky* categories of obscenity or fighting words, the singular issue involved determining the constitutionality of profanity regulation and, thus, whether "the States, acting as guardians of public morality, may properly remove this offensive word from the public vocabulary" (pp. 22–23). Responding in the negative, Justice Harlan maintained that

> The State has no right to cleanse public debate to the point where it is
> grammatically palatable to the most squeamish among us. . . . [W]hile
> the particular four-letter word being litigated here is perhaps more
> distasteful than most others of its genre, it is nevertheless often true
> that one man's vulgarity is another's lyric. (p. 25)

This anticensorship rule means that the government may not suppress speech simply because it disapproves of a message or finds it offensive. As Justice Brennan explained in *Texas v. Johnson* (1989, p. 414), the case invalidating a conviction for burning a flag during the Republican National Convention, it is a "bedrock principle" of the First Amendment that "the government may not prohibit the expression of an idea simply because society finds the idea . . . offensive or disagreeable." The Court is aware that such offensive ideas can be emotionally disturbing to people but it counsels those disturbed to "avert their eyes" or to counter the offensive speech with more speech. The Supreme Court has, therefore, removed profanity from *Chaplinsky's* list, deeming it a fully protected class of expression.

Importantly, the state may still regulate speech it finds offensive, but it must only do so in a round-about way, such as by regulating its secondary effects. Indeed, this has emerged as the rule, most notably in efforts to zone adult entertainment. Central to the Court's adult-entertainment case law is the interpretation of adult-entertainment zoning ordinances as content-neutral rather than content-based. A content-neutral law controls expression without regard to the speech itself or the speech's impact. In this sense, laws that regulate the time, place, and manner of speech, but not the actual speech itself, are content neutral. Therefore, an adult-entertainment zoning law that regulates the location of a business is said to regulate only the secondary effects of such speech, rather than the speech itself. In contrast, a content-based law singles out certain messages, topics, or forms of expression for regulation and restriction. In theory, the controlling question for determining whether a law is content neutral should be whether the application of the law turns on the message or content of the speech. The Supreme Court's analysis, however, is often inconsistent with this approach. Instead of analyzing the law on its face to determine whether it singles out certain speech, the Court often considers the intent or purpose of the legislation. In these instances, a content-based law that is motivated by an apparent content-neutral purpose—such as the regulation of only the time, place, and manner of speech—is considered content neutral, even if the law is facially content based.

The U.S. Supreme Court's most complete discussion of this analysis took place in *City of Renton v. Playtime Theatres, Inc.* (1986). In that case, the Court upheld the zoning ordinance in Renton, Washington, which effectively concentrated all adult-entertainment businesses in certain areas of the city. The city's ordinance prohibited such theaters from locating less than 1,000 feet from residential zones, single- or multiple-family dwellings, churches, or parks, and less than one mile from schools. The Court held the law to be content-neutral because the City Council intended only to regulate the negative secondary effects of adult entertainment, rather than the actual expression, by restricting the locations in which such businesses operated. In other words, the legislative intent, rather than the statutory language, contributed to the law's content neutrality.

Having established that the ordinance was content-neutral, the Court then turned to the two-part test for content-neutral laws—whether the law was designed to serve a substantial government interest, and whether it permitted adequate alternative avenues of communication. It was clear to the Court that the ordinance served a substantial government interest. In *Renton*, the city articulated several intangible secondary effects including "degradation of the community standard of morality," a "degrading effect upon the relationship between spouses," and a "loss of sensitivity to . . . the concept of non-aggressive, consensual sexual relations" (*Renton v. Playtime Theatres, Inc.*, 1986, p. 59). The city also articulated several quantifiable secondary effects, including increases in crime, prostitution, rape, incest, and assaults in the area. The Court majority made no distinction between the two types of secondary effects. The Court only noted that the zoning ordinances were passed after a "long period of study and discussion of the problems of adult movie theaters" (p. 60). In terms of the second prong, the Court noted that the city had made "some areas" open to adult-entertainment businesses wishing to engage in protected expression and that these areas provided a "reasonable opportunity" to operate such businesses. Then, in determining whether reasonable alternative avenues existed, the Court determined that even though "practically none" of the land zoned for adult businesses was "for sale or lease" there still existed reasonable alternative avenues for speech (p. 51). The Court was not concerned about the land's lack of commercial or economic viability. It only required that the land was theoretically open to adult businesses in the zoning scheme. In evaluating the case, courts make special note of the significance of the statute's purpose. Lines of cases have rejected efforts to bar offensive speech and conduct similar to those zoned out. Most notably, in *Schad v. Borough of Mount Ephraim* (1981), the Court struck down an effort to prohibit nude dancing by enacting a zoning ordinance prohibiting any live entertainment, adult or otherwise. This line of cases is quite significant, for it reveals the extent to which some laws could, in a real sense, regulate speech when that regulation can be deemed as incidental to another compelling concern.

The Emerging (and Often Ignored) Right to Receive Information

Generally, the Supreme Court interprets the First Amendment of the U.S. Constitution to imply a negative right that prevents the government from placing obstacles in the path of constitutionally protected speech. This interpretation is consistent with the widely accepted view that the Constitution focuses on the right to be free from government intrusions (negative rights) and that it generally does not confer an affirmative right to command government action or aid (positive rights). As a result, First Amendment jurisprudence focuses on the rights of the speaker, on preventing the government from restraining protected speech. To say, then, that people have a right to express ideas is not the same as saying that people have a right to access those ideas, but the former has generally implied the latter. This line of thinking appropriately suggests that it is generally unnecessary for those who oppose regulation of speech to rest their arguments on the right to receive information where the rights of speakers themselves are strong enough to be undiminished. Not surprisingly, then, the notion of a right to receive speech tends to be invoked where courts have, in the past, limited speakers' rights. Given that these instances involve speech that gains less protection, it is not surprising to find that the right to receive information tends to be less robust in those contexts. Given that, as we will see in the next chapter, adolescents' First Amendment rights are subject to important restrictions and thus likely to raise concerns about the right to receive information, it is important to understand the important strands of cases dealing with this right.

The line of cases that views the right to receive information as a corollary of the right to speak (meaning that audience rights stem from speaker rights) provides the strongest protection for the right to hear. The common theme in this line of cases involves the government's attempt to prevent otherwise protected speech, such as through specific criminal statutes, censorship of mail, and limitations on the expressions of corporations. In balancing the competing interests in such cases, the Court finds that the government customarily has no place regulating the dissemination of information. Several important cases contributed to this development.

The right to receive information to prevent governmental obstacles to the dissemination of information roots back to the 1940s. The first time the Court considered the right to receive information was in *Martin v. City of Struthers* (1943). That case involved a Jehovah's Witness who walked door to door ringing doorbells to publicize a religious meeting, and in doing so, violated a city ordinance barring the distribution of handbills, circulars, or other advertisements through door-to-door solicitation. In announcing it opinion, the Court stressed the broad scope of the freedom of speech and press and found that it "embraces the right to distribute literature and necessarily protects the right to receive it" (*Martin v. City of Struthers*, 1943, p. 143). To reach this conclusion, the Court balanced the rights of the speaker and the rights of the individual householder against the interests of the entire community. The Court found that the ordinance stood as a barrier to protected communications, that individual householders must be given the opportunity to choose whether to listen to the speaker's message, rather than having the community choose for them. The Court characterized the door-to-door distributors as useful members of society engaged in the dissemination of ideas in accordance with the best tradition of free discussion. The Court emphasized that "freedom to distribute information to every citizen wherever he desires to receive it is so clearly vital to the preservation of a free society that, putting aside reasonable police and health regulations of time and manner of distribution, it must be fully preserved" (pp. 146–47).

Although not expressly relying on the right to receive information in its holding, *Martin* represents the first step towards the Court's recognition of the right. The Court envisioned the right to receive information as one that allows a free exchange of ideas without government intervention to mold the nature of those ideas or to protect citizens from undesirable information. The focus on the exchange of ideas was central to another case from this era, *Thomas v. Collins* (1945). In that case, a Texas district court had enjoined a union president and labor organizer from soliciting members for labor union membership. The labor organizer's actions had violated a Texas statute because he had failed to obtain an organizer's card. Because Thomas had not registered with the state, the district court prevented him from making a public speech regarding the merits of joining a union. The Supreme Court emphasized Thomas's right to speak and the workers' right to hear his message. The Court found the restraint "so destructive of the right of public discussion" as to constitute unconstitutional restraint on free speech (*Thomas v. Collins*, 1945, p. 537). Courts and commentators often cite both *Martin* and *Thomas* as the precursors to the right to receive information and use them to strike down restraints on free speech.

It would be two decades before the Court would actually use the right to receive information as the basis of an opinion protecting free speech. The Court did so in *Lamont v. Postmaster General* (1965). At issue in *Lamont* was a statute that required postal workers to separate and hold "communist political propaganda" until delivery was requested by the recipient. The Court struck down the restriction on mail delivery as an unnecessary restraint on free speech and the corollary right to receive information. The Court found that, by requiring an additional step by the addressee to obtain his mail, the "regime of this Act is at war with the 'uninhibited, robust, and wide-open' debate and discussion that are contemplated by the First Amendment" (*Lamont v. Postmaster General,* 1965, p. 308). The Court equated the government's attempt in *Lamont* to control the flow of the mail to the attempt in *Thomas* to control the flow of ideas; the government was indirectly burdening the flow of information as it did in *Thomas*. This burden constituted an impermissible restraint on the recipient's right to receive information. This was the first case in which an intended recipient of speech, rather than a speaker, sought to invalidate a law for violating the recipient's First Amendment rights and the first case in which the Court held that requiring an affirmative action to obtain delivery of information unconstitutionally abridged the addressee's First Amendment right to receive speech.

This line of cases gained increasing significance that very same year when the Court announced one of the most important cases detailing the nature of the right to privacy. In *Griswold v. Connecticut* (1965), directors of the Planned Parenthood who had given information, instruction, and other medical advice to married couples concerning birth control were convicted under a Connecticut law that criminalized the use and dissemination of contraceptives. In ruling for the directors, the Court demonstrated its concern not only with protecting the First Amendment rights of doctors and patients, but also the right to privacy for actions occurring in a citizen's home. The Court found that the government had created a barrier between a citizen and constitutionally protected information relating to the private affairs of a husband and wife, thus violating the citizen's right to receive information. The Court found that

> The State may not, consistently with the spirit of the First Amendment, contract the spectrum of available knowledge. The right of freedom of speech and press includes not only the right to utter or to print, but the right to distribute, the right to receive, the right to read and freedom of inquiry, freedom of thought, and freedom to teach. (p. 482)

The Court construed the right to receive requested, constitutionally protected information as one form of facilitating a citizen's right to privacy in conducting his personal affairs.

The right to receive information also gained significance in the manner it was the express basis of the holding in leading obscenity cases. We already have seen that the Constitution generally does not protect materials that meet the legal definition of obscenity *(Roth v. United States,* 1957; *Miller v. California,*

1973). Yet, the Court ventured into new territory and recognized the right to receive ideas in this area of jurisprudence that does not typically protect such ideas. In *Stanley v. Georgia* (1969), the Supreme Court overturned a statute criminalizing "mere private possession" of legally obscene material for personal use. The appellant, who had been convicted under the statute after the police found three obscene movies in his bedroom, argued, among other things, that he possessed "the right to read . . . what he pleases" (*Stanley v. Georgia*, 1969, p. 565). The Court agreed. The majority limited the question to whether "mere private possession of obscene material" could be made a crime, and concluded that it could not, based on the primacy of an individual's "fundamental" right "to read or observe what he pleases" (p. 568). "This right to receive information and ideas," the majority emphasized, "is fundamental to our free society" and that right to receive ideas applies "regardless of their social worth" (p. 564). The Court based its holding on the right to receive information, coupled with the "fundamental . . . right to be free, except in very limited circumstances, from unwanted governmental intrusions into one's privacy" (p. 564). Given the nature of the regulation regarding speech that is not constitutionally protected and the Court's statement that "it is now well established that the Constitution protects the right to receive information and ideas," the Court gave the right its strongest endorsement in an area where it typically views the government's interests in restricting speech as paramount (p. 564). Through *Stanley*, then, the Court consistently reaffirmed the First Amendment right to receive information as an individual right against the government's interest, even the broad "public interest," in suppressing obscene speech.

The right to receive ideas also finds support in leading cases involving commercial speech, all of which highlight the significance of limiting the state's paternalistic role. Most notably, a statute in this area's leading case, *Virginia State Board of Pharmacy v. Virginia Citizens Consumer Council, Inc.* (1976), prevented pharmacists from "publishing, advertising, or promoting" the price of a prescription drug (p. 750). The Court found that the statute impermissibly restrained commercial speech and the patients' right to receive information. This case both affirmed the protection of commercial speech and the Court's continued protection of the right to receive information. The Court opined that freedom of speech presupposes a willing speaker and that, "where a speaker exists, as is the case here, the protection afforded is to the communication, to its source and to its recipients both" (p. 756). Finding a firm basis in the free flow of ideas and information, the Court concluded that commercial speech gains protection in order to shelter consumers' right to information. Sheltering consumers from information was one form of a paternalistic government the Court was unwilling to accept. Rather than allowing consumers to evaluate the information prohibited by the statute, the government was making that decision for consumers, thus keeping them in ignorance. The Court found this type of restriction an unacceptable way for the government to achieve its interests, as it held that governmental barriers to dissemination of this kind of information must not be tolerated. The Court adopted a similar rationale in *First National Bank v. Bel-*

lotti (1978). In that case, the Court addressed the constitutionality of a Massachusetts statute that prohibited businesses from publicizing views regarding questions posed on an election ballot. Protecting corporate expression and the rights of businesses to disseminate information, the Court struck down the law. In discussing the reasoning behind the holding, the Court found that "the First Amendment goes beyond protection of the press and the self-expression of individuals to prohibit government from limiting the stock of information from which members of the public may draw" (*First National Bank v. Bellotti*, 1978, p. 783). The public has a right to gather all possible information, despite its source, to make an effective judgment in private affairs, thus promoting and enhancing the idea of self-government.

The concept of the right to receive information captured the approval of every justice who participated in the Supreme Court's consideration of *Bolger v. Youngs Drug Products Corporation* (1983), even though the concept was not expressly before the Court in that case. This right sounds an implicit theme both in the majority opinion and in a concurring opinion. The precise question before the Court in *Bolger* involved the right of a contraceptive manufacturer to mail to the public unsolicited pamphlets, described as "informational," which concerned the general availability of prophylactics and the prevention of sexually transmitted diseases. The Court upheld the rights of the commercial speaker, holding that the importance of conveying "truthful information relevant to important social issues" outweighed the government's asserted interests (*Bolger v. Youngs Drug Products Corporation*, 1983, p. 69). The Court examined the importance of the right of parents to receive information that might help them in carrying out some of their most difficult responsibilities, concluding that the statute prohibiting the unsolicited mailing of contraception advertisements was defective in part because it denied parents access to important information and in part because it denied teenagers access to critical knowledge (pp. 74–75). The concurring opinion emphasized that although parents might be entitled to the government's support in limiting the kinds of materials that reached the family mailbox, as the government had argued in the case, the statute at issue inhibited the interests of parents because the law denied "parents access to information about birth control that might help them make informed decisions" about what to tell their children (p. 79). The Court, then, has embraced a right to receive at least some types of information, including information some would deem problematic in the hands of adolescents.

The second line of cases presents the rare case where the government, as a result of limitations on broadcast frequencies, will require the press to act affirmatively and make information available to the public. For example, in a handful of cases, the Court has used the right to receive information to require an affirmative act by speakers. The leading case in this area, *Red Lion Broadcasting v. Federal Communications Commission* (1969), involved a Constitutional challenge to the federal regulations and statutes requiring that broadcasted discussions of public issues be presented on broadcast stations, and that each of those issues must be given fair coverage, such as requiring broadcasters to provide candidates with equal air time to discuss their views. Relying heavily on the scarcity of broadcast frequencies, the Court upheld the constitutionality of the statutes. The Court found that the laws enhanced the freedoms associated with freedom of speech and the press. The crux of the argument rested on the notion that the right of free speech does not allow a broadcaster to ignore the free speech of others given the scarcity of the broadcast frequencies. The Court posited that "it is the purpose of the First Amendment to preserve an uninhibited marketplace of ideas in which truth will ultimately prevail, rather than to countenance monopolization of that market, whether it be by the Government itself or a private licensee" (*Red Lion Broadcasting v. Federal Communications Commission,* 1969, p. 390). Essentially, the government's mandate required an affirmative act on the part of the broadcasters, essentially taking away the broadcasters' right to make certain choices relating to content. The Court found that "it is the right of the public to receive suitable access to social, political, esthetic, moral, and other ideas and experiences which is crucial here. That right may not constitutionally be abridged either by Congress or by the FCC" (p. 390). In another medium, this analysis would more than likely fail, and actually has failed (see *Miami Herald Publishing Co. Division of Knight Newspapers, Inc. v. Tornillo,* 1974). Broadcast media is different from other media, a difference that allows the government to intervene and ensure dissemination of all viewpoints.

A third line of cases permits audience use of the right to receive information to claim access to information in the government's possession. Cases involving library censorship provide the most illustrative examples. The leading case in this area, *Board of Education v. Pico* (1982), involved libraries under state control. In this case, the Court encountered a local New York board of education decision to remove certain "objectionable" books from the libraries of the junior and senior high schools. The school board made a decision to remove the books in order to "protect the children in our schools from this moral danger" (*Board of Education v. Pico,* 1982, p. 857). All of the books were constitutionally protected and did not fall into any of the categories of unprotected speech. Although the Court recognized the school board's broad discretion in making content-based education decisions, it also confirmed secondary students' right to receive information through reading as an essential part of a student's freedom to inquire. The Court reaffirmed the Constitutional protection of the right to receive information:

> This right is an inherent corollary of the rights of free speech and press that are explicitly guaranteed by the Constitution, in two senses. First, the right to receive ideas follows ineluctably from the sender's First Amendment right to send them: The right of freedom of speech and press embraces the right to distribute literature, and necessarily protects the right to receive it. The dissemination of ideas can accomplish nothing if otherwise willing addressees are not free to receive and consider them. It would be a barren marketplace of ideas that had only sellers and no buyers. (p. 867)

Once the library makes the books available, their removal may implicate the right to receive information. Generally, once the government chooses to make the information available, the right to receive that information hampers the government from later taking that information away from the public.

Although the above opinions may represent a strong application of the right to receive information, it is important to note their limits. First, the decisions themselves often are quite narrow. In *Pico*, for example, the Court qualified the right by narrowly holding that the student's First Amendment right is only violated when the decision to remove a book is provoked by the school board's aversion to the ideas pronounced in the works in question. Although even the dissent recognized the right to receive ideas in a narrow set of circumstances, the Court's reasoning in *Pico* narrowed the right it was exploring to the context of school libraries. As a result, many of the cases that do not directly present issues of the right to express opinions are sometimes vulnerable and context driven.

A second limitation of the line of cases finding a right to information returns us to our discussion of government subsidies. Recall, for example, that the Supreme Court in *Rust v. Sullivan* (1991) upheld the regulations that prohibit employees of Title X funded clinics from discussing abortion with their patients. The Court rejected the First and Fifth Amendment challenges brought by clinics and their doctors, reasoning that the regulations were merely a constitutional refusal by government to subsidize the delivery of abortion information. According to the majority, the government is not denying a benefit to anyone, but instead simply insists that public funds be spent for their authorized purposes. Although the regulations subsequently were repealed, the *Rust* decision remains a powerful defense of government restrictions on speech. Similarly, in *United States v. American Library Association, Inc.* (2003), the Court sustained a facial challenge to the constitutionality of the Children's Internet Protection Act (CIPA). CIPA was designed to assist federal public libraries in providing Internet access to library patrons. The government had conditioned funding on the library's installing filtering software designed to prevent access to obscenity and any other information deemed harmful to children. The primary issue in the case revolved around whether CIPA's filtering requirement violated the First Amendment rights of the libraries to choose content and also the First Amendment rights of the patrons to receive information. The Supreme Court, in a plurality opinion, upheld the constitutionality of CIPA, finding no impermissible restraints on First Amendment rights. Only the concurring opinion recognized the right to receive information, but it ultimately found the limitation permissible in light of finding no other means to filter the undesired information in furtherance of the CIPA's goals.

Lastly, a few years after *Stanley* and *Lamont*, the Court decided *Kleindienst v. Mandel* (1972), a case illustrative of the limited right to receive ideas when the speaker has no right to express those ideas. In that case, Mandel, a scholar residing in Belgium, was invited to speak at numerous symposiums and engagements about his Marxist theories. The claimants—Mandel, various professors, and U.S. citizens—challenged the government's denial of his visa. The crux of the claim was that the professors were denied the freedom to engage in a free and open academic exchange with Mandel, violating their First Amendment rights to hear Mandel express his views. The Court recognized the interest of the public right to receive information, but it still upheld the government's plenary authority to control the country's borders. The government's interest prevailed even though denial of Mandel's visa stemmed from a dislike of his political views. The Court simply declined to balance the right to receive information against the "plenary" power of the government to exclude aliens. This holding demonstrates one situation in which the balance between the public interest and Congress' plenary power favors the latter. Although the case appears to give short shrift to any right to receive information, the Court did recognize the right to receive information and rejected the government's claim that the entry involved only action, not speech, and that American scholars had alternative access to Mandel's ideas. The Court relied instead on the Attorney General's determination that Mandel had abused his privilege in previous visits: "What First Amendment or other grounds may be available for attacking exercise of discretion for which no justification whatsoever is advanced is a question we neither address nor decide in this case" (*Kleindienst v. Mandel*, 1972, p. 770). Even cases like *Kleindienst*, then, affirm that the implicit right to know accompanies the explicit right to speak.

Discerning Free Speech Methodologies

We already have discerned important fluctuations in the extent to which the Court differently protects different speech. The Court does seem to favor consistently some speech over others; but the Court also often shifts the extent to which it views speech, and the medium of such speech, as worth protecting. The Court routinely floats different principles for different problems. Conceptually, however, we can decipher two broad approaches used to determine the type of speech deemed worthy of protection under the First Amendment: absolutism and balancing. The Court recognizes that each approach has its benefits and limitations, but jurisprudence does seem to move entire areas of speech protections toward categorical balancing.

As we have seen in our brief review of commentators' efforts to develop First Amendment jurisprudence, absolutism has had convincing champions. It seems quite appealing to have categories determined in advance; it provides predictability and curbs the discretion of lawmakers, administrators and the judiciary to limit speech recognized as worth protecting. The Court's First Amendment jurisprudence, however, has never guaranteed any inviolate sphere of speech. The Court has never embraced this approach in spite of the apparent absolutism from the phrase "no law abridging the freedom of speech." Case law makes quite clear that even political speech, the speech deemed most fundamental to democratic life, can be prohibited by the government when the government presents a compelling state interest. The Court, for example, has upheld a state's prohibition of campaign solicitation within 100 feet of a polling place (*Burson v. Freeman*, 1992) and has upheld federal ceilings on campaign contributions (*Buckley v. Valeo*, 1976). Such cases highlight well the limit of even the most protected speech and the reality that no speech enjoys absolute protection.

Instead of adopting absolutism, the Court embraces balancing methodologies to discern what type of speech deserves protection. Ultimately, this approach places great weight on judges to interpret cases through a sensitive weighing of fact-specific values rather than being constrained by strict rule-based precedents. Although judges who engage in balancing still observe *stare decisis*, unfettered balancing can lead judges to distinguish prior free speech cases on the basis of specific facts. This fact-specific approach has important limitations. It fails to offer adequate certainty to speakers who cannot know how judges are likely to decide under specific circumstances. The approach can also lead to an under-valuing of free speech given the apparent discretion given to individual judges. In addition, granting this discretion to unelected judges has the disadvantage of being somewhat undemocratic. Such criticisms have considerable merit. When no rules fetter the balancing process, judges and other administrators run the risk of inserting their own ideological predispositions into free speech analyses. Yet, the balancing approach may provide judges with the flexibility needed to decide difficult cases correctly. Equally importantly, not forcing rigid decision making may facilitate democratic deliberation as it allows speech into civic discourse. Given the potential dangers and benefits to balancing, then, it is not surprising to find an emergence of several balancing approaches that aim to temper limitations.

The Court uses two main balancing methodologies: ad hoc and categorical. In ad hoc balancing, the Court weighs the value of speech against the various other competing interests in a particular case, such as the need for social order, an unsullied reputation, a proper use of public resources, privacy, or crime reduction. Under this approach, the Court determines which of two conflicting interests demands the greater protection under the presented circumstances. Although the Supreme Court must always weigh fact-specific values in resolving free speech cases, the Court often adopts a categorical First Amendment methodology. Under this approach, the Court balances the value of free speech against competing interests only in an initial case that defines a category of speech as constitutionally unprotected or protected under a rule asserted at the conclusion of the balancing. Jurists then apply the rule to subsequent cases and need not engage in ad hoc balancing because prior cases establishing the category already have weighted relevant values. Consequently, jurists confronting important First Amendment cases must determine whether speech falls into a previously identified, unprotected category, but need not place a "value" on that particular speech in light of the specific facts of each case. A look at Supreme Court precedents reveals considerable use of a categorical balancing methodology, so much so that, as we have seen, several categories emerge that are deemed as either inside or outside of First Amendment protection. These categories, however, still do appear in a state of flux, for the legal system needs to respond and adapt to technological and social developments.

Determining the State's Burden in its Efforts to Limit Speech

Great significance attaches to the extent to which a category of speech is deemed worthy of protection. If the speech is to be protected highly, the government undertakes a heavier burden in efforts to limit it. This simple rule emerges from the manner the Court's current constitutional doctrine tends to describe disputes between the state and individuals as clashes between an individual's constitutional "right" and a societal interest in limiting that right for the broader good. The greater the intrusion on constitutionally favored rights, the greater the state's burden to justify such an intrusion. The Court has developed constitutional doctrine that provides a metric to analyze efforts that seek to limit different rights. Generally, as the Court progressively deems burdened rights as more fundamental or otherwise more worth protecting, the Court requires progressively stronger governmental reasons to justify an action. This metric supports and develops a standard of review that may seem rather simple and easily applicable, but great debate continues regarding whether the Court (and different justices constituting it) systematically uses different standards of protection.

Standards of Review in Constitutional Cases

As a whole, constitutional jurisprudence reveals three analytic levels that include their own standards of review meant to guide courts as they sort legal disputes into categories that require varying degrees of justification for governments to burden or alter the involved rights. The first, "strict scrutiny," is the highest standard that the Court employs to assess the validity of government regulations and is the most exacting standard of constitutional review. To survive constitutional challenge under the strict scrutiny test, the regulation must be narrowly tailored to advance a compelling state interest. Very few laws survive this test, which represents very active judicial review and scrutiny of a state's claims and the law itself. The test is so difficult to satisfy that it has become famously known as strict in theory and fatal in fact. Second and in contrast, the weakest or least demanding test is the "rational basis" test. Under the rational basis test, the Court simply asks whether it is conceivable that a regulation or classification bears a rational relationship to a legitimate governmental end permitted by the Constitution. So long as it is arguable, or "rational," that the legislative branch of government had a legitimate basis for creating the classification, a court will support the law. Couched between these two extremes is the third, "intermediate scrutiny" test. By the terms of that test, the government must satisfy the courts that a regulation is substantially related to an important asserted governmental objective or social policy. Though descriptively vague, intermediate scrutiny becomes conceptually clearer when viewed in conjunction with the two alternative standards of review. Application of either rational basis review or strict scrutiny virtually preordains a case's outcome. Intermediate scrutiny falls between these two extremes: rather than assuming a strong initial advantage for either side, this level of scrutiny seeks to even the playing field on which conflicting state and private interests battle. The approach ultimately balances the asserted state interests against the asserted private interests. Under this standard of review, the Court possesses a great deal of freedom, as it is free to balance the private and state interests involved with no clear rules detailing its approach. The likely implementation of intermediate scrutiny thus adds to the already significant discretion courts retain in assessing the constitutionality of a law.

Standards of Review in Free Speech Cases

Much significance attaches to determinations of which tests courts will apply to resolve constitutional disputes. In First Amendment contexts, since we are dealing with fundamental rights (i.e., constitutionally protected rights), strict scrutiny applies. But that hardly resolves the matter. For a statute or regulation to survive scrutiny, it still must pass the often difficult characterization stage that helps determine whether the contested speech is worth protecting. And the law also must undergo the challenging assessment of the government's interests and the mechanisms designed to further them. These are challenging concepts to apply.

As expected, strict scrutiny only applies if the speech is determined to fit within the category of speech deemed worth protecting. This is where the cases we have examined above gain significance: they help guide us in our understanding of what speech the legal system views as falling under the First Amendment's reach. When dealing with free speech deemed worth protecting, the courts essentially grapple with the sensitive question of how to keep censorship within tolerable limits. Once it has been found that a law infringes on freedom of expression worth protecting, standard First Amendment doctrine requires courts to determine whether the law is "content-based" or "content-neutral." Content-based laws regulate the ideas being expressed, while content-neutral laws regulate the time, place, or manner of expression. The distinction between content-based and content-neutral laws has played a crucial role in determining the standards of review that are used to measure the constitutionality of laws that affect the freedom of expression.

Government regulations linked to the content of speech receive very close judicial scrutiny. In contrast, when government regulates speech in a manner unrelated to content, the level of scrutiny decreases. Further, under the current doctrine, the format for assessing the constitutionality of content-based laws differs from the format that is used to evaluate content-neutral laws. The constitutionality of content-based laws depends on the value of the category of speech that is being regulated. As we have seen, political, artistic, literary, and scientific speech are considered to be "high value" speech, and accordingly laws that infringe on such speech must meet the "strict scrutiny" standard of review. In contrast, commercial speech has been considered to be of middling value, and courts typically subject laws suppressing such speech to intermediate scrutiny. The Supreme Court has granted low value to other categories of speech, such as obscenity and fighting words, which renders laws limiting such speech essentially constitutional without much further analysis (with the notable exception highlighted below that the laws still must not inadvertently chill protected speech in the process).

Because censorship regulates speech based on content, the Court typically applies "strict scrutiny" analysis that invalidates a law unless it serves a "compelling" governmental interest and uses the "least speech-restrictive means" to further that interest. The application of strict scrutiny to content regulations reflects the skepticism with which courts view regulations that restrict a fundamental right, such as the freedom of expression. For example, the government may regulate the content of constitutionally protected speech in order to promote a compelling interest if it chooses the least restrictive means to further the articulated interest. The Supreme Court sometimes includes a requirement that a law be "narrowly tailored" to serve the government's interest. The narrowly tailored requirement, like the least restrictive means requirement, ensures that content-based regulations do not burden more speech than is necessary to accomplish the government's purpose.

Content-neutral laws are evaluated in a different manner. The constitutionality of laws that restrict the time, place, or manner of expression essentially calls for intermediate scrutiny. The need to use that standard was announced in *United States v. O'Brien* (1968), which called for an intermediate scrutiny with the additional proviso that any content-neutral law must "leave open ample alternative channels of communication." In particular, the *O'Brien* test has been used to evaluate the constitutionality of laws regulating symbolic speech and laws regulating the time, place, or manner of expression that occurs in places considered part of the "public forum." A lower standard of review—the rational basis test—applies to laws regulating expression that occurs in places that are not part of the public forum, subject to the same proviso that even regulations of some nonpublic forums must leave open substantial alternative channels of communication.

Current doctrine's requirements that content-based laws be analyzed one way and content-neutral laws be analyzed another way, renders crucial the ability to tell the difference between these types of laws. Some cases involve laws that are purely content-based or purely content-neutral. However, it is not always possible to classify a law as purely content-based or purely content-neutral. In fact, many laws regulating expression can be deemed both content-based and content-neutral. For example, zoning laws that disperse sexually oriented businesses, campaign finance reform laws that limit the amount of money a person or a political party may contribute to a candidate, policies and regulations restricting access of religious groups to public schools and universities, laws prohibiting electioneering at polling places on the day of an election, and laws that regulate indecent or pornographic speech over specific media are both content-based and content-neutral on their face. In addition, many laws are content-neutral on their face, but also content-based in fact. These include laws and injunctions limiting protests at health care facilities, public nudity laws as applied to nude dancing establishments, and laws prohibiting flag and cross burning. Despite the development of rules, then, First Amendment jurisprudence still remains quite complicated and, in many instances, still undetermined and unpredictable.

Constitutional concerns still may arise after the courts have resolved issues of content and appropriate levels of scrutiny. Most notably, the Court deems laws problematic if they have used vague or overbroad language to define the regulated speech. Although these doctrines are conceptually distinct from the least restrictive means requirement, they too concern regulatory means that unnecessarily suppress or chill speech. Litigants challenging censorship laws often invoke the doctrines of vagueness or overbreadth. An overbreadth challenge asserts that the restriction is not limited to the furtherance of some sufficiently important state interest, but rather sweeps within its prohibition speech that is otherwise constitutionally protected and which does not threaten any valid state interest. Such an attack contends either that the interest asserted in support of the restriction is not compelling, or that the restriction is not narrowly tailored to the asserted state interest. A vagueness challenge asserts that the scope of the restriction lacks the clarity necessary when restricting free speech. All laws entail some degree of ambiguity, and this does not automatically doom a law. When a law restricts free speech, however, courts have imposed a stricter standard of clarity to minimize the risk of selective enforcement, of deterring speakers uncertain about the scope of the restriction, and of trapping innocent offenders. Together, these doctrines again reveal the extent to which the legal system seeks to ensure that the government does not inappropriately censor speech worth protecting.

Determining the Extent to Which Evidence Matters

In addition to placing responsibility for protecting speech rights on the judiciary, First Amendment jurisprudence embodies a particular doctrinal imperative of accurate factual determinations regarding claims that state action infringes speech, because the government raises the constitutional stakes when it places speech in jeopardy. The requirement of accuracy roots in the fact-based structure of First Amendment doctrine. Although free speech jurisprudence sometimes recognizes the intrinsic value of free expression, it often rests instead on the furtherance of instrumentalist or consequentialist goals, the realization of which may be assessed empirically: promoting a robust "marketplace of ideas," enabling self-governance and political participation, fostering individual development, or serving as a check on the processes of government. Speech doctrine similarly requires courts to make empirical assessments of facts in order to weigh competing interests. First Amendment balancing tests, such as the *O'Brien* test, require courts to assess the severity of social harms and the importance of legitimate government interests, as well as to predict potential burdens on speech. Overbreadth challenges and sensitivity to "chilling effects" require courts to determine whether state action may inhibit the constitutionally protected speech of third parties. And despite the near-absolute proscription on prior restraints, courts may allow some form of prior restraint based on contextual assessments of the potentially suffered degree of harm. Even when reviewing content-based restrictions, courts must make fact determinations regarding the existence of compelling state interests and the fit between these interests and the government's response. Even the "clear and present danger" rule defining incitement requires determinations of "imminence" and "danger." Thus and especially in the strict and intermediate scrutiny contexts, findings of fact lending themselves to empirical assessments often are determinative of the constitutionality of a government action.

The Norm of Accuracy

Because of the centrality of factual assessment to First Amendment decision making, the Supreme Court has developed, in a number of doctrinal contexts, a norm of accuracy. This norm is perhaps best illustrated by the Supreme Court's use of the rule in *Bose Corp. v. Consumers Union of United States, Inc.* (1984) and its progeny. It was in *Bose*, a case in which an audio equipment manufacturer sued a consumer publication, alleging that it published an unflattering, inaccurate, and biased review of a set of the plaintiff's speakers, that the Supreme Court imposed a constitutional "duty" on appellate courts hearing speech cases to conduct an independent review of factual records developed by federal or state courts and administrative agencies (*Bose Corp. v. Consumers Union of United States, Inc.*, 1984, pp. 498–511; see also *Hurley v. Irish-American Gay, Lesbian and Bisexual Group*, 1995, pp. 566–68). This duty has been interpreted by lower courts to require plenary (sometimes called "*de novo*," "free," or "independent") review in all cases involving First Amendment issues to ensure that the judgment does not constitute a forbidden intrusion on free expression. This review of the facts underlying the application of a constitutional standard is often characterized as the review of "constitutional fact." Under constitutional fact doctrine, a reviewing court must consider the factual record in full when it seeks to determine whether a constitutional standard has been satisfied. When a court reviews the rulings or decision of a controversy *de novo*, it conducts an independent determination that accords no deference to any prior resolution of the same controversy. The standard affords a court the broadest scope of review.

This independent review of the record is a strong exception to the default approach, the abuse of discretion standard that generally accepts prior determinations of fact. This independent judgment rule actually is grounded entirely on concerns assertedly peculiar to the First Amendment. In *Landmark Communications, Inc. v. Virginia* (1978, p. 843), for instance, the Court stated that "[d]eference to a legislative finding cannot limit judicial inquiry when First Amendment rights are at stake." In other contexts, the typical decision making rule grants great deference to the fact-finders (Levesque, 2006). Yet, in First Amendment cases, the Court embraces the notion that the First Amendment's reach ultimately is defined by the facts it is held to embrace and that courts must review these facts independently, "to be sure that the speech in question actually falls within the unprotected category and to confine the perimeters of any unprotected category within acceptably narrow limits" (*Bose Corp. v. Consumers Union of United States, Inc.*, 1984, p. 505).

First Amendment doctrine further requires exacting and accurate adjudication for other reasons. First Amendment jurisprudence imposes stringent restrictions on the procedures that govern First Amendment litigation. The Supreme Court has long held that, in First Amendment cases, "the procedures by which the facts of the case are determined assume an importance fully as great as the validity of the substantive rule of law" (*Speiser v. Randall*, 1958, p. 520). In these cases, "the possibility of mistaken fact-finding . . . creates the danger that the legitimate utterance will be penalized" (p. 526). For example, an accuracy norm underlies procedures that allow for judicial consideration of the speech rights of third parties. The same norm allows for judge-made prophylactic rules, such as those against "chilling effects," that extend protection to speech too far in order to protect covered speech. The nearly absolute bar on prior restraint similarly reflects the norm. The Supreme Court has long viewed laws requiring speakers to obtain permits or licenses before using public forums as "prior restraints," and has looked with disfavor on schemes vesting officials with broad discretion to regulate speech in such forums. The requirement of accuracy also takes the form of the need for precision and persistent distrust of official discretion in First Amendment contexts. The Court continues to demonstrate its skepticism of discretion in the manner it strikes down laws with vaguely defined standards that delegate to public officials virtually unbridled discretion to determine who may speak. From its earliest First Amendment speech and assembly cases, the Supreme Court has recognized that laws vesting official actors with broad discretion to regulate or restrict speech threaten the constitutional imperative that the government should not restrict expression because of its message, its ideas, its subject matter, or its content. Concern for "unbridled discretion" links closely to the Court's general intolerance for vagueness where laws criminalize or otherwise regulate speech.

The Quantum of Evidence

On the surface, the norm of accuracy seems quite attractive and comforting. It leads us to believe that decisions will be based not on a judge's personal preferences, but rather on facts, such as what is derived from "neutral" or "scientific" data. Yet, in practice, even the Court has exhibited remarkable inconsistency in its use of evidence. Indeed, the Supreme Court's use of empirical evidence in constitutional adjudications has generated considerable controversy, and the extent to which the Court values empirical analyses shifts from context to context and even from one justice to another.

The Supreme Court's analyses of empirical evidence in its First Amendment cases reveals considerable variation. In some instances, the Court eschews any independent review and defers to the factual findings of legislators. Cases in the area of obscenity provide the clearest example of this immense deference. As we have seen, the Court officially endorsed the obscenity exception in *Roth v.*

United States (1957), and it did so by providing weakly supported arguments. The Court claimed that obscene speech is "utterly without redeeming social importance" without further explaining why other types of low-value speech continue to receive First Amendment protection (p. 484). The Court merely provided historical support for its conclusion. Perhaps most importantly, the Court declared obscenity unprotected without requiring any empirical proof that the speech's harmfulness. The Court ignored briefs that had inundated the Court with empirical studies. The Court's willingness to declare obscene speech unconstitutional without empirical proof of its harmfulness became even more transparent in *Paris Adult Theatre I v. Slaton* (1973, p. 60), decided a quarter century after *Roth*. In that case, the Court upheld a Georgia law prohibiting the exhibition of obscene films at adult theaters by stating that "it is not for us to resolve empirical uncertainties underlying state legislation" and that "we do not demand of legislatures 'scientifically certain criteria of legislation'" (*Paris Adult Theatre I v. Slaton*, 1973, p. 60, quoting *Ginsberg v. New York*, 1968, pp. 642–43; quoting *Noble State Bank v. Haskell*, 1911, p. 110). Indeed, the Court even willingly deferred to the "unprovable assumptions" of legislators (*Paris Adult Theatre I v. Slaton*, 1973, p. 61).

It is important to emphasize that these cases involve complex doctrinal moves. Supreme Court precedent, notably under the *Ginsberg* decision we examined earlier, does not require the State to provide "empirical" evidence that exposure to sexually explicit materials may harm children, because legislators are permitted to assume such harm based on common cultural understandings. This creates, for example, a problem with reliance on *Ginsberg* to support child protective laws based on evidence of psychological harm. As previously noted, *Ginsberg* did not involve strict scrutiny or a compelling governmental interest. In addition, the Court based the independent governmental interest in protecting children on concerns about "ethical and moral development." Ethical and moral questions are by their nature not susceptible to empirical or scientific proof; rather, their answers exist in the eyes of the beholder. This apparently is what the Court meant in *Ginsberg* when it held that "it is very doubtful" if the legislative finding regarding the effect of sexually explicit materials on children "expresses an accepted scientific fact" (*Ginsberg v. New York*, 1968, p. 641). Thus, empirical attacks on the government's purported independent interest in protecting children miss the point. They challenge an unmade assertion and fail to address the law's true concern: whether the State has a legitimate or compelling interest in inculcating moral and ethical values in children by controlling their access to indecent materials as a step towards creating a morally virtuous citizenry.

In other contexts when First Amendment rights were at stake, the Court has refused to defer to legislative fact-finding. In *Sable Communications of California v. Federal Communications Commission* (1989), the Court struck down a flat congressional ban on the interstate transmission of indecent commercial telephone messages. The Court did so on "narrow tailoring" grounds (the second part of the Court's "strict scrutiny" test), accepting without question the government's "compelling interest in protecting the physical and psychological well-being of minors" (*Sable Communications of California v. Federal Communications Commission*, 1989, p. 126). In *Sable*, the Court for the first time elevated the government interests recognized in *Ginsberg* to the level of compelling interests, sufficiently powerful to satisfy strict scrutiny, the highest standard of review. The Court apparently took this important doctrinal step summarily; it did not detail the criteria for defining compelling interests and avoided discussing the inapplicability of its precedents. The Court, however, apparently ruled after conducting a close review of the materials, a review pursuant to its need to not readily defer to government judgments in First Amendment cases. More recently, in *44 Liquormart, Inc. v. Rhode Island* (1997), the Court again refused to take a deferential view even as to commercial advertising, which the Court has long treated as less valuable than other speech. The Court, then, can readily consider the extent of evidence supporting rationales for limiting speech in its considerations of legislative mandates.

The above characterization, however, masks important controversies. For example, the Supreme Court's two decisions on the constitutionality of the federal "must-carry" rules—*Turner Broadcasting System, Inc. v. FCC* (1994) and *Turner Broadcasting System, Inc. v. FCC* (1997)—emphasize both the importance of independent judicial review of legislative fact-finding in First Amendment cases and the need for deference toward this fact-finding. The Court stated, in both cases, that reviewing "courts must accord substantial deference to the predictive judgments of Congress," but also that this "substantial deference does not mean" that Congressional judgments "are insulated from meaningful judicial review altogether" (*Turner Broadcasting System, Inc. v. FCC*, 1994, pp. 665–66; *Turner Broadcasting System, Inc. v. FCC*, 1997, pp. 195–96). Yet, the Turner cases stand out for the extent to which the government's evidence concerning the impact of cable television on broadcast television took center stage. The Court remanded the first to the lower courts to develop that evidence more fully. The Court noted that

> Without a more substantial elaboration in the District Court of the predictive or historical evidence upon which Congress relied, or the introduction of some additional evidence to establish that the dropped or repositioned broadcasters would be at serious risk of financial difficulty, we cannot determine whether the threat to broadcast television is real enough to overcome the challenge to the provisions made by these appellants. (*Turner Broadcasting System, Inc. v. FCC*, 1994, p. 667)

When the case returned to the Supreme Court, the justices embarked on an exhaustive examination of the economic facts that had been developed in the judicial and legislative record (*Turner Broadcasting System, Inc. v. FCC*, 1997, pp. 197–213).

The Court continues to wrestle with the use of empirical findings in its First Amendment cases. Despite the claim that facts matter, for example, the Court sometimes rules on questionable or insufficient evidence both in what would seem to be highly protected and not so protected speech. For example, in *City of Erie v. Pap's A.M.* (2000) the Justices split over the adequacy of the evidence supporting the legislative judgment that prohibiting nude dancing and dispersing adult businesses would diminish crime and support property values in the surrounding neighborhoods. Justice Souter, in particular, clearly noted that the "principal reason" for his dissent was the "insufficiency" of the evidence offered by the municipality. The controversy was quite significant given the view that the cited studies had obtained questionable findings with considerably flawed methods and that the more empirically credible studies demonstrate either no negative secondary effect associated with adult businesses or an actual reversal of the presumed negative effects (Paul, Linz, & Shafer, 2001; Linz, Land, Williams, Paul, & Ezell, 2004).

Similar use of evidence has been noted in what would have been thought to be highly protected by the First Amendment—political speech. This deference was most apparent in *Nixon v. Shrink Missouri Government PAC* (2000), a leading case sustaining state law limitations on campaign contributions ranging from $250 to $1000. The Court required essentially no evidence to sustain contribution limits instituted by a Missouri ballot measure. The Court upheld the limits based on a few newspaper articles citing voter discontent with money in politics, the Missouri electorate's approval of the measure (as suggestive of the appearance of corruption), and an affidavit by a Missouri legislator stating that "large contributions have real potential to buy votes" (*Nixon v. Shrink Missouri Government PAC*, 2000, pp. 393–94). The Court also considered whether contribution limits were so low as to hinder a candidate's ability to raise the funds necessary to run an effective campaign. Concluding that the limits were not so low as to render political association ineffective, drive the candidate's voice below the level of notice, and render contributions pointless, the Court established a very high threshold for constitutional challenges to the level of contribution limits. *Shrink Missouri* essentially halted a lower court trend that had sought to enhance the evidentiary standard required to uphold campaign restrictions. In doing so, the Court emphasized the variability of the state's burden of proof in freedom of expression cases. The Court forthrightly stated that "the quantum of empirical evidence needed to satisfy heightened judicial scrutiny of legislative judgments will vary up or down with the novelty and plausibility of the justification raised" (*Nixon v. Shrink Missouri Government PAC*, 2000, p. 391). For our purposes, that the Court would significantly lower the evidentiary threshold for contribution limits to political campaigns, arguably the bedrock of highly protected political speech, signals a challenge ahead for those who would seek certainty in the Court's use of empirical evidence.

Conclusions

The breadth and depth of First Amendment jurisprudence defies simple rules. Despite complexity, this area of jurisprudence does reveal and reflect some widely accepted principles that guide responses to governmental efforts to regulate speech. Perhaps the most fundamental of these principles maintains that our constitutional scheme considers free speech a preferred value because free thought and the dissemination of ideas are crucial to the development of human capacity. Free speech, according to the Court, supports both the smooth functioning of our democratic society and, because of that, the flourishing of human personality. Although initially narrowly conceived as a mechanism to foster effective government, free speech jurisprudence now recognizes that the free speech clause supports the main structural mechanisms by which democracy determines its purposes so that people may thrive. Justice Harlan famously made this observation in *Cohen v. California* (1971, p. 24):

> The constitutional right of free expression is powerful medicine in a society as diverse and populous as ours. It is designed and intended to remove governmental restraints from the arena of public discussion, putting the decision as to what views shall be voiced largely into the hands of each of us, in the hope that use of such freedom will ultimately produce a more capable citizenry and more perfect polity and in the belief that no other approach would comport with the premise of individual dignity and choice upon which our political system rests.

Under our system of government, our free speech jurisprudence permits the most direct expression of human personality in society, and, as such, concerns itself with the development of human identity, respect for human dignity, and formation of a more capable and better polity. Our system assumes that the law must protect us from itself for it to allow us to become capable citizens with a strong sense of dignity and choice in matters affecting ourselves and our surroundings.

The centrality of free speech to our government and human development does not mean that speech must be absolutely free from regulation, let alone "free" in terms of our government's actively contributing to speech's dissemination. The Constitution focuses on "abridgment," and the Court interprets this command as not necessarily rendering an abridgment of protected speech unconstitutional.

The Court adopts a variety of approaches to determine the propriety of a restraint on the freedom of speech. The Court uses a categorical approach that provides a continuum of protection, based on the extent to which the Court deems the speech protected by the Constitution. Despite numerous qualifications, some categories of messages are constitutionally disfavored and may be regulated by the state in a broad range of circumstances; other kinds of messages can be regulated but only on a more limited basis. Indeed, analyzing a free speech law issue requires a quick run through our checklist of "unprotected" categories to determine if any of them covers the speech at issue. Determining whether an expressive activity falls within or outside the scope of First Amendment protection, however, only begins the analysis. If the speech is worth protecting, the Court adopts a balancing approach that essentially weighs two competing interests: the government's concern about protecting a particular interest and the individual's and society's interests in expression. The Court has approached this balancing by developing a number of rules to determine the extent to which a party will have the burden to challenge or support alleged abridgements. Where the Court has found that the speech lacks First Amendment value, the Court has understandably given legislatures broad discretion to regulate the speech. But where the speech has constitutional value courts independently judge whether the speech may nonetheless be controlled or even banned. Thus, even when the Court fully protects speech, the government may be entitled to impose some restrictions based on the methods of communication (such as prohibit bullhorns at midnight) or on a combination of the message and the surrounding circumstances (such as a relationship between the speech and some specific governmental activity, e.g., the speech of military personnel on the battlefield, of prisoners in prison, or of students in schools). These developments reveal that the traditional focus of free speech doctrine on what was protected has evolved into a modern doctrine equally concerned with how the government has crafted its regulations controlling the contested speech. Although over a hundred years in the making, this development is not surprising. Emphasizing what the government has done as much as the speaker tracks and mirrors the text of the First Amendment itself. Despite necessary complexities, then, it becomes increasingly possible to discern how the Court determines whether certain types of speech gain protection, how the speech gains protection, and the type of evidence the Court typically considers to determine whether and how to protect certain types of expressions.

7

The Free Speech Rights of Adolescents

The legal system intensely protects the right to speak and the freedom to develop one's own thoughts, but such protections may exclude adolescents. The legal system considerably varies its treatment of adolescents' First Amendment rights. Sometimes the law lumps adolescents with adults and bestows them both with similar rights. As a result, adolescents sometimes are free to think as they please, express their firmly held beliefs, and hold rights equal to those of adults. We have seen how adolescents have the right to speak racist and hateful speech in public (*R.A.V. v. City of St. Paul*, 1992) and retain the right to not express beliefs in custodial contexts like public schools (*West Virginia State Board of Education v. Barnette*, 1943). In other instances, however, the legal system treats adolescents like children who must be controlled and protected. As we have seen, states may limit adolescents' access to indecent speech (*FCC v. Pacifica Foundation*, 1978). Most notably, however, the state allows others to limit the extent to which adolescents develop the capacity to think for themselves. The legal system pervasively grants parents broad rights to control their children's education, direct their general upbringing, and even provide adolescents with speech the state itself deems inappropriate (*Ginsberg v. New York*, 1968). At other times, adolescents have their rights protected simply because society values the rights of adults more than it values the need to limit adolescents' access to potentially harmful materials or curb adolescents' disturbing expressions. We have seen, for example, how expressions that may be harmful to minors may not be limited if the restrictions infringe on the rights of adults to access that information, such as in cases involving Internet pornography (*Reno v. American Civil Liberties Union*,

1997). Adolescents' First Amendment speech rights, then, add several layers of complexity and variability to an already complicated jurisprudence.

The results of legal approaches to adolescents may suggest a lack of clear rules and unpredictable results, but the above variations reveal overarching principles that will re-occur throughout our analysis of the jurisprudence of adolescents' First Amendment speech rights. First, the Supreme Court acknowledges the government's power to censor materials that may reach adolescents. This governmental power may deny minors access to speech that it cannot deny to adults because the state retains the power to enact child-protection censorship. Second, the Court acknowledges that minors have free speech rights that occasionally can trump the government's interest in censorship. Third, the Court recognizes that censorship aimed to protect minors raises serious constitutional concerns when it incidentally denies adults access to speech or infringes on parental rights. Thus, two powerful countervailing forces counsel against limiting the rights of adolescents to certain speech: the rights of adolescents themselves as well as the rights of adults. These potentially clashing rights and interests ensure that First Amendment free speech claims involving adolescents remain rather complex and almost inevitably marked by bitter controversy.

The variability in the legal system's treatment of adolescents' free speech rights reveals how the legal system regulates adolescents' rights—both in the form of adolescents' own expressions and access to the expressions of others—quite differently than it does the rights of adults. This different treatment is not peculiar to First Amendment jurisprudence. The difference roots deeply in the manner the law presumptively conceives of adolescents' rights. The law confers adolescents with a special status simply because of their particular vulnerabilities, their place in society, and the type of society adults wish to assert. This status means that the legal system does not, in many ways, recognize adolescents as fully constitutional persons in the sense that the law deems adolescents generally incompetent to control their own rights. Adolescents' First Amendment freedoms provide no exception to the law's conception of adolescents' abilities and place in society.

Despite the inherent complexity of adolescents' own rights involved in free speech jurisprudence and the recurring complaint that this area of law lacks clarity and predictability, we still can articulate what governments *generally* may or may not do to protect minors from harmful speech and from inappropriate government censorship. To do so, we first explore the jurisprudence that permits censorship through child-protective efforts. We then explore adolescents' own right to express themselves. Lastly, we examine the extent to which adolescents have rights to certain forms of information. Our discussions necessarily reach broadly, for much of this area still remains tentative and subject to important challenges as it seeks to adapt to rapid social changes. Although wanting, current doctrine still points to important conclusions that can help us envision ways to address the free speech rights of adolescents and shape their responses to diverse informational environments. Efforts to understand adolescents' free speech rights, then, necessarily require us to examine how the law addresses tensions arising from the need to protect minors and foster their healthy development.

Protecting Adolescents from Harmful Speech

Numerous laws specifically aim to protect adolescents from harm. These "harmful to minors" laws range widely. Most notably, their existence justifies our massive child protection system to protect children from maltreatment and even provides the foundational rationale for the juvenile justice system which seeks to protect minors from the harms of punitive responses to problem behavior (Levesque, 2002a). In the context of free speech, the most notable, obvious and least controversial laws concerned with protecting minors from harmful speech involve those that prohibit the production, sale, and possession of child pornography. We have seen in the previous chapter the key rationales that support efforts to censor everyone from materials deemed obscene. More problematic to regulate, however, are materials deemed indecent to adults and (potentially) obscene as to minors, which exemplify this very large genre of "harmful to minors" laws. Efforts to censor such materials are of considerable significance. They reveal the fundamental tension between protecting minors while not infringing on the rights of adults and the rights of minors themselves, and that tension demonstrates the limits that can be placed on adolescents' First Amendment rights.

The Development and Reach of Child Protection Rationales

Jurisprudentially, the state's right to censor materials deemed harmful as to minors stems from the foundational child protection case that halted the expansive reach of the rights of parents to control their children's upbringing. In that case, *Prince v. Massachusetts* (1944), the legal guardian (an aunt acting as parent) of a 9-year-old girl permitted her to distribute religious pamphlets in the streets. The guardian was convicted for violating child labor laws, given that those who distributed pamphlets accepted donations. On appeal to the Supreme Court, the Court used the opportunity to find, for the first time, the state's "compelling interest in the protection of children from 'harmful' speech" (*Prince v. Massachusetts*, 1944, p. 160). The Court created a special exception solely for minors because the "State's authority over children's activities is broader than over like actions of adults" (p. 168). The Court stated that it is in "the interest of youth itself, and of the whole community, that children be both safeguarded from abuses and given opportunities for growth into free and independent well-developed men and citizens" (p. 165). Unlike cases before it, *Prince* confirmed the significance of the state in fostering the healthy development of youth, something important not just for the individuals themselves but also for civil society.

  Prince did much more than underline the importance the Court places on the state's role in the protection of children, including protection from harmful speech. The Court provided the rationale for doing so and emphasized the limit of that rationale. Thus, while recognizing the role of the state when parents have failed or when parents need extra assistance to parent, the *Prince* Court still affirmed that parents play the central role in the upbringing of children and that the state should not seek to usurp this role. The Court cautioned against granting the state too much power to restrict the rights of parents. It emphasized that it is "cardinal . . . that the custody, care and nurture of the child reside first in the parents, whose primary function and freedom include preparation for obligations the State can neither supply nor hinder" (*Prince v. Massachusetts*, 1944, p. 166). In addition and pervasively ignored by courts and commentators, the Court highlighted that the need for that protection was to provide "opportunities for growth into free and independent well-developed men and citizens" (p. 165). Following *Prince's* dictates, parents and the state would share the responsibility to foster and shape adolescent development, but parents would retain power by default.

The Court returned to child protection jurisprudence and squarely addressed it in the context of censorship in its 1968 seminal decision, *Ginsberg v. New York* (1968). *Ginsberg* upheld the conviction of a New York bookseller who sold "girlie magazines" to minors. Although these magazines were fully protected speech as to adults, the Court concluded that the state could deny them to minors. The Court used a variant of the standard definition of obscenity to find it permissible to bar the sale to minors of materials deemed obscene as to minors. Following *Prince*, the *Ginsberg* Court recognized two distinct interests that the state could advance to justify developing a rule that could define what was obscene depending on the recipient's minority status. The Court noted that it consistently had recognized parental claims to authority in their own households to direct the rearing of their children and had conceded the legislature's ability to support parents' efforts to discharge their responsibilities for their children's well-being. Despite the primacy of parental rights, the Court highlighted the state's own independent interest in the well-being of its youth. That interest grants power to the state to control the conduct of children which reaches beyond the scope of its authority over adults. It was this power, in addition to the power to assist parents in discharging their duties, that allowed the state to ban the sale to minors of sexually explicit materials which might harm their "ethical and moral development" (*Ginsberg v. New York*, 1968, pp. 640–41).

Regrettably, the *Ginsburg* Court neglected to delineate what precisely makes adolescents different from adults. The Court did reason, however, that parental control over minors and minors' unique vulnerability renders minors' First Amendment rights less robust than those of adults. Yet, the Court offered no evidentiary analysis to support its reasoning. The Court simply rejected the contention that a state seeking to regulate such harms must demonstrate the harm's existence with "scientific" evidence. Instead, the Court concluded that it would uphold the statute so long as "it was not irrational for the legislature to find that exposure to materials condemned by the statute is harmful to minors" (*Ginsberg v. New York*, 1968, pp. 640–41). *Ginsberg* thus firmly established the power of the state to protect children from the "harms," purported or real, caused by exposure to sexual speech and also endorsed the dual nature of the state's interests in this regard. In so doing, the Court simply presumed that children differ from adults and that these differences justify greater speech regulation. The Court, without considering the broad variability in adolescents' abilities and needs, simply concluded that minors are less developed than adults and consequently are more vulnerable to harms.

The Court continues to cite its *Prince* and *Ginsberg* conclusions that affirm and justify child-protection censorship to support the constitutionality of child-protection censorship. But the Court has yet to explore vigorously what makes adolescents different from adults in free speech contexts. Indeed, this area of jurisprudence has yet to explore adult-minor differences outside of indecent, sexual speech. Understanding the rationales for treating minors differently requires a turn to another constitutional context the Court developed a decade after *Ginsberg*, to *Bellotti v. Baird* (1979). *Bellotti* concerned a minor's right to obtain an abortion without parental consent. It was in that groundbreaking case that the Court reasoned that minors are "not beyond the protection of the Constitution" but that their constitutional rights "cannot be equated with those of adults" (*Bellotti v. Baird*, 1979, pp. 633–34). To explain this disparate treatment, the Court focused on three characteristics that distinguish minors from adults: "the peculiar vulnerability of children; their inability to make critical decisions in an informed, mature manner; and the importance of the parental role in child-rearing" (p. 634). The Court elaborated on each of these characteristics as it defined them in restrictive ways. The "peculiar vulnerabilit[ies]," the Court noted, refer to minors' special "needs for 'concern, ... sympathy, and ... paternal attention'" (p. 635). Minors' inability to make critical decisions in an informed, mature manner reflects their lack of "experience, perspective, and judgment to recognize and avoid choices that could be detrimental to them" (p. 635). The importance of the parental role justifies limits on minors' freedoms because parental guidance "is essential to the growth of young people into mature, socially responsible citizens" (p. 638). This three-pronged line of inquiry has been used in a wide variety of contexts, most notably in recent death penalty cases (*Roper v. Simmons*, 2005), to determine whether minors should be treated like children and offered special protections. Equally importantly and often ignored, the Court uses the same line of inquiry to determine whether minors, especially mature minors, should perhaps receive the same rights and protections enjoyed by adults but not the protections granted children. This actually was *Belotti*'s ruling: If minors can support claims that they are appropriately mature, they retain the right to control their own rights rather than have an adult determine whether they can exercise their fundamental right.

The factors used to determine whether to treat minors as children or adults reveal why the legal system may permit child-protection censorship. The factors also reveal, of course, why some minors should not be treated like children. The "peculiar vulnerabilities" of minors may suggest that minors need government protection from speech if their lack of emotional and intellectual maturity renders them vulnerable to harm. The relative ability of minors "to make critical decisions in an informed, mature manner" may suggest that the government should limit minors' access to dangerous ideas if minors cannot responsibly evaluate them. The "importance of the parental role in child rearing" suggests that parents may need assistance of government censorship to fulfill their child-rearing responsibilities. These factors tend to combine to create persuasive justifications supporting child-protection censorship. Not surprisingly, these rationales find parallels in *Ginsberg's* (1968, p. 639) reference to the state's "independent interest in [protecting] the well-being of its youth" and to the right of parents "to the support of laws designed to aid discharge of [their child-rearing] responsibility." The Court, then, allows for treating adolescents differently when the government has an independent interest in protecting minors from speech that could harm them, and the government shares a vicariously derived interest in supporting parents with their child-rearing responsibilities, which the government can further by denying children access to materials that their parents do not want them to see.

Although the Court often presents state and parental interests as two independent rationales that allow the legal system to censor materials that may reach adolescents, the application of these rationales reveals an assumed congruence. We have seen how *Ginsberg* does not even require a state to provide empirical evidence to prove that exposure to sexually explicit materials may harm children. The Court permits legislators to assume such harm based on common cultural understandings. For example, the Court observed that most parents did not want their children to see these publications, and the legislature could appropriately wish to help those parents. When the Court cited the state's independent interest in the well-being of its youth, it did not specify just what harm the state was preventing, and the most thoughtful source it quoted offered

> A distinction between the reading of pornography, as unlikely to be per se harmful, and the permitting of the reading of pornography, which was conceived as potentially destructive. The child is protected in his reading of pornography by the knowledge that it is pornographic, i.e., disapproved. It is outside of parental standards and not a part of his identification processes. To openly permit implies parental approval and even suggests seductive encouragement. If this is so of parental approval, it is equally so of societal approval—another potent influence on the developing ego. (*Ginsberg v. New York*, 1968, p. 642 n.10)

As the Court's use of sources reveals, the Court essentially found that pornographic materials themselves do not cause harm to its young readers; harm derives from materials presented in a certain context. The context, the Court suggested, should be one in which the readers do not perceive the wrong moral norms. The law prohibits the sale of pornography to children more to protect a moral stance than to keep the materials out of their hands. Otherwise, parents would no longer be free to purchase such materials for their children. In this instance, the law concerns itself with moral harm rather than the inducement of bad conduct. Moral harm arises from the failure of the state to support the belief that parents want to disapprove and from the failure of the state to provide a firm statement that the state itself disapproves.

We already have seen that concerns about moral harms are not conducive to empirical assessment; the power the Court grants parents compounds the significance of this view. *Ginsberg* grants parents, if they wish, the right not to compete with the marketplace of ideas for influence on their children. This has not been a fleeting notion. The role of parents in controlling their children's marketplace of ideas would again be raised and disagreements roundly defeated in *Wisconsin v. Yoder* (1972). *Yoder* concerned the right of Amish parents to remove their children from school after eighth grade. The parents' central claim involved the fear that "high school tends to emphasize intellectual and scientific accomplishments, self-distinction, competitiveness, worldly success, and social life with other students," all of which the parents had found incompatible with Amish values (*Wisconsin v. Yoder*, 1972, p. 211). The Court ruled in favor of the parents, and did not even consider the rights of the adolescents to express their own views on the matter. Even more strikingly, the Court expressly ruled in favor of the parents because the children had reached adolescence and were susceptible to mainstream ideas. *Yoder* thus stands for the general rule that parents have the right to limit their adolescents' access to ideas, even ideas society has developed vast systems to inculcate and otherwise has deemed as instrumental for proper individual and civic development. By default and by state support, constitutional jurisprudence ensures that parents enjoy the plenary right to dictate the informational environments that will influence their children's lives.

The Limits of Child Protection Rationales

Together, the above line of cases provides strikingly broad rulings and sweeping rationales largely immune from empirical challenges. Yet in terms of First Amendment law, the emerging doctrine reveals at least two important limits to this broad control over adolescents in the name of child protection. The *Ginsberg* case and its progeny again are illustrative. The first limit derives from the manner *Ginsberg* only involved a prohibition on sales to minors of speech deemed constitutionally unprotected as to them; the case did not involve any restrictions on adults' access to protected speech. Cases limiting adults' access tend to lead to different outcomes. In 1957, for example, the Court had held, in *Butler v. Michigan* (1957, p. 383), that the state may not absolutely prohibit the sale of "lewd" material that might harm children, because the state may not "reduce the adult population of Michigan to reading only what is fit for children." The distinction is of significance in that modern indecency cases and cases involving child protection from harmful ideas increasingly involve the rights of adults. The second limitation deals with the Court's standard of review. Because the *Ginsberg* restrictions did not infringe on the rights of adults, the legal analysis supporting censorship did not involve the application of strict scrutiny or any level of heightened scrutiny under the modern doctrinal framework. Instead, because it placed the restricted speech in the "obscenity/unprotected speech" category, the *Ginsberg* Court essentially applied a form of rational basis review rather than the strict scrutiny review when it had noted that the legislature had not acted in an "irrational" manner (*Ginsberg v. New York*, 1968, p. 641). These often ignored characteristics of the *Ginsberg* ruling—the low standard for review and the highly respected rights of adults—reveal the limits of child protection rationales.

The significance of the limits *Ginsberg* exemplified quickly came to light in the recent high number of cases involving restrictions on sexual speech—imposed in the name of protecting children—in more modern communications media, specifically cable television and the Internet. These cases reveal that the Court generally accepts, with little skepticism, the government's asserted child protection justifications. The Court, however, now focuses quite closely on whether the challenged regulations are "narrowly tailored," a necessary part of the "strict scrutiny" test applicable to protected speech. In *Denver Area Educational Telecommunications Consortium v. FCC* (1996), the Court faced a challenge to a congressional statute imposing various restrictions on the transmission of indecent materials on leased access and public access cable television channels. No member of the Court seriously questioned the strength or legitimacy of the government's interest in protecting children. The divisions within the Court centered on issues of tailoring and defining the proper standard of review, and establishing the nature of the constitutional rights of cable operators. The Court eventually struck down two of three restrictions; it rejected attempts to censor speech and upheld only the right of cable operators to prohibit the airing of offensive programming.

Similarly, in *Reno v. American Civil Liberties Union* (1997) the Court struck down the *Communications Decency Act* (CDA), a federal statute that effectively prohibited the transmission or posting on the Internet of indecent speech directed at, or available to, minors. Once again, the Court accepted without question "the governmental interest in protecting children from harmful materials" (*Reno v. American Civil Liberties Union*, 1997, p. 875), but also found that the CDA was not narrowly tailored. Among the Court's most compelling examples of the failure of the statute to limit its reach to protected speech was the rights of parents to provide information to their adolescent children:

> Under the CDA, a parent allowing her 17-year-old to use the family computer to obtain information on the Internet that she, in her parental judgment, deems appropriate could face a lengthy prison term.... Similarly, a parent who sent his 17-year-old college freshman information on birth control via e-mail could be incarcerated. (*Reno v. American Civil Liberties Union*, 1997, p. 878)

The cases reveal well how few doubt the state's interest in protecting minors, but that interest may give way to other concerns when the Court engages in a higher level of scrutiny and must consider the rights of adults.

Just as the *Ginsberg*-type justifications for censoring have faced limits when censorship curbs the rights of adults, so have they not sufficed to support censoring materials other than sexually indecent materials. Several examples illustrate the flurry of recent legislative and judicial activity and the somewhat remarkable extent to which the legal system *resists* censorship efforts in the name of protecting minors from harm. The first notable example involves concern over violent video games, a concern that swelled after a series of killings by adolescents. Despite widespread concern, subsequent efforts to limit minors' access to violent video games have been notably unsuccessful. Two circuit courts recently arrived to the same conclusion as both struck down efforts to limit access to violent video games. Importantly, one leading court reasoned that children would be ill prepared for adulthood if raised in an "intellectual bubble" and compared violent video games to "[c]lassic literature and art" (*American Amusement Machine Association v. Kendrick*, 2001, pp. 573, 575, 557, 558). The other court invalidated an ordinance prohibiting the sale of violent video games to minors, finding it inconsequential that modern technology "increased viewer control" and commenting that "literature is most successful when it 'draws the reader into the story . . . [and] makes him identify with the characters'" (*Interactive Digital Software Association v. St. Louis County*, 2003, p. 957). Just as courts have rebuked legislative attempts to curb access, courts have refused to impose liability on video game distributors and manufacturers for peddling violence that allegedly caused harms. Courts have found that the First Amendment bars these efforts by private parties seeking to impose tort liability on the video game industry (see, e.g., *James v. Meow Media, Inc.*, 2002; *Wilson v. Midway Games, Inc.*, 2002; *Sanders v. Acclaim Entertainment, Inc.*, 2002). The harm linked to violent media does not suffice to curb adolescents' own rights, which, as we have seen, have a tendency to enjoy very limited protection.

The second notable example of the legal system's resistance to censorship in the name of child protection comes from responses to a wealth of federal legislation seeking to curb violent and indecent television programming. The early cases that provided considerable support have given way to changed circumstances and much less solicitude to regulators. We saw in the previous chapter that the Court has long supported the FCC's authority to regulate indecency on broadcast television. The landmark Supreme Court decision on the regulation of broadcast indecency, *FCC v. Pacifica Foundation* (1978), upheld an FCC sanction against the Pacifica Foundation for broadcasting George Carlin's "Filthy Words" monologue. The Court held that the FCC had the power to regulate broadcast material that was indecent but not obscene, even though the First Amendment protects nonobscene speech. The Court justified its holding on two principal grounds. First, the broadcast media are uniquely pervasive in the lives of all Americans, present not only in public but in the privacy of homes. Second, broadcasting is uniquely accessible to children, and special restrictions on indecent broadcasting were justified in light of this unique accessibility since certain forms of protected speech may nonetheless be withheld from children. The

Pacifica decision thus enabled the FCC to regulate broadcasts despite Supreme Court precedent protecting these forms of speech.

The potentially expansive role of the FCC, however, has been quite limited in other contexts. Broadcasting has been given a lower level of First Amendment protection, which allows for more restrictions. That reduced protection derives from the unique characteristics of the broadcast medium, which do not necessarily transfer to other media. Notably, Congress attempted to respond to the rise in media indecency by enacting stringent regulations for cable television. One of the illustrative examples of these new efforts included a law designed to protect children from "signal bleed," those fleeting moments when inappropriate images and sounds on scrambled cable stations escape unscrambled. The Court found this law unconstitutional in *United States v. Playboy Entertainment Group, Inc.* (2000). In that case, the adult entertainment company challenged part of the legislation that required cable companies to fully scramble sexually oriented programming or limit their transmissions to between 10 p.m. and 6 a.m. when children would not likely be watching. Congress had hoped that the "full scrambling" requirement would address signal bleed. The Court found that these requirements would effectively block signals but ruled that the requirements abridged the First Amendment on grounds that there existed an effective less restrictive alternative; households simply could order signal blocking. Such targeted blocking allowed the government to support parental authority without denying adult speakers and willing listeners their First Amendment rights. Given alternative ways to establish legislative goals, the Court struck down the provision. It found that the statute was not narrowly tailored to advance the admittedly compelling goal of facilitating parental control over their children's access to sexual images or sounds via signal bleed. *Playboy Entertainment Group*, then, stands for firm limits on the state's effort to protect children when the rights of adults are involved and parents can protect children on their own volition. The case also importantly reveals the extent to which the Court may be willing to reject the assumption that parents will want to limit their children's market of ideas—all of which ends up shielding adolescents from state censorship.

The child protective rationales announced in *Ginsberg* also have helped generate a series of federal laws aimed to regulate the Internet. Despite the persuasiveness of child protection needs, the laws have been subjected to numerous legal challenges that tend to find those needs insufficient to stifle the rights of adults. Congress's first major foray into the field was the CDA of 1996 (2000), which regulated the display and distribution of "indecent" materials to minors. The Supreme Court invalidated this act because of its vague terms and failure to use the least restrictive means to accomplish the government's purpose (*Reno v. ACLU*, 1997). Congress responded two years later with a more carefully drawn law, the Child Online Protection Act (COPA, 2000). Despite this effort, a lower court enjoined COPA's enforcement and the Supreme Court affirmed the court's holding (*Ashcroft v. ACLU*, 2004). The Supreme Court, reiterating that a trial court granting such an injunction must conclude that the plaintiffs are likely to prevail on the merits of their claim, held that the plaintiffs had satisfied the appropriate standard. The majority focused on the likelihood that the statute burdens some speech that is protected for adults. The Court reasoned that it was important to let the injunction stand pending a full trial because of the potential harm in chilling protected speech that could result from the prosecution of distributors of Internet materials under COPA. In remanding the case, the Court indicated that it would be possible, although not likely, for the government to meet its burden of showing that COPA is necessary for Congress to accomplish its goal of safeguarding children from harmful materials via the Internet.

Importantly, the limits in the manner *Ginsberg*-type approaches to child protective efforts do not mean that the legal system cannot use the power of the purse to curb speech. Indeed, Congress has had slightly more success with the Children's Internet Protection Act (CIPA, 2000), which denies federal funds to public libraries that fail to place filters on their publicly accessible computers. But that ruling relied on the conclusion that the limitation was a valid exercise of Congressional spending power. By upholding CIPA in *United States v. American Library Association* (2003), the Court recognized the latitude Congress has to attach reasonable conditions to the receipt of federal funds, as long as the conditions do not abridge constitutional rights. This standard was met since libraries could already adopt filters on their own without implicating the First Amendment and, given that the filters can be disabled for adult patrons, the filtering software did not prevent adult library patrons from gaining access to some constitutionally protected expression or abridges libraries' First Amendment rights. Declining to apply heightened judicial scrutiny in reviewing the law, a majority of the justices concluded that libraries should be able to block online pornography since they can exclude pornography from print collections without being subjected to heightened scrutiny. As we have seen in the previous chapter, these approaches to countering limits on the government's power to censor gain increasing significance, but the general rule remains that the legal system will closely scrutinize efforts to censor materials alleged to be harmful to minors, especially when those rights may infringe the rights of adults.

Protecting Adolescents' Right to Speak

We have seen that a hallmark principle underlying the protection of free speech stresses the need to permit a free trade in ideas, even ideas that the overwhelming majority of people might find distasteful or discomforting. The belief is that such freedom permits the development of individuality, respects diversity, and prepares individuals for engagement in democratic society. As a result, the First Amendment ordinarily denies a state the power to prohibit the dissemination of information that a vast majority of its citizens believes to be false and fraught with evil consequence. As expected, the extent to which adolescents may benefit from this protection varies from context to context and from one form of speech to another. This section examines the rights of minors addressed by the Court in its censorship jurisprudence. Although sporadic, the cases have produced a wide range of analyses addressing religious, political, sexual, and racial issues. Admittedly, these areas do not neatly replicate key areas of concern for addressing the censorship of adolescents. Nor do they tend to address directly adolescents' media rights. But doctrine works by analogy and precedent, which makes these lines of cases important to understand if we are to envision adolescents' rights and consider how the law protects adolescents' freedoms. How the law treats adolescents' informational environments dictates how it approaches adolescents' media use. Viewed in light of its potential impact on adolescents' relationships with their social world, adolescents' right to speak clearly reaches the heart of adolescents' developing identity, which often is ignored in analyses of media rights. Together, these cases offer a sense of the extent to which jurisprudence shields adolescents from censorship and, in a deeper sense, recognizes their personhood and fosters their development—the central concern of media and informational rights we will develop in the chapter that follows.

Political Expression

The Court explicitly includes adolescents within its formulation of political expressions that receive considerable constitutional protection. The leading case addressing adolescents' political expression, *Tinker v. Des Moines Independent Community School District* (1969), spiritedly affirmed that adolescents do have First Amendment rights and that they do not lose those rights even in authoritarian governmental institutions. In *Tinker*, a number of students, including a 13-, 15-, and 16-year-old, donned black armbands to protest the United States' involvement in the Vietnam War. Des Moines school officials, fearing possible controversy and disruption, directed the students to stop wearing the armbands at school, suspended them when they refused to do so, and told them they could return if they followed the principals' directives. Rather than rule in favor of the school officials, the Supreme Court supported the students' right to express their political views in a peaceful manner. The Court held that wearing an armband to express a viewpoint constituted a symbolic act closely related to "pure speech," and was, therefore, clearly protected under the First Amendment. The Court famously wrote that neither "students nor teachers shed their constitutional rights of freedom of speech or expression at the schoolhouse gate" (*Tinker v. Des Moines Independent Community School District*, 1969, p. 506). State institutions are not immune from constitutional scrutiny simply because they have adolescents in their care. In addition and often ignored, by ruling that crossing the threshold into the school did not mean that adolescents' constitutional rights evaporated, the Court affirmed that adolescents retained arguably even stronger rights when out of public schools.

Although *Tinker* remains perhaps best remembered for its ringing endorsement of students' freedoms, the decision contains much more. The Court did more than underscore the need to restrict a school official's discretionary authority over students' political speech—even symbolic speech in the form of black armbands. In explaining its holding, the Court stressed that the schools apparently had sought to prohibit only the wearing of armbands symbolizing opposition to the Vietnam War and not other politically controversial symbols. The Court found the prohibition of expression of one particular opinion constitutionally impermissible, at least without strong evidence of its necessity. The Court ostensibly provided school officials with a high standard to follow if they wished to limit the rights of students to express their political beliefs. The Court rejected the school officials' attempts to defend their actions based on their fear of disturbances arising from displays of black armbands. The Court acknowledged that words spoken in school, whether in or out of the classroom, might disrupt the normal school routine, but insisted that the Constitution obliges schools to take that risk. School officials may censor student speech only when they can show that it "materially and substantially" interferes with the work of the school, school discipline, or the rights of others in the school community (*Tinker v. Des Moines Independent Community School District*, 1969, p. 509). The Court emphasized that an "undifferentiated fear or apprehension of disturbance does not suffice to overcome the right to freedom of expression" and that punishment may not be based only on "a mere desire to avoid the discomfort and unpleasantness that always accompany an unpopular viewpoint" (p. 508).

Tinker's powerful recognition of adolescents' constitutional rights certainly is significant, but that significance derives from the rationale supporting efforts to limit the state's ability to censor political expression. The Court framed the limit in terms of the state's role in fostering adolescents into responsible citizenship. The Court noted that our government may not fashion adolescents as "closed-circuit recipients of only that which the State chooses to communicate," that adolescents "may not be confined to the expression of those sentiments that are officially approved," and that states had no business conducting its schools so as to "foster a homogeneous people" (*Tinker v. Des Moines Independent Community School District*, 1969, p. 511). In further explaining that schools could not censor some but not other politically controversial symbols, the Court stressed the need for openness to competing ideas as it tied the students' protest to the citizen-critic model. It is this openness to competing ideas, said the Court, "that is the basis of our national strength and of the independence and vigor of Americans who grow up and live in this relatively permissive, often disputatious, society" (pp. 508–09). As the Court noted, "That the [Boards of Education] are educating the young for citizenship is reason for scrupulous protection of Constitutional freedoms of the individual, if we are not to strangle the free mind at its source and teach youth to discount important principles of our government as mere platitudes" (p. 507). The Court concluded that "the vigilant protection of constitutional freedoms is nowhere more vital than in the community of American schools" (p. 512). This view envisions classrooms as the premier site for fostering the "marketplace of ideas." Borrowing from cases that had found unconstitutional efforts to prevent the appointment or retention of public school employees who advocated or taught the forcible overthrow of government, the Court reasoned that the nation's future depends on leaders trained through wide exposure to that robust exchange of ideas which discovers truth "out of a multitude of tongues, [rather] than through any kind of authoritative selection" (p. 512, quoting *Keyishian v. Bd. of Regents*, 1967, p. 603). The Court firmly embraced the need to protect adolescents' expression in the name of diversity, individual development, and democratic nation building.

A generous reading of *Tinker's* approach to adolescents' freedom of expression emphasizes the democratic values at stake in students' speech and requires that the government provide substantial justification for burdening the speech activity. *Tinker* furnishes strong support to the proposition that the First Amendment entitles student speech activity to robust protection. The majority's approach emphasizes the importance of student speech, the limits on school authority, and the need for judicial review. Instead of conceptualizing the protection of student expression as in tension with the mission of schools, the Court regards safeguarding speech as a crucial part of educating students about the Constitution's foundational premises. However, linking adolescents' rights to expression, especially while in schools, to civic engagement and preparation for life in a pluralistic society does not mean that adolescents have free reign to express themselves in and out of educational institutions. Indeed, *Tinker* may have protected the rights of adolescents generously, but the Court would not necessarily be generous to *Tinker*.

Tinker may well remain one of the most important Supreme Court case that protects the First Amendment constitutional rights of students and delineates the political rights of adolescents, but even the *Tinker* opinion itself noted critical limitations of adolescents' rights, and, as we will see later in this chapter, those limitations become more obvious when the Supreme Court later cites to *Tinker* to narrow adolescents' First Amendment freedoms. The *Tinker* opinion makes clear that consideration of the school's educational mission led the Court to apply a test that does not accord students the same speech rights as those possessed by the person on the street. The Court essentially established a test that balances students' First Amendment rights with the necessity for school officials to maintain an orderly school environment. The Court stated that schools may punish student speech only on proof that the speech would "substantially interfere with the work of the school or impinge upon the rights of other students" (*Tinker v. Des Moines Independent Community School District*, 1969, p. 509). Thus, as the Court expanded students' rights under the First Amendment, the Court correspondingly narrowed its decision by highlighting the need to affirm "the comprehensive authority of the States and of school officials, consistent with fundamental constitutional safeguards, to prescribe and control conduct in the schools" (p. 507). Under this view, courts should defer to the expertise and authority of school officials in deciding when expression needs to be prohibited and punished. The focus on the comprehensive authority reflects the ingrained belief that adults and state officials occupy the best position to determine the extent of adolescents' freedoms.

Read in the spirit of freedom and democratic ideals, *Tinker* clearly did not aim to deliver school officials unbridled discretion in efforts to reconcile the conflict between students' speech rights and the authority of the schools to abridge such rights, but the application of the *Tinker* rule bestows schools with considerable power. *Tinker* determines that school officials must now connect a student's speech with the school disruption, thus ending the long-established principle that a school official's good judgment was all that was needed to justify his or her actions. Now, a challenge to a school rule places the burden on the administration to demonstrate a constitutionally sufficient justification to regulate student behavior. But, in determining whether school officials are justified in "forecasting" disruption, *Tinker* requires only that a court find that their anticipation of potential disorder was not unreasonable. This standard renders it difficult for a court to find fault with a school administration when its regulation has acted as a prior restraint and precluded the anticipated disturbance from occurring. In *Tinker*, the state (in this case, the public school) had only to demonstrate a "legitimate" interest in regulation, rather than the "compelling" interest that often must be shown in such circumstances.

Tinker and its progeny may have appropriately recognized that the First Amendment rights of students are somewhat abridged inside of schools, but recall that the Court had created a distinction between expression taking place off-campus and that which occurs inside the schoolhouse gates. In delineating the rights of adolescents in schools, the Court revealed the fundamental point that adolescents' political expressions outside of schools deserve protection as the Court declared that adolescents have constitutional rights that do not evaporate simply because they are in state-controlled schools. The Court actually has not squarely addressed the political expression rights in pubic, noncustodial contexts. Clearly, the limits placed on adults' speech freedoms would apply, but whether adolescents retain peculiar rights because of their minor status remains unknown and untested at the Supreme Court level. It may seem that adolescents' rights outside of school are rather strong, but judging from other forms of speech, the Constitution permits numerous restrictions. Those restrictions are permissible because minors can be viewed not only as different from adults but also like adults. These limitations are most obvious in several forms of expression we now turn to examine.

Sexual Expressions

Adolescent sexuality contributes to one of the most contentious areas of jurisprudence seeking to address concerns about adolescents' inappropriate expressions. As with other areas of adolescents' rights, we find considerable limits, and those limits take different forms depending on contextual differences. The different contexts in which expressions are made—such as public expressions and expressions made in custodial contexts (namely educational institutions)—lead to different analyses but they reveal strikingly similar outcomes in the manner the legal system regulates expressions. Indeed, this area of law tends to treat adolescents as de facto children, which grants adults considerable control over adolescents' sexual expressions.

We already have seen that child pornography receives little First Amendment protection. Considering their rights compared to adults, it is clear that adolescents may not be obscene or even express what would be indecent if they were adults. We already have visited the leading case in this area, *New York v. Ferber* (1982), that addressed the extent to which society may suppress materials harmful to minors. That case, however, also incidentally involved the rights of minors to express their sexuality. *Ferber* had held not only that society may limit materials harmful to minors but also that society must limit materials derived from minors. Indeed, it was the involvement of minors in the production of the materials that provided the Court with its strongest rationale for limiting the expression. The *Ferber* Court clearly separated the exception for child pornography from the obscenity standard announced in *Miller v. California* (1973). The standard set forth in *Miller* did not reflect the state's particular and more compelling interest in prosecuting those who promote the sexual exploitation of children. Further, the *Ferber* exception differed from the *Miller* requirements because it did not require prurient interest and patently offensive material; nor did the material at issue need to be considered as a whole. The purpose of the exception carved out in *Ferber* was to help prevent the abuse of children engaged in sexual conduct for commercial purposes. In fact, *Ferber* reaffirmed that where the speech is neither obscene nor the product of sexual abuse, it does not fall outside the First Amendment's protection. And this view was again affirmed in the Court's rejection of a federal law banning "virtual" child pornography (adults depicted as children *Ashcroft v. Free Speech Coalition*, 2002). These cases reiterate that speech may not be prohibited because it concerns subjects offending our sensibilities, but offending speech can be limited if it involves the expressions of minors. Together, these cases restrict materials that would appear to be most readily subjected to censorship—child pornography—to a very narrow class that only prohibits the expression of minors.

In addition to cases allowing censorship of adolescents' expressions deemed obscene because adolescents rather than adults express them, important cases address adolescents expressing sexual language that some may deem to be inappropriate and thus subjected to censorship. The two leading cases in this area return us to the public schools. In the first case, *Bethel School District No. 403 v. Fraser* (1986), Matthew Fraser, a high school honor student, delivered a nominating speech on behalf of a classmate at a school-sponsored assembly. To communicate the qualities of his candidate, Fraser used crude, if humorous, sexual innuendos. School officials found his use of language unacceptable under this section of their school policy: "Conduct which materially and substantially interferes with the educational process is prohibited, including the use of obscene, profane language or gestures" (*Bethel School District No. 403 v. Fraser*, 1986, p. 678). Fraser was suspended for a few days and kept from speaking at his graduation as scheduled.

The Supreme Court ruled that the First Amendment did not protect students' use of vulgar and offensive language in public discourse. The Court upheld the punishment and emphasized the need for judicial deference to educational institutions given the importance of schools in "inculcating" the "habits and manners of civility" (pp. 680–81). The Court reasoned that "The undoubted freedom to advocate unpopular and controversial views in schools and classrooms must be balanced against the society's countervailing interest in teaching students the boundaries of socially appropriate behavior" (p. 681). Importantly, the Court distinguished *Tinker* on the basis that it had involved political speech, whereas the expression in *Fraser* was sexual in nature. The Court noted:

> During Fraser's delivery of the speech, a school counselor observed the reaction of students to the speech. Some students hooted and yelled; some by gestures graphically simulated the sexual activities pointedly alluded to in respondent's speech. Other students appeared to be bewildered and embarrassed by the speech. One teacher reported that on the day following the speech, she found it necessary to forgo a portion of the scheduled class lesson in order to discuss the speech with the class. (*Bethel School District No. 403 v. Fraser*, 1986, p. 678)

Given the facts offered in evidence, the Court easily could have focused on the effect of the speech by using *Tinker's* "substantial disruption" test in order to find the students' speech unprotected expression. Instead, the Court elected to focus on the sexual content of the speech to reject the idea that states must closely protect student speech in schools; schools need freedom to regulate student speech on school grounds. The Court concluded that "[a] high school assembly or classroom is no place for a sexually explicit monologue. . . . It was perfectly appropriate for the school to disassociate itself to make the point to the pupils that vulgar speech and lewd conduct is wholly inconsistent with the 'fundamental values' of public school education" (*Bethel School District No. 403 v. Fraser*, 1986, pp. 685–86). Although the Court noted the importance of permitting the expression of a variety of viewpoints in the schools, it emphasized that "the undoubted freedom to advocate unpopular and controversial views in schools and classrooms must be balanced against the society's countervailing interest in teaching students the boundaries of socially appropriate behavior" (p. 681). Without hesitation, the Court deferred to the school authorities' conclusory determination that Fraser's speech seriously disrupted the school's educational activities. Reasoning that the school's fundamental role was to instruct students about the "essential lessons of civil, mature conduct," the Court held that a school may suppress speech that does not directly inculcate such lessons (p. 683). The majority stated that "it is a highly appropriate function of public school education to prohibit the use of vulgar and offensive terms in public discourse" and that "it was perfectly appropriate for the school to disassociate itself" from it (pp. 683–686). The Court found a "marked distinction" between the double entendres contained in Fraser's speech and the political message communicated through the students' armbands in *Tinker*.

Fraser was not just different from *Tinker* in terms of the Court's ruling. *Fraser* fundamentally moved away from the *Tinker* model in the manner it embraced the need for judicial deference to the authority and expertise of school officials. The Court notably began its opinion by evoking the *parens patriae* doctrine from the pre-*Tinker* era and its interest in controlling adolescent behavior. As with the *Tinker* dissent, the *Fraser* Court wished "'to disclaim any purpose … to hold that the Federal Constitution compels the teachers, parents, and elected school officials to surrender control of the American public school system to public school students'" (*Bethel School District No. 403 v. Fraser*, 1986, p. 686). The Court reasoned that the school's legitimate interest in protecting the student audience from exposure to lewd, vulgar, and plainly offensive speech justified the school's disciplinary action. It further reiterated the proposition that speech protected by the First Amendment for adults is not necessarily protected for children, arguing that in the public school context school authorities may take the sensibilities of fellow students into consideration when regulating speech activities. As a result, courts give great deference to the authority and expertise of school officials when regulating student expression. The required evidence need not be robust. The *Fraser* Court noted that "the pervasive sexual innuendo in Fraser's speech was plainly offensive to both teachers and students—indeed to any mature person" (p. 683). And, in this instance, the speech could not have been that offensive to many of the students because Fraser ultimately delivered a commencement speech after being elected as a write-in candidate. But, again, it would be adults' opinions, rather than those of students, that would control whether students may express themselves in these contexts.

The second leading case in this area, *Hazelwood School District v. Kuhlmeier* (1988), involved the extent to which school officials could exercise control over the content of an official high school newspaper produced as part of a school journalism class. Following the accepted practice in the Hazelwood School District, the journalism teacher submitted printer proofs of the forthcoming edition of the school newspaper (ironically named *Spectrum*) to the principal for review prior to publication. Without providing the student writers with any notice or opportunity to respond, the principal directed deletion of two articles (one dealing with teen pregnancy and another with teen experiences with parental divorce) from the newspaper because they were "inappropriate, personal, sensitive, and unsuitable" (*Hazelwood School District v. Kuhlmeier*, 1988, p. 278). Three student staff members on the *Spectrum* brought suit in federal court alleging that the principal's acts of censorship violated their First Amendment rights. The Court reasoned that, when student expression is part of a curriculum-related activity, school officials may exercise editorial control over the "style and content" of the student speech "so long as their actions are reasonably related to legitimate pedagogical concerns" (p. 273). Because writing for the *Spectrum* was deemed to be a part of the school's educational curriculum, which the school was entitled to regulate in any reasonable manner, the Court followed *Fraser*'s reasoning and deferred to the school authorities' determination regarding the inappropriateness of the articles. The Court created a distinction between school-sponsored and incidental expression, and held that a school may regulate speech which a reasonable person would deem to be school-sponsored. The Court recognized that "a school need not tolerate student speech that is inconsistent with its 'basic educational mission,' even though the government could not censor similar speech outside the school" (p. 273). Applying the new standard and without explaining the legal limits of the pedagogical-concerns exception to *Tinker*, the Court found that the principal's stated concerns about disruption were reasonable and thus a lawful response to that threat.

The *Hazelwood* Court granted school officials sweeping authority to censor expression in school-sponsored activities. The Court did so by extending *Fraser*'s deference to school authorities' regulation of student speech by making a distinction between tolerating and promoting student speech. According to the Court, the First Amendment requires schools to tolerate personal student speech that happens to occur on the school premises but is unrelated to the curriculum. On the other hand, if student speech activity is curriculum-related, it might be perceived by students, staff, and outsiders as having the school's sanction. As a consequence, schools have the authority to regulate (or even prohibit) such speech. Under the *Hazelwood* standard, however, the school's decision to suspend the students in *Tinker* arguably would have been upheld. A reasonable application of *Hazelwood* could view any student speech inside the classroom, including the wearing of armbands, as school-sanctioned or approved and, therefore, subject to regulation. As the Court in *Hazelwood* stated, "these activities may fairly be characterized as part of the school curriculum, whether or not they occur in a traditional classroom setting, so long as they are supervised by faculty members and designed to impart particular knowledge or skills to student participants and audiences" (*Hazelwood School District v. Kuhlmeier*, 1988, p. 271). In effect, *Hazelwood* just about overruled *Tinker* by severely circumscribing the decision's applicability.

The Court's invocation of the rational basis standard translates into very limited judicial review of the school authorities' conduct. Under *Hazelwood*, courts have no obligation to weigh or investigate the government's interest in excluding student speech or the availability of less restrictive alternatives to an outright bar. A school's speech regulation has a reasonable relation to the school's curriculum unless it completely lacks "any valid educational purpose" (*Hazelwood School District v. Kuhlmeier*, 1988, p. 273). Only then is the First Amendment "so 'directly and sharply implicate[d]' as to require judicial intervention to protect students' constitutional rights" (p. 273). Under the *Hazelwood* standard, if student expression interferes with the school's power "to assure that participants learn whatever lessons the activity is designed to teach," school officials may restrict it (p. 271). Thus, although the Court in *Fraser* had declared that students have an "undoubted freedom to advocate unpopular and controversial views in schools and classrooms" (*Bethel School District No. 403 v. Fraser*, 1986, p. 681), the practical effect of the *Fraser/Hazelwood* judicial deference to school officials leaves little real protection for student expression not endorsed by school authorities.

The *Fraser/Hazelwood* framework largely ignores the reality that schools, as a practical matter, are the only forum in which minors may express themselves publicly. Under *Fraser* and *Hazelwood*'s broad definition of "curriculum" and their concomitant deference to school authorities, the schools have wide power to regulate and exclude student speech. The Court in *Frazer* and *Hazelwood* significantly disappointed the expectations of those who read *Tinker* as providing robust free speech rights for students. The cases gave short shrift to *Tinker's* claim that (1) students are "persons" under the Constitution with fundamental rights the state must respect; (2) school officials are bound by the Constitution, and their discretionary functions performed under state authority must be within the limits of the Bill of Rights; and (3) schools may punish student speech only with proof that the speech would "'substantially interfere with the work of the school or impinge on the rights of other students'" (*Tinker v. Des Moines Independent Community School District*, 1969, p. 509). Instead the Court stressed the doctrine of *parens patriae*, deference to school officials, and minimal constitutional protection for student speech. Adolescents essentially possess the same minimal rights in schools as they do in their own homes; adults determine the limits of adolescents' expressions. These cases reveal that, even though *Tinker* may not have been technically over-ruled, the Court has yet to give its legacy full expression.

Religious Expression

Jurisprudence addressing adolescents' rights to religious expressions, especially the right not to express a religious conviction not their own, dates back to the foundational cases dealing with adolescents' rights. More than fifty years ago, in *West Virginia State Board of Education v. Barnette* (1943), the Court recognized the importance of protecting students' First Amendment rights in the primary and secondary school setting. In *Barnette*, members of a Jehovah's Witness congregation, on behalf of children in public schools in West Virginia, challenged a state law requiring all students to salute the flag and recite the pledge of allegiance. The Jehovah's Witnesses argued that the state regulation conflicted with their religious beliefs and improperly subjected children, including their own children, to possible exclusion from school. The Court held that requiring school children to salute the United States flag violated the First Amendment by compelling "affirmation of a belief and an attitude of mind" (*West Virginia State Board of Education v. Barnette*, 1943, pp. 633, 642). The Court recognized that school officials have an important interest in promoting citizenship but declined to uphold the school's authority to punish students exercising their religious faith.

Although commentators deem *Barnette* the starting point for examinations of adolescents' free speech rights and religious freedom, this area of jurisprudence quickly becomes complex as it needs to consider the fullness of the First Amendment. In addition to free speech protections, the Constitution's First Amendment contains two clauses directly relating to religion: the free exercise clause and the establishment clause. Specifically, the free exercise clause guarantees freedom of religious expression to individuals, while the establishment clause prohibits governments from becoming involved in religious affairs and prohibits religious officials from exerting undue influence over the government. For our purposes, the First Amendment's religion clauses gain significance to the extent that they protect free speech by maintaining a balance between church and state. In the balancing, the Court still deals with fundamental issues raised in *Barnette*. The Court seeks to determine the extent to which a state fosters an orthodoxy that would place at risk the freedom of belief and conscience that provides the sole assurance that religious faith is authentic, not imposed.

The Supreme Court has struggled to refine the tests used to determine violations of the religious clauses. For a period of time, the Court referred to the separation between church and state as a wall dividing the two institutions. No state or federal government could pass laws that aided religion or preferred one religion over another. More recently, however, the wall of separation has become more metaphorical and a blurred distinction has replaced what was once believed to be a necessarily solid line. The Court exemplifies this blurring by the manner it relies on three different approaches to determine the constitutionality of government actions regarding the establishment of religion. The Supreme Court enunciated its first establishment clause test in *Lemon v. Kurtzman*, 1971, p. 625), a case involving the use of public funds to pay for teachers' salaries, textbooks, and school supplies to private schools, some of which were religious. Although the Court unanimously found the assistance unconstitutional, it offered a variety of opinions that ultimately resulted in the "*Lemon* test." Under that test, a government practice violates the establishment clause if it (1) lacks a secular purpose, (2) has the primary effect of advancing or inhibiting religion, or (3) excessively entangles government with religion.

The Court announced yet another test in *Lee v. Weisman* (1992), a case known for developing a "coercion test" to address the extent to which a public school could permit prayers at graduation ceremonies. Under that test, a governmental action violates the establishment clause if the religious practice conveys the message that the government is establishing, or at least favoring, a chosen religion, which implicitly impinges on the free exercise of religion. Unconstitutional coercion occurs when the government directs a formal religious exercise that forces the participation of objectors. A third test, known as the "endorsement test," attempts to determine whether the government endorses religion through governmental action. This test slightly alters the first two prongs of the *Lemon* test and some consider it a modification of *Lemon*. Instead of focusing solely on the presence of a secular purpose, the endorsement test requires a court to scrutinize whether the government's purpose endorses, condemns, favors, prefers, or promotes a certain religious belief over another. Under this approach, the government acts unconstitutionally when its endorsement of religion sends a message to nonadherents that they are outsiders, not full members of the political community, and an accompanying message to adherents that they are insiders, favored members of the political community. Although announced in a concurring opinion, the Court subsequently adopted the test, as revealed in the most recent Supreme Court case examining prayer in a public high school, *Santa Fe Independent School District v. Doe* (2000). As our brief review reveals, the Court tends to analyze government practices challenged on establishment clause grounds under these three complementary, and occasionally overlapping, tests. This approach obviously renders this area of law somewhat unpredictable and makes brief reviews highly incomplete and perhaps even misleading. We thus necessarily narrow our review to leading cases that delineate the contours and limits the Constitution places on adolescents' religious expressions.

Given that schools provide the context in which adolescents most often interact directly with state institutions, it is not surprising to find that legal disputes involving religion and adolescents largely take place in school contexts. Both individuals and groups can make religious claims on public schools. Those claims may either seek to prohibit religious expression or to allow it. Individual claims or objections by students may involve a wide range of issues, such as by allowing religious meetings during noninstructional time, wearing religious clothing or symbols, making speeches, or distributing literature. Students also may make claims through their religious organizations. Those claims most frequently involve the provision of meeting space in school facilities, availability of resources, and distribution of religious materials. In addition to individual students, religious organizations also may make demands of school officials, such as requesting meeting space on school premises and distribution of religious materials. School responses to those organizations may be objected to by the organizations themselves if schools fail to accommodate their needs, or by parents or students who seek to limit a school's accommodation. Given the high volume of litigation in this area, a good handful of these cases eventually have made their way to the Supreme Court. These cases provide the necessary starting point for our analyses.

In *Lee v. Weisman* (1992), the Court addressed school prayer outside the classroom when it confronted the issue of whether the inclusion of prayers by clergy members during a school graduation ceremony violated the establishment clause. In this case, at the invitation of a principal, a rabbi delivered a nonsectarian invocation and a benediction during a middle school graduation ceremony. As a result, Daniel Weisman, the parent of a student participating in the ceremony, sought to bar other public school officials from inviting clergy to deliver invocations and benedictions at any future public school graduation. In its review of the case, the Court interpreted the Constitution to guarantee that the government will not coerce a person into participating in religious exercises. Further, the Court found that the school district's supervision of a public school graduation placed considerable public and peer pressure on the attending students to stand as a group or to maintain respectful silence during the invocation. As such, for many of the students attending the graduation the act of standing or remaining silent constituted participation in the rabbi's prayer. The Court found that a state contravenes the establishment clause when it places school children in this position. Although the parties stipulated the voluntariness of the graduation and promotional ceremonies, the Supreme Court acknowledged that "the Constitution forbids the State to exact religious conformity from a student as the price of attending her own . . . graduation" (*Lee v. Weisman,* 1992, p. 86). The "State had in every practical sense compelled attendance and participation in an explicit religious exercise at an event of singular importance to every student, one the objecting student had no real alternative to avoid" (p. 598). Given that state officials directed the performance of a formal religious exercise during the ceremony, the Court held that the establishment clause forbade clergy members from offering prayers as part of an official school ceremony because students cannot be compelled to participate in religious exercises.

Santa Fe Independent School District v. Doe (2000) presents the Court's most recent decision regarding the separation between church and state as it applies to school prayer. *Santa Fe* involved prayer at the football games of a Texas high school. In order to continue the ritual of prayer before football games, the school board had implemented a policy that allowed the students to vote in two elections: one to determine whether a brief invocation and/or message should be delivered during the pre-game ceremonies of the home varsity football games, and another to choose a student, from a list of volunteers, to deliver the invocation or message throughout the year. The district apparently did so to avoid being viewed as establishing religion. The Supreme Court rejected the school district's argument that its policy for student-initiated prayer represented private speech, not government speech, endorsing religion. The Court noted that the invocations were "authorized by a government policy and [took] place on government property at government-sponsored school-related events" (*Santa Fe Independent School District v. Doe*, 2000, pp. 302). Although the Court specifically noted that not every message given under the same circumstances would be considered government speech, a pre-game prayer could not be considered a public forum with minimal state involvement, particularly when only one student was allowed to speak throughout the year.

A key factor for the Court seemed to be the majoritarian process developed to allow prayer and the effect of this process on minority beliefs. The student election, said the Court, "effectively silenced" the views of the minority, put the minority at the mercy of the majority, and failed to protect diverse student speech. In fact, far from making the prayer permissible, the election actually intensified the offense of the minority. The Court found the majoritarian process especially troublesome because it was coupled with one of the factors from *Lee*: state direction of a religious message. The pre-game prayer clearly bore the state's imprint. The elections occurred because the school board allowed them. The school board even directed that the student council would hold the elections with the advice and supervision of the principal. Further, the policy itself invited and encouraged religious messages. Invocations were the only type of message mentioned directly and the purposes of the policy made it clear that a solemn, nonreligious message would be out of place. In addition, according to the policy, the message or invocation had to be consistent with the goals and purposes of the policy, implying that a religious message was necessary. Most importantly, however, students understood that the policy was about prayer. The Court found the imprint of the state to be present in other ways as well: the name of the school was displayed prominently on the jerseys of the football team, on the band and cheerleaders' uniforms, and on the field. The prayer was "delivered to a large audience assembled as part of a regularly scheduled, school-sponsored function conducted on school property" (*Santa Fe Independent School District v. Doe*, 2000, p. 307). The imprint of the state, combined with the election used to initiate prayer, contributed to the audience's impression that the prayer was an expression of the views of the majority, delivered under the sanction of the school board.

The Court also found coercion, the second factor from *Lee*, to be present in *Santa Fe*, despite the fact that the prayers were held at an extracurricular event. The Court rejected the claim that the football game events were voluntary. Some students, namely, the football players, the band, and the cheerleaders, were essentially required to attend. Football games and other extracurricular activities are also part of the complete educational experience. In addition, the Court noted that the games are large gatherings of students and faculty, both past and present, as well as family and friends, all rooting for a common cause. The Court explained that the Constitution forbids the school from forcing students to either choose to attend (or not) a social event to avoid a religious message. Even if the choice were truly voluntary, the Court found that the policy was improper because it coerced students to participate in an act of religious worship. Although striking down this particular policy, the Court still recognized the importance of public worship in many communities and the desire to use public prayer to mark certain occasions. The Court reaffirmed that not all religious activity in public schools is unconstitutional—voluntary prayer remains within the bounds of the First Amendment. The Court also noted the distinction between the public and private sphere, emphasizing that the responsibility and choice of religious beliefs are committed to the private sphere. By passing the policy, the district forced the debate into the public sphere. By doing so, the policy encouraged divisiveness along religious lines in a public school setting, which the First Amendment forbids.

Unlike the case of graduation prayer or prayers at sporting events, no Supreme Court case directly addresses religious speech in the classroom, such as oral reports and presentations. Rather than involving the religious clauses, controversies arising in these contexts typically use the *Tinker-Hazelwood* dichotomy between personal student expression and school-sponsored speech. The reason for not involving the religion clauses is simple. In cases involving student-initiated prayer at graduations, the school usually defends the religious expression against the claim of an establishment clause violation. The plaintiffs argue that the speech violates the establishment clause because it is school-sponsored speech endorsing religion, and the school defends the speech on the grounds that the messages are private expression, not school-sponsored speech. By contrast, in cases involving classroom speech, the school usually has excluded or otherwise restricted the student religious speech, and the student challenges the exclusion on free speech grounds. These classroom speech cases usually involve students below high school age, and the school typically will argue that prohibiting the religious speech is necessary to avoid a perception by students that the school endorses the speech. The student, by contrast, typically argues that the religious speech is private expression and, thus, protected by *Tinker*. As expected from our discussions of *Tinker's* progeny, students tend to lose these cases.

Since cases involving religious meetings on school grounds sometimes turn on whether they can be framed as private expressions, they raise their own peculiar issues. In *Good News Club v. Milford Central School* (2001), a Christian club sought the use of school facilities to hold weekly meetings that involved prayer, Bible reading, Bible verse memorization, and playing Bible games. The school board prohibited the Club from using the school's facilities because its activities were not limited to a religious perspective on the secular subject of morality. The Supreme Court addressed whether the public school could prohibit a religious club from using its building based on the club's religious message and the religious nature of its meeting. The Court held that the school could not prohibit the group from meeting if it permitted other non-religion-based groups to meet in the building. Such viewpoint discrimination violates the First Amendment rights of those who wished to participate in the religious club's activities.

The majority focused on whether the school violated the free speech rights of the club by excluding the club from meeting after hours and whether the Board's establishment clause concern justified the prohibition. After acknowledging that the parties had stipulated to the school's being a limited public forum, the Court held that a school practiced viewpoint discrimination when the school prohibited the use of its facilities or denied funds based on the organization's espoused Christian message. Speech discussing permissible subject matter could not be excluded from a limited forum just because the speech had a religious viewpoint. Excluding the club from using school facilities constituted viewpoint discrimination and violated the First Amendment rights of those who wished to participate in the club's activities. The school board argued that its restrictions were necessary in order to avoid violating the establishment clause. The Court responded that although avoiding an establishment clause violation may provide a compelling justification for content-based discrimination, it was not a compelling justification in this case.

The Court provided five reasons to support its conclusion. First, it held that allowing the Club to meet on school grounds actually ensured neutrality in its treatment towards religious groups, rather than threatening neutrality. Second, the Court held that the proper establishment clause coercion analysis focused not on the children, but on the local community. Thus, the Court examined whether the local community would feel coercive pressure or misconstrue the school as endorsing the club's activities. Because children cannot attend the club without a parental permission slip, parents choose whether or not their children may attend the club's meeting. The parents, as adults in the community, were unlikely to be confused as to whether the school was endorsing religion. Third, the Court held that any emphasis the Court placed on the impressionability of children in establishment clause precedent was inapplicable in this case. The Court reasoned that it had never extended establishment clause jurisprudence to private religious conduct during non-school hours simply because the activities took place where elementary school children were present. Because non-schoolteachers taught the lessons after school, and students could only attend with parental consent, the Court found no establishment clause violation. Fourth, the Court dismissed the possibility of coercion because there was no evidence that children were permitted to loiter outside the classroom after the school day. The Court relied on several factors in concluding that young children would not misperceive the club's activities as government-endorsed: the instructors were not schoolteachers, the children were of different ages, and the club met in a resource room, not in an elementary school classroom. Finally, the Court held that just as the children might perceive acceptance of the Club's request as governmental endorsement, so they might also perceive rejection of the club's request as governmental hostility toward religion. The Court refused to employ a standard "in which a group's religious activity can be proscribed on the basis of what the youngest members of the audience might misperceive" (*Good News Club v. Milford Central School*, 2001, p. 119). The Court found that the countervailing interest of the free speech rights of the Club and its members outweighed any establishment clause defense.

Several opinions in the case addressed the peculiar position of the minors. Although agreeing with the Court's conclusion, one opinion did not agree with the standard used to analyze the school's establishment clause defense. The opinion stated that the Court should have evaluated "whether a child, participating in the Good News Club's activities, could reasonably perceive the school's permission for the Club to use its facilities as an endorsement of religion" (*Good News Club v. Milford Central School*, 2001, p. 127). It also stated that the Court should have examined additional factors, including the time of day of the meetings, age of the children, nature of the meetings, and other case specific circumstances to determine the children's perceptions of the Club's activities. Similarly, another opinion outlined the problems associated with permitting religious proselytizing in an elementary school setting, which include that younger students are more impressionable and more likely to misperceive the Club's activities as being endorsed by the government. Although these opinions would seem persuasive, the majority of the Court did not view them as significant enough to be addressed in its ruling. Rather, the majority decided the case by ignoring the special position of minors who could feel compelled to express religious views that were inconsistent with their own privately held beliefs. The Court sided with the parents of minors who wished to express and protect their religious views.

As expected, the right to express (or not) religious beliefs is limited not only in schools but also in homes through the power of parents to direct their children's religious upbringing. This is the rule that has emerged from cases granting parents the power to send their children to sectarian schools, a power that has taken a new meaning with the development of school choice programs built on vouchers. *Pierce v. Society of Sisters* (1925, pp. 534–35) started the trend. In that case, Oregon sought to require, by referendum, that all children attend public schools. The Court responded to a challenge to that statute by ruling that the Oregon law was an unconstitutional violation of the substantive due process rights of the parents:

We think it entirely plain that the Act of 1922 unreasonably interferes with the liberty of parents and guardians to direct the upbringing and education of children under their control . . . . The fundamental theory of liberty upon which all governments in this Union repose excludes any general power of the state to standardize its children by forcing them to accept instruction from public teachers only. The child is not the mere creature of the state; those who nurture him and direct his destiny have the right, coupled with the high duty, to recognize and prepare him for additional obligations. (*Pierce v. Society of Sisters*, 1925, pp. 534–35)

The Court did, however, preserve the authority of the state to mandate compulsory education and to regulate private schools, to which parents now had a constitutional blessing to send their children:

No question is raised concerning the power of the State reasonably to regulate all schools, to inspect, supervise, and examine them, their teachers and pupils; to require that all children of proper age attend some school, that teachers be of good moral character and patriotic disposition, that certain studies plainly essential to good citizenship must be taught, and that nothing be taught which is manifestly inimical to the public welfare. (p. 534)

It would take half a decade for the Court to recognize the right to the "free exercise" of religion directly involving minors. The Court did so in *Wisconsin v. Yoder* (1972, p. 234), when it held that "the First and Fourteenth Amendments prevent the state from compelling the parents of Amish children to cause their children to attend formal high school to age 16." Importantly, *Yoder* was a "parental rights" case, not a "minors' rights case," and it did not involve the right to "free exercise" in school. That case simply gave parents the free exercise right to impose their religious rights on their children.

In *Zelman v. Simmons-Harris* (2002), the Court would grant parents even greater power to choose schools for their children so that they (the parents) may exercise their religious rights in schools. That case gave parents the power by permitting voucher programs to include sectarian schools. In *Zelman*, the Ohio legislature enacted the Cleveland Scholarship and Tutoring Program, which allows parents of K-8 school students to use vouchers worth up to $2,250 for tuition at a private or religious school of choice. Putting an end to several years of legal battles, the Court concluded that the use of public money to underwrite tuition at private and religious schools did not violate the establishment clause of the Constitution as long as parents make the decision regarding where to use the voucher. Given the range of options and the responsibility of the parent to choose from among them, the Supreme Court concluded that the Cleveland program was neutral with regard to religion, even though the majority of voucher recipients chose religious schools. The Court wrote, "we believe that the program challenged here is a program of true private choice . . . and thus constitutional . . . the Ohio program is neutral in all respects toward religion" (*Zelman v. Simmons-Harris*, 2002, p. 651). The neutrality meant that parents, if they chose to do so, controlled their adolescents' religious development, expression, and rights. These cases reveal the prevailing tendency of the legal system to grant parents broad control over adolescents' religious environments.

Hateful Expression

Leading cases involving hate and violent expression squarely address the rights of adolescents. Yet, their findings and analyses clearly indicate that the age of the individuals involved did not influence the Court's analysis. The legal system treats adolescents' hateful expression conducted in public as it would the expression of adults. The problem of regulating such speech in the public marketplace is different, of course, from its regulation in schools, where socialization is one of the lessons taught and balanced against the need to respect personal opinions and individualism. The difference is worth emphasizing, and we approach it by differentiating expressions in and outside of custodial contexts, where adolescents are directly under the authority of adults (as in schools) rather than in public spaces like streets.

The Supreme Court confronted the need to address "hate speech" in *R.A.V. v. City of St. Paul* (1992). Events leading to this groundbreaking case started when Robert A. Viktora and several other St. Paul teenagers fashioned a cross of broken chair legs and burned it inside the fenced yard of a Black family that lived across the street. Viktora was convicted under St. Paul's Bias-Motivated Crime Ordinance which states:

> Whoever places on public or private property a symbol, object, appellation, characterization or graffiti, including, but not limited to, a burning cross or Nazi swastika, which one knows or has reasonable grounds to know arouses anger, alarm or resentment in others on the basis of race, color, creed, religion or gender commits disorderly conduct and shall be guilty of a misdemeanor. (*R.A.V. v. City of St. Paul*, 1992, p. 330)

The Court unanimously struck down the statute on First Amendment grounds. The Court did so because the statute regulated the content of speech, as opposed to merely the time, place or manner of speech. Although all of the justices found the ordinance unconstitutional, many sharply disagreed on their reasoning. The majority agreed that the ordinance could not prohibit expression solely because of its content. The City of St. Paul could not selectively regulate only those fighting words that provoke violence on the basis of race, color, creed, religion or gender while permitting fighting words on other topics. The First Amendment, could, however, permit St. Paul to impose special prohibitions on those speakers who express views on disfavored subjects if the content discrimination was reasonably necessary to achieve St. Paul's compelling interests. The Court did not view the discrimination as necessary, given that even an ordinance not limited to the favored topics would have precisely the same beneficial effect. It found that the only interest distinctively served by the content limitation was the city council's display of special hostility towards the singled-out biases. Such singled-out biases are precisely what the First Amendment forbids. The government is entitled to express that hostility—but not through the means of imposing unique limitations on speakers who (however benightedly) disagree. The majority, then, relied on an "underbreadth" rationale, reasoning that if some fighting words are to be regulated then all fighting words also must be regulated. Numerous concurrences offered variations on other reasons for holding the statute unconstitutional, such as the claim that the First Amendment protects words that hurt (like racial epithets). Despite disagreements, the opinions confirmed the view that the government generally disfavors efforts aimed to suppress some expression of hate while ignoring others.

The Court had an opportunity to clarify the deep divisions on the content-based regulation of speech in a case dealing with a Wisconsin statute which enhanced the sentences for persons who intentionally selected a victim because of their race, religion, color, disability, sexual orientation, national origin, or ancestry. In *Wisconsin v. Mitchell* (1992) the state of Wisconsin challenged its highest court's ruling that had struck down a penalty enhancement statute. In that case, the lower court had overturned the state's effort to punish an offender more severely because his motives were hateful. Mitchell, who is black, joined a group of young black men who were discussing a scene from the movie "Mississippi Burning" where a white man beat a young black boy who was praying. In apparent response to that film, Mitchell had encouraged a group of boys to severely beat a boy who was merely passing by them on the other side of the street.

Relying on *R.A.V.*, the Wisconsin Supreme Court invalidated the penalty-enhancement statute, arguing that the penalty-enhancement statute was invalid because it would punish the defendant for the content of his thought and because the statute would chill speech given that speech will often be used to prove the element of bias. The Supreme Court reversed the Wisconsin decision and held that the penalty-enhancement statute passed constitutional muster. The Court distinguished *R.A.V.* by noting that the ordinance struck down in that case was explicitly directed at expressions, at "speech" or "messages." The statute in *Mitchell* sought to enhance the sentences for conduct, such as assault, which is unprotected by the First Amendment. The message of the *R.A.V.* majority and *Mitchell*, then, is that states can proscribe both "fighting words" and bigoted conduct. Attempts to bar only a certain type of expression most likely will be struck down as inappropriate.

Mitchell, however, was not the Court's last word. Recently, the Court examined the constitutionality of a statute that prohibited the burning of a cross to intimidate. *Virginia v. Black*, (2003, p. 347–48) involved the constitutionality of a Virginia statute that made it a felony "for any person . . . with the intent of intimidating any person or group . . . to burn . . . a cross on the property of another, a highway or other public place" and specified that any such burning was to be "prima facie evidence of an intent to intimidate a person or group." After a cross was burned at a 1998 Ku Klux Klan rally in a privately owned open field in Virginia, the leader of the rally was tried and convicted for violating the statute. In a separate incident in Virginia, two individuals attempted to burn a cross on the yard of an African-American neighbor. Both of these individuals were charged with attempted cross burning; one individual pleaded guilty, and the other was convicted after a trial. The Supreme Court of Virginia vacated the convictions on the ground that the statute was facially invalid under the First Amendment. It reasoned that the statute assertedly discriminated on the basis of speech content by choosing to ban only cross burning because of that act's distinctive message and that the prima facie evidence revealed that it was overbroad, as the enhanced probability of prosecution chilled the expression of protected speech. Given precedent, the ruling appeared quite reasonable.

The Supreme Court offered a complicated response as it held that a state actually could ban cross burning carried out with the intent to intimidate, for cross burning was a particularly virulent form of intimidation which the state could properly choose to regulate, instead of prohibiting all intimidating messages; and a statute banning cross burning carried out with the intent to intimidate did not single out for opprobrium only that speech directed toward one of various specified disfavored topics. The Court found nothing objectionable to the state's choosing to regulate a subset of intimidating messages in light of cross burning's long and pernicious history as a signal of intimidations and impending violence. A ban on cross burning carried out with the intent to intimidate was fully consistent with the Court's *R. A. V.* decision. Unlike the statute at issue in *R. A. V.*, the Virginia statute did not single out for opprobrium only that speech directed toward one of the specified disfavored topics; and the Court had struck down the Virginia provision that made the act of cross burning prima facie evidence of an intent to intimidate. It does not matter whether an individual burns a cross with intent to intimidate because of the victim's race, gender, or religion, or because of the victim's political affiliation, union membership, or homosexuality. In addition, *R.A.V.* had not held that the First Amendment prohibited all forms of content-based discrimination within a proscribable area of speech. Rather, the Court specifically had stated that a particular type of content discrimination does not violate the First Amendment when the basis for it consists entirely of the very reason its entire class of speech is proscribable. For example, it is permissible to prohibit only that obscenity that is most patently offensive in its prurience—in other words, that which involves the most lascivious displays of sexual activity. Similarly, Virginia's statute did not run afoul of the First Amendment insofar as it banned cross burning with intent to intimidate, as long as it did not assume that cross burning necessarily meant to intimidate. According to the Court, even when speech can be regulated because it creates a substantial evil such as intimidation, the state may not suppress it merely because it has that tendency: the speaker must intend that result. The Court rejected the notion that cross burning can have but one intent—the intent to intimidate—recognizing that cross burning sometimes is engaged in to communicate an ideology, albeit an ideology of hate, and that the Constitution protects the expression of that ideology by operation of the bedrock principle that government never may censor speech simply because of society's abhorrence of the ideas expressed (*Virginia v. Black*, 2003, pp. 356–57). Thus, just as a state may regulate only that obscenity which is the most obscene due to its prurient content, so too may a state choose to prohibit only those forms of intimidation that are most likely to inspire fear of bodily harm.

The protections relating to hate speech, coupled with the rights of parents to develop and guide the upbringing of their children, reveal that adolescents are indeed quite free to express hate as long as their parents allow them to do so. The Supreme Court has yet to scrutinize cases involving hate in schools. Given that hate speech can be disruptive and counter to pedagogical concerns, however, it would seem to not garner much protection under neither *Tinker* nor *Hazelwood*, and thus fall under the discretion of school officials. Importantly, though, this is clearly an area of developing law, as evidenced by the emergence of efforts to confront harassment and bullying (see Levesque, 2000). The recent efforts to address those forms of harms highlight that hateful expressions may well exist in schools. But to the extent the states respond to those harms, it is clear that school officials retain broad discretion, as evidenced by the leading Supreme Court case that established a very high threshold for students to reach if they wanted to litigate claims against schools for failing to recognize and respond to sexual harassment by peers (*Davis v. Monroe County Board of Education*, 1999).

Protecting Adolescents' Right to Receive Information

Despite its importance, the right to receive information remains a relatively unexplored component of the freedom of speech even when adults assert such a claim. As we have seen in chapter 6, we can attribute this lack of attention to the manner this right is frequently taken for granted and subsumed within the speaker's right to express their views. Where the rights of the speakers themselves are pure and undiminished, it is generally unnecessary for those who oppose regulation of speech to rest their arguments on the right to receive information. The cases we have examined involving adolescents' rights to expression generally fail to consider the rights of listeners. When the Court does consider the rights of listeners in those cases, it tends to do so to limit adolescents' own control of their rights—as seen in cases involving sexuality, religion, and hate. This theme especially emerged in state-controlled contexts, given that other contexts most often involved the rights of parents to censor their children and control their interactions. The Supreme Court, however, has reviewed and decided important cases that do implicate adolescents' right to receive information. These cases help us gain a fuller appreciation of adolescents' free speech rights for they provide us with an important glimpse at how the law envisions adolescents' informational environments and who best controls them.

Consistent with the view that the legal system disfavors minors in their quests to exercise constitutional rights, the Court perceives adolescents' right to receive information as more limited than the corresponding rights of adults.

Where young persons assert rights to speech, and make related autonomy claims, the traditional limitations on the core rights of the minors again figure prominently in their right to receive information. As we have seen in the context of speech deemed harmful to minors, the Supreme Court accepts without question the notion that the state has a greater interest, and therefore broader authority, in regulating minors' exposure to certain speech than with regard to adults. This regulation takes two forms—one where adolescents are subjected to the authority of parents and the other where the state limits adolescents' access. Barring a narrow set of circumstances, minors have no constitutional rights inside their parents' homes vis-à-vis their parents, at least in part because their parents are not state actors. For example and as we have seen in *Wisconsin v. Yoder* (1972), while parents may force their children to observe the family's faith and cultural traditions, the state may not do so directly. At home, minors possess neither freedom of speech nor its reciprocal right, the right to receive information, unless their parents choose to grant them such privileges.

When the state itself regulates access to information, adolescents actually do gain some rights. Adolescents' right to receive information mainly arises in the context of governmental activities designed to promote the marketplace of ideas. This area of jurisprudence focusing on state censorship actually is the only one where the Court considers (but does not fully recognize) adolescents' independent right to information. As expected, however, other cases recognizing the rights of parents to information or the state's freedom to subsidize particular viewpoints at the expense of others also may implicate minors' rights, even though those rights are given short shrift or ignored.

The pivotal role of the right to receive information when evaluating presumptively truncated free speech rights of minors clearly emerged in the flurry of judicial opinions issued in *Board of Education, Island Trees Union Free School District No. 26 v. Pico* (1982). The Court relied heavily on its long history of holdings recognizing that the right to receive information "is an inherent corollary of the rights of free speech," that the right "follows ineluctably from the sender's First Amendment right to send" ideas (*Board of Education, Island Trees Union Free School District No. 26 v. Pico*, 1982, pp. 867–68). The Court also noted that the right has a second source as well. It stems directly from the liberty claims of the listeners: "The right to receive ideas is a necessary predicate to the recipient's meaningful exercise of his own rights of speech, press, and political freedom" (p. 867). Without reservation, the Court applied the right of minors to receive ideas as presented by the students who had challenged the book removals from their school library. The plurality maintained that allowing access to ideas in a school library was an important aspect of preparing students "for active and effective participation in the pluralistic, often contentious society in which they will soon be adult members" (p. 868). The Court relied on a line of precedents beginning with *Barnette* for the principle that, although schools have a duty to inculcate values, they may not impose orthodoxy in matters of opinion. The Supreme Court remanded the case for a hearing into the school board's motives for denying students access to books that a citizens' group argued were "anti-American, anti-Christian, anti-Semitic [*sic*], and just plain filthy" (p. 853).

The *Pico* decision was far from unanimous, which rendered the right to information less than firm, at least in the context of schools. The concurrence, for example, disagreed on the issue of whether the First Amendment creates in students a right to receive information. Rather, it perceived the tension in the case to be between the school's broad power to inculcate students with ideas and the constitutional prohibition on "certain forms of state discrimination between ideas" (*Board of Education, Island Trees Union Free School District No. 26 v. Pico*, 1982, p. 878). This view lead to the conclusion that the tension should be resolved by articulating a rule that the government may not remove books from a school library for the purpose of suppressing ideas because of a distaste for the ideas themselves. Similarly, a powerful dissent highlighted the inherent selectivity in elementary and secondary education as the critical difference between the government as educator and the government as sovereign:

> When [the government] acts as an educator, at least at the elementary and secondary school level, [it] is engaged in inculcating social values and knowledge in relatively impressionable young people. Obviously there are innumerable decisions to be made as to what courses should be taught, what books should be purchased, or what teachers should be employed. . . . In the very course of administering the many-faceted operations of a school district, the mere decision to purchase some books will necessarily preclude the possibility of purchasing others. The decision to teach a particular subject may preclude the possibility of teaching another subject. A decision to replace a teacher because of ineffectiveness may by implication be seen as a disparagement of the subject matter taught. In each of these instances, however, the book or the exposure to the subject matter may be acquired elsewhere. The managers of the school district are not proscribing it as to the citizenry in general, but are simply determining that it will not be included in the curriculum or school library. (pp. 909–10)

The dissent conceded that a politically motivated Democratic school board could not remove all books written by or in favor of Republicans, and that a racially motivated all-white school board could not remove all books authored by blacks or in favor of racial equality. But that concession was viewed as largely theoretical, given that such "extreme examples" rarely occur in real life. Thus, notwithstanding the distinction between a school's suppression of students' individual expression and a school district's decision to remove books from a school library, the plurality and dissent apparently agreed on the impropriety of schools' attempting, through suppression, to shape racial or political opinions. They disagreed on whether such suppression had been or could be demonstrated on the facts in *Pico*.

The extent to which *Pico* clearly recognized the right to receive information eventually would contribute to considerable debate, but the concept of the right to receive information captured the approval of every Justice who participated in the Supreme Court's consideration of *Bolger v. Youngs Drug Products Corporation* (1983). Even though the concept was not expressly before the Court in that case, the right to receive information emerged as an important theme both in the majority opinion and the concurrence. The precise question before the Court in *Bolger* involved the right of a contraceptive manufacturer to mail to the public unsolicited pamphlets described as "informational" which concerned the availability of prophylactics generally and the prevention of sexually transmitted diseases. The Court upheld the rights of the commercial speaker, holding that the importance of conveying "truthful information relevant to important social issues" outweighed the government's asserted interests (*Bolger v. Youngs Drug Products Corporation*, 1983, p. 69). In doing so, however, the Court also examined the importance of the right of parents to receive information that might help them in carrying out some of their most difficult responsibilities, concluding that the statute prohibiting the unsolicited mailing of contraception advertisements was defective in part because it denied parents access to important information and in part because it denied teenagers access to critical knowledge. The Court did so by citing to *Erznoznik v. City of Jacksonville*, 1975, p. 213–14), which had struck down an ordinance prohibiting drive-in movie theaters from showing any movies containing nudity if visible from the street. The statute in *Erznoznik*, like the one in *Bolger*, was the type of statute that "also quite clearly denies information to minors, who are entitled to 'a significant measure of First Amendment protection'" (*Bolger v. Youngs Drug Products Corporation*, 1983, pp. 74–75 n.30 citing *Erznoznik v. City of Jacksonville*, 1975, p. 212). The concurrence joined by emphasizing that, although parents might be entitled to the government's support in limiting the kinds of materials that reached the family mailbox, as the government had argued in the case, the statute at issue inhibited the interests of parents because the law denied "parents access to information about birth control that might help them make informed decisions" about what to tell their children (*Bolger v. Youngs Drug Products Corporation*, 1983, p. 79). The Court thus recognized a right to receive at least some types of information.

The right to receive information recognized in *Bolger* and other cases like it, however, seem to render control of that right to parents and other adults. The right to know, like the right to speak itself, is a right that individuals may exercise solely against their government. Despite strong preference for the parental right to control the information their children receive, the Court has rejected state action that would make materials entirely unavailable to minors regardless of the minors' own parents' preferences for openness. The notion that parents may elect to make controversial materials available to their children when the state restricts direct access by minors has been a foundation of judicial reasoning in cases upholding state regulation of speech for the purpose of protecting children. In *Ginsberg v. New York* (1968, p. 639), for example, the Supreme Court underscored that state regulation barring sale of so-called "girlie magazines" to minors did not have the effect of making the materials completely unavailable to minors. Parents remained free under the statute to buy the prohibited magazines for their children; but parents were not free to prohibit other parents from obtaining the materials for their own children. Regardless, adolescents themselves do not have direct, unrestricted access to the materials.

The Supreme Court has yet to squarely consider cases where the minors and their parents advocated different positions with regard to speech rights. The Supreme Courts First Amendment cases exploring the rights of minors involve fact situations that align parents' and children's interests—parents argue that their children possessed speech rights in situations where their children shared their belief system. Some parental rights cases famously offer dissenting opinions urging consideration of children's independent rights. The classic, illustrative case, *Wisconsin v. Yoder* (1972), allowed parents to remove their adolescent children from public schools; the Court explicitly allowed parents to do so because the children were reaching adolescence and could be highly influenced by mainstream culture. A vigorously dissenting opinion argued that the children should be consulted in such cases, but (and contrary to commentators' claims) did not go as far as to urge the Court to recognize that adolescents have a right against their parents in such contexts.

In addition to First Amendment contexts involving adolescents, the Supreme Court has considered the legal rights of adolescents in the broader context of the public's right to receive information. The analysis of this right appears in the most basic atmosphere for receiving information—the educational setting. The Court actually first recognized the right to receive information in the educational setting in *Meyer v. Nebraska* (1923) as well as its close progeny (see *Pierce v. Society of Sisters*, 1925). In *Meyer*, Nebraska enacted a statute making teaching any subject in a language other than English a misdemeanor. Meyer was convicted under the statute for teaching his daughter German. The Court struck down the statute as it found that the concept of liberty "without doubt" includes "the right of the individual... to acquire useful knowledge" (*Meyer v. Nebraska*, 1923, p. 399). Moreover, the Court said,

> This liberty may not be interfered with, under the guise of protecting the public interest, by legislative action which is arbitrary or without some reasonable relation to some purpose within the competency of the state to effect.... The American people have always regarded education and acquisition of knowledge as matters of supreme importance, which should be diligently promoted. (Id., pp. 399–400)

In *Meyer*, the relationship between the right to know and the right to speak was symbiotic. Although it is possible to see *Meyer* as turning exclusively on the teacher's right to speak, the reversal of Meyer's conviction vindicates both aspects of this liberty interest. Importantly, the *Meyer* Court does not explicitly address whether the teacher had standing to raise the student's right to receive the German language training. But a later case, *Griswold v. Connecticut* (1965), not only settles the issue in favor of the speaker's standing to raise the constitutional rights of the listener, it actually cites *Meyer* as a case in which this was done appropriately. *Griswold* dealt directly with the right to receive information, in this instance the right of individuals to information regarding contraceptives. Importantly, though, *Griswold*'s value to this discussion is somewhat limited by the fact that, ultimately, the holding turned on the unconstitutionality of state prohibition on contraception as an invasion of privacy, rather than merely the right to receive information about contraception. The relationship between privacy and the right to receive information is of significance not just for adults but also for ensuring adolescents' rights. These admittedly controversial cases reveal that if the First Amendment is to accord a central status to the many benefits of the marketplace of ideas, like self-realization and autonomy, and whether laws enrich or impoverish the universe of speech, individuals need an uninhibited flow of information and opinion to aid them in making life-affecting decisions, in governing their own lives and in preserving the goal of democratic self-governance expressed through the speech clause.

As the education cases suggest, the public may have a right to receive information, but the Court does allow the state to control the nature of that information. This rule also emerges in the context of state subsidies. Although it would seem that the government would encourage the flow of information, we have seen in chapter 6 that the government itself can engage in viewpoint discrimination in its support of ideas. The First Amendment does not place limits on the government's ability to use its spending power to influence private or public speech. We already have examined how the rule limits the broader right to information; the rule's application to adolescents does not provide an exception. Most notably, the rule has been accepted in the context of state-supported services for adolescents. Interestingly, the challenge came in the context of information the Court has recognized as private and important for self-determination: sexuality education and reproductive services. The most illustrative example involves the *Adolescent Family Life Act* ("AFLA"; 1982), which provides grants to public or nonprofit private organizations for services and research in the area of premarital adolescent sexual relations and pregnancy. The types of programs funded vary from media campaigns such as billboard advertisements, to after-school mentoring programs, to sex educational programs in public and private schools. The AFLA expressly requires the promotion of family support and the involvement of religious, charitable, and voluntary organizations; it expressly forbids funds from being used to fund, promote, or encourage abortion. In its current form, the Act provides the major source of funding for sex education and requires supported organizations to provide only abstinence-based education rather than comprehensive education. Although the government clearly engages in viewpoint discrimination, the Act has not been challenged seriously on Free Speech grounds simply because such challenges are barred given that *Rust v. Sullivan* (1991) and its progeny allow the government to selectively fund programs and send its own desired messages. The Act, however, was challenged on First Amendment establishment clause grounds for, it was argued, the funding was skewed toward organizations that would adopt abstinence-based missions, such as religious institutions. The Supreme Court, in *Bowen v. Kendrick* (1988) strongly rejected those challenges as it found no conflict in the fact that the desired effects of the AFLA legislation advancing certain morals coincided with religious groups' morals and that the religious groups received funds to promote that message. Thus, even when directly implicating potentially powerful rights like religious freedom, the right to information remains insufficient to overcome limitations when the state—like parents—would rather not provide adolescents with disfavored ideas.

Conclusions

Addressing adolescents' rights means transposing and fitting a group of multiple values on the already existing web of First Amendment concerns. Primary among those other values is the pervasive view that adolescents' right to express themselves essentially derives from and is protected by adults. Our legal system generally frames adolescents' First Amendment freedoms in a manner that grants adults general control over the manner and extent to which adolescents may express themselves or receive certain ideas. This approach merely reflects the general jurisprudential conception of adolescents' rights. That conception simultaneously views adolescents as in need of protection from adults' realities as well as in need of exposure to some of those realities so that they may develop the inner-directed capacity to engage in markets of ideas. That capacity serves as the center of First Amendment jurisprudence that builds and accepts an image of decision makers as free, autonomous, hearty, and self-reliant individuals participating in free exchanges of ideas.

The legal system differently images adults and adolescents, and the assumptions about their capacities direct the development of different legal responses that fail to reflect the manner both adults and adolescents engage with ideas. For adults, the legal assumptions reflect much less actually-attainable goals than aspirations that allow the legal system to address often conflicting values. Social science understandings of human development and capacity reasonably question whether even those considered adults are sufficiently mature or enlightened or disposed temperamentally or culturally to resist corrupted ideas or glean truths in the market of free speech. Citizens may well not, in fact, be autonomous. Rather, their choices seem constrained or manipulated by government, economic forces, the media, and other socializing institutions. Indeed, in many respects, those institutions exist to guide and constrain behaviors, thoughts, and emotions. In this regard, the law's ideals of autonomy profoundly fail to reflect the assumed courage and self-reliance required for participation in free speech. The law's vision of adolescents does no better; the law misconstrues adolescents as badly as it does adults. Although the broad assumptions about adolescents' incapacities fail to reflect their diverse realities, when compared to adults, the legal system's image of adolescents probably more closely reflects the realities of citizen's interactions in the market of ideas. Yet, the legal system actively seeks to constrain adolescents and assumes their incapacity to function in the market of ideas.

We have seen the broad rights parents retain as well as the law's pervasive assumption that adolescents are in some form of custody, that adults control them. Leading cases involving adolescents' right to expression support this view. Adolescents essentially have no freedom of expression rights within their families. In addition, adolescents generally have no right to receive information if parents wish not to provide such information. This is not surprising. The Constitution protects against state action, and parents' actions do not constitute such actions. Parents are free to do as they wish, as long as they are not abusive. Although some may contend that adolescents should retain independent rights within their families, Supreme Court cases have yet to champion this approach in any meaningful and persuasive fashion, even in its dissenting opinions.

When adolescents could be deemed as public actors in public places, adolescents still retain very few independent rights to receive or express ideas. The clearest example we have seen of this infirmity involves adolescents in state care. The leading examples involve public schools; but such infirmities clearly transfer to other areas of state-controlled care, such as the child welfare system and juvenile justice system, which are so controlling in this regard that they proceed without much First Amendment challenge. Although the leading case affirming adolescents' First Amendment rights that they would control themselves actually emerged in the context of state care (in public schools), the Court subsequently interpreted that position much more narrowly than some had hoped. Cases since then confirm that adolescents actually have few rights to control their expressions and even fewer rights to control the ideas they may seek and receive. These decisions envision schools as authoritarian institutions (much like prisons, the military as well as the juvenile and child welfare systems) and they openly express judicial deference to the choices of school officials. Simply put, in the decades since *Tinker*, the courts clearly have ruled that students leave most of their constitutional rights at the schoolhouse gate and any other gate the state erects. The judiciary's acceptance of the need for deference to state authority leaves relatively little room for protecting adolescents' control of their own constitutional rights while in state care. Despite the authority schools and other state institutions enjoy, the cases still reveal that state officials should not attempt to interfere with adolescents' overall development in critical areas that should be left to parents, religious or cultural communities, and other institutions considered free from state control. The clearest example we have seen in this regard has been the manner the Court envisions adolescents' religious rights while in state care. In such instances, the Court tends to view adolescents less as public actors in public places and more as private actors in public places. But, rather than view adolescents in such contexts as private actors who can control their own rights, the legal system increasingly views them as private actors whose rights and protections derive from parents and other communities—parents ultimately control their children's educational environments, and communities can either support or ignore such efforts. Thus and typically, this means that adolescents' own rights, in the sense of having control over such rights, generally get short shrift.

Unlike the legal infirmities of adolescents' rights in families and in state controlled institutions, adolescents apparently have considerable free speech rights when acting as private actors in public, non-state controlled places; and the Court in those instances is more likely to treat adolescents' rights like those of adults. This rule derives from the belief that adolescents have a right to engage in the marketplace of ideas. Indeed, the few cases involving expression, both in the sense of receiving and expressing ideas, in this context reveal a focus on the presented speech at the virtual exclusion of considerations that we are dealing with minors. Hate speech cases provide the clearest examples. Although it may be tempting to view these rights as expansive, they still are restricted to the extent that the state also limits adults' rights in these contexts. In addition, adolescents' rights still may be restricted because of adolescents' minority status. In many instances, adolescents still end up controlled by the state and parents in that adolescents may be assumed as in need of protection. This was the ruling of the leading case, *Prince v. Massachusetts* (1944), which embraced child protection rationales to control both the rights of parents and their children. The same rule supported laws that limit adolescents' sexual expressions (*Ginsberg v. New York*, 1968). The limitations are quite real, but these contexts reveal the remarkable extent to which adolescents can gain freedoms when they act in broader society.

The tension that emerges from the manner the law treats and expects adolescents to behave while in controlled institutions (e.g., schools and families) and in broader society without those controls (on the streets) creates challenges for First Amendment jurisprudence. We have seen how that jurisprudence rightly views free speech, including the right to information, as both intrinsically and instrumentally valuable. Intrinsically, free speech promotes and reflects human personality and fosters the essence of human dignity. Autonomy to think, listen, and speak for oneself is essential to a free and self-determining personhood, the true foundation of liberty. Free speech also properly is viewed as valuable for the consequences it furthers. Most notably, free speech promotes the formation and structuring of political will, which directs the scope and purposes of democracy and civil society. First Amendment law continues to expand what is worth championing. No longer limited to championing free speech's role in furthering our political democracy, First Amendment law now recognizes the role free expression plays in private as well as broader public spheres, including the search for truth, self-realization, self-fulfillment, as well as community organization, transformation and continuation. These webs constitute the necessary building blocks of human development.

For our purposes, First Amendment freedoms of expression must be interpreted to refer to development of the individual's powers and abilities (such as what is meant when a person realizes their own full potential) and to the individual's control of their own destiny through making life-affecting decisions. This reflects a move in First Amendment jurisprudence that recognizes that, although democratic and community values matter much, so does the foundational principle of individual self-realization, one on which we should keep our focus as we consider adolescent development and its place in civil society. That is, the value of self-realization supports both democracy and free speech. Similarly, democracy and free speech support self-realization: adolescents who have relative freedom to develop their own unique selves may make better democratic citizens. Similarly, democracy and free speech support one another in that the protection of free speech safeguards democratic processes. None of these values—democracy, self-fulfillment, etc.—are isolated values. When people fulfill themselves by speaking, writing, and receiving ideas they also serve the social, public values of free speech. As we have observed, the complexity of social reality defies attempts to confine the significance of free speech to any one value, a reality complicated even further by adolescents' peculiar place in society.

Just as First Amendment jurisprudence necessarily involves layers of complexities in itself and even more layers when addressing adolescents' legal realities, adolescent' social realities bring yet another important dimension. Adolescents may be more free to express and receive speech than legal commentaries reveal and popular opinion suggests. Indeed, as the first part of this book has revealed, adolescents receive incredibly huge doses of information which they are assumed to not be able to use responsibly, such as information regarding sexuality and drug use. Indeed, adolescents are assumed to not have the ability to control the use of that information. This reality finds reflection in the growing concern over the media's impact on adolescents. If any conclusions can be drawn from the mixture of law and reality, it is that finding safe and appropriate places for adolescents within the First Amendment constitutes a difficult and ever-changing task. In one direction, it could result in unnecessary censorship. In another, it could expand First Amendment protection beyond established constitutional frameworks. And these directions go in different ways as jurisprudence seeks to respond to changing social circumstances. These changing directions and circumstances mean that efforts to direct the structure and process of adolescents' free speech rights merit attention. Even though solutions may well elude us, our concluding chapter examines the implications of these tensions resulting from these myths and realities and charts ways to begin reframing the rights of adolescents.

8

Conclusions
Taking Developmental Science
and Free Speech Rights Seriously

The meteoric rise in the volume and quality of impressive media research reveals much about the manner adolescents respond to information and the remarkable extent to which information meant for mass consumption influences adolescent development. Despite disputes over the implications of established findings, available evidence does reveal that the media play a central role in adolescents' socialization. Some media effects are direct and immediate, others are more long term and indirect, and all interact with adolescents' dispositions and factors within adolescents' environments. Given the pervasiveness of diverse media, these findings are unsurprising. The media simply constitute a component of the informational environments that always have played powerful roles in adolescent life.

Research appropriately highlights the need to consider media influences on adolescent development, but, as we have seen, research agendas investigating media consumption and influences tend to embrace narrow lines of inquiry. Narrow approaches are understandable given methodological limitations, practical considerations, and the sheer complexity of adolescent development. But research still tends to focus on selected media content, most notably sexual activity, drug use, violence and, more recently, body images. Research has yet to tackle systematically how multiple forms of media content influence adolescents as multidimensional beings, as individuals whose approaches to identified concerns interact with one another and with other environmental forces. Media-effects research also still pervasively ignores other environmental factors that structure information and shape adolescents' processing of information. That is, research does convincingly reveal links between media use and selected behavioral outcomes (like drug use, sexual activity, and eating habits), but research only recently addresses how adolescents think and process information from media in light of other sources of information (e.g., peers, parents, and schools). Although impressive, media research tends to remain narrow in scope.

The significance of narrow efforts extends widely. For our purposes, the significance of narrow research derives from the manner such efforts stifle appropriate legal responses. No real effort has focused on determining how policy responses to the media, either broadly or narrowly defined, have anything much to do with our current understanding of adolescents' development and their place in civil society. Often driven by research with narrow concerns and findings, policy responses to the media's influence are similarly piecemeal and fail to consider the fuller complexities of adolescent life. As a result, legal responses, including cases that respond to them, fail to consider the fullness of adolescents' rights and the very reason the Constitution does not limit free speech rights to a particular group.

The discussion that follows brings together the conclusions we have drawn and seeks to envision the jurisprudential posture the legal system would adopt if it were to take developmental sciences more seriously. To do so, we examine why current policies tend to ignore the fullness of adolescent development, including the various ways media and informational environments influence adolescent life. That discussion bolsters the rest of our analyses for it reveals the need for alternative ways to approach adolescents' rights. Our discussion of adolescents' rights begins with the Constitution itself, highlighting how the free speech principles identified in chapter 6 relate to adolescent life. The discussion reframes the current piecemeal approaches to adolescents' media and free speech rights, as explored in chapter 7, which tend to compare adolescents to adults. Rather than offering adults as the benchmark to determine whether the legal system should recognize and respect adolescents' rights, the analyses look at the constitutional principles that govern free speech rights to develop principles that would foster the development of legal rules that remain faithful to the Constitution's plain dictate that everyone deserves its protections.

The Law's Need and Failure to Consider Adolescents' Informational Environments

Embarking on an effort to reconsider the free speech rights of adolescents first requires understanding the compelling need to do so. The history of laws regulating adolescents reveals that legal responses derive from images of adolescents and perceptions of their place in society. Entrenched social forces, supported by our legal system, ensure that those images and perceptions acquire a life of their own, which severely restrains efforts that seek to change them and the policies that flow from them. Yet, as we will see, reform efforts are far from futile when they address adolescents' needs, the foundation of constitutional rights, and adolescents' peculiar place in civil society. Those efforts are shaped by the current failure to recognize and consider adolescents' needs. Those failures necessarily serve as springboards that shape outcomes, but they remain insufficient to prompt reform. Regardless of adolescents' needs, legal responses to those needs rely on perceptions of those needs and on the factors the law must consider in its effort to accommodate those perceptions.

Accounting for Failures in Recognition

The previous chapters suggest five factors that help account for the failure to examine more fully the regulation of adolescents' more general media and informational environments. The first factor deals with the misperception that some forms of media directly and inevitably cause certain outcomes. The belief that some media content is harmful, for example, narrows interest to those contents and efforts to curb access to those specific media contents. As a result, policy efforts focus on specific needs and respond to specific findings often championed by research and advocacy groups. Although this narrowing approach may be worthwhile to the extent that it seeks to address pressing social problems, it has the unfortunate effect of playing down the reality that no specific medium or media content acts alone in its influence on adolescent development. There is actually nothing novel about concluding that the media are but one aspect of adolescents' informational environments and that the media are nondeterminative. Leading commentators who examine media effects cautiously present their findings in ways that mark and highlight empirical nuances, qualifications, and limitations. Regrettably, policy responses tend not to be so careful in their use of evidence; the use of evidence by policy makers seems to come when extreme events and examples provide a window of opportunity to drive policy making. And court decisions that build jurisprudence necessarily respond to those policies. As a result, reform efforts still adopt piecemeal approaches as the legal response to research often takes a life of its own. No comprehensive effort drives responses to adolescents' media and informational environments.

The second factor that helps account for the failure to take a broader look at media and informational environments deals with the misperception that the legal system already formally addresses adolescents' media rights. Yet, as we have seen, much actually remains to be determined. Some media "expressions," like those from movies and music, are highly unregulated, as are experiences emanating from dominant media outlets, like the Internet, phones, and cable television. This under-regulation has reverberating effects on informational systems, with, for example, the Internet allowing individuals an instantaneous mode of communication with others via e-mail, automatic mailing lists, chat rooms, and the World Wide Web. As a result, media often deemed out of the reach of adolescents actually enter their social world. Simply having one peer with access to a type or content of media essentially ensures that peers within that social network will receive those ideas, even if it means that they will receive fettered accounts. The misperception that laws already address media environments reveals the need to reconsider the media's place within the context of broader informational environments. This misperception is quite significant. The misperception that the legal system already addresses adolescents' media, or that it easily could if lawmakers wanted to, gives way to the reality that appropriate responses must take a broader look at free speech rights, a look that considers how laws pervasively do not address the media, how adolescents interact with their informational environment, and how the media suffuse adolescent life.

The third factor deals with popular perceptions and social traditions affirming that parents control, guide, and even determine adolescents' media environments. Although parents can and often do play powerful roles in adolescents' lives, perceptions of that power frequently overestimate parental influences and the need to champion parental claims to their children's media environments and orientations toward various media. Indeed, our close look at media environments, the impact of media, and the development of orientations toward the media suggested many reasons to question the real extent to which parents directly control adolescents' media experiences. By the time children reach adolescence, adolescents have gained considerable access and exposure to various media. That media access includes materials their parents would rather not have them have access to or materials that their parents allow them to have access to without realizing or sufficiently caring about the influence of that media. Reviews repeatedly reveal that parents typically do not exert much control over their children's media consumption, even though they report that they exert control (Gentile & Walsh, 2002). Much evidence refutes the misperception that parents control their adolescents' informational environments. This failure to recognize the complexity of factors shaping adolescents' access to media highlights the need to re-evaluate the wide range of influences on adolescents.

The third factor helps account for the fourth: the wide power the law bestows upon parents to raise their children as they see fit and the prevailing tendency to treat adolescent minors as children under law. As we have seen, parents do retain wide latitude but the legal system, depending on different contexts, still allows adolescents to exercise their own rights and seeks to protect those rights from state-sponsored encroachment. In addition, the law now recognizes that the veil of privacy drawn over family relations might obscure other important values and rights that deserve recognition, such as liberty, equality, and protection of dependent family members. As a result, even in contexts where parents retain great control, the law allows for intervening to protect the rights of adolescents or to address potential conflicts that may arise when the rights of parents interfere with the broad interests of civil society, local communities, or others who interact with adolescents. Of course, where parents do not retain direct control, such as when adolescents are "on the streets," the law generally responds to adolescents as independent actors and plays down parental claims, such as when adolescents' speech crosses from protected speech to punishable speech activity. The criminal justice system often assumes that adolescents act with the same information as adults, as exemplified by recent efforts to dismantle the juvenile court system and by police and prosecutors' interactions with minors (Levesque, 2006). Equally important, the law influences media and other informational environments which, in turn, influence parents and adolescents—and the direction of influence on adolescents does not necessarily flow directly through parents, as seen by the laws' regulation of media and adolescents' peers. The erroneous assumption that parents control and foster their adolescents' media environments, then, has reverberating consequences for the manner the state approaches adolescents when they are either in or out of families. Rejecting the misperception that the law always treats adolescents as minors reveals the need to consider the media's direct and indirect routes of influence on adolescents. Appropriately addressing those routes requires accepting adolescents' fundamental social, developmental, and legal realities that impact adolescents' development, their environments, and the demands of living in a civil, pluralistic society.

The above factors all contribute to the final misperception: the belief that adults must shield minors from the media and even from the First Amendment itself. The rise in "harmful to minors" laws we examined in chapter 7 illustrates the point. Commentators and the law tend to champion a need for censorship in the name of child protection. Like adults, adolescents certainly could benefit from censorship of numerous forms of speech, as we saw in the long list of exceptions to free speech highlighted in chapter 6. Those exceptions apply to everyone. But, the extent to which adolescents need more intrusive and vigorous protection from speech actually is quite debatable. If it were not debatable, then the law would not increasingly grant parents censorship control rights over adolescents since doing so clearly remains an ineffective way to remove ideas from adolescents' informational environments. Indeed, that move allows for considerable slippage and seepage. That move's effect reveals that current laws generally seem more intent on protecting parental rights than on protecting adolescents from harm. As a result, these laws leave adolescents not well protected from speech that could harm them and fails to provide adolescents with information that could help them respond to actual harms. These counter-intuitive results have yet to dislodge the misperception that the law actively seeks to protect adolescents from harm and that adolescents' rights must remain limited for the sake of effective child protection.

The Need to Address Failures

Suggesting pervasive misperceptions of adolescents' place in media, law, and policy, not to mention challenging perceptions of parents' control of their children's informational environments, undoubtedly constitutes a controversial stance. Yet, the misperceptions undergird the need to evaluate the media's role in adolescent development and policies affecting adolescents. These misperceptions, however, do not by themselves support a need for evaluating and suggesting reform in the regulation of media and adolescence. The legal system always makes broad assumptions about individuals and their circumstances that allow the system to function smoothly even when social science findings and reality challenge those assumptions. In this instance, however, several features of the historical moment merge with the realities behind misperceptions and render urgent a close look at intersections among media control and technologies, adolescent development, families, communities and the law.

Adolescents face changed (and troubled) realities in their families, communities, and peer relationships. Adolescents live in distressed families and communities that limit opportunities. For example, compared with their economically advantaged counterparts, adolescents who live in poverty are exposed to more family turmoil, violence, separation from their families, instability, and chaotic households that offer less social support (Evans, 2004). Poor adolescents confront widespread environmental inequities; neighborhoods with limited institutional resources, strained relationships, and without norms of collective efficacy, foster instability leading to negative behavioral and emotional outcomes (Leventhal & Brooks-Gunn, 2000). Importantly, families not in poverty also struggle to nurture, care, and even provide basic physical necessities (Bradley & Corwyn, 2002; Levesque, 2002a).

It is difficult to argue that adolescents are thriving. A large number of adolescents are growing up without opportunities for pondering the meaning of life to them, and communities fail to address such needs (Levesque, 2002c). Evidence of the resulting failure to support adolescent development abounds, particularly in rates of adolescents' victimizations, school failures, and unmet mental health needs (Levesque, 2002a). Minority youth face increasing disparities in their mental health and in access to mental health services; these are related to the multiple challenges they already face in socioeconomic status, but are aggravated by the lack of culturally competent services that can address their specific mental health needs within the context of their culture, family, and community (Pumariega, Rogers, & Rothe, 2005). Even if adolescents were able to grow in stable families and communities with strongly established social groups, these groups, which may have the best intentions, may in fact harm adolescent development, foster biases against individuals or members of other groups, and, by doing so, place a burden on broader society. Adolescents, families, and communities cannot ignore adolescents from their own and other communities. Adolescents face many communal challenges as communal institutions themselves face challenges. These challenges inevitably involve free speech, such as information needed to receive assistance and know that it is available, as well as to determine the dangers that lurk from having access to potentially harmful communities and to respond effectively to such threats.

In addition to changes in social relationships, shifts in governments' role in providing for basic human needs urge reconsideration of the media's role in adolescence. As communities and private communal groups evidence difficulties confronting challenges, policies increasingly shift the responsibility for social provision to them. For example, the shift's new rigor in supporting religious institutions' efforts to provide social services increasingly means a shedding of broader public responsibility and accountability for social provision. In addition to proving potentially problematic for adolescents, the change may prove problematic for the very fabric of society. The push for using public dollars to pay for private and religious schools, for example, challenges the shared context that connects private and public lives. Unlike before, current reforms call for focusing public funding to educate adolescents outside of the common, public system.

This channeling dismantles the very idea of a common school capable of integrating students from a variety of backgrounds and committed to inculcating a shared American tradition (Levesque, 2002b). Although some private schools may actually do as well or better than regular public schools in socializing their students to the values appropriate to citizenship (Godwin, Godwin, & Martinez-Ebers, 2004), the ideal of a common education no longer exists. This dismantling means a move away from the traditional, primary purpose of public education, which was to prepare students to participate effectively as citizens in the U.S. constitutional democracy. Information carried through various media, as well as the emergence of dominant media that shape youth culture, now performs much of the homogenizing, standardizing function once claimed for the common school controlled by parents and communities. As we have seen, the media transmit values that may not reflect well those endorsed by more traditional institutions, and it is unclear how new media environments can help foster effective citizenship in the absence of a concerted effort to restructure social and legal responses to the media's new role.

The privatization shift occurring in the more traditional areas of information provision, like schooling, also runs deep in other social service provision areas, and privatization's unintended results on adolescents' informational environments find parallels in those shifts. Most notably, the recent injection of private options into the delivery of welfare services becomes worrisome if viewed from the perspective of information transmittal. This is true, for example, in terms of the rampant discrimination already revealed by numerous evaluations of child welfare services and in terms of who receives services, the type of services, and what recipients must do to receive services (Levesque, 2000). The risk of discrimination may increase to the extent that increasing reliance on private groups to provide services may lead to unwitting (and witting) exclusions and coercions that violate the freedoms that have imbued the nation's ideals. These developments all directly implicate adolescents' right to information, the right to speak, and the freedom to develop their own potentials. As we have seen, privatization means that the government may now support, at the exclusion of other efforts, programs that censor information and reveal only what the state deems worth presenting to adolescents who must make private choices that will influence their life course. Although several important rationales support this form of censorship, it is clear that some adolescents will be deprived of potentially important informational resources while others will benefit from other ways of gaining access. Thus, although privatization may not be framed as First Amendment concerns, its consequences clearly involve informational rights and environments.

The media's role in the context of adolescents' broader informational environments also requires a close examination because of revolutionary developments in laws and policies regulating media. The legal system historically has been receptive to the ready availability of self-help remedies as evidence that state agents lack any compelling interest to restrict speech. Self-help remedies used to take simple and direct forms (such as looking away from offensive materials). The approach was so simple that courts never really trumpeted the fact that they used self-help to limit state censorship efforts. The advent of technologies capable of filtering potentially problematic speech, however, recently has encouraged courts to view self-help in a different light. Courts increasingly cite such technological self-help as evidence that state agents have sought unjustifiably restrictive means of achieving their ends. The Supreme Court, for instance, recently confirmed its willingness to compare the restrictiveness of the state's remedy for the supposed ills of free speech with the restrictiveness of alternative, self-help remedies (*United States v. Playboy Entertainment Group*, 2000, p. 814). The Court, moreover, has embraced self-help's new role with such evident vigor and consciousness that it has opened the door to revising the proper limits of state action: "Technology expands the capacity to choose; and it denies the potential of this revolution if we assume the Government is best positioned to make these choices for us" (*United States v. Playboy Entertainment Group*, 2000, p. 818).

These developments are particularly relevant to adolescents. Cases embracing self-help stand for the proposition that parental authority can serve as a form of self-help sufficiently effective to invalidate the state's claim to further its compelling interest in protecting minors from harmful speech. This trend even is revealed in free speech contexts outside of the media, such as cases involving religious club meetings in public schools (*Good News Club v. Milford Central School*, 2001). The result is an increase in information potentially available to adolescents, an increase that does not necessarily foster ways to ensure that adolescents who are exposed to information have the ability to respond to it effectively. That result acquires a new sense of urgency in light of leading commentators' lament that mass-media marketing—the advertising and promotion of products for consumption by children—already has displaced parental authority as the primary force in socializing our children, which profoundly impacts the social and cultural environment of childhood (Woodhouse, 2004). We need not take such an extreme stance to recognize that the media and marketing now compete with the family and governments to create and manipulate youth culture and reshape the ecology of adolescence. But, the media's potential power, coupled with the law's increasing attachment to principles of self-help, highlights how emerging technologies and informational markets challenge embraced approaches to protecting adolescents. Ironically, the increasing use of self-help remedies comes at a time when they may no longer serve their protective purposes.

As the above changes continue to alter adolescents' circumstances, the legal system itself has changed. The law increasingly recognizes that adolescents are persons worthy of constitutional protection in their own right. For example, the legal system now bestows on adolescents procedural rights when they become involved in the juvenile justice system. The legal system also has recognized that adolescents have rights within schools. As we have seen, the legal system protects adolescents' expression of religious speech and seeks to prevent state officials from supporting environments that would coerce adolescents into supporting or professing certain religious beliefs (*Santa Fe School District v. Doe*, 2000). These recognitions parallel those we have examined in the context of families, where the Court recognizes that adolescents have independent claims to privacy. All of these developments in the regulation of adolescents' private and public lives reflect a recognition of the need to protect adolescents from harm and to prepare them for responsible citizenship. These developments, however, remain far from systematic, coherent, and as liberative and as fearful as perceived by those who champion a more aggressive turn to parental rights (Hafen & Hafen, 1996). Many incongruities still mark the legal systems' responses to adolescents, and the developments in law and policy do not necessarily respond well to the current understanding of adolescent development, adolescents' place in society, and the changing world adolescents inhabit.

The extent to which the legal system fails to respond to adolescents' peculiar needs (and thus those of society) reveals yet another reason to reconsider the legal regulation of media and informational environments with an eye toward laws and policies affecting adolescents. The legal system evinces considerable trouble responding to the current understanding of adolescent development. Much of the failure is understandable in light of the nature of law: law cannot respond to and address only one issue without considering that issue's impact on others. Given the real extent to which adolescents must rely on others to meet their needs, the need to consider other peoples' rights and responsibilities is particularly present in the context of jurisprudence regulating adolescents. That is, the legal system necessarily responds to political concerns, social goals, and familial concerns, as well as to adolescents' needs. However, when the legal system assumes realities of adolescent life, it cannot achieve greater efficiency and ensure justice when it takes into account misperceptions rather than reality. In thinking of adolescents, the traditional view supposes that adolescents are passive recipients of social beliefs and traditions. Although that view appropriately highlights the relative power of social forces and their dominance over adolescents, it fails to consider how adolescents actively participate in their development. As we already have seen in chapters 2 through 5 and will see more clearly below, research highlighting how adolescents idiosyncratically evoke, interpret, and respond to their social environments continues to revolutionize the study of adolescent development. This new understanding of the adolescent period, and research supporting that conceptualization, further supports the need to examine the legal regulation of adolescents' informational environments.

The above misperceptions, diversities, failures, and complexities do much more than suggest a need for the current evaluation. They also complicate our effort. The resulting complications, however, render our task neither impossible nor futile. The previous chapters do suggest that a sharper focus on adolescents' basic rights and a firmer social science understanding of adolescence could better effect the desired outcomes of secure, healthy, and responsible adolescent development, including development that allows for freedoms deemed the bedrock of our civil society. The focus, importantly, includes responding to the complexities in which adolescents find themselves. Thus, the focus does not entail a need to unnecessarily limit the firmly established rights of parents and communities to influence their children's informational environments and development. Instead, the focus relies on the need to clarify and support those rights and rejects the popular dichotomy that envisions and assumes a necessary clash between adolescents' rights and those of their communities.

The point deserves emphasis given that the need to balance the rights of parents with those of others may get lost on those adhering to a firm parental rights model that confers the control of adolescents' rights to parents. Although the following analysis considers extending innovations in adolescents' rights, even these expansions remain far from radical and not beyond the realm of possibility. Likewise, although the analysis suggests alternative directions to achieve similar ends, the proposals still remain consistent with numerous legal principles and mandates—offered directions receive support from existing legal structures that remain largely undeveloped or simply ignored. The proposal, then, is simple: Legal and policy mandates may be better developed, respect adolescents' basic rights, reflect the realities of adolescent life, and foster healthy individual and social development while addressing adolescents' informational needs and responding to their media environments. To achieve those ends, the following analysis provides one version of possible steps forward.

The Place of Free Speech Principles in Adolescent Development

It may seem odd to propose that approaches to adolescents' rights must remain faithful to constitutional principles. No commentators and no courts overtly argue that the Constitution should be set aside when they determine the rights of adolescents. Yet, in practice and implicitly, they pervasively do set aside the Constitution when they fashion the rights of adolescents. Current approaches to adolescents' rights do so by the manner they use adults as the starting point of discussion. Even recent efforts that adopt a children's rights perspective that focuses on basic needs end up focusing on differences and on adult's rights. These analyses typically begin with the presumed differences and needs of minors compared to adults and then move on to consider how to address those differences. Even the Supreme Court routinely begins with the specifics of adults' rights and whittles them down to those of adolescents. In doing so, the Court typically (but not always) considers adolescents' peculiar circumstances and how those circumstances affect adults' rights. As a result, sometimes adolescents' circumstances suffice to support denying adolescents the rights adults receive, while at other times the circumstances justify treating adolescents no differently from adults. In its determinations, the Court pervasively looks to adult conceptions of rights rather than the principles that animate adults' constitutional rights. When the legal system adopts this adult-centered approach, it pervasively fails to remain faithful to adolescents' own constitutional rights. When applied to adolescents' peculiar position in society, such approaches distort analyses and outcomes that eventually do a disservice to adolescents as well as to constitutional rights themselves.

Conceptions of adolescents' rights that seek to remain faithful to constitutional principles must emanate from the same principles that animate the rights the Constitution ostensibly affords to everyone. Given that these constitutional principles must guide legal developments, determinations of the nature and extent of specific rights must involve how best to respect these principles that recognize adolescents' peculiar circumstances. The proposed approach begins with constitutional principles and considers how to apply them to adolescents. The approach accepts that adolescents have fundamental rights worth protecting and seeks to determine how to protect those rights. At its core, the proposed jurisprudential posture of adolescents' rights rejects the established vision of minors as infirm holders of reduced rights. The approach does examine how different adolescents are from adults, but it does so to understand how to fashion approaches that respect the same constitutional principles guiding the formulation of adults' rights, rather than to compare adolescents to adults for the purposes of noting that adolescents are inferior and concluding that their rights must also be reduced because adolescents do not measure up to adults.

Proposing that analyses of adolescents' constitutional rights should remain true to the principles that motivate these rights for everyone does not make for a simple and straightforward jurisprudence. It would be inappropriate to expect simple rules and outcomes for adolescents. We already have seen that, for free speech, the Court and commentators have identified several motivating principles. The application of these general principles to specific facts support multiple results for adults. Principles simply guide; they do not dictate. But just as fidelity to constitutional principles secures and balances adults' rights with those of others so that both individuals and society could flourish, remaining faithful to foundational principles should ensure that analyses of adolescents' rights are more mindful of adolescents' realities and of our democratic, civil society's constitutional building blocks. As we revisit principles guiding freedom of speech laws in light of developmental research, then, we embrace the Constitution's view that adolescents deserve rights and protections that secure them a place in our democratic, constitutional system.

Free Speech Principles and Adolescents' Development

As we have seen in chapter 6, several principles guide First Amendment free speech law, and the traditional principles that shape analyses continue to expand and protect wider spheres of speech. Viewed in its most narrow, traditional sense, the First Amendment relies on three principles that vindicate vigorous speech protections. First, free speech facilitates the search for truth and tests ideas in the marketplace of ideas. Second, free speech buttresses democratic self-governance through the sharing of information and viewpoints. Third, free speech fosters self-fulfillment through its support of autonomous expression. These closely intertwined justifications do not dictate the same result in every case, for their relevance also varies from case to case. Together, however, the justifications emerge as the central principles that have motivated the Court's constitutional analysis of adults' speech rights. The Court and leading commentators have yet to apply these same principles to adolescents. Instead, they have focused on parental rights and the need to protect adolescents from speech, as we have seen in "harmful to minors" laws. But the three free speech principles actually do readily apply to adolescents. Indeed, the principles seem to be of great relevance to fostering adolescent development and actually must work together to shape the responsible individual and civic development the Court views as the purpose of our laws' commitment to adapting individuals to life in modern civil society.

Engaging Markets of Ideas

If speech must be free to ensure the pursuit of truth, then adolescents' claim to free speech appears remarkably strong. The adolescent period actually is marked by the manner youths actively devote their time to the pursuit and meaning of truth (Levesque, 2002c). The period of adolescence involves rapid development and education geared toward developing ways to seek and evaluate information. Whether consciously or unconsciously, adolescents devote a significant portion of their daily attention to the acquisition of knowledge and the development of beliefs. The shaping of these emerging understandings and beliefs relies on speech among adolescents and between adolescents and adults. Developmentally primed for this engagement and interaction with others, adolescents are fundamentally open to the marketplace of ideas, arguably even more so than most adults. Adolescents embrace, reject, and consider ideas to determine their current and possible sense of self. The leading framework for understanding identity formation, Erikson's identity development theory (1966, 1968), emphasizes the dynamic, progressive organization of the child's drives, abilities, beliefs, and individual history leading to the adolescent's development of the internal self-structure known as identity. As adolescents actively engage in the process of sorting out their identities, looking to others for ideas about potential alternatives (B. B. Brown, 2004). As they share personal thoughts and feelings and learn to become sensitive to the needs, desires, and thoughts of others, adolescents gain deeper understandings of themselves and others. Experts consider this exploration a necessary precursor to successful identity development; healthy adolescents engage in identity exploration as they actively seek out information and test hypotheses about their theory of self (Dunkel & Lavoie, 2005).

The above process of identity exploration and formation actually constitutes the central task of adolescence. Identity formation involves the successful negotiation of a variety of activities and relationships during adolescence, including school achievement, social relations with others, and development of career interests and choices, along with a great deal of exploration of different activities and roles (Harter, 1999). These activities and rules contribute to the formation of one's gender, ethnicity, and sexual orientation, all of which are important to adolescents' developing identity. Integrating these experiences and characteristics into a coherent sense of self is fundamental to identity formation as identity development proceeds through different phases throughout the adolescent period (Berzonsky & Adams, 1999). The process of identity development rests on the active engagement of one's social environment.

Adolescents' focus on identity likely stems in part from the cognitive changes as well as their understanding of the imminence of their adulthood and the end of their childhood. The formation of a sense of identity—an integrated composite of personality, tastes, values, skills, and behaviors—develops in adolescence partly because it rests on certain cognitive advancements and changing social roles. By mid-adolescence, adolescents increasingly engage in abstract thinking, consider the hypothetical as well as the real, engage in more sophisticated and elaborate information-processing strategies, and reflect on themselves and complicated problems (Keating, 2004). These thought processes actually do not emerge at adolescence, but adolescents' increasing ability to organize and reflect on available information allows them to engage more readily in these higher-order thinking processes. Adolescents gain the capacity to engage in levels of abstract thinking and coordination of multiple perspectives that permit them to consider overarching principles and alternative hypothetical worlds. These new capacities merge with changing social roles and prompt the identity formation process. Imminent independence from parents, and the resulting need to make important decisions about work, friendships, lifestyle, and family, focuses adolescents' attention on the search for who they are and what they wish to become. Although parents figure prominently in guiding explorations and development, adolescents increasingly rely on peer and media interactions to accomplish the task of identity development. Who those peers are, and the informational context in which they interact, inevitably influences who adolescents become (Reis & Youniss, 2004; J. D. Lee, 2005).

Although sorting out one's identities constitutes a lifelong project, the concept of self most thoroughly and self-consciously emerges during adolescence and influences the life course. Engaging in markets of ideas gains significance for adolescents to the extent that no other age period is as central or intense as identity formation during adolescence. The unfolding of identity formation during adolescence dramatically affects their entire life course (Côté & Levine, 2002). The development of a subjective sense of an invigorating sameness and continuity is essential to healthy development and to securing a responsible place in civil society. Facing and adopting a firm sense of self-identity enables individuals to make important life choices that will serve their unique needs and talents, gives them a kind of stability and security that equips them to remain faithful to their commitments and handle life's vicissitudes, and prepares them to enter intimate relationships. Healthy, responsible development arises from an active choice-making process and from the necessity to confront, evaluate, and make choices based on available information and resources. This exploration is central to acquiring an understanding of self that equips adolescents to make decisions driven by genuine personal preference rather than externally imposed obligations and expectations.

Speech itself plays such an integral role in identity development and actually has a special value to adolescents largely absent for adults. Engaging in the process of identity formation means working through what one believes in matters of both fact and principle. While parental upbringing plays a large role in shaping this identity, the period of adolescence means a turn to independent, nonparental sources. Adolescent development, then, by its nature points adolescents toward the marketplace of ideas to work out who they are and what they think. Adolescents engage in the marketplace of ideas in a genuine search for truth (Levesque, 2002c). Adolescents enter the marketplace to consider various viewpoints and characterizations of facts and benefit from participation.

It would be naive to conclude that the enhanced value of speech during adolescence does not bring with it potential dangers. The law often interprets adolescents' openness to ideas as a unique vulnerability. Just like adults, minors may make mistakes. But, from a market perspective, this potential for mistakes does not, by itself, devalue adolescents' market participation. Healthy adolescent development actually depends on opportunities to practice and engage in processes of trial and error. Those experiences facilitate the development of self-knowledge, a better sense of the world, and greater moral understanding. From a speech perspective, then, the potential harms associated with speech mistakes appear quite milder than those that may arise from other contexts. Sexual activity and delinquency clearly are the two contexts of mistakes leading to harm that most likely come to mind. Yet, the legal system is not known for protecting adolescents from the harms of sexual activity and delinquent behavior (Levesque, 2000, 2002a). Indeed, research clearly indicates that addressing those harms means revamping adolescents' access to information (Levesque, 2003) and the manner adolescents receive educations (Levesque, 2002b) in ways that view adolescents as active participants who shape their environments. Even if the above examples did not exist and the law did properly protect adolescents from decision making, it is important to recall that the legal system seeks to distinguish exchanges of ideas from actions. Following the principle that the law generally protects speech but not necessarily its resulting actions, adolescents' speech rights would seem to warrant considerable protection. From the perspective of free speech principles, then, speech retains a special value to adolescents as a relative safe practice ground for choice, the essence of the market-of-ideas rationale for protecting speech.

Fostering Self-Governance and Civic Participation

If governments must protect free speech to ensure self-governance and foster civic participation, then adolescents own a strong claim to free speech. Of course, if self-governance referred simply to voting, it would be a challenge to relate the rationale to adolescents, given that voting constitutes the only constitutional reference to minors' status, which also happens to be the only status that the Constitution uses to exclude individuals from otherwise universal civic participation. As we have seen, however, the self-governance rationale for protecting speech dramatically expands beyond narrow views of political participation. The Court now conceives the justification more broadly as it extends protections to speech that serves the ends of self-government indirectly, as well as to speech designed directly to affect the democratic process. Self-government exists only insofar as citizens acquire the intelligence, integrity, sensitivity, and generous devotion to the general welfare that casting a ballot presumably expresses. Adolescents' speech experience critically affects their future and current speech habits as well as their expectations as democratic participants.

Contemporary models of political and civic socialization adopt developmental approaches that emphasize adolescents' active role in contributing to their communities and that highlight the socializing role of peers, media, and adults (Sapiro, 2004). These approaches differ considerably from earlier models dominated by the view that the "system" was handed down, relatively intact, from one generation to the next through families and schools. In addition to rejecting a vertical transmission perspective of socialization, new perspectives broaden the meaning of politics from a focus on the electoral arena to one that includes civic and community life. Developmental models focus on the opportunities adolescents have to experience membership in local groups, organizations, and institutions and to practice the skills needed for citizenship in modern society. Models also highlight the influences of media and informational environments on civic engagement. Together, diverse fields of inquiry (e.g., political science, communication, education, sociology, and developmental psychology) now reveal three essential components of civic participation. These components all have deep developmental roots that emerge from adolescents' abilities to access and process information about their place in society.

The Essential Components of Civic Participation

The first developmental component essential to responsible citizenship and civic participation directly centers on information and the accumulation of civic knowledge (Galston, 2001, 2004). Few dispute the nature of civic knowledge needed for living in a modern democracy. This knowledge involves what citizens ought to know and the processes set in place to ensure that sources of information and ideas are not monopolized by the government or a single dominant group, such as a political party or religious organization. Useful civic knowledge includes understanding the governments' purposes and appreciating the government's powerful impact on our daily lives. Civic knowledge allows individuals to recognize their voluntary but responsible role in civil society that provides a check on governmental power. It includes the recognition that governments, as instruments for social control, can foster justice as well as injustice. It allows for appreciating the role of democratic self-governance and knowing that knowledgeable citizens can act individually and collectively to protect rights, ensure observance of democratic values, and promote the common good. At its core, then, civic participation in modern, civil society rests on the accumulation of knowledge about what it means to be good citizens.

Civic skills comprise the second developmental component of responsible citizenship, and they are necessary for effective use of civic knowledge (Verba, Schlozman, & Brady, 1995). Both intellectual and participatory skills are necessary for citizens to exercise their rights and discharge their responsibilities as members of self-governing communities. Both types of skills allow citizens to use knowledge to negotiate systems. Prominent among the intellectual skills needed are those dealing with active exchanges of ideas: deliberation, communication, and persuasion. These competencies make effective action possible and lead to a greater sense of empowerment. Given that effective civic participation rests on collective decision making, participatory skills also constitute an important set of skills for civic participation, such as skills needed for interacting with other citizens to promote personal and common interests. The ability to participate in this manner necessarily relies on intellectual skills that allow citizens to identify and describe; explain and analyze; and evaluate, take, and defend positions on public matters. Both sets of skills necessarily involve learning to identify and process information. Opportunities to practice these skills during adolescence lead them to see themselves as politically engaged and helps motivate them toward greater engagement (Kirlin, 2002).

The third essential developmental ingredient that contributes to civic participation emerges from the development of skills that foster engagement. Engagement skills contribute to the development of values and self-concepts that support civic dispositions integral to the maintenance and improvement of democratic society. These dispositions take both individual and collective forms. Civil society relies on each individual's development of moral responsibility, self-discipline, and respect for the worth and human dignity of every individual. Collectively, civil society rests on public spiritedness, civility, respect for the rule of law, critical mindedness, and willingness to listen, negotiate, and compromise. The quality of democratic life rests on the extent to which claims of support for democracy are accompanied by deeper-rooted orientations of tolerance, trust, and a participatory outlook (Carpini, 2004). The deeper those orientations, the greater the chances are that effective democracy will emerge at the societal level. The character of the citizen body itself—citizens' shared dispositions or commitments—provides the barometer of the quality of democratic life. Both individualistic and collectivistic aspects of civil dispositions rely heavily on information. Democracy thrives when it makes information available and helps citizens develop the ability to process information thoughtfully. When democracy thrives, thoughtful citizens foster respect for the dignity and worth of every human being and a tolerance of difference, a willingness to engage in public policy issues beyond the act of voting, a readiness to exercise civil rights when they are threatened, a commitment to civil and rational discourse, and concern for the common good. This readiness emerges only with deep commitments, and such commitments only arise after fully engaging ideas. The development of civic dispositions, then, ensures effective civic participation, a foundational principle guiding free speech protections.

Fostering Civic Engagement

The three fundamental components of civic participation—knowledge, skills, and dispositions—underscore the legal system's need to adopt a developmental view if it ever wishes to foster positive civic engagement. Those key components develop slowly over time and with practice in families, schools, communities, and broader informational environments. They develop as adolescents gain a sense of who they are and of their place in society. Not surprisingly, adolescents initially view citizenship as good behavior, obeying laws, and doing what is expected (Conover & Searing, 2000). This obedience-oriented view changes as adolescents develop. The span of adolescence coincides with the development of a more critical appraisal of citizenship, one that allows for the exercise of good judgment, all of which relies on access and sorting through information. The transformation derives from informal and formal discussion and debates that bring adolescents into the process of civic engagement, that teach them that it matters to be informed and to hold an opinion, and that provide opportunities for involvement (Eccles & Barber, 1999; Flanagan, Gill, & Gallay, 2005). Participation in youth activities directly relates to the development of psychological strengths and a positive citizenship identity (Markstrom, Li, Blackshire, & Wilfong, 2005; Youniss, McLellan, Su, & Yates, 1999). As we have seen, this identity involves a moral commitment to others and a desire to act for the greater good, which links to participating in civic activities that enable adolescents to experience a sense of the collective (Perkins, Brown, & Taylor, 1996; Youniss et al., 1999). These formulations are consistent with Erikson's (1966) theory of development which posits that an identity search begins in early adolescence and that internal and external experiences during childhood and adolescence accumulate and lead to a commitment to particular values and beliefs.

Given the above findings, it seems fair to conclude that the availability of community-based organizations remains a primary factor influencing participation. These organizations foster civic responsibility when they provide pro-social reference groups where adolescents learn what it means to belong to a community and to matter to fellow members of that community. Effective youth activities provide adolescents with experiences related to initiative, identity exploration and reflection, emotional learning, developing teamwork skills, and forming ties with community members (D. M. Hansen, Larson, & Dworkin, 2003). In addition, they provide opportunities for bonding and connecting with others, for developing a sense of collective identity that sets them on a path towards lifelong civic participation (Smith, 1999). By participating in local community organizations and institutions, by exercising rights and fulfilling obligations in those groups, adolescents become aware that their own goals are realized when the group's goals are achieved. In this way, adolescents come to see themselves as societal members who share an interest in the common good (Menezes, 2003; Villarruel, Perkins, Borden, & Keith, 2003). Not surprisingly, a host of important retrospective studies with adults, as well as prospective studies with adolescents, have shown that engagement in extracurricular and community-based organizations and activities predicts civic engagement in adulthood, with sports providing a possible exception to this rule and with race and socioeconomic status shaping important variations (Verba et al., 1995; Flanagan, Bowes, Jonsson, Csapo, & Sheblanova, 1998; Frisco, Muller, & Dodson, 2004). These associations are consistent with the theory of social capital that views social connections and social organizations as creating norms and infrastructures to support civic engagement (Putnam, 2000). The consistency of these findings suggests that efforts to increase civic participation would benefit from a focus on adolescents, a focus that would increase adolescents' opportunities to engage actively with their communities.

Parents and peers also play significant roles in fostering civic participation. Researchers have long noted the important role parents play in the transmission of values (Grusec & Kuczynski, 1997). The socialization of civic values provides no exception. Civically engaged adolescents tend to have similarly engaged parents (Flanagan et al., 1998). Researchers now recognize that a dialectical relationship occurs between child and parent that affects both of their views of civic responsibilities (McDevitt & Chafee, 2000). Even when parents are not involved in community activities, their support strongly strengthens their children's involvement (Fletcher, Elder, & Mekos, 2000). Importantly, it is not just the adults in these institutions who matter; peers also potentially play a strong socializing force conducive to civic participation (Flanagan et al., 2005). Friends play supportive roles, whether their interactions take place within a structured program or in more informal settings. Positive relationships with peers predict civic behaviors, such as a greater likelihood of participating in community service activities (Wentzel & McNamara, 1999; Yates & Youniss, 1998). Adolescents involved in service learning, for example, reveal an increase in positive self-concept and political engagement when they have a high degree of voice and ownership over programs (Morgan & Streb, 2001). Importantly, family and peer relationships need not be situated in civic activities to influence concerns about civic life. Much of what becomes relevant to formal politics and political processes resonates with adolescents' everyday peer and family relationship experiences: experiences of inclusion and exclusion, stereotypes and prejudice, membership in and identification with a group, rights and responsibilities, self-determination and tolerance for difference, status and power, trust and loyalty, and of fairness in process and justice in outcome. Adolescents experience politics every day.

The media constitute another key aspect of adolescents' communities and increasingly plays an active role in the manner information, and the ability to use information effectively, grounds civic participation. Informational media use, such as reading newspapers, watching news programs, and gathering and exchanging information over the Internet, links to pro-civic consequences as it contributes to a wide range of participatory behaviors (Norris, 1996; McLeod,

Scheufele & Moy, 1999). Even social dramas that depict life-world controversies contribute to civic participation (Shah, 1998). Together, these media promote civic engagement as they allow users to gain knowledge, reinforce social linkages, and coordinate actions. The greater the connectedness with others, the more the communications can provide a means for individuals to link community information to opportunities for discussion, reflection, and recruitment (Shah, Cho, Eveland, & Kwak, 2005). Importantly, the use of media for entertainment and diversion—such as the use of the Internet for recreation and anonymous socialization and television for watching reality-based programs that present the world as full of deception, wrong-doing, and betrayal—seem to not contribute civic benefits and may even have adverse civic consequences (Shah, Kwak, & Holbert, 2001). As with all other media, content matters as does adolescents' use of such media. The dispositions adolescents bring to the media, and their ability to engage effectively, have important consequences. Fostering civic participation requires considering how the law will shape the media's role in adolescents' informational environments contributing to civic participation.

A developmental view of civic participation reveals that multiple social contextual influences and individual-level factors contribute to the development of civic engagement envisioned by our legal system's ideals. Our best evidence reveals that both public and private character traits central to democratic life necessarily derive from dispositions fostered during adolescence. A person's crucial orientations to life incubate during adolescence, and one's civic orientation is no different. The development of an ideology is part of adolescents' identity-making processes. As adolescents reflect on who they are and the future to which they aspire, they inevitably think about what they stand for and take stock of their societies. During adolescence, political views merge with personal values as they shape their language for explaining social issues. A large body of political socialization research indicates that a number of crucial political behaviors and attitudes are already shaped at an early age, and that they gain increasing stability during the life cycle (Stolle & Hooghe, 2004). The literature suggests that identity exploration tends to produce a greater sense of autonomy in subsequent decision making. That is, those who make commitments after engaging in a process of identity exploration are more likely to experience choice making as a deliberate, self-reflective selection among options and to perceive themselves as the authors of their own choices. The state might seek to cultivate this sense of self-determination in its citizens in order to promote their effective democratic participation both as voters and, more indirectly, through their exercise of individual rights. Embracing a faith or other value after a process of exploration and resolution arguably better comports with our conception of what constitutes the exercise of civil rights in our constitutional system than does embracing the same faith or values out of an unreflective sense of obligation. A legal system overtly committed to ensuring civic participation would take adolescents quite seriously, as an important group with rights to participate in the exchange of ideas contributing to the Constitution's vision of individual and community life.

Nurturing Self-Fulfillment

Researchers and theorists have yet to address directly the nature of adolescents' self-fulfillment. The study of adolescents' positive mental health and optimal functioning generally frames approaches in terms of what would constitute the acquisition of necessary skills and experiences for a positive transition to adulthood. The stance is significant: it is future-oriented and implicitly uses another age group to measure success. Although basing adolescents' notions of well-being on what they will be like as adults, the approach is far from peculiar; well-being necessarily involves delayed gratification, unwelcomed experiences, and honing of skills to increase the chances of long-term well-being (Seligman & Csikszentmihalyi, 2000). Thus, the manner one deals with and controls current experiences and the attributions placed on those experiences largely determines mental health. From this view, optimal mental health in adolescence involves possessing appropriate coping skills, retaining a positive self-image, and maintaining a self-understanding that allows for engaged and proactive involvement in determining one's development and interactions with others. These components of optimal functioning, and factors that contribute to its promotion, reveal the significant role played by information and the freedom to engage different points of view

The Essential Components of Positive Adaptations

Self-fulfillment, regardless of age, rests on positive mental health and adaptation to one's environment. This orientation fundamentally involves a sense of agency. Agency entails experiencing one's thoughts and actions as originating voluntarily within the self (Ryan, 1993). This sense of agency is critical to intrinsic motivation, the experience of wanting to do and being invested in an activity. Research examining motivation illustrates the significance of agency for positive mental health. Adolescents can be motivated because they value certain activities or because of powerful external coercion; that is, they can have internal motivation or externally pressured motivation. Self-authored motivation leads to more interest, confidence, and excitement which in turn results in enhanced performance, persistence, creativity and general well-being (Ryan & Deci, 2000). Acting on intrinsic motivation describes the inclination toward assimilation, mastery, spontaneous interest, and exploration deemed essential to cognitive and social development and the principal source of enjoyment and vitality throughout life, including adolescence (Csikszentmihalyi & Rathunde, 1993).

A second factor, fundamentally related to the first, involves a concerted engagement in the environment. This engagement must involve paying close attention to the constraints, rules, challenges, and complexities found in the environment. Adolescents who experience chronic interest in everyday life experiences, unlike those who experience widespread boredom, experience greater well-being, as evidenced, for example, by global self-esteem, locus of control, and emotions regarding one's future prospects. Adolescents' generalized chronic experience of interest, an innate physiological function, actually signals their psychological health, while chronic boredom points to psychic dysfunction (Hunter & Csikszentmihalyi, 2003). This sense of engagement, of effective adaptation in the environment, often is framed in terms of one's level of "competency." Standards on which to determine competence may take at least two directions. Competence may be broadly defined in terms of reasonable success with major developmental tasks expected of a person in the context of his or her culture, society, and time. Or, it may be more narrowly defined in terms of specific domains of achievement, such as academics, peer acceptance, or athletics. In general, however, competency refers to good adaptation, rather than superb achievement and engagement with the social environment. Competency carries a dual meaning that the person has a track record of achievement and that the influential factors impacting the capacity to perform will persist in the future. Optimally functioning adolescents have a sense of competency that allows them to engage with their environments.

The third factor central to optimal functioning involves efforts directed toward a goal, which might include dealing with setbacks, re-evaluations, and adjustment of strategies. To a large extent, this factor involves a sense of resilience. While there exists no universal definition of resilience, the term generally refers to manifested competence in the context of significant challenges to adaptation or development. Resilient individuals are those who successfully cope with or overcome risk and adversity or who have developed a sense of competence in the face of severe stress and hardship (Rutter, 1987). Thus framed, the identification of resilience requires two judgments. First, there must have been a threat to the individual, such as the extent to which they live in a high-risk environment. Second, the individual must have adapted or developed in a competent manner despite the adversity. Adolescents who can set themselves on a path of self-fulfillment possess the characteristics and skills that enable them to attain personal success despite seemingly poor odds.

Taken together, the three factors reveal much about conceptions of positive mental health central to self-fulfillment. Definitions of positive health tend to take an adult-centered standard. For example, risks are seen as creating problems not necessarily for the adolescent period but arguably more so for the time when adolescents reach adulthood. As such, conceptions of mental health are future-oriented. Definitions also focus on individuals in context. Mental health tends to be viewed in terms of responses to social environments. Evaluations of optimal functioning, although framed in terms of self-determination and individual initiative, still must consider social interactions. Positive mental health essentially involves individuals' active engagement with their surroundings. Healthy adolescents are those deemed involved in creating their own social world. Feeling good about the self, excited, proud, sociable, and active are the strongest predictors of trait happiness (Csikszentmihalyi & Hunter, 2003). Lastly, despite impressive progress in understanding the nature of positive mental health, research remains in its infancy and has yet to attract the amount of research that its centrality to human development would warrant.

Fostering Fulfilling Adaptation

Given the continued lack of focus on the nature of positive mental health, it is not surprising to find that the promotion of positive adolescent development also garners little interest and research. Existing studies of adolescent and child development, however, do offer important starting points. Particularly important to consider is research exploring conditions that foster resilience (Luthar, Cicchetti, & Becker, 2000), intrinsic motivation, and positive emotional experiences some view as "flow" (Csikszentmihalyi & Rathunde, 1993), as well as recent research focusing on shaping communities to foster positive youth development (Larson, 2000).

Research concerned with resilience focuses on the psychological and social forces that allow adolescents to overcome adversity and successfully adjust to conditions that could otherwise contribute to dysfunction. Although this research does not focus directly on optimal functioning, it does suggest important factors that permit adolescents to adapt positively to their circumstances. The central finding of resiliency research reveals that resilience to adversity depends as much on the characteristics of the important contexts in which adolescents develop (family, school, and community) as on the characteristics of the adolescents themselves (Garmezy, 1991; Radke-Yarrow & Brown, 1993). The most important factor associated with resilient behavior highlights the necessary interaction between individuals and social forces. Good cognitive development or intellectual functioning frequently serves as the most broad and salient predictor of competence, the ability to respond to challenges. For example, generally good cognitive skills predict more than academic achievement; they also predict other aspects of competence as well, such as the ability to follow rules, direct attention, and control impulses. This more social aspect of competence reveals that adolescents' social interactions matter in fostering competence. It also reveals that the caretaking roles adults assume can foster competence and hold important potential for adolescents to overcome some of the hardships that life may press upon them, a point highlighted by efforts to enact policies and programs to protect and foster good cognitive development as ways of building human capital (i.e., early intervention efforts receive enormous popularity and relative success; see Ramey & Ramey, 1998). In short, resilient outcomes depend on specific mechanisms and processes that help link resilient behaviors with prosocial adult responses in a variety of contexts.

In addition to research on resilience, important insights emerge from examinations of ways adolescents become motivated, directed, socially competent and psychologically rigorous adults. Rather than focusing solely on the individual, this area of research focuses on how individuals approach situations and how specific supportive conditions must be present to maintain and enhance positive, engaged, competent, and intrinsically motivated approaches to one's environment. The general finding suggests that social-contextual events, such as feedback, rewards, and communications, conduce toward feelings of competence during actions and can enhance intrinsic motivation, but behavior will be experienced as intrinsically motivated if it is experienced as self-determined. Thus, optimal challenges and effective feedback that fosters autonomous behaviors and beliefs facilitate intrinsic motivation and positive mental health (Ryan & Deci, 2000).

Numerous areas of research support the above claims. Choice, acknowledgment of feelings, and opportunities for self-direction enhance intrinsic motivation and positive adaptation because they foster feelings of autonomy. For example, teachers who are autonomy supportive (in contrast to controlling) catalyze in their students' greater intrinsic motivation, curiosity, and desire for challenge; all of which allows students to learn more effectively (Utman, 1997). Likewise, autonomy-supportive parents, relative to controlling parents, provide types of environments in which children exhibit more intrinsic motivation (Grolnick, Deci, & Ryan, 1997; Assor, Roth, & Deci, 2004). These findings generalize to other domains, such as music and sports, in which supports for autonomy and competence by parents and mentors incite more intrinsic motivation and greater success (Grolnick et al.,1997).

Not surprisingly, then, the combination of warm, structured child-rearing practices in parents with reasonably high expectations for competence strongly ties to success in multiple domains and to resilience among children at risk. In general, the more involvement, structure, and autonomy-granting opportunities adolescents receive from their parents, the more positively teens evaluate their own conduct, psychosocial development, and mental health (Gray & Steinberg, 1999; Kerr & Stattin, 2000), and the lack of such opportunities between sibling relationships also contributes to adolescents' adjustment problems (Conger, Conger, & Scaramella, 1997). The same has been found for student success in schools, with such opportunities deemed as contributing, for example, to more engagement, better performance, lower dropout rates, and higher-quality learning (Ryan & Deci, 2000). Whether in school or in families, adolescents who receive support, feel challenged, and experience a sense of autonomy rate more highly on measures of optimal development (Hektner, 2001). Similar findings even have been reported with adolescents' engagement in their communities; meta-analyses reveal that structured youth activities reach effectiveness in fostering positive growth when they foster independence, self-efficacy, assertiveness, decision making, and internal locus of control (Hattie, Marsh, Neill, & Richards, 1997). The abilities of communities to foster adolescents' sense of engagement with their social world, and even to do so perhaps more effectively than schools and some parents, has led leading researchers to focus on community programs and youth activities to enhance adolescents' positive mental health (e.g., Larson, 2000). A central thrust of these efforts focuses on applying the findings and principles we identified above to shape healthy development (Lerner & Castellino, 2002). Not surprisingly, the research finds that teachers, parents, and communities can promote positive youth development by maintaining an environment rich in interpersonal support, autonomy, and opportunities to pursue challenges related to future goals (Hektner, 2001). Adolescents reporting the most intrinsic and optimal motivation do so in contexts surrounded by structures that support self-determination.

The Significance of Diversity

Identifying some behaviors, thoughts, and emotions as foundational for optimal development contributing to self-fulfillment readily raises issues of bias. Considering what is optimal obviously may differ in relation to potential racial/ethnic, gender, sexual orientation, and other dimensions of cultural diversity. The above research reveals that researchers may have identified underlying developmental factors that may express themselves differently. Cultural and developmental influences produce variations in the salience of certain goals and experiences which, in turn, yield different satisfaction of basic needs and different levels of well-being and self-fulfillment. This reality means that any understanding (and promotion) of self-fulfillment must consider contextual forces.

Although the adolescent period may be distinct relative to other age groups, adolescents by no means constitute a monolithic group. Adolescents exhibit variations and inhabit different environments that deserve emphasis to the extent that they determine the variety of challenges to adolescents' mental health. A most significant consideration involves the impact of living in a cultural or community context that differs from larger society. The primary example involves adolescents living in highly dangerous inner-city neighborhoods where survival depends on views that may be deemed inappropriate in mainstream society (Coll et al., 1996). Some argue, for example, that adolescents raised in ghettos are barred from opportunities in mainstream society and that they may seek achievement in alternative economic and social structures represented by illegal activities (e.g., Ogbu, 1981; Bourgois, 1995). Likewise, adolescents and parents from these environments may use different criteria to measure successful developmental outcomes, such as the "Revised American Dream" that results from severe restrictions in opportunities (Burton, Obeidallah, & Allison, 1996). This research finds interesting parallels with research examining civic participation, which finds urban youth involved less in traditional civic activities but still quite concerned about, albeit different, civic matters (Sherrod, 2003).

If we consider self-fulfillment in terms of mental health, it is clear that responding to different environmental considerations necessarily impacts adolescents' self-fulfillment. Most notably, the health of minority adolescents is generally poorer than the health of their dominant-culture peers (McLoyd & Steinberg, 1998; D. K. Wilson, Rodrigue, & Taylor, 1997). To complicate matters even more, adolescents experiencing extreme levels of stress (e.g., minorities in violent urban settings) seem to defy existing theories of resiliency. Adolescents suffering from chronic exposure to stressors and identified as resilient to those stressors (through academic performance and relative lack of externalizing behaviors) do not report higher levels of hypothesized protective resources such as perceived self-worth, competence, and social support; nor do they report lower levels of depression or anxiety (D'Imperio, Dubow, & Ippolito, 2000). Although potentially protective resources are themselves compromised by chronically disadvantaged neighborhoods, these environments do help shape protective factors. Minority adolescents expressing greater religiosity and concern for correcting social inequalities, for example, tend to score high on measures of well-being (Moore & Glei, 1995). Despite these more positive findings, research continues to document links between adolescents' perception of their neighborhoods as more threatening and increases in adolescents' numerous negative outcomes, especially their symptoms of depression, opposition defiant disorder, and conduct disorder (Aneshensel & Sucoff, 1996). Not surprisingly, environmental factors shape the experience and expression of self-fulfillment.

The adolescent experience also varies tremendously according to gender, which inevitably influences manifestations of self-fulfillment. Gender differences are manifested in behavior, beliefs about health and health-related behavior, health-related knowledge, and behavioral determinants. Moreover, gender differences interact with culture, ethnicity, minority/immigrant status, and socio-economic status to create unique mental health risks for different groups of adolescents. These differences are important in that they reveal more variation within groups than between groups (Eccles, Barber, Jozefowicz, Malenchuk, & Vida, 1999). These differences suggest that declines in factors relating to mental health are not inevitable consequences of adolescence or gender development; the differences also show that some factors that place some groups at risk for some things buffer them from other problems. For example, girls have many strengths that serve them well as they move through adolescence. Girls are more confident than males in stereotyped female gender-role domains, such as general social skills and general academic abilities, and these strengths allow them to adjust to schooling better than boys who are more likely to drop out or get into trouble (Eccles et al., 1999). However, narrow standards for girls' appropriate gender roles place a majority of girls at risk to suffer from subclinical eating concerns, body dissatisfaction, and what researchers view as normal discontent which places them at greater risk for depression (Striegel-Moore & Cachelin, 1999). The role gender plays in adolescent development emphasizes well the need to consider adolescents' place vis-à-vis other adolescents.

Subpopulations of adolescents also reveal different issues regarding their mental health. Although many adolescents express different mental health needs, particularly adolescents who are homeless (Berdahl, Hoyt, & Whitbeck, 2005), immigrant (Harris, 1999; McLatchie, 1997), or non-heterosexual (Meyer, 2003), adolescents in foster care and those in detention continue to receive the most attention. Although even literature relating to these two latter groups remains limited, it nevertheless provides important examples of the unique risks for morbidity they express, often to a greater degree. Although the majority of studies examining the health of adolescents in foster care tend not to separate adolescents from young children, the surveys that do exist provide important information regarding adolescents' need for mental health services. A leading study of adolescents entering foster care found that three-quarters required urgent mental health referrals (Chernoff, Combs-Orme, Risley-Curtiss, & Heisler,

1994). Adolescents in custody for delinquent behavior also reveal mental health needs. Reports from detention facilities indicate that more than half of adolescents experience depression, one-fifth are actually suicidal or self-violent, one-third exhibit disruptive behaviors, and one-fifth have thought disorders (Snyder & Sickmund, 1995). In addition, incarcerated adolescents reveal high-risk sexual and substance use behaviors, with one-third entering detention testing positive for a least one illicit drug (Snyder & Sickmund, 1995) and with nearly one-quarter reporting a history of sexually transmitted disease (Canterbury et al., 1995). The status of some adolescents (which when taken together actually begins to constitute the majority), then, exacerbates differences other adolescents experience as normative. Importantly for our concerns, the diversity in the status of adolescents results in an increasing need to consider ways to foster their self-fulfillment and a need to revisit informational environments.

Reaching for Fidelity to Free Speech Principles

If developmental sciences tell us anything about the values underlying rationales to protect First Amendment Speech freedoms, it certainly is that they have considerable relevance to healthy adolescent development. Our examination revealed strong parallels and relationships between the values that undergird First Amendment free speech jurisprudence and the emerging research findings that indicate what constitutes and supports healthy adolescent development. These are somewhat surprising given that developmental research seems to have developed without overtly considering free speech jurisprudence, and that jurisprudence clearly has developed in the absence of developmental research. Yet, as we have seen, the parallels should not surprise us. Our society's deep attachment to the democratic principles of respect for individual development and concern for responsible citizenship no doubt infiltrate who we are and our conceptions of healthy development. It remains to be seen whether the legal system could benefit from taking developmental findings seriously enough to reshape the law's response to adolescents' informational environments.

The legal system undoubtedly has much to consider in its responses to adolescents' speech rights (including media rights), and the extent to which developmental sciences can assist may remain an open matter. The diversity of legal approaches to address different types of speech and media, the obvious attachment of free speech issues to deep moral and political concerns, and the long history of ignoring developmental findings suggest that empirical accounts may not contribute greatly to the legal regulation of speech that affects adolescents' experiences. Yet, regardless of the political and moral stances taken by policy makers, and those who interpret and implement existing laws, all must address adolescents' peculiar place in society and how adolescents' rights must be balanced against those of their parents, communities and civil society. This reality suggests that there still remains hope that adolescents, parents, and society can benefit from existing developmental sciences' findings relating to adolescents and their informational environments. Hope rests in the ability to integrate social science findings into the values found in existing jurisprudence and policy rationales that could be extended to adolescents. On a more practical level, re-conceptualizing the legal regulation of adolescents in ways consistent with social science suggestions requires a close examination of the rights of adolescents in different contexts and across different relationships.

The need for a more nuanced balancing and the preceding chapters' discussions contribute basic principles that can serve as foundations to guide policies and reforms that more effectively balance the rights of adolescents, parents, communities, and broader society. The principles rest on the need to champion respect for adolescents and ensure young peoples' membership in a society that takes adolescents' interests seriously and that fosters citizens who also take their own and societal interests seriously. The following discussion examines these principles. In addition, the analysis enumerates the principles' divergences from misperceptions of current law and policy, evaluates available social science suggestions regarding the appropriateness of the principles, and responds to potential criticisms levied against efforts that would seek to take the principles more seriously.

Although the principles that follow emerge and receive support from our previous discussions, two caveats immediately arise as we move from a more descriptive to a more proscriptive analysis. First, the highlighted principles simply are meant to serve as guiding tools. None has particular talismanic qualities given that all principles deserve consideration and their content obviously must be weighted differently depending on contextual requirements and peculiar exigencies arising from the need to balance adolescents' rights with other people's interests and those of civil society. Second, offered principles all inter-relate and even overlap. Models certainly could be much more conceptually tidy and their factors shaped to maximize their independence, but such contorted models and efforts would not necessarily offer much practical utility. The conflictual and mutual interactions among the worlds of law, media, and adolescence present complex and, when in need of rebalancing, highly context-dependent outcomes. Bearing in mind these realities, we now revisit our previous discussions to detail future directions in the law's approach to adolescents' informational environments, including their media access.

Recognize Adolescents' Competencies

Reconsidering adolescents' free speech rights requires reassessing the extent to which parents, society, and the law should give weight to adolescents' abilities and rights to make significant life choices and, often ignored, to make the choices that will set them on particular developmental trajectories. As we have seen in chapters 6 and 7, traditional jurisprudential trends in adolescents' rights generally bestow parents with the control of adolescents' rights. For example, parents generally control the context of family life. Where parents do not have control, the state generally controls adolescents' rights. Adults' pervasive control over adolescents' rights renders it difficult to envision a system that also bestows on adolescents control over their own rights. Yet, modern jurisprudence increasingly accords adolescents more control over their own rights and recognizes adolescents' ability to act autonomously. These innovative developments firmly attach to traditional jurisprudence and continue to serve the very fundamental reasons for giving parental rights much of their valence and the government so much power—protecting adolescents and producing socially responsible citizens (Levesque, 2000). In terms of law, then, taking adolescents' competencies seriously might mean beginning to bestow more control of adolescents' rights (such as to increased access to media and information) directly on adolescents themselves rather than continuing to confer the control of those rights on parents or the state. This shift would be done in the name of protecting adolescent development and civil society.

Assumptions about minors' decision-making competence frame the law's attitude toward the question of whether some adolescent decisions should be treated no differently than adult decisions. Depending on different contexts, ranging from families, schools, streets, stores, clinics, theaters, and pool halls to doctors' offices, the law sometimes must explicitly or implicitly judge the competence of minors to make significant decisions about the course of their lives. To the extent that minors exhibit decisional competence no more infirm than that displayed by adults, it would seem to follow that competence to make those decisions should be respected, at least no less than those deriving from similarly situated adults' decisional competence. As with adults, respecting adolescents' decisions can mean depriving them of beneficial consequences from a decision on the grounds that those consequences are outweighed by negative consequences either to the decision maker or to others. Respecting their decision might also mean allowing negative consequences that may befall them. Given the risks involved, the determination of appropriate competency undoubtedly remains quite tricky. In determining general rules and discovering general assumptions, however, the developmental sciences have much to offer.

More similarities than differences mark adolescents' and adults' decisional capacities. The cognitive elements of decision making support the conclusion that the decision-making competencies of older adolescents do not differ greatly from those of adults (Scott, Reppucci, & Woolard, 1995). For non-cognitive factors, the differences between older adolescents and younger adolescents are more prominent than the differences between older adolescents and young adults (Steinberg & Cauffman, 1996; Scott, Reppucci, & Woolard, 1995). Adolescents' perceptions of risk also may not be as defective as once thought. In fact and compared to young adults, adolescents may be less susceptible to risk and to thoughts that they are invulnerable. Recent risk research examining natural hazards and behavior-linked risks finds adolescents less likely than young adults to see themselves as invulnerable, and their perceptions of the magnitude of their personal risk for experiencing negative outcomes actually decrease as they move out of adolescence (Millstein & Halpern-Felsher, 2002). Adults, then, may well rival adolescents' level of "immaturity."

Yet, adolescents are not adults. Despite positive accounts of adolescents' level of decisional capacities, relatively massive amounts of research document well how adolescents still engage in problematic and even dangerous activities *despite* knowing the high risks involved. Chapters 2 through 5 persuasively documented both the failure of adolescents to make appropriate decisions, and adolescents' vulnerability to social influences. This research fits quite nicely with growing evidence that maturational brain processes continue well through adolescence (Keating, 2004; Dahl & Spear, 2004). This research certainly highlights adolescents' neurological limitations and indicates their difficulty with "hot cognitions," thinking that needs to be made under strong feelings or high arousal (such as under peer pressure; Steinberg, 2005). Although this line of research remains more speculative than popular commentaries suggest, it contributes substantial speculation about the connections between the plasticity of adolescents' brain maturation and their behavioral and emotional development. It even has led some commentators to suggest that adolescents must be protected from media influences so that such influences do not adversely affect adolescents' neurobiological development (Saunders, 2005). Our broader understanding of adolescent development and influences on them, however, does not necessarily support an aggressive turn to limiting adolescents' access to life experiences; it does not do so for the simple reason that adolescents are not children at least as much as they are not adults.

Research highlighting limitations in adolescents' decision making capacities does not vitiate the findings indicating the opposite, those relating more to "cold cognitions." And policy suggestions that focus on limitations similarly run the risk of ignoring adolescents' abilities, especially their ability to make sound decisions and their need to learn how to make such decisions. Taken together, both lines of research (one highlighting limitations and one demonstrating impressive capabilities) reveal that understanding decision making means focusing on contexts. We know that different contexts may demand considerable skills that challenge anyone's ability to make sound decisions and that other contexts can reveal how adolescents may not be particularly deficient in needed skills and so incompetent in their abilities that they cannot make decisions and influence their own behavior. This more integrative view indicates how, as a period for reorganizing psychological, social, and neurobiological regulatory systems, adolescence constitutes a period fraught with both risks and needed opportunities for developing effective competencies. This more integrative view reinforces the proposition that our society, including our legal system, needs to structure adolescents' experiences in ways that foster the development of competent decision making.

Decisions involving media and informational matters provide no exception to the need to examine adolescents' decisional capacities and other abilities in the context of their other dependencies. In terms of adolescents' media environments, existing research reveals many complexities and important conclusions. First, parents highly influence adolescents' developmental experiences, but that influence wanes. As we also have seen, by adolescence, parents lose their grip on their children's exposure to media and access to speech. Available peer groups and informational environments (such as schools and social service providers) also impact adolescents' development, attitudes, and behaviors. Thus, regardless of whether we desire it, adolescence involves increasing freedom to explore media and information. Second, understanding social influences, including media influences, on adolescents requires realizing the many recursive influences on those who interact with adolescents, such as the manner peers and broader communities impact parents which, in turn, impact adolescents who then impact communal, peer and parents' own dispositions. This means that if we want to consider how the media influence adolescents' decisions, we must focus beyond the media itself and include parent, peer, cultural, and numerous other social and personal influences. Third, we have learned that development, including the development of competence, involves an active process, a process of exploration in available social environments. Indeed, the healthiest forms of identity and competence emerge through active exploration of alternatives and settling on one's own sense of self. Active exploration allows for the development of a more fully conscious, self-directed, and self-regulating mind. Adolescents actually engage and shape their social worlds, including their social environments, and the extent to which they are able to do so contributes to and reveals their competence.

The above research findings suggest that matters involving the media and informational environments may not involve issues of competence as traditionally described by available research attempting to index competencies in legal decision-making. The research does suggest, however, the need to at least consider how the legal system could better address adolescents' needs as it grants adolescents greater control over their own rights and as adolescents respond to media environments and contexts that could be influenced by others' media exposure. A close look at current laws regulating adolescents' media environments and identity development reveals that providing greater respect for adolescents' abilities to make decisions regarding information is both feasible and far from radical. In fact, providing adolescents with greater opportunities to exercise their competence to follow their choices, especially those that involve "cold cognitions," is much less extremist and less radical than the traditional trends that viewed adolescents as possessions over which parents and others can exercise power and control.

The legal system already recognizes adolescents' competencies and the need to support the development of competency through ensuring access to information. Innovative policies already ensure that adolescents have exit options in the form, for example, of judicial relief or social service delivery when adolescents' rights would otherwise be violated by parents or others acting in ways that exert too much control over adolescents' decision making and informational resources. The highly charged example of parents' rights to control their children's reproductive freedoms—their right to access information and services from medical providers—offers the starkest example of the many ways law skirts around parental rights to provide adolescents with ways to exercise their own rights when they would conflict with those of their parents (Levesque, 2000). We have seen other examples. Mundane but pervasive examples involve the power of school officials to regulate informational environments and the important limits placed on school officials in the name of adolescents' informational rights (*West Virginia State Board of Education v. Barnette*, 1943; *Tinker v. Des Moines Independent Community School District*, 1969; *Board of Education, Island Trees Union Free School District No. 26 v. Pico*, 1982). All of these developments directly protect adolescents' free speech rights as they shield them from environments that would infringe on those rights. Importantly, the developments reveal that adolescents have the competence to hold convictions, and that the legal system views such convictions as worthy of respect. These laws may remain controversial, but they still respect traditional concerns to the extent that they take seriously society's interest in assisting adolescents' development and that they recognize the importance of the need to justify denying adolescents access to informational resources and benefits simply because they are not considered adults.

Beyond general informational rights, competency may figure prominently in the central way the legal system censors adolescents' media access. We have seen that concerns about harms figure prominently in First Amendment jurisprudence controlling the media that may reach adolescents. Early jurisprudence, especially the *Ginsberg*-line of cases, allowed the state to censor media, a censorship based on the compelling argument that some forms of sexualized media could cause moral harm to minors. The Court even adopted the approach in the absence of empirical evidence and, more importantly, noted that such evidence need not even be considered since what constituted harm in that instance rested on a moral standard not conducive to empirical inquiry. We have seen that concerns about harm actually are difficult to address. It seems clear, though, that different results would emerge if the censorship were evaluated from a moral standpoint that considers adolescents' positions in society, their competencies, and their compelling need for First Amendment protection. It would seem that there would not be much difference between that type of harm and all of the other types of potential harms (from portrayals of violence, drugs, etc.) that could result from media use but do not lead to the same high level of media censorship. Thus, taking adolescent's competencies more seriously would move the early, established cases that allow for censorship toward the more recent cases that, in other contexts, reject censorship, as we have seen in cases that protect media producing violence and even indecent sexual materials. Thus, the law already allows for a judicial posture that reduces censorship of adolescents' exposure to what may be construed as harmful materials. The hesitancy to limit exposures does not deal directly with issues of competency, but it is clear that if the interest in protecting adolescents were more compelling, if it were really thought that adolescents would be harmed and be incompetent to deal with the media, then that would justify censorship. The extent to which censorship is resisted in these cases reveals the extent to which the legal system believes adolescents are not so impressionable, vulnerable, and incompetent to deal with the censored media content.

Although the legal system increasingly recognizes the peculiar legal needs of adolescents and adolescents' potential competencies, the recognition that adolescents possess significant competence has not erased continued challenges that derive from efforts to protect them from harm and to foster their healthy social development. For example, we found very few cases that directly address adolescents' right to media, and those cases tend to be narrowly decided and result from censorship of information that the government already has in its possession. In those contexts, adolescents face limitations similar to those of adults; the right to information has yet to be developed. This important limit to adolescents' right to media is but one example of the many limits our legal system places on free speech (as reviewed in chapters 6 and 7). These limitations reveal the complexities that jurisprudence and litigation must address even when similar issues involve adults. These limits are important to consider in that they reveal how adolescents' increased control over their own rights as they become subjects of rights does not translate into abandoning them to their own rights. Like adults, adolescents still remain social beings with social responsibilities. Providing adolescents with greater autonomy to exercise their free speech rights requires accepting the state's legitimate control of adolescents and adults. The next issue becomes, then, helping to determine when, and in what contexts, adolescents should be allowed to express and experience speech environments and express beliefs as they would see fit.

Support Adolescents' Dynamic Self-Determination

Recognizing that adolescents may be competent enough to hold convictions worth protecting and that they may be deemed legally competent to control their rights in some contexts underscores only part of what the legal system may need to consider if we are to take adolescents' free speech rights seriously. Taking their rights seriously would mean that the legal system would respect their right to self-determination and structure their social environment in ways that would foster self-determination simply because it remains unlikely, and inappropriate in most contexts, to bestow adolescents with entire control of their rights. Adolescents' rights and obligations require balancing with those of others. In envisioning the balancing, the need to enhance dynamic self-determination provides a key principle to guide the development of policies regulating adolescents' informational environments, including adolescents' media access.

As with other legal developments discussed above, legal systems already attempt to foster self-determination. The use of the maturity standard illustrates the feasibility of the approach. The standard, for example, has been used to determine access to medical services, including access to abortion, medical testing, and treatment. Following initial reluctance to interfere with parents' duty to raise their children, courts have taken a more active role during the latter half of this century in compelling medical care for children, objections by parents notwithstanding. In some instances, courts have been willing to order life-saving and even life-enhancing medical treatment, no matter how remote the threat of death nor how dangerous the procedure, so long as the medical treatment offers hope of being in the child's best interests—in other words, so long as the medical treatment may possibly lead the child toward normalcy and happiness (Levesque, 2002a). These developments allow for infringing on the fundamental rights of parents. Thus, as adolescents' rights have been deemed fundamental and adolescents have been able to determine the results evolving from those rights, so has jurisprudence and legislation increasingly allowed adolescents access to services, courts, and extra procedural protections to enhance respect for their fundamental rights.

Although legal systems increasingly recognize adolescents' right to self-determination, the principle remains applied narrowly and in limited contexts. For example, current conceptions of the maturity standard generally do not allow for more direct intervention into family dynamics and reallocation of familial dynamics consistent with adolescents' levels of maturity. Nor has the principle typically been used to regulate adolescents' educational environments and their access to such environments. In those instances, bright lines dictate how groups of adolescents gain rights. Few jurisdictions expansively recognize the need to better adolescents' sense of self-determination as part of the effort to respect adolescents' individual rights.

Given the limited attention formally paid to adolescents' self-determination, it seems fruitful to examine instances where the legal system distinguishes less between adolescents and adults and more between adolescents and civic concerns. Such instances highlight the critical point that respecting adolescents' self-determination needs does not mean that adolescents' rights would necessarily trump those of their parents and community, but it does mean that adolescents could be treated as individuals able to determine their attitudes about important matters to them and suffer the consequences when those attitudes lead to harm to themselves or to others.

The Supreme Court's response to the recent slew of statutes to stem hate crimes reveals the contours of the limits of self-determination. Both of the leading cases that set the standards involved adolescents and, interestingly, the fact that adolescents were involved simply did not matter to the resolution of constitutional issues. The first case, *R.A.V. v. City of St. Paul* (1992), which reversed the conviction of Caucasian juveniles who shaped broken chair legs into a cross and burned it inside the fenced yard of an African-American couple, stands for the freedom to express one's thoughts and act on them within the context and confines of content-based expressive conduct. The second case, *Wisconsin v. Mitchell* (1993), which upheld the state's penalty-enhancement statute for hate crimes, stands for the state's freedom to regulate proscribed conduct and to impose higher sentences for crimes motivated by thoughts and beliefs. The distinction between the cases is important because the perpetrators of hate crimes cannot shield themselves with First Amendment speech protections when they commit crimes in order to express their hatred for a group. The holding in *Mitchell* punishes more severely those who succumb to these protected predilections. The approach is rather significant—it allows individuals to express themselves and it assumes that they can determine their actions—regardless of whether they are adolescents. The approach also is significant for one of the key jurisprudential principles on which it stands: faith in the marketplace of ideas. While it could be argued that *R.A.V.* supports those views and beliefs in the marketplace of ideas that nurture hate crimes, the Court emphasizes that diverse communities have the responsibility, if not the obligation, to confront bias-motivated hate messages and that confronting those messages will ensure that hate does not win out in the marketplace of ideas. And, in these cases, no doubt existed that society had an obligation to protect adolescents' marketplace of ideas. Society has an obligation to ensure support for adolescents' responsible self-determination.

Although the above cases highlight well the significance granted to the market of ideas in order to support adolescent development, other settings also have been known to take it seriously. Public school settings, for example, were the first place to recognize adolescents' free speech rights, and that recognition was based on the market-of-ideas rationale, as well as on the need to prepare adolescents for responsible citizenship. Although the development of that principle has taken different turns in schools, the principle still finds expression in some recent cases. Most obvious are the school cases that allow the proselytizing of some students by other students. In those cases, the courts evince a greater willingness to make age-based distinctions and show less deference to parents' desire to protect their children from potentially different ideas as children mature. These cases reflect a greater level of attention to adolescents' changing needs and roles. They note a decrease in vulnerability to confusion or trauma associated with ideological discussions among peers and an increased value of these interactions as adolescents approach adulthood. The Court recognizes that adolescents have the ability to engage their peers' marketplace of ideas.

Cases involving adolescents' media also reveal the significance of adolescents' self-determination. These cases recognize much more than adolescents' ability to engage their peers' marketplace of ideas; they recognize their ability, and even need, to engage some adults' informational marketplace. A highly influential jurist, Judge Richard Posner, recently addressed the issue in the context of allowing adolescents access to video games that a state had argued was inappropriate for minors. He reached essentially the same conclusion in even more pointed terms, arguing that children must be provided some access to information—even controversial information—because "[p]eople are unlikely to become well-functioning, independent-minded adults and responsible citizens if they are raised in an intellectual bubble" (*American Amusement Machine Association v. Kendrick*, 2001, p. 577). Another federal circuit court followed a similar reasoning as it rejected a law seeking to protect minors from "slasher" films (*Video Software Dealers Association v. Webster*, 1992, p. 689), and it more recently struck down as unconstitutional an ordinance that banned selling or renting violent video games to minors without parental consent (*Interactive Digital Software Association v. St. Louis County*, 2003). Perhaps even more controversial, another circuit court affirmed a lower federal court's recognition of the need to protect the right of minors to discuss sexual issues such as birth control, abstinence, sexual intercourse, pregnancy, sexually transmitted diseases, and rape in an online forum (*Cyberspace Communications, Inc. v. Engler,* 1999). These are considerably intriguing developments that build on the Supreme Court's major case addressing media violence and the First Amendment: *Winters v. New York* (1948). It was in that case that the Court struck down a statute prohibiting the distribution of magazines containing criminal news and stories of bloodshed because they were believed to be "vehicles for inciting violent and depraved crimes against the person" (*Winters v. New York,* 1948, p. 518). The Court noted that these magazines "are as much entitled to the protection of free speech as the best of literature" and famously pointed out that "What is one man's amusement, teaches another's doctrine" (p. 510). That the Supreme Court itself has never held that speech containing violent sentiments or imagery lies outside the First Amendment's protection as applied to either adults or children certainly has lead other courts addressing similar issues to swing in this direction. Not limiting access to materials, even those without "any possible value to society," so that individuals may acquire one's "doctrine" (p. 510), reveals the significance self-determination plays in our legal system and its visions of human development.

Consider the Centrality of Adolescents' Participation

The next principle, the need to ensure adolescents' participation in decisions and matters that affect their lives, emerges from the free speech rationale that urges us to take seriously adolescents' civic participation and self-determination. At its core, the participation principle challenges the traditional view that others should control adolescents' decisions and ignore adolescents' potential role in decisions that affect them. The effort seeks to foster adolescents' participation in decision making and develop decision-making skills that enable adolescents to become responsible societal members.

We already have seen that existing social science evidence emphasizes the need to promote adolescent development through fostering their participation in outcome determination. The finding emerges repeatedly in terms of family life and other social institutions that govern adolescents, especially schools and juvenile justice systems. The findings consistently indicate that healthy adolescent development results from social and familial contexts that support autonomy, provide structure, and supply warm and involved socializing agents. These contexts offer informational feedback, rationales, and administer consistent consequences as they encourage self-initiation, minimize use of controls, and adopt adolescents' perspectives. The healthy outcome of autonomy allows adolescents to act on their own volition while still relying on others for support, unlike the frequently fused and confused concept of independence, which implies detachment and minimal reliance on others. Although the process continues over the entire life course, we have seen that the need for participating seems particularly central to the adolescent period. Adolescents evince a high need to belong, a need for attachment to others that the media facilitate. The nature of that engagement changes as age significantly structures the manner young people negotiate their environment, the most obvious being the developmental process of separation from parental influence coupled with the increase in the role of peers that help rechannel the nature and saliency of media. Understanding the role of media and informational environments in adolescents' experiences, then, requires a close look at how adolescents are allowed to engage in the community, peer groups, and families in which they find themselves.

The law increasingly allows for adolescents' participation, although still in a limited manner. Respect for the principle of participation most frequently involves efforts to provide adequate information in interventions and foster inclusion into society. For example, the law already mandates the principle in educational provisions, such as through the focus on inclusion, respect for cultural and religious differences, and recognition of students' rights to free speech. Likewise, laws provide adolescents in other settings with opportunities to express and explore options, such as in requiring medical decision-making procedures that counsel before the provision of services or materials. In addition and as we have seen above, the law provides some adolescents with access to genuine avenues of complaint for situations in which they feel mistreated, ignored or abused. In sum, the basic principle reflected in due process—the right to be heard and recognized and to participate in governmental processes that impact one's rights—increasingly applies to adolescents and different parts of their lives that do not directly involve courts.

The social sciences recognize the central need for participation in adolescents' social environments, but legal contexts involving information do not foster adolescents' participation as much as research suggests it could. A key example involves recent limitations placed on the nature of discussions between service providers (including school counselors) and adolescents seeking reproductive services and receiving sexuality education. We know that patients, for example, are likely to give great weight to physicians' expressions of state preferences, not because they are persuaded by the messages, but merely because the messages are delivered by physicians (Levesque, 2002c). The asymmetrical, highly emotional quality of doctor-patient interaction makes it probable that patients—particularly those who are nonwhite, poor, elderly, female, or adolescent—will be intimidated by physician expressions of the state's viewpoint and respond with confusion and deference. Although adolescents may be vulnerable to the inability to interact in the way the Supreme Court assumes they can, we already have seen that adolescents do have a level of competence that could allow them to sort out differences in information. As we have seen, evidence does support the contention that adolescents are not so incapable of complex thought that the state needs to preselect information for their welfare. Importantly, the skills needed to evaluate the information seem much more attainable during adolescence than skills the Supreme Court has recognized in mature teenagers, such as their ability to make abortion and contraception decisions without state or parental input.

Although not taken as seriously as it could, the participation principle actually operates at several levels and numerous rights support its conceptualization. The principle receives support, for example, from the recognized adolescents' rights to receive adequate information, be heard in matters that concern them, and exercise freedom of expression. It also receives support from the principles we already have discussed, such as those that encourage policies that allow adolescents to share in decision-making processes and gradually control the outcome of important decisions as adolescents achieve legal independence. In terms more central to adolescents' media rights, we already have seen that the most effective ways to increase healthy responses to media is to include adolescents in decision making about the media and to foster the development of media-processing skills.

Attempts to use the legal system to foster adolescents' ability to engage responsibly with the media are surprisingly scarce. The most obvious way to take this principle seriously would be to encourage its use in educational institutions. We already have seen that educational responses can foster healthy media habits and the influence of media deemed problematic. Yet states have yet to respond even though the federal government's Goals 2000—landmark legislation that sets national education objectives—requires schools to incorporate media literacy in their curriculum. It is true that all fifty states now have educational standards that include some type of media-literacy requirements. States embed media-literacy requirements in standards for languages, social studies, health, and several other content areas; and media-literacy standards themselves often remain hidden among other standards and requirements. A look at state statutes reveals, however, that states simply tend to encourage districts to teach media literacy and that efforts are far from comprehensive (J. A. Brown, 2001). As a result, media education has not flourished and continues to lack structural support, which limits the extent and duration of media curriculum endeavors. The reason for the wide variety of programs (if they do exist) derives from the manner the United States embraces a decentralized approach to education, with more than 15,000 relatively autonomous districts and systems that leave the development of media studies to entrepreneurial teachers or principals (J. A. Brown, 2001). The absence of legal mandates leaves schools on their own, which increases the chances that they will funnel resources, teacher training, and curricula development to other areas (Levesque, 2002b). Despite the paucity of efforts, though, existing requirements still reveal a fundamental point: states can enact laws that would foster the development of skills necessary to respond to problematic media and informational environments.

Importantly, requiring media literacy may not be as important as the manner schools provide adolescents with ways to approach information. As the famous school cases we have seen in chapter 7 recognize, schools must be permitted to educate students for citizenship and instill fundamental societal values. Schools have the obligation to prepare students for positive public discourse and compliance with fundamental societal values. We have seen that the determination of what manner of speech in the classroom or in the school assembly is inappropriate properly rests with the school board. But the broad goals of fostering responsible citizenship highlight how, even though a school's power may seem almost plenary, school authority to regulate speech faces important limits. Even though schools may retain the broad discretion to structure adolescents' informational environments, it does not mean that the discretion cannot be harnessed to ensure that adolescents develop skills to engage information.

The legal system clearly allows schools to retain considerable power and can foster adolescents' engagement with the marketplace of ideas. Despite high deference paid to the rights of parents, for example, schools still retain considerable control and may provide even explicit materials that some parents may find objectionable. *Brown v. Hot, Sexy & Safer Prods., Inc.* (1995) illustrates the potentially significant role of schools. In that case, students were compelled to attend a mandatory AIDS-awareness school assembly program that described and demonstrated certain sexual acts that the plaintiff students and parents found highly offensive. The First Circuit court dismissed the action, finding that the plaintiff students and parents failed to state a claim for relief. The court reasoned that previous Supreme Court holdings gave parents the right to choose a school for their children, but did not give parents the right to exercise control over the curriculum at a public school to which they have chosen to send their children. The Court's observation that parents do not have a fundamental right to tell public schools what to teach their children, coupled with the offensive and objectionable nature of certain public school curricula, highlights the potentially powerful role of schools in fostering adolescents' abilities to gain access to and understand even controversial information that even their parents would rather not have placed in their environment.

Affirm the Significance of Adolescents' Best Interests

Reconsidering the types of informational environments that would protect adolescents' free speech rights, even when adolescents do not control those rights, necessarily involves considering the "best interests" standard that frequently guides the law's response to adolescents. Both traditional and innovative efforts follow the rule that those who control adolescent development and adolescent's rights should act in adolescents' best interests. Without that fundamental rule, the power granted to others loses its legitimacy, for it would be strange for a democratic regime to support the right to exploit others for one's own gain without providing the other any say in the matter. The rule may be obvious, but, if taken seriously, the rule's results may lead to peculiar and unexpected situations that hold institutions and individuals legally accountable when they otherwise generally escape accountability. As we have seen, however, it remains difficult and disingenuous to argue that society and individuals actually follow the best-interest mandates.

The failure to follow the best-interests mandate appears especially true in the context of adolescents' informational environments. For example, states do not act on adolescents' best interests when they allow or encourage discrimination in education, medical neglect, problem family dynamics and even family violence, all of which link directly to adolescents' access to information. Likewise, society can stand idly by even when respecting speech also means fostering intolerance, prejudice, and hate activity, even though the legal system, as we have seen, hopes, but the law does not require, that society will help foster appropriate responses to problematic manifestations of speech. When states deny the basic interests of adolescents in those circumstances, they pursue the best interests of parents, communities, and institutional actors who deny adolescents' rights, rights that adolescents would otherwise enjoy but for their status as adolescents. As the state allows these conditions to continue, however, its actions become increasingly difficult to justify on either traditional or modern jurisprudential grounds. If anything, then, the focus on adolescents' best interests is far less peculiar than the failure to put adolescents' interests first when those interests arguably should take precedence in a civil society that aims to protect the rights of all its citizens. Society, law, and policy typically frame the harms adolescents suffer in the above circumstances simply as collateral costs in a system geared toward having private citizens (parents) responsible for the upbringing of children and the inability to address all harms individuals suffer.

Our review of efforts to address the negative consequences of media exposure reveals a remarkable failure to focus on adolescents' best interests. Media literacy and other media-related efforts continue to sprout in an effort to address how adolescents receive and respond to the media's negative and positive aspects. Yet, these efforts tend to be ignored. Research has managed to identify potential problems in media accessed by adolescents but it has yet to demonstrate and help implement comprehensive ways to address the intricacies of concerns. The legal system and commentators also have not done much either to advance efforts. Indeed, we now know that no comprehensive analysis addresses adolescents' media rights, whether it be in schools, out of schools, in homes, in communities, or in peer relationships. In addition, the laws that exist surprisingly deal more with protecting the rights of adults than with protecting the rights and best interests of adolescents, despite the prevailing belief that adolescents are more worthy of protection and regulation

Despite these failures, we have seen how the legal system could respond more effectively to the harms we now recognize as linked to respect for speech. The most promising aspect of the best-interests standard involves the hope that it can address private as well as public actions, one of the key limitations of free speech jurisprudence and legislation. This is not to say that the legal system would radically transform First Amendment jurisprudence. But, it is to say that taking adolescents seriously when they are in state institutions and have protections against state action, for example, will impact their private relationships, which tend to be immune unless the recipients are harmed seriously enough to involve the child welfare or criminal justice system.

The place of schools in adolescents' informational environments is again illustrative. Given that the media contributes greatly to societal messages that shape adolescents' environments and that those messages tend to contradict other efforts that seek to ensure responsible development, it would seem that schools would need to consider more systematically the media's role in adolescent life. It has long been assumed that schools have an obligation to impart appropriate, accurate, and useful information and skills that will prepare adolescents for responsible relationships, a mandate accepted and fostered by our legal system (Levesque, 2002b). Making that assumption a reality would seem to at least include efforts to address the significant role diverse media play in adolescents' socialization. The rationale for doing so becomes increasingly obvious and exemplified by the societal approaches to information regarding sexuality. Adolescents rely on peers and the media for their information and guidance, peers rely on media, the media has yet to curb its conflicting images of sexuality, and parents play a diminishing role in their adolescents' sexuality education. If schools could incorporate how the media impact adolescents' sexuality, schools could go a long way toward providing more effective sexuality education and preparing adolescents for responsible relationships. Yet, as we have seen, sexuality education programs increasingly move away from efforts that consider how powerful socializing institutions influence adolescents. Efforts to address the media's role in the sexual education of adolescence, then, require a rethinking not only of sexuality education programs but also of media education programs, adolescents' media rights, and adolescents' broader rights to participate in society and their families.

Service provision programs also reveal the need to consider the extent to which actions are made in the best interests of adolescents. Commentators lament the failure of the federal government to mount more comprehensive sexuality education programs. They frequently highlight how the federal government acts irresponsibly as it increases funding for abstinence-only-until-marriage sex education and service provisions in the face of soaring rates of sexually transmitted diseases and other harms adolescents suffer as a result of inappropriate knowledge about sexuality (Brindis, 2002). Yet, as we have seen, adolescents have a considerable amount of access to information through a pervasively unregulated media. That information, however, is problematic. Most notably, the information provided remains biased; it is not the type that leads to "responsible" sexual behavior. To make matters even more troublesome, a number of factors suggest that the media will not change any time soon, a reality stemming from the media's need to provide sexual titillation to sell products and attract consumers and the need to steer away from controversial or otherwise unpleasant issues that may alienate viewers and advertisers. The issue thus becomes not necessarily adolescents' access to information, but a lack of access to appropriate information. In addition, the issue becomes not only access to appropriate information but also access to the kinds of skills and environments that allow adolescents to make use of appropriate information and act on their own best interests.

One of the major faults of current sexuality education programs involves the failure to take into account the popular culture outside schools and the discontinuity between classroom experiences and outside experiences. The social norms created by mass media both fail to reinforce and often actively contradict the educational lessons taught in schools. The social norms, such as those that seem irresponsible, extend beyond the media. Rather than attempt to limit access to media, efforts should be made to have adolescents recognize that they are valued members of our communities who are expected to act responsibly in all aspects of their daily lives, not just their sexuality. We should follow this insight and consider providing adolescents with access to the education, tools, and services to reach those goals. Dealing with problematic media influences, then, necessitates dealing with the structure of adolescent life, most notably the position of adolescents in society and their eventual roles. Distal social contexts, such as race, gender, age, and social class play important roles in determining access and influence. Different teens have and see different opportunity structures, such as whether they intend to go to college, seek a realistic career, get married, and so forth. In addition, these social contexts are mediated by many institutions, such as peers, schools, and families. Thus, the sexual content offered by various forms of media may constrain what adolescents learn and respond to, but the effect of that content depends on who adolescents are when they come to use the media and conceptions of adolescents' rights shapes who adolescents are.

Matters under familial control clearly offer a more fundamental challenge. The current focus on the best interest of the child places very high obstacles for efforts that would aim to intervene directly in family life: adolescents must suffer, or be at risk for suffering, a recognized form of harm (such as child abuse). It is important to keep in mind that thinking of state intervention as direct involvement in families takes an unnecessarily narrow view of state intervention in family life and misses what may be the vast majority of laws that do regulate families. We have seen, for example, that changing schools and peer relations means impacting families, as does changing the nature of social service delivery. Realizing the powerful nature of social forces outside of families—especially of the media—does not mean that policies must sever the powerful bonds between parents and adolescents. Rather, recognizing the role of social forces outside of families simply means that they must be considered to ensure that adolescents have options when their relationships fail to operate in adolescents' best interests and help them determine what is potentially so important and central to their humanity.

Although matters under familial control provide important challenges, it is important to keep in mind the limits of efforts to control adolescents in the name of acting in their best interests. We have seen, for example, that the Court acknowledges that censorship may serve a compelling governmental interest in child protection. In a very recent opinion, the Court stated that the "interest in protecting young library users from material inappropriate for minors is legitimate, and even compelling, as all Members of the Court appear to agree" *(United States v. American Library Association, Inc.*, 2003, p. 215). The compelling interest in protecting the physical and psychological well-being of minors can be rather significant, but it leaves much room for free speech, even for protecting the free speech rights of minors. Indeed, efforts to carve out exceptions to the First Amendment for minors predominantly fail. The Supreme Court has made it quite clear that the state does not possess unlimited power to shield minors from ideas of which it disapproves. The Court, in *Erznoznik v. City of Jacksonville* (1975-), explicitly made this point by striking down an ordinance prohibiting drive-in movie theaters from showing any movies containing nudity if visible from the street:

> Speech that is neither obscene as to youths nor subject to some other legitimate proscription cannot be suppressed solely to protect the young from ideas or images that a legislative body thinks unsuitable for them. In most circumstances, the values protected by the First Amendment are no less applicable when government seeks to control the flow of information to minors. (pp. 213–14)

The underpinnings of the First Amendment reinforce the correctness of these statements. If one of the core purposes of the First Amendment is to prevent the government from using censorship to impose its own political and moral values on the population, then entirely exempting adolescents from that protection would create a gaping hole in that purpose, especially given the formative nature of the adolescent period. Whatever the state's general power to protect children from harm and act in their best interests, much cannot qualify as a relevant kind of "harm" when the issue involves the nature of First Amendment limits on the state's power to suppress speech.

Conclusions

The media and their distribution of ideas shape us and the future of our democracy. As it has throughout the history of our nation, the media play key roles in determining the nature of communities, family dynamics, interpersonal relationships, and even social policies. As we have seen, despite efforts to exclude some forms of media from adolescents' lives, the media play central but often enshrouded roles in shaping everyone's cultural and personal identities. We continue to witness rapid changes in the legal foundation of adolescents' media and broader informational environments, and evidence suggests that we have reached a critical juncture. The rapid changes in the regulation of media and the impact of those changes on adolescents lead us to conclude that we cannot hope to address adolescents' and society's needs without more deliberate responses to adolescents' place in the law. We cannot rely on the received faith that adolescents' interests are addressed adequately as we address the rights and needs of those who control adolescents' informational environments. Given the law's impressive reach, we cannot cling to traditional paradigms and assumptions about the inherently private nature of speech that results in efforts to leave speech alone and, for adolescents, subject to the will of those who traditionally have controlled them. We cannot do so simply because the legal system requires close scrutiny to ensure that it furthers freedoms rather than stifles them. A close look at how the legal system approaches adolescents' media and informational environments reveals many inadequacies. The failure to address more directly adolescents' needs, abilities, and peculiar place in families, communities, and the law becomes quite suspect when we consider two points. First, issues relating to the freedom of speech clearly involve rights that deserve protection of the highest order. Although we have seen that recent Supreme Court cases do not grant free speech rights absolute power over other potentially competing rights and societal interests, these rights nevertheless remain highly regarded and respected. Second, the Supreme Court recognizes that states must respect free speech rights, even when the rights holders are adolescents. The Court continues to extend important due process rights to adolescents, affirm fundamental (but highly controversial) privacy rights, and even recognize adolescents' rights involving freedom of conscience. The Court also recognizes the rights of adolescents to express themselves and increasingly refuses to curtail adult's access to media when challenged on the grounds that states must do so to protect minors from harmful media. The fact that media can be harmful to adolescents no longer suffices to limit adults' and everyone's access to that media. These extensions of adolescents' rights, however, have yet to take full shape and have been explored only in limited contexts. In fact, we have seen that much of the analyses of adolescents' rights involve analyses of other groups' rights, namely the rights of adults.

The need to address adolescents' free speech rights more directly makes critical the type of analyses just offered. Available developmental science reveals that the traditionally accepted and often affirmed principles that support vigorous free speech actually have relevance for adolescents' lives. Indeed, research indicates that those rationales may actually have greater relevance for adolescents than they do for adults: adolescents thirst for ideas and readily engage the marketplace of information, seek to develop their sense of self through engaging with ideas, and shape their sense of civic responsibility that will guide their future participation in society and families. Likewise, available developmental science evidence and innovative laws indicate a need to rethink adolescents' rights and offer paths to greater legal recognition. Equally importantly, existing laws already provide mechanisms consistent with new conceptions of adolescents' rights, and the existence of several innovative efforts to address adolescents' rights suggests that efforts are far from futile. As we have seen, effective efforts genuinely involve adolescents in the planning and implementation of efforts and laws and recognize how groups and communities channel and constrain behaviors. These developments reveal how it increasingly makes sense to ensure the fundamental democratic principle that all have a right to self-determination, to participate in society in a democratic manner that appreciates individuals' basic interests, and to exert more control over the rights that would benefit them. All of these ingredients have been identified as important to positive individual fulfillment and to effective adaptations to civil society, two central rationales supporting vigorous free speech protections that form the basis of a truly democratic society.

Although the developmental sciences may suggest and the law may support and even require the development of the types of principles presented above, we also have seen that much controversy would attach to such efforts. This is unsurprising given that the development of adolescents' rights always has engendered much controversy. We also have seen that recognizing adolescents' informational rights may prove a difficult challenge for a society that places much weight on the rights of parents to determine their children's upbringing. Rather than ignoring objections to efforts seeking to grant greater respect to adolescents, our analyses reveal the need to accept those challenges and properly respond to them. The ability to respond highlights a key consideration in the law's role in adolescents' lives and informational concerns adolescents' confront. The legal system can help recognize issues and structure responses. That the legal system can guide such intervention in adolescents' lives as it regulates media is just as critical an area of reform and inquiry as are efforts to protect adolescents from overt violations and discriminations now deemed routine matters of child welfare law as well as educational and juvenile justice systems. In fact, close examination of existing legal rules reveals that laws already exist that may be harnessed to help foster healthy and supportive adolescent development, including support for the development of their identity and the impact of that identity on their social dispositions. Indeed and again, free speech, as we have seen at the end of chapter 6, serves as the center point of rights necessary for healthy adolescent development in modern civil society.

A close look at what the law can help accomplish also highlights its limits. Given the needs of civil society, of a society poising itself to foster and respect free speech, the law cannot embark wholeheartedly on many suggestions offered by those who seek to harness governmental resources to limit adolescents' access to information. The legal system cannot do so even though the social sciences do support the claim that the media links to an impressive array of negative outcomes for society and even adolescents themselves. Although the media does link to negative outcomes, we have seen that the links do not appear as direct as current discourse suggests. In fact, adolescents' responses to the media include many potentially positive outcomes. The existence of either possible outcome may reveal limitations in the law's potential responses, but it also suggests the law's central challenge: how the law can and must structure adolescents' informational environments.

Understanding the potential role of law has meant that our investigation necessarily ventured beyond current constitutional, jurisprudential, and legislative mandates. It has meant first understanding the role of media in adolescent life. The investigation revealed that much depends on adolescents' internal and external resources. No single psychological, social, or cultural factor explains adolescents' dispositions and the impact of those dispositions on adolescents' developmental outcomes. Rather, a constellation of forces work together to achieve negative and positive developmental outcomes. Drawing from available developmental sciences exploring the nature of adolescence and the possible influence of media on adolescent development led us to offer legal principles to help guide responses to adolescents' peculiar place in society and law. Considering these principles in our efforts to respond to adolescents can help ensure that we recognize adolescents' abilities and peculiar social condition in a manner that will enhance respect for adolescents' own needs.

It may be naive to suggest that greater recognition of adolescents' individual needs and concerns may lead to positive outcomes, not the least of which includes allowing adolescents to negotiate their own paths to meaningful lives and sort through information often deemed harmful. Parents, not society, traditionally have held that burden. But time, society, families, and the law continue to change. Our understanding of those changes reveals a pressing need to move beyond simple causal models in order to fully understand both adolescents' development and the impact of the media on adolescents' developmental outcomes. The media infuse adolescents' environments, and it is that infusion that impacts developmental outcomes. The current social science understanding of those environments led to our development of important guiding principles, which find remarkable parallels with those that our legal system views as foundational to participating in modern civil society. Although media and informational choices, and the provision of environments to help support and foster choices, surprisingly have not been part of the discourse on adolescents' rights and youth policy, we have seen that jurisprudential and legislative developments, coupled by rapidly changing social conditions affecting adolescents, place us at a critical juncture we can no longer ignore. Achieving the goals of our civil, pluralistic society requires recognizing that everyone deserves real opportunities to develop and follow their convictions in a society that understands and responds to the potential of those convictions in everyone's lives.

States educate, regulate family life, and supervise adolescent development. Governments have an interest in raising healthy, well-rounded young people into mature citizens. Despite these interests, the current approach to adolescents' media rights seeks to limit adolescents' access to media, flatly fails to do so, and does not offer adolescents ways to protect themselves from potential harms. As we have seen, the media shape more than individuals; it shapes society, its perceptions, and its definitions of culture. Properly used, the media can teach adolescents about the complexities of life and may be used to ensure adolescents' participation in society. This approach to the media can be much more effective than efforts that seek to keep information from adolescents and that make adolescents outsiders and nonparticipants in what otherwise would be their own cultural life. Our Constitution always has had a simple policy response to the social ills created by unsettling speech: the First Amendment cure for problematic speech is more and varied expression. At its core, the First Amendment affirmatively encourages speech and demands that people, include adolescents, participate in social life and maximize the pursuit of their own defined developmental trajectories.

References

Abrams v. United States, 250 U.S. 616 (1919).

Ackard, D. M., Neumark-Sztainer, D., Story, M., & Perry, C. (2003). Overeating among adolescents: Prevalence and associations with weight-related characteristics and psychological health. *Pediatrics, 111,* 67–74.

Ackard, D. M., & Peterson, C. B. (2001). Association between puberty and disordered eating, body image, and other psychological variables. *International Journal of Eating Disorders, 29,* 187–194.

Adolescent Family Life Act, Pub. L. No. 97-35, 95 Stat 578 (codified as amended at 42 U.S.C. 300z-300z-10) (1982).

Agliata, D., & Tantleff-Dunn, S. (2004). The impact of media exposure on males' body image. *Journal of Social and Clinical Psychology, 23,* 7–22.

AIDS Alert. (2000). Youth programs take pop-culture approach. *AIDS Alert, 15,* 88–89.

Akers, R. L. (1998). *Social learning and social structure: A general theory of crime and deviance.* Boston: Northeastern University Press.

Allbutt, H., Amos, A., & Cunningham-Burley, S. (1995). The social image of smoking among young people in Scotland. *Health Education Research, 10,* 443–54.

Allen, M., D'Alessio, D., & Brezgel, K. (1995). A meta-analysis summarizing the effects of pornography II: Aggression after exposure. *Human Communication Research, 22,* 258–283.

Allen, M., Emmers, T., Gebhardt, L., & Giery, M. A. (1995). Exposure to pornography and acceptance of rape myths. *Journal of Communication, 45,* 5–26.

Allison, K. W., Crawford, I., Leone, P. E., Trickett, E., Perez-Febles, A., Burton, L. M., et al. (1999). Adolescent substance use: Preliminary examinations of school and neighborhood context. *American Journal of Community Psychology, 27,* 111–141.

Aloise-Young, P., Shenanigan, K., & Graham, J. (1996). Role of self-image and smoker stereotypes in smoking onset during early adolescence: A longitudinal study. *Health Psychology, 15,* 494–497.

Alstead, M., Campsmith, M., Halley, C. S., Hartfield, K., Goldbaum, G., & Wood, R. W. (1999). Developing, implementing, and evaluating a condom promotion program targeting sexually active adolescents. *AIDS Education and Prevention, 11,* 497–512.

Alvermann, D. E., & Hagood, M. C. (2000). Critical media literacy: Research, theory, and practice in "new times." *Journal of Educational Research, 93,* 193–206.

American Academy of Pediatrics (2000). Joint statement on the impact of entertainment violence on children: Congressional Public Health Summit. (2000, July 26). Retrieved January 29, 2006, from http://www.aap.org/advocacy/releases/jstmtevc.htm

American Amusement Machine Association v. Kendrick, 244 F.3d 572 (7th Cir. 2001).

American Psychiatric Association. (2000). *Diagnostic and statistical manual of mental disorders* (4th ed., text revision). Washington, DC: Author.

American Social Health Association. (1996). *Gallup study: Teenagers know more than adults about STDs.* Durham, NC: Author.

Amos, A., Currie, C., Gray, D., & Elton, R. (1998). Perception of fashion images from youth magazines: Does a cigarette make a difference? *Health Education Research, 13,* 491–501.

Anda, R., Williamson, D., Escobedo, L., Mast, E., Giovino, G., & Remington, P. (1990). Depression and the dynamics of smoking: A national perspective. *Journal of the American Medical Association, 264,* 1541–1545.

Anderson, C. A. (1997). Effects of violent movies and trait irritability on hostile feelings and aggressive thoughts. *Aggressive Behavior, 23,* 161–178.

Anderson, C. A., Berkowitz, L., Donnerstein, E., Huesmann, L. R., Johnson, J. D., Linz, D., et al. (2003). The influence of media violence on youth. *Psychological Science in the Public Interest, 4,* 81–110.

Anderson, C. A., & Bushman, B. J. (2001). Effects of violent video games on aggressive behavior, aggressive cognition, aggressive affect, physiological arousal, and prosocial behavior: A meta-analytic review of the scientific literature. *Psychological Science, 12,* 353–359.

Anderson, C. A., & Bushman, B. J. (2002). Media violence and the American public revisited. *American Psychologist, 57,* 448–450.

Anderson, C. A., Carnagey, N. L., & Eubanks, J. (2003). Exposure to violent media: The effects of songs with violent lyrics on aggressive thoughts and feelings. *Journal of Personality and Social Psychology, 84,* 960–971.

Anderson, C. A., & Dill, K. E. (2000). Video games and aggressive thoughts, feelings, and behavior in the laboratory and in life. *Journal of Personality and Social Psychology, 78,* 772–790.

Anderson, C. A., Flanagan, M., Carnagey, N. L., Benjamin, A. J., Jr., Eubanks, J., & Valentine, J. C. (2004). Violent video games: Specific effects of violent content on aggressive thoughts and behavior. *Advances in Experimental Social Psychology, 36,* 199–249.

Anderson, C. A., & Huesmann, L. R. (2003). Human aggression: A social-cognitive view. In M. A. Hogg & J. Cooper (Eds.), *Handbook of social psychology* (pp. 296–323). London: Sage.

Anderson, R. E. (2002). Youth and information technology. In J. T. Mortimer & R. W. Larson (Eds.), *The changing adolescent experience: Social trend and the transition to adulthood* (pp. 175–207). Cambridge, MA: Cambridge University Press.

Aneshensel, C. S., & Sucoff, C. A. (1996). The neighborhood context of adolescent mental health. *Journal of Health and Social Behavior, 37*, 293–310.

Archibald, A. B., Graber, J. A., & Brooks-Gunn, J. (1999). Associations among parent-adolescent relationships, pubertal growth, dieting, and body image in young adolescent girls: A short-term longitudinal study. *Journal of Research on Adolescence, 9*, 395–415.

Arnett, J. J. (1995). Adolescents' uses of media for self-socialization. *Journal of Youth and Adolescence, 24*, 519–534.

Arnett, J. J. (2001). Adolescents' responses to cigarette advertisements for five "Youth Brands" and one "Adult Brand." *Journal of Research on Adolescence, 11*, 425–443.

Ashcroft v. ACLU, 542 U.S. 656 (2004).

Ashcroft v. Free Speech Coalition, 535 U.S. 234 (2002).

Assor, A., Roth, G., & Deci, E. L. (2004). The emotional costs of parents' conditional regard: A self-determination theory analysis. *Journal of Personality, 72*, 47–88.

Atkin, C., & Marshal, A. (1996). Health communication. In M. B. Salwin & D. W. Stacks (Eds.), *An integrated approach to communication theory and research* (pp. 479–497). Englewood Cliffs, NJ: Prentice-Hall.

Attewell, P. (2001). The first and second digital divides. *Sociology of Education, 74*, 252–259.

Attie, I., & Brooks-Gunn, J. (1989). Development of eating problems in adolescent girls: A longitudinal study. *Developmental Psychology, 25*, 70–79.

Avenevoli, S., & Merikangas, K. R. (2003). Familial influences on adolescent smoking. *Addiction, 98*, 1–20.

Aubrey, J. S., Harrison, K., Kramer, L., & Yellin, J. (2003). Variety versus timing: Gender differences in college students' sexual expectations as predicted by exposure to sexually oriented television. *Communication Research, 30*, 432–460.

Austin, E., & Johnson, K. (1997). Immediate and delayed effects of media literacy training on third graders' decision making for alcohol. *Health Communication, 9*, 323–349.

Backer, T., Rogers, E., & Sopory, P. (1992). *Designing health communication campaigns: what works?* Newbury Park, CA: Sage Publications.

Backinger, C. L., Fagan, P., Matthews, E., & Grana, R.(2003). Adolescent and young adult tobacco prevention and cessation: current status and future directions. *Tobacco Control, 12*, iv46–iv53.

Baker, C. E. (1989). *Human liberty and freedom of speech.* New York: Oxford University Press.

Baker, C. E. (1997). Giving the audience what it wants. *Ohio State Law Journal, 58*, 311–417.

Balfour, D. J. K., & Ridley, D. L. (2000). The effects of nicotine on neural pathways implicated in depression: A factor in nicotine addiction? *Pharmacology Biochemistry and Behavior, 66*, 79–85.

Ballard, S. M., & Morris, M. L. (1998). Sources of sexuality information for university students. *Journal of Sex Education and Therapy, 23*, 278–287.

Bandura, A. (1965). Influence of models' reinforcement contingencies on the acquisition of imitative response. *Journal of Personality and Social Psychology, 1*, 589–595.

Bandura, A. (1977). *Social learning theory.* Englewood Cliffs, NJ: Prentice Hall.

Bandura, A. (1994). Social cognitive theory of mass communication. In J. Bryant & D. Zillmann (Eds.), *Media effects: Advances in theory and research* (pp. 61–90). Hillsdale, NJ: Erlbaum.

Bandura, A. (2001). Social cognitive theory of mass communication. *Media Psychology, 3*, 265–299.

Barker, E. T., & Galambos, N. L. (2003). Body dissatisfaction of adolescent girls and boys: Risk and resource factors. *Journal of Early Adolescence, 23*, 141–165.

Barongan, C., & Nagayama Hall, G. C. (1995). The influence of misogynous rap music on sexual aggression against women. *Psychology of Women Quarterly, 19*, 195–207.

Bartecchi, C., MacKenzie, T., & Schrier, R. (1995). The global tobacco epidemic. *Scientific American, 1995*, 44–51.

Barth, R. P., Fetro, J. V., Leland, N., & Volkan, K. (1992). Preventing adolescent pregnancy with social and cognitive skills. *Journal of Adolescent Research, 7*, 208–232.

Barthel, D. (1992). When men put on appearance: Advertising and the social construction of masculinity. In S. Craig (Ed.), *Men, masculinity, and the media: Vol. 1: Research on men and masculinity series* (pp. 137–153). Thousand Oaks, CA: Sage Publications.

Bartholow, B. D., & Anderson, C. A. (2002). Effects of violent video games on aggressive behavior: Potential sex differences. *Journal of Experimental Social Psychology, 38*, 283–290.

Bartholow, B. D., Anderson, C. A., Benjamin, A. J., & Carnagey, N. L. (2005). Individual differences in knowledge structures and priming: The weapon priming effect in hunters and nonhunters. *Journal of Experimental Social Psychology, 41*, 48–60.

Bartholow, B. D., Dill, K. E., Anderson, K. B., & Lindsay, J. J. (2003). The proliferation of media violence and its economic underpinnings. In I. E. Sigel (Series Ed.) & D. A. Gentile (Vol. Ed.), *Advances in applied developmental psychology: Media violence and children* (pp. 1–18). Westport, CT: Greenwood Publishing.

Basil, M. (1997). The danger of cigarette "special placements" in film and television. *Health Communication, 9*, 190–98.

Bauman, K. E., Carver, K., & Gleiter, K. (2001). Trends in parent and friend influence during adolescence: The case of adolescent cigarette smoking. *Addictive Behaviors, 26*, 349–361.

Bauman, K. E., Foshee, V. A., Linzer, M. A., & Koch, G. G.. (1990). Effect of parental smoking classification on the association between parental and adolescent smoking. *Addictive Behavior, 15*, 413–22.

Bauman, K. E., LaPrelle, J., Brown, J. D., Koch, G. G., & Padgett, C. A. (1991). The influence of three mass media campaigns on variables related to adolescent cigarette smoking: Results of a field experiment. *American Journal of Public Health, 81*, 597–604.

Baxter, R. L., De Riemer, C., Landini, A., Leslie, L., & Singletary, M. W. (1985). A content analysis of music videos. *Journal of Broadcasting and Electronic Media, 29*, 333–340.

Beebe, T. J., Asche, S. E., Harrison, P. A., & Quinlan, K. B. (2004). Heightened vulnerability and increased risk-taking among adolescent chat room users: Results from a statewide school survey. *Journal of Adolescent Health, 35*, 116–123.

Belch, M. A, Krentler, K. A., & Willis-Flurry, L. A. (2005). Teen Internet mavens: Influence in family decision making. *Journal of Business Research, 58*, 569–575.

Bellotti v. Baird, 443 U.S. 622 (1979).

Belson, W. A. (1978). *Television violence and the adolescent boy*. Hampshire, England: Saxon House, Teakfield.

Berdahl, T. A., Hoyt, D. R., & Whitbeck, L. B. (2005). Predictors of first mental health service utilization among homeless and runaway adolescents. *Journal of Adolescent Health, 37*, 145–154.

Berkowitz, L. (1984). Some effects of thoughts on anti- and prosocial influences of media events: A cognitive-neoassociational analysis. *American Psychologist, 45*, 494–503.

Berkowitz, L. (1993). *Aggression: Its causes, consequences, and control*. New York: McGraw-Hill.

Berndt, T. J. (1996). Exploring the effects of friendship quality on social development. In W. M. Bukowski, A. F. Newcomb, & W. W. Hartup (Eds.), *The company they keep: Friendship in childhood and adolescence* (pp. 346–365). Cambridge, UK: Cambridge University Press.

Berzonsky, M. D., & Adams, G. R. (1999). Reevaluating the identity status paradigm: Still useful after 35 years. *Developmental Review, 19*, 557–590.

Bethel School District No. 403 v. Fraser, 478 U.S. 675 (1986).

Biener, L., & Siegel, M. (2000). Tobacco marketing and adolescent smoking: More support for a causal inference. *American Journal of Public Health, 90*, 407–11.

Biglan, A., Ary, D. V., Smolkowski, K., Duncan, T., & Black, C. (2000). A randomized controlled trial of a community intervention to prevent adolescent tobacco use. *Tobacco Control, 9*, 24–32.

Biocca, F., Brown, J., Shen, F., Bernhardt, J. M., Batista, L., Kemp, K., et al. (1997). Assessment of television's anti-violence messages: University of North Carolina at Chapel Hill study. In *National Television Violence Study* (Vol. 1, pp. 413–530). Thousand Oaks, CA: Sage.

Blasi, V. (1977). The checking value is First Amendment theory. *American Bar Foundation Research Journal, 1977*, 521–582.

Blasi, V. (1985). The pathological perspective and the First Amendment. *Columbia Law Review, 85*, 449–514.

Blasi, V. (2004). Holmes and the marketplace of ideas. *The Supreme Court Review, 2004*, 1–46.

Blum, R. W., Beuhring, T., Shew, M. L., Bearinger, L. H., Sieving, R. E., & Resnick, M. D. (2000). The effects of race/ethnicity, income, and family structure on adolescent risk behaviors. *American Journal of Public Health, 90*, 1879–1884.

Blumenthal, S., & Pike, D. (1996). Ten things every woman should know about depression. *Ladies Home Journal, 208*, 132–138.

Blyth, D. A., Simmons, R. G., Bulcroft, R., Felt, D., Van Cleave, E. F., & Bush, D. M. (1981). The effects of physical development on self-image and satisfaction with body-image for early adolescent males. *Research in the Community and Mental Health, 2*, 43–73.

Blyth, D. A., Simmons, R. G., & Zakin, D. F. (1985). Satisfaction with body image for early adolescent females: The impact of pubertal timing within different school environments. *Journal of Youth and Adolescence, 14*, 207–225.

Board of Education, Island Trees Union Free School District No. 26 v. Pico, 457 U.S. 853 (1982).

Bolger v. Youngs Drug Products Corporation, 463 U.S. 60 (1983).

Bollinger, L. (1986). *The tolerant society: Freedom of speech and extremist speech in America*. New York: Oxford University Press.

Bork, R. (1971). Neutral principles and some First Amendment problems. *Indiana Law Journal, 47*, 1–35.

Boroughs, M., & Thompson, J. K. (2002). Exercise status and sexual orientation as moderators of body image disturbance and eating disorders in males. *International Journal of Eating Disorders, 31*, 307–311.

Borzekowski, D., Flora, J., Feighery, E., & Schooler, C. (1999). The perceived influence of cigarette advertisements and smoking susceptibility among seventh graders. *Journal of Health Communication, 4*, 105–118.

Borzekowski, D. L. G., Robinson, T. N., & Killen, J. D. (2000). Does the camera add 10 pounds? Media use, perceived importance of appearance, and weight concerns among teenage girls. *Journal of Adolescent Health, 26*, 36–41.

Bose Corp. v. Consumers Union of United States, Inc., 466 U.S. 485 (1984).

Botta, R. (1999). Television images and adolescent girls' body image disturbance. *Journal of Communication, 49*, 22–41.

Botvin, G. J., Botvin, E. M., Baker, E., Dusenbury, L., & Goldberg, C. J. (1992). The false consensus effect: Predicting adolescents' tobacco use from normative expectations. *Psychological Reports, 70*, 171–178.

Botvin, G. J., Epstein, J., Schinke, S., & Diaz, T. (1994). Predictors of cigarette smoking among inner-city minority youth. *Developmental and Behavioral Pediatrics, 15*, 67–73.

Bourgois, P. (1995). *In search of respect: Selling crack in el barrio.* New York: Cambridge University Press.

Bowen v. Kendrick, 487 U.S. 589 (1988).

Bradley, R. H., & Corwyn, R. F. (2002). Socioeconomic status and child development. *Annual Review of Psychology, 53*, 371–399.

Brandenburg v. Ohio, 395 U.S. 444 (1969).

Breslau, N., Kilbey, M., & Andreski, P. (1993). Vulnerability to psychopathology in nicotine-dependent smokers: An epidemiologic study of young adults. *American Journal of Psychiatry, 150*, 941–946.

Breslau, N., & Peterson, E. L. (1996). Smoking cessation in young adults: Age at initiation of cigarette smoking and other suspected influences. *American Journal of Public Health, 86*, 214–20.

Brindis, C. (2002). Advancing the adolescent reproductive health policy agenda: Issues for the coming decade. *Journal of Adolescent Health, 31*, 296–309.

Brodie, M., & Foehr, U. (2001). Communicating health information through the entertainment media. *Health Affairs, 20*, 192–200.

Brown, B. B. (2004). Adolescents' relationships with peers. In R. M. Lerner & L. D. Steinberg (Eds.), *Handbook of adolescent psychology* (2nd ed., pp. 363–394). New York: Wiley.

Brown, C., Madden, P. A. F., Palenchar, D. R., & Cooper-Patrick, L. (2000). The association between depressive symptoms and cigarette smoking in an urban primary care sample. *International Journal of Psychiatry in Medicine, 30*, 15–26.

Brown, J. A. (1998). Media literacy perspectives. *Journal of Communication, 48*, 44–47.

Brown, J. A. (2001). Media literacy and critical television viewing in education. In D. G. Singer & J. L. Singer (Eds.), *Handbook of children and the media* (pp. 681–697). Thousand Oaks, CA: Sage Publications.

Brown, J. D. (2000). Adolescents' sexual media diets. *Journal of Adolescent Health, 27*, 35–40.

Brown, J. D. (2002). Mass media influences on sexuality. *Journal of Sex Research, 39,* 42–45.

Brown, J. D., Halpern, C. T., & L'Engle, K. L. (2005). Mass media as a sexual super peer for early maturing girls. *Journal of Adolescent Health, 36,* 420–427.

Brown, J. D., & Keller, S. N. (2000). Can the mass media be healthy sex educators? *Family Planning Perspectives, 32,* 255–256.

Brown, J. D., L'Engle, K. L., Pardun, C. J., Guo, G., Kenneavy, K., & Jackson, C. (2006). Sexy media matter: Exposure to sexual content in music, movies, television, and magazines predicts black and white adolescents' sexual behavior. *Pediatrics, 11,* 1018–1027.

Brown, J. D., & Newcomer, S. (1991). Television viewing and adolescents' sexual behavior. *Journal of Homosexuality, 21,* 77–91.

Brown, J. D., & Schulze, L. (1990). The effects of race, gender, and fandom on audience interpretation of Madonna's music videos. *Journal of Communication, 40,* 88–102.

Brown, J. D., & Witherspoon, E. M. (2002). The mass media and American adolescents' health. *Journal of Adolescent Health, 32,* 153–170..

Brown v. Hot, Sexy & Safer Prods., Inc., 68 F.3d 525 (1995).

Browne, K. D., & Hamilton-Giachritsis, C. (2005). The influence of violent media on children and adolescents: A public-health approach. *Lancet, 365,* 702–10.

Bryant, J., & Rockwell, S. C. (1994). Effects of massive exposure to sexually oriented prime-time television programing on adolescents' moral judgment. In D. Zillman, J. Bryant, & A. C. Huston (Eds.), *Media, children and the family: Social scientific, psychodynamic, and clinical perspectives* (pp. 183–195). Hillsdale, NJ: Erlbaum.

Buckingham, D. (1998). Media education in the UK: Moving beyond protectionism. *Journal of Communication, 48,* 5–15.

Buckley v. Valeo, 424 U.S. 1 (1976).

Bucy, E. B., & Newhagen, J. E. (2004). *Media access: Social and psychological dimensions of new technology.* Mahwah, NJ: Erlbaum.

Buddeberg-Fischer, B., Klaghofer, R., Gnam, G., & Buddeberg, C. (1998). Prevention of disturbed eating behaviour: A prospective intervention study in 14- to 19-year-old Swiss students. *Acta Psychiatrica Scandinavica, 98,* 146–155.

Buerkel-Rothfuss, N., & Strouse, J. S. (1993). Media exposure and perceptions of sexual behaviors: The cultivation hypothesis moves to the bedroom. In Greenberg, B. S., Brown, J. D. & Buerkel-Rothfuss, N. L. (Eds.), *Media, sex and the adolescent* (pp. 225–247). Cresskill, NJ: Hampton Press.

Bufkin, J., & Eschholz, S. (2000). Images of sex and rape: A content analysis of popular film. *Violence Against Women, 6,* 1317–1344.

Bukowski, W. M., Hoza, B., & Boivin, M. (1993). Popularity, friendship, and emotional adjustment during early adolescence. *New Directions for Child Development, 60,* 23–37.

Burns, D. M., & Johnson, L. D. (2001). Overview of recent changes in adolescent smoking behavior. In D. M. Burns, R. H. Amacher, & W. Ruppert (Eds.), *Smoking and tobacco control monograph 14: Changing adolescent smoking prevalence, where it is and why.* (NIH Publication No. 02-5086, pp. 1–8). Washington DC: U.S. Department of Health and Human Services.

Burson v. Freeman, 504 U.S. 191 (1992).

Burton, L. M., Obeidallah, D. A., & Allison, K. W. (1996). Ethnographic perspectives on social context and adolescent development among inner-city African-

American teens. In R. A. Jessor, A. Colby, & R. A. Shweder (Eds.), *Ethnography and human development: Context and meaning in social inquiry* (pp. 395–418). Chicago: University of Chicago Press.

Bushman, B. J. (1995). Moderating role of trait aggressiveness in the effects of violent media on aggression. *Journal of Personality and Social Psychology, 69,* 950–960.

Bushman, B. J. (1998). Effects of television violence on memory of commercial messages. *Journal of Experimental Psychology: Applied, 4,* 291–307.

Bushman, B. J., & Anderson, C. A. (2001). Media violence and the American public: Scientific facts versus media misinformation. *American Psychologist, 56,* 477–489.

Bushman, B. J., & Anderson, C. A. (2002). Violent video games and hostile expectations: A test of the general aggression model. *Personality and Social Psychology Bulletin, 28,* 1679–1686.

Bushman, B. J., & Cantor, J. (2003). Media ratings for violence and sex: Implications for policymakers and parents. *American Psychologist, 58,* 130–41.

Bushman, B. J., & Huesmann, L. R. (2001). Effects of televised violence on aggression. In D. G. Singer & J. L. Singer (Eds.), *Handbook of children and the media* (pp. 223–254). Thousand Oaks, CA.: Sage Publications.

Butler v. Michigan, 352 U.S. 380 (1957).

Byely, L., Archibald, A. B., Graber, J., & Brooks-Gunn, J. (2000). A prospective study of familial and social influences on girls' body image and dieting. *International Journal of Eating Disorders, 28,* 155–164.

Byrne, D., Byrne, A., & Reinhart, I. (1995). Personality, stress and the decision to commence cigarette smoking in adolescence. *Journal of Psychosomatic Research, 39,* 53–62.

Byrne, D., & Mazanov, J. (1999). Sources of adolescent stress, smoking and the use of other drugs. *Stress Medicine, 15,* 215–27.

Calfin, M. S., Carroll, J. L., & Shmidt, J. (1993). Viewing music-videotapes before taking a test of premarital sexual attitudes. *Psychological Reports, 72,* 475–481.

Calvert, S. (1999). *Children's journeys through the information age.* Boston: McGraw Hill.

Calvert, S., Jordan, A. B., & Cocking, R. R. (2002). *Children in the digital age: The role of entertainment technologies in children's development.* Westport, CT: Praeger.

Calvert, S. L., & Tan, S. (1994). Impact of virtual reality on young adults' psychological arousal and aggressive thoughts: Interaction versus observation. *Journal of Applied Developmental Psychology, 15,* 125–139.

Campbell, A. J. (1999). Self-regulation and the media. *Federal Communications Law Journal, 51,* 711–772.

Canterbury, R. J., McGarvey, E. L., Sheldon-Keller, A. E., Waite, D., Reams, P., & Koopman, C. (1995). Prevalence of HIV-related risk behaviors and STDs among incarcerated adolescents. *Journal of Adolescent Health, 17,* 173–7.

Cantor, J. (2000). Media violence. *Journal of Adolescent Health, 27,* 30–34.

Cantor, J. (2001). The media and children's fears, anxieties, and perceptions of danger. In D. G. Singer & J. L. Singer (Eds.), *Handbook of children and the media* (pp. 207–221). Thousand Oaks, CA: Sage.

Cantor, J., & Wilson, B. (2003). Media and violence: Intervention strategies for reducing aggression. *Media Psychology, 5,* 363–404.

Capaldi, D. M., Dishion, T. J., Stoolmiller, M., & Yoerger, K. (2001). Aggression toward female partners by at-risk young men: The contribution of male adolescent friendships. *Developmental Psychology, 37,* 61–73.

Carpini, M. X. D. (2004). Mediating democratic engagement: The impact of communications on citizens' involvement in political and civic life. In L. L. Kaid (Ed.), *Handbook of political communication research* (pp. 395–434). Mahwah, NJ: Erlbaum.

Carver, C. S., Ganellen, R. J., Froming, W. J., & Chambers, W. (1983). Modeling: An analysis in terms of category accessibility. *Journal of Experimental Social Psychology, 19*, 403–421.

Cash, T. F., & Pruzinsky, T. (2002). *Body image: A handbook of theory, research, and clinical practice.* New York: Guilford Press.

Catalano, R. E., & Hawkins, J. D. (1996). The social development model: A theory of antisocial behavior. In J. D. Hawkins (Ed.), *Delinquency and crime: Current theories* (pp. 149–197). New York: Cambridge University Press.

Cates, W. (1999). Estimates of the incidence and prevalence of sexually transmitted diseases in the United States. *Sexually Transmitted Diseases, 26*, S2–S7.

Cattarin, J. A., & Thompson, J. K. (1994). A three-year longitudinal study of body image, eating disturbance, and general psychological functioning in adolescent females. *Eating Disorders, 2*, 114–125.

Cattarin, J. A., Thompson, J. K., Thomas, C., & Williams, R. (2000). Body image, mood, and televised images of attractiveness: The role of social comparison. *Journal of Social & Clinical Psychology, 19*, 220–239.

Centers for Disease Control and Prevention. (1998). Tobacco use among high school students—United States, 1997. *Morbidity and Mortality Weekly Report, 47*, 229–233.

Centers for Disease Control and Prevention. (2000). CDC surveillance summaries. *Morbidity Mortality Weekly Report, 49*, SS-10.

Centers for Disease Control and Prevention. (2002). Trends in sexual risk behaviors among high school students—United States, 1991–2001. *Morbidity and Mortality Weekly Report, 51*, 856–859.

Centers for Disease Control and Prevention. (2005a). *WISQARS* (Web-based Injury Statistics Query and Reporting System). Retrieved June 17, 2005.

Centers for Disease Control and Prevention. (2005b). *Targeting tobacco use: The nation's leading cause of death 2005.* Atlanta, GA: Author. Retrieved February 2, 2006, from http://www.cdc.gov/nccdphp/publications/aag/osh.htm

Central Hudson Gas & Electric Corp. v. Public Service Commission of New York, 447 U.S. 557 (1980).

Chafee, Z. (1920). *Freedom of speech.* Cambridge, MA: Harvard University Press.

Chafee, Z. (1941). *Freedom of speech in the United States.* Cambridge, MA: Harvard University Press.

Champion, H., & Furnham, A. (1999). The effect of the media on body satisfaction in adolescent girls. *European Eating Disorders Review, 7*, 213–228.

Chaplin, L. N., & John, D. R. (2005). The development of self-brand connections in children and adolescents. *Journal of Consumer Research, 32*, 119–129

Chaplinsky v. New Hampshire, 15 U.S. 568 (1942).

Chassin, L., Presson, C. C., Rose, J. S., & Sherman, S. J. (1998). Maternal socialization of adolescent smoking: Intergenerational transmission of smoking-related beliefs. *Psychology of Addictive Behaviors, 12*, 206–216.

Chassin, L., Presson, C. C., & Sherman, S. J. (1995). Social psychological antecedents and consequences of adolescent tobacco use. In J. L. Wallander & L. J. Siegel (Eds.), *Adolescent health problems: Behavioral perspectives advances in pediatric psychology* (pp. 141–159). New York: Guilford Press.

Chernoff, R., Combs-Orme, T., Risley-Curtiss, C., & Heisler, A. (1994). Assessing the health status of children entering foster care. *Pediatrics, 93*, 594–601.

Child Online Protection Act, Pub. L. No. 105–277, 112 Stat. 2681 (codified at 47 U.S.C. § 231) (2000).

Children's Internet Protection Act, Pub. L. No. 106-554, 114 Stat. 2763 (2000).

Christ, W. G., & Potter, W. J. (1998). Media literacy, media education, and the academy. *Journal of Communication, 48*, 5–15.

Christenson, P. G., & Roberts, D. F. (1998). *It's not only rock & roll: Popular music in the lives of adolescents.* Cresskill, NJ: Hampton Press.

City of Erie v. Pap's A.M., 529 U.S. 277 (2000).

City of Renton v. Playtime Theatres, Inc., 475 U.S. 41 (1986).

Clarke, G. N., Hawkins, W., Murphy, M., & Sheeber, L. (1993). School-based primary prevention of depressive symptomatology in adolescents: Findings from two studies. *Journal of Adolescent Research, 8*, 183–204.

Cockerill, I. M., & Riddington, M. E. (1996). Exercise dependence and associated disorders: A review. *Counseling Psychology Quarterly, 9*, 119–129.

Cohane, G. H., & Pope, H. G., Jr. (2001). Body image in boys: A review of the literature. *International Journal of Eating Disorders, 29*, 373–379.

Cohen v. California, 403 U.S. 15 (1971).

Coll, C. G., Crnic, K., Lamberty, G., Wasik, B. H., Jenkins, R. G., Vasquez, H., et al. (1996). An integrative model for the study of developmental competencies in minority children. *Child Development, 67*, 1891–1914.

Collins, R. L., Eilliott, M. N., Berry, S. H., Kanouse, D. E., Kunkel, D., Hunter, S. B., et al. (2004). Watching sex on television predicts adolescent initiation of sexual behavior. *Pediatrics, 114*, e280–e289 (doi:10.1542/peds.2003-1065-L).

Communications Decency Act of 1996, Pub. L. No. 104-104, 110 Stat. 133 (codified at 47 U.S.C. §§ 230, 560–61) (2000).

Comstock, G. A., & Paik, H. (1991). *Television and the American child.* San Diego, CA: Academic Press.

Comstock, G. A., & Strasburger, V. C. (1990). Deceptive appearances: Television violence and aggressive behavior. *Journal of Adolescent Health Care, 11*, 31–44.

Conger, K. J., Conger, R. D., & Scaramella, L. V. (1997). Parents, siblings, psychological control and adolescent adjustment. *Journal of Adolescent Research, 12*, 113–138.

Connolly, J., & Goldberg, A. (1999) Romantic relationships in adolescence. The role of friends and peers in their emergence and development. In W. Furman, B. B. Brown, & C. Feiring (Eds.), *The development of romantic relationships in adolescence* (pp. 266–290). Cambridge, UK: Cambridge University Press.

Conover, P. J., & Searing, D. D. (2000). A political socialization perspective. In L. M. McDonnell, P. M. Timpane & R. Benjamin (Eds.), *Rediscovering the democratic purposes of education* (pp. 91–124.). Lawrence, KS: University of Kansas Press

Corrado, R. R., Roesch, R., Hart, S. D., & Gierowski, J. K. (Eds.). (2002). *Multi-problem violent youth: A foundation for comparative research on needs, interventions, and outcomes.* NATO Science Series. Amsterdam: IOS Press.

Côté, J. E., & Levine, C. G. (2000). *Identity formation, agency, and culture: A social psychological synthesis.* Mahwah, NJ: Erlbaum.

Courtright, J. A., & Baran, S. J. (1980). The acquisition of sexual information by young people. *Journalism Quarterly, 57*, 107–114.

Covey, L. S., Glassman, A. H., & Sterner, F. (1998). Cigarette smoking and major depression. *Journal of Addictive Diseases, 17,* 35–46.

Coyne, S. M., Archer, J. A., & Eslea, M. (2004) Cruel intentions on television and in real life: Can viewing indirect aggression increase viewers' subsequent indirect aggression? *Journal of Experimental Child Psychology, 88,* 234–253.

Coytaux, R., Altman, D. G., & Slade, J. (1995). Tobacco promotions in the hands of youth. *Tobacco Control, 4,* 253–257.

Crosby, R. A., DiClemente, R. J., Wingood, G. M., Salazar, L. F., Rose, E., Levine, D., et al. (2005). Condom failure among adolescents: Implications for STD prevention. *Journal of Adolescent Health, 36,* 534–536.

Csikszentmihalyi, M., & Hunter, J. (2003). Happiness in everyday life: The uses of experience sampling. *Journal of Happiness Studies, 4,* 185–199.

Csikszentmihalyi, M., & Rathunde, K. (1993). The measurement of flow in everyday life: Towards a theory of emergent motivation. In J. E. Jacobs (Ed.), *Nebraska symposium on motivation* (Vol. 40, p. 57–97). Lincoln, NE: University of Nebraska Press.

Cusumano, D. L., & Thompson, J. K. (1997). Body image and body shape ideals in magazines: Exposure, awareness and internalization. *Sex Roles, 37,* 701–721.

Cusumano, D. L., & Thompson, J. K. (2001). Media influence and body image in 8- to 11-year-old boys and girls: A preliminary report on Multidimensional Media Influence Scale. *International Journal of Eating Disorders, 29,* 37–44.

Cyberspace Communications, Inc. v. Engler, 55 F. Supp. 2d 737 (1999), aff'd, 238 F.3d 420 (2000).

Dahl, R. E., & Spear, L. (Eds.). (2004). Adolescent brain development: Vulnerabilities and opportunities. *Annals of the New York Academy of Sciences* (Vol. 1021). New York: New York Academy of Sciences.

Dalton, M. A., Sargent, J., Beach, M., Titus-Ernstoff, L., Gibson, J. J., Ahrens, M. B., et al. (2003). Effect of viewing smoking in movies on adolescent smoking initiation: A cohort study. *Lancet, 362,* 281–285.

Dalton, M. A, Tickle, J. J., Sargent, J. D., Beach, M. L., Ahrens, M. B., Heatherton, T. F. (2002). The incidence and context of tobacco use in popular movies from 1988–1997. *Preventive Medicine, 34,* 516–523.

Davis, S., & Mares, M.-L. (1998). Effects of talk show viewing on adolescents. *Journal of Communication, 48,* 69–86.

Davis v. Monroe County Board of Education, 526 U.S. 629 (1999).

DeJong, W., &. Winsten, J. A. (1999). The use of designated drivers by U.S. college students: A national study. *Journal of American College Health, 47,* 151–6.

Delgado, R. (1982). Words that wound: A tort action for racial insults, epithets, and name-calling. *Harvard Civil Rights-Civil Liberties Law Review, 17,* 133–181.

Delgado, R., & Stefancic, J. (2004). *The boundaries of free speech: Understanding words that wound.* Boulder, CO: Westview Press.

Dempsey, J. M., & Reichert, T. (2000). Portrayal of married sex in the movies. *Sexuality & Culture: An Interdisciplinary Quarterly, 4,* 21–36.

Dent, C., & Biglan, A. (2004). Relation between access to tobacco and adolescent smoking. *Tobacco Control, 13,* 334–338.

Denver Area Educational Telecommunications Consortium v. FCC., 518 U.S. 727 (1996).

Dietz, W. H. (1998). Health consequences of obesity in youth: Childhood predictors of adult disease. *Pediatrics, 101,* 518–525.

DiFranza, J. R., & Coleman, M. (2001). Sources of tobacco for youths in communities with strong enforcement of youth access laws. *Tobacco Control, 10,* 323–8.

DiFranza, J. R., Savageau, J. A., & Aisquith, B. F. (1996). Youth access to tobacco: The effects of age, gender, vending machine locks, and "it's the law" programs. *American Journal of Public Health, 86,* 221–224.

D'Imperio, R. L., Dubow E. F., & Ippolito, M. F. (2000). Resilient and stress-affected adolescents in an urban setting. *Journal of Clinical Child Psychology, 29,* 129–142.

Dishion, T. J., McCord, J., & Poulin, F. (1999). When interventions harm. Peer groups and problem behavior. *American Psychologist, 54,* 755–764.

Distefan, J. M., Gilpin, E. A., Sargent, J. D., & Pierce, J. P. (1999). Do movie stars encourage adolescents to start smoking? Evidence from California. *Preventive Medicine, 28,* 1–11.

Distefan, J. M., Pierce, J. P., & Gilpin, E. A. (2004). Do favorite movie stars influence adolescent smoking initiation? *American Journal of Public Health, 94,* 1239–1244.

Dodge, K. A., Pettit, G. S., Bates, J. E., & Valente, E. (1995). Social information processing patterns partially mediate the effect of early physical abuse on later conduct problems. *Journal of Abnormal Psychology, 104,* 632–643.

Donaldson, S. I. (1995). Peer influence on adolescent drug use: A perspective from the trenches of experimental evaluation research. *American Psychologist, 50,* 801–802.

Donnerstein, E., & Smith, S. (2001). Sex in the media: Theory, influences and solutions. In D. S. Singer & J. L. Singer (Eds.), *Handbook of children and the media* (pp. 289–307). Thousand Oaks, CA: Sage.

Doolittle, J. C. (1980). Immunizing children against possible antisocial effects of viewing television violence: A curricular intervention. *Perceptual and Motor Skills, 51,* 498.

Downs, A. C., & Harrison, S. K. (1985). Embarrassing age spots or just plain ugly? Physical attractiveness stereotyping as an instrument of sexism on American television commercials. *Sex Roles, 13,* 9–19.

Drewnowski, A., Kennedy, S. H., Kurth, C. L., & Krahn, D. D. (1995). Effects of body image on dieting, exercise and anabolic steroid use in adolescent males. *International Journal of Eating Disorders, 17,* 381–387.

Duffy, M., & Gotcher, J. M. (1996). Crucial advice on how to get the guy: The rhetorical vision of power and seduction in the teen magazine YM. *Journal of Communication Inquiry, 20,* 32–48.

Duncan, T. E., Tildesley, E., Duncan, S. C., & Hops, H. (1995). The consistency of family and peer influences on the development of substance use in adolescence. *Addiction, 90,* 1647–1660.

Dunkel, C. S., & Lavoie, J. C. (2005). Ego-identity and the processing of self-relevant information. *Self & Identity, 4,* 349–359.

Duran, R. L., & Prusank, D. T. (1997). Relational themes in men's and women's popular magazine articles. *Journal of Social and Personal Relationships, 14,* 165–189.

Durant, R. H., Rich, M., Emans, S. J., Rome, B. S., Alfred, E., & Woods, B. R. (1997). Violence and weapon carrying in music videos: A content analysis. *Archives of Pediatrics and Adolescent Medicine, 151,* 443–448.

Durant, R. H., Romes, E. S., Rich, M., Allred, E., Emans, J. S., & Woods, E. R. (1997). Tobacco and alcohol use behaviors portrayed in music videos: A content analysis. *American Journal of Public Health, 87,* 1131–1135.

Eccles, J. S., & Barber, B. L. (1999). Student council, volunteering, basketball, or marching band: What kind of extracurricular involvement matters? *Journal of Adolescent Research, 14*, 10–43.

Eccles, J., Barber, B., Jozefowicz, D., Malenchuk, O., & Vida, M. (1999). Self-evaluations of competence, task values, and self-esteem. In N. G. Johnson, M. C. Roberts & J. Worell (Eds.), *Beyond appearance: A new look at adolescent girls* (pp. 53–83). Washington, DC: American Psychological Association.

Eckhardt, L., Woodruff, S. I., & Elder, J. P. (1997). Related effectiveness of continued, lapsed, and delayed smoking prevention intervention in senior high school students. *American Journal of Health Promotion, 11*, 418–421.

Eder, E., Evans, C. C., & Parker, S. (1995). *School talk: Gender and adolescent culture.* New Brunswick, NJ: Rutgers University Press.

Eggermont, S. (2005). Young adolescents' perceptions of peer sexual behaviors: The role of television viewing. *Child: Care, Health and Development, 31*, 459–468.

Elder, J. P., Wildey, M., deMoor, C., Sallis, J. F., Eckhardt, L., Edwards, C., et al. (1993). The long-term prevention of tobacco use among junior high students: Classroom and telephone interventions. *American Journal of Public Health, 83*, 1239–1244.

Ellickson, P. L., Collins, R. L., Bogart, L. M., Klein, D. J., & Taylor, S. L. (2005). Scope of HIV risk and co-occurring psychosocial health problems among young adults: Violence, victimization, and substance use. *Journal of Adolescent Health, 36*, 401–409.

Ellickson, P. L., Tucher, J. S., & Klein, D. J. (2001). High-risk behaviors associated with early smoking: Results from a 5-year follow-up. *Journal of Adolescent Health, 28*, 465–473.

Else-Quest, N. M., Hyde, J. S., Goldsmith, H. H., & Van Hulle, C. A., (2006). Gender differences in temperament: A meta-analysis. *Psychological Bulletin, 132*, 33–72.

Emerson, T. (1963). Toward A General Theory of the First Amendment. New York: Vintage.

Ennett, S. T., Flewelling, R. L., Lindrooth, R. C., & Norton, E. C. (1997). School and neighborhood characteristics associated with school rates of alcohol, cigarette, and marijuana use. *Journal of Health and Social Behavior, 38*, 55–71.

Epel, E. S., Spanakos, A., Kasl-Godley, J., & Brownell, K. D. (1996). Body shape ideals across gender, sexual orientation, socioeconomic status, race, and age in personal advertisements. *International Journal of Eating Disorders, 19*, 265–273.

Erikson, E. (1966). Eight ages of man. *International Journal of Psychiatry, 2*, 281–300.

Erikson, E. H. (1968). *Identity, youth, and crisis.* London: Farber.

Eron, L. D., Huesmann, L. R., Lefkowitz, M. M., & Walder, L. O. (1972). Does television violence cause aggression? *American Psychologist, 27*, 253–263.

Erznoznik v. City of Jacksonville, 422 U.S. 205 (1975).

Escamilla, G., Crdock, A. L., & Kawachi, I. (2000). Women and smoking in Hollywood movies: A content analysis. *American Journal of Public Health, 90*, 412–414.

Escobedo, L. G., Reddy, M., & Giovino, G. A. (1998). The relationship between depressive symptoms and cigarette smoking in U.S. adolescents. *Addiction, 93*, 433–440.

Evans, G. W. (2004). The environment of childhood poverty. *American Psychologist, 59*, 77–92.

Evans, N., Farkas, A., Gilpin, E., Berry, C., & Pierce, J. P. (1995). Influence of tobacco marketing and exposure to smokers on adolescent susceptibility to smoking. *Journal of the National Cancer Institute, 87*, 1538–1545

Evans, W. N., & Farrelly, M. C. (1998). The compensating behavior of smokers: Taxes, tar, and nicotine. *Rand Journal of Economics, 29*, 578–95.

Everett, S. A., Schnuth, R. L., & Tribble, J. L. (1998). Tobacco and alcohol use in top-grossing American films. *Journal of Community Health, 23*, 317–24.

Everett, S. A., Warren, C. W., Sharp D., Kann, L., Husten, C. G., & Crosset, L. S. (1999). Initiation of cigarette smoking and subsequent smoking behavior among U. S. high school students. *Preventive Medicine, 29*, 327–333.

Fabes, R. A., & Strouse, J. (1987). Perceptions of responsible and irresponsible models of sexuality: A correlational study. *Journal of Sex Research, 23*, 70–84.

Fairburn, C. G., Cooper, Z., Doll, H. A., Norman, P. A., & O'Connor, M. E. (2000). The natural course of bulimia nervosa and binge eating disorder in young women. *Archives of General Psychiatry, 57*, 659–665.

Farrelly, M. C., Healton, C. G., Davis, K. C., Messeri, P., Hersey, J. C., & Haviland, M. L. (2002). Getting to the truth: Evaluating national tobacco countermarketing campaigns. *American Journal of Public Health, 92*, 901–907.

FCC v. Pacifica Foundation, 438 U.S. 726 (1978).

Federal Trade Commission (2004). *Marketing violent entertainment to children: A fourth follow-up review of industry practices in the motion picture, music recording & electronic game industries: A report to congress.* Retrieved January 9, 2006, from http://www.ftc.gov/opa/2004/07/040708kidsviolencerpt.pdfFerguson, C. J., (2002). Media violence: Miscast causality. *American Psychologist, 57*, 446–447.

Feshbach, S., & Singer, R. D. (1971). *Television and aggression: An experimental field study.* San Francisco: Jossey-Bass.

Fichtenberg, C. M., & Glantz, S. A. (2002). Youth access interventions do not affect youth smoking. *Pediatrics, 109*, 1088–92.

Field, A. E., Camargo, C. A., Jr., Taylor, C. B., Berkey, C. S., Frazier, A. L., Gillman, M. W., et al. (1999). Overweight, weight concerns, and bulimic behaviors among girls and boys. *Journal of the American Academy of Child & Adolescent Psychiatry, 38*, 754–760.

Field, A. E., Camargo, C. A., Jr., Taylor, C. B., Berkey, C. S., Roberts, S. B., & Colditz, G. A. (2001). Peer, parent, and media influences on the development of weight concerns and frequent dieting among preadolescent and adolescent girls and boys. *Pediatrics, 107*, 54–60.

Field, A. E., Cheung, L., Wolf, A. M., Herzog, D. B., Gortmaker, S. L., & Colditz, G. A. (1999). Exposure to the mass media and weight concerns among girls. *Pediatrics, 102*, E36.

Finkelhor, D., Mitchell, K. J., & Wolak, J. (2000). *Online victimization: A report on the nation's youth.* Alexandria, VA: National Center for Missing and Exploited Children.

Fischer, P. M., Schwartz, M. P., Richard, J. W., & Goldstein, A. O. (1991). Brand logo recognition by children aged 3 to 6 years. *Journal of the American Medical Association, 266*, 3145–3148.

First National Bank v. Bellotti, 435 U.S. 765 (1978).

Flanagan, C., Bowes, J., Jonsson, B., Csapo, B., & Sheblanova, E. (1998). Ties that bind: Correlates of adolescents' civic commitments in seven countries. *Journal of Social Issues, 54*, 457–475.

Flanagan, C. A., Gill, S., & Gallay, L. S. (2005). Social participation and social trust in adolescence: The importance of heterogeneous encounters. In A. Omoto (Ed.),

Processes of community change and social action (pp. 149–166). Mahwah, NJ: Erlbaum.

Flay, B. R., Hu, F. B., & Richardson, J. (1998). Psychosocial predictors of different stages of cigarette smoking among high school students. *Preventive Medicine, 27,* A9–A18.

Fletcher, A., Elder, G., & Mekos, D. (2000). Parental influences on adolescent involvement in community activities. *Journal of Research on Adolescence, 10,* 29–48.

Flint, A. J., Yamada, E. G., & Novotny, T. E. (1998). Black-white differences in cigarette smoking uptake: Progression from adolescent experimentation to regular use. *Preventive Medicine, 27,* 358–364.

Flynn, B. S., Worden, J. K., Secker-Walker, R. H., Pirie, P. L., Badger, G. J., Carpenter, J. H., et al. (1994). Mass media and school interventions for cigarette smoking prevention: Effects 2 years after completion. *American Journal of Public Health, 84,* 1148–1150.

Flynn, B. S., Worden, J. K., Secker-Walker, R. H., Pirie, P. L., Badger, G. J., & Carpenter, J. H. (1997). Long-term responses of higher and lower risk youths to smoking prevention interventions. *Preventive Medicine, 26,* 389–394.

Forster, J. L., Klepp, K. I., & Jeffery, R. W. (1998). Sources of cigarettes for tenth graders in two Minnesota cities. *Health Education Research, 4,* 45–50.

44 Liquormart, Inc. v. Rhode Island, 517 U.S. 484 (1996).

Fouts, G., & Burggraf, K. (1999). Television situation comedies: Female weight, male negative comments, and audience reactions. *Sex Roles, 42,* 925–932.

Fowles, J. (1999). *The case for television violence.* Thousand Oaks, CA: Sage.

Fox, J. A., & Zawitz, M. W. (2001). *Homicide statistics calculated from data provided in homicide trends in the United States.* Washington, DC: Bureau of Justice Statistics.

Freedman, J. L. (2002). *Media violence and its effects on aggression.* Toronto: University of Toronto Press.

Freedman, R. (1990). Cognitive-behavioral perspectives on body image change. In C. F. Cash & T. Pruzinaky (Eds.), *Body image: Development, deviance, and change* (pp. 273–295). New York: Guilford Press.

French, S. A., Leffert, N., Story, M., Neumark-Sztainer, D., Hannan, P., & Benson, P. L. (2001). Adolescent binge/purge and weight loss behaviors: Associations with developmental assets. *Journal of Adolescent Health, 28,* 211–221.

French, S. A., Perry, C. L., Leon, G. R., & Fulkerson, J. A. (1995). Changes in psychological variables and health behaviors by dieting status over a three-year period in a cohort of adolescent females. *Journal of Adolescent Health, 16,* 438–447

French, S. A., Story, M., Remafedi, G., Resnick, M. D., & Blum, R. W. (1996). Sexual orientation and prevalence of body dissatisfaction and eating disordered behaviors: A population-based study of adolescents. *International Journal of Eating Disorders, 19,* 119–126.

Frisco, M. L., Muller, C., & Dodson, K. (2004). Participation in voluntary youth-serving associations and early adult voting behavior. *Social Science Quarterly, 85,* 660–676.

Funk, J. B., Bechtoldt-Baldacci, H., Pasold, T., & Baumgardner, J. (2004). Violence exposure in real-life, video games, television, movies, and the Internet: Is there desensitization? *Journal of Adolescence, 27,* 23–39.

Funk, J. B., Flores, G., Buchman, D. D., & Germann, J. N. (1999). Rating electronic games: Violence is in the eye of the beholder. *Youth & Society, 30,* 283–312.

Furnham, A., & Calnan, A. (1998). Eating disturbance, self-esteem, reasons for exercising and body weight dissatisfaction in adolescent males. *European Eating Disorders Review, 6,* 58–72.

Galston, W. A. (2001). Political knowledge, political engagement, and civic education. *Annual Review of Political Science, 4,* 217–234.

Galston, W. A. (2004). Civic education and political participation. *PS: Political Science & Politics, 37,* 263–266.

Gan, S.-L, Zillman, D., & Mitrook, M. (1997). Stereotyping effect of Black women's sexual rap on White audiences. *Basic and Applied Social Psychology, 19,* 381–399.

Garmezy, N. (1991). Resiliency and vulnerability to adverse developmental outcomes associated with poverty. *American Behavioral Scientist, 34,* 416–430.

Garner, A., Sterk, H. M., & Adams, S. (1998). Narrative analysis of sexual etiquette in teenage magazines. *Journal of Communication, 48,* 59–78.

Gentile, D. A. (2003). *Media violence and children: A complete guide for parents and professionals.* Westport, CT: Praeger.

Gentile, D. A., & Anderson, C. A. (2003). Violent video games: The newest media violence hazard. In D. A. Gentile (Ed.), *Media violence and children: A complete guide for parents and professionals* (pp., 131–152). Westport, CT: Praeger.

Gentile, D. A., Lynch, P. J., Linder, J. R., & Walsh, D. A. (2004). The effects of violent video game habits on adolescent aggressive attitudes and behaviors. *Journal of Adolescence, 27,* 5–22.

Gentile, D. A., & Walsh, D. A. (2002). A normative study of family media habits. *Applied Developmental Psychology, 23,* 157–178.

Gerbner, G., Gross, L., Jackson-Beeck, M., Jeffries-Fox, S., & Signorielli, N. (1978). Cultural indicators: Violence profile no. 9. *Journal of Communication, 28,* 176–207.

Gerbner, G., Gross, L., Morgan, M., & Signorielli, N. (1994). Growing up with television: The cultivation perspective. In J. Bryant & D. Zillmann (Eds.), *Media effects: Advances in theory and research* (pp. 17–41). Hillsdale, NJ: Lawrence Erlbaum.

Gilpin, E. A., Choi, W. S., Berry, C., & Pierce, J. P. (1999). . How many adolescents start smoking each day in the United States? *Journal of Adolescent Health, 25,* 248–55.

Ginsberg v. New York, 390 U.S. 629 (1968).

Glantz, S. A. (2003). Smoking in movies: a major problem and a real solution. *Lancet, 362,* 258–259.

Glantz, L. H.. (1997). Controlling tobacco advertising: The FDA regulations and the First Amendment. *American Journal of Public Health, 87,* 446–451.

Goddard, E. (1990). *Why children start smoking.* London, England: HMSO (Her Majesty's Stationery Office).

Godwin, R. K., Godwin, J. W., & Martinez-Ebers, V. (2004). Civic socialization in public and fundamentalist schools. *Social Science Quarterly, 85,* 1097–1111.

Goldstein, A. O., Sobel, R. A., & Newman, G. R. (1999). Tobacco and alcohol used in G-rated children's animated films. *Journal of the American Medical Association, 281,* 1131–1136.

Good News Club v. Milford Central School, 533 U.S. 98 (2001).

Gooding v. Wilson, 405 U.S. 518 (1972).

Gordon, S., & Gilgun, J. F. (1987) Adolescent sexuality. In V. B. Van Hasselt & M. Hersen (Eds.), *Handbook of adolescent psychology* (pp. 147–167). New York: Pergamon Press.

Gostin, L. O., Arno, P. S., & Brandt, A. M. (1997). FDA regulation of tobacco advertising and youth smoking: Historical, social, and constitutional perspectives. *Journal of the American Medical Association, 277*, 410–418.

Graber, J. A., Brooks-Gunn, J., Paikoff, R. L., & Warren, M. P. (1994). Prediction of eating problems: An 8-year study of adolescent girls. *Developmental Psychology, 30*, 823–834.

Graber, J. A., Lewinsohn, P. M., Seeley, M. S., & Brooks-Gunn, J. (1997). Is psychopathology associated with the timing of pubertal development? *Journal of the American Academy of Child & Adolescent Psychiatry, 36*, 1768–1776.

Grandpre, J., Alvaro, E. M., Burgoon, M., Miller, C. H., & Hall, J. R. (2003). Adolescent reactance and anti-smoking campaigns: A theoretical approach. *Health Communication, 15*, 349–366.

Gray, D., Amos, A., & Currie, C. (1996). Exploring young people's perception of smoking images in youth magazines. *Health Education Research, 11*, 215–230.

Gray, D., Amos, A., & Currie, C. (1997). Decoding the image—consumption, young people, magazines and smoking. An exploration of theoretical and methodological issues. *Health Education Research, 12*, 505–517.

Gray, M. R., & Steinberg, L. (1999). Unpacking authoritative parenting: Reassessing a multidimensional construct. *Journal of Marriage and the Family, 61*, 571–587.

Gray, N. J., Klein, J. D., Noyce, P. R., Sesselberg, T. S., & Cantrill, J. A. (2005). Health information-seeking behavior in adolescence: The place of the Internet. *Social Science & Medicine, 60*, 1467–1478.

Greenberg, B.S., Brown, J. D., & Buerkel-Rothfus, N. (Eds.). (1993). *Media, sex and the adolescent*. Cresskill, NJ: Hampton Press.

Greenberg, B. S., & Busselle, R. W. (1996). Soap operas and sexual activity: A decade later. *Journal of Communication, 46*, 153–160.

Greenberg, B. S., Linsangan, R., Soderman, A., Heeter, C., Lin, C., Stanley, C., et al. (1993). Adolescents' exposure to television and movie sex. In B. S. Greenberg, J. D. Brown & N. Buerkel-Rothfuss (Eds.), *Media, sex and the adolescent* (pp. 61–98). Cresskill, NJ: Hampton Press.

Greenberg, B. S., Siemicki, M., Dorfman, S., Heeter, C., Stanley, C., Soderman, A. et al. (1993). Sex content in R-rated films viewed by adolescents. In B. S. Greenberg, J. D. Brown, & N. Buerkel-Rothfuss (Eds.), *Media, sex, and the adolescent* (pp. 45–58). Cresskill, NJ: Hampton Press.

Greenberg, B. S., & Rampoldi-Hnilo, L. (2001). Child and parent responses to age-based and content-based television ratings. In D. S. Singer & J. L. Singer (Eds.), *Handbook of children and the media* (pp. 621–634). Thousand Oaks, CA: Sage.

Greenfield, P. M. (2004). Inadvertent exposure to pornography on the Internet: Implications of peer-to-peer file-sharing networks for child development and families. *Applied Developmental Psychology, 25*, 741–750.

Greeson, L. (1991). Recognition and ratings of television music videos: Age, gender, and sociocultural effects. *Journal of Applied Psychology, 21*, 1908–1920.

Greeson, L. E., & Williams, R. A. (1986). Social implications of music videos for youth: An analysis of the content and effects of MTV. *Youth and Society, 18*, 177–189.

Griesler, P. C., & Kandel, D. B. (1998). Ethnic differences in correlates of adolescent cigarette smoking. *Journal of Adolescent Health, 23,* 167–180.

Griesler, P. C, Kandel, D. B., & Davies, M. (2002). Ethnic differences in predictors of initiation and persistence of adolescent cigarette smoking in the National Longitudinal Survey of Youth. *Nicotine Tobacco Research, 4,* 79–93.

Griswold v. Connecticut, 381 U.S. 479 (1965).

Groescz, L. M., Levine, M. P., & Murnen, S. K. (2002). The effect of experimental presentation of thin media images on body satisfaction: A meta-analytic review. *International Journal of Eating Disorders, 31,* 1–16.

Grolnick, W. S., Deci, E. L., & Ryan, R. M. (1997). Internalization within the family: The self-determination theory perspective. In J. E. Grusec & L. Kuczynski (Eds.), *Parenting and children's internalization of values: A handbook of contemporary theory* (pp. 135–161). New York: Wiley.

Gross, E. F., (2004). Adolescent Internet use: What we expect, what teens report. *Journal of Applied Developmental Psychology, 25,* 633–649.

Grunbaum, J. A., Kann, L., Kinchen, S., Ross, J., Hawkins, J., Lowry, R., et al. (2004). Youth Risk Behavior Surveillance—United States, 2003, *Morbidity and Mortality Weekly Report,* May 21, 2004 / 53(SS02);1–96.

Grusec, J. E., & Kuczynski, L. (Eds.) (1997). *Parenting and children's internalization of values: A handbook of contemporary theory.* New York: Wiley.

Gunter, B., Oates, C., & Blades, M. (2005). *Advertising to children on TV: Content, impact, and regulation.* Mahwah, NJ: Erlbaum.

Hafen, B. C., & Hafen, J. O. (1996). Abandoning children to their autonomy: The United Nations Convention on the Rights of the Child. *Harvard International Law Journal, 6,* 449–491.

Haferkamp, C. J. (1999). Beliefs about relationships in relation to television viewing, soap opera viewing, and self-monitoring. *Current Psychology, 18,* 193–204.

Hague v. Committee for Industrial Organization, 307 U.S. 496 (1939).

Hamilton, J. (1998). *Channeling violence: The economic market for violent television programming.* Princeton, NJ: Princeton University Press.

Hanna, E. Z., & Grant, B. F. (1999). Parallels to early onset alcohol use in the relationship of early onset smoking with drug use and DSM-IV drug and depressive disorders: Findings from the National Longitudinal Epidemiologic Survey. *Alcoholism: Clinical and Experimental Research, 23,* 513–522.

Hannegan v. Esquire, 327 U.S. 146 (1946).

Hancox, R. J., Milne, B. J., & Poulton, R. (2004). Association between child and adolescent television viewing and health: A longitudinal birth cohort study. *Lancet, 364,* 257–262.

Hansen, C. H. (1989). Priming sex-role stereotypic event schemas with rock music videos: Effects on impression favorability, trait inferences, and recall of subsequent male-female interaction. *Basic and Applied Social Psychology, 10,* 371–391.

Hansen, C. H., & Hansen, R. D. (1988). How rock music videos can change what is seen when boy meets girl: Priming stereotypic appraisal of social interactions. *Sex Roles, 19,* 287–316.

Hansen, C. H., & Hansen, R. D. (1990). Rock music videos and antisocial behavior. *Basic and Applied Social Psychology, 11,* 357–369.

Hansen, D. M., Larson, R. W., & Dworkin, J. B. (2003). What adolescents learn in organized youth activities: A survey of self-reported developmental experiences. *Journal of Research on Adolescence, 13,* 25–56.

Hargreaves, D., & Tiggemann, M. (2002a). The effect of television commercials on mood and body dissatisfaction: The role of appearance-schema activation. *Journal of Social and Clinical Psychology, 21,* 287–308.

Hargreaves, D., & Tiggemann, M. (2002b). The role of appearance schematicity in the development of adolescent body dissatisfaction. *Cognitive Therapy and Research, 26,* 691–700.

Hargreaves, D., & Tiggemann, M. (2003). The effect of "thin ideal" television commercials on body dissatisfaction and schema activation during early adolescence. *Journal of Youth and Adolescence, 32,* 367–373.

Haridakis, P. M., & Rubin, A. M. (2003). Motivation for watching television violence and viewer aggression. *Mass Communication & Society, 6,* 29–56.

Harris, K. M. (1999). The health status and risk behaviors of adolescents in immigrant families. In D. J. Hernandez (Ed.), *Children of immigrants: Health, adjustment, and public assistance* (pp. 286–347). Washington, DC: National Academy Press.

Harrison, K, & Cantor, J. (1997). The relationship between media consumption and eating disorders. *Journal of Communication, 47,* 40–67.

Harrison, K., & Cantor, J. (1999). Tales from the screen: Enduring fright reactions to scary media. *Media Psychology, 1,* 97–116.

Harter, S. (1999). *The construction of self: A developmental perspective.* New York: Guilford.

Hartup, W. W. (1996). The company they keep: Friendships and their developmental significance. *Child Development, 67,* 1–13.

Hattie, J., Marsh, H., Neill, J., & Richards, G. (1997). Adventure education and Outward Bound: Out-of-class experiences that make a lasting difference. *Review of Educational Research, 67,* 43–87.

Hazan, A. R., & Glantz, S. A. (1995). Current trends in tobacco use in prime-time fictional television. *American Journal of Public Health, 85,* 116–117.

Hazan, A. R., Lipton, H. L., & Glantz, S. A. (1994). Popular films do not reflect current tobacco use. *American Journal of Public Health, 84,* 998–1000.

Hazelwood School District v. Kuhlmeier, 484 U.S. 260 (1988).

Hearold, S. (1986). A synthesis of 1043 effects of television on social behavior. In G. Comstock (Ed.), *Public communication and behavior* (Vol. 1., pp 65–133). San Diego, CA: Academic Press.

Heath, S. B., & McLaughlin, M. W. (Eds.). (1993). *Identity and inner-city youth: Beyond ethnicity and gender.* N.Y.: Teachers College Press.

Heffernan, K. (1994). Sexual orientation as a factor in risk for binge eating and bulimia nervosa: A review. *International Journal of Eating Disorders, 16,* 335–347.

Heinberg, L. J., & Thompson, J. K. (1992). Social comparison: Gender, target importance ratings, and relations to body image disturbance. *Journal of Social Behavior and Clinical Psychology, 14,* 325–340.

Heinberg, L. J., & Thompson, J. K. (1995). Body image and televised images of thinness and attractiveness: A controlled laboratory investigation. *Journal of Social & Clinical Psychology, 14,* 325–338.

Heins, M. (2001). *Not in front of the children: "Indecency," censorship and the innocence of youth.* New York: Hill and Wang.

Hektner, J. M. (2001). Family, school, and community predictors of adolescent growth-conducive experiences: Global and specific approaches. *Applied Developmental Science, 5,* 172–183

Hellenga, K. (2002). Social space, the final frontier: Adolescents and the Internet. In J. T. Mortimer & R. W. Larson (Eds.), *The changing adolescent experience: Social trend and the transition to adulthood* (pp. 208–249). Cambridge, MA: Cambridge University Press.

Henke, L. L. (1995). Young children's perceptions of cigarette brand advertising symbols: Awareness, affect, and target market identification. *Journal of Advertising, 24,* 13–28.

Hess v. Indiana, 414 U.S. 105 (1973).

Hobbs, R. (1998). The seven great debates in the literacy movement. *Journal of Communication, 48,* 16–32.

Hoek, J. (1999). Effects of tobacco advertising restrictions: Weak responses to strong measures? *International Journal of Advertising, 18,* 23–39.

Hogben, M., & Byrne, D. (1998). Using social learning theory to explain individual differences in human sexuality. *Journal of Sex Research, 35,* 58–71.

Hofferth, S. L., & Sandberg, J. F. (2001). How American children spend their time. *Journal of Marriage and the Family, 63,* 295–308.

Howard, D. E., & Wang, M. Q. (2005). Psychosocial correlates of U.S. adolescents who report a history of forced sexual intercourse. *Journal of Adolescent Health, 36,* 372–379.

Hu, F. B., Flay, B. R., Hedeker, D, & Siddiqui, O. (1995). The influences of friends' and parental smoking on adolescent smoking behavior: The effects of time and prior smoking. *Journal of Applied Social Psychology, 25,* 2018–2047.

Huesmann, L. R. (1986). Psychological processes promoting the relation between exposure to media violence and aggressive behavior by the viewer. *Journal of Social Issues, 42,* 125–139.

Huesmann, L. R. (1988). An information processing model for the development of aggression. *Aggressive Behavior, 14,* 13–24.

Huesmann, L. R. (1999). The effects of childhood aggression and exposure to media violence on adult behaviors, attitudes, and mood: Evidence from a 15-year cross-national longitudinal study. *Aggressive Behavior, 25,* 18–29.

Huesmann, L. R., & Eron, L. D. (1986). *Television and the aggressive child: A cross-national comparison.* Hillsdale, NJ: Erlbaum.

Huesmann, L. R., Eron, L. D., Berkowitz, L., & Chaffee, S. (1991). The effects of television violence on aggression: A reply to a skeptic. In P. Suedfeld & P. Tetlock (Eds.), *Psychology and social policy* (pp. 191–200). New York: Hemisphere.

Huesmann, L. R., & Guerra, N. G. (1997). Children's normative beliefs about aggression and aggressive behavior. *Journal of Personality and Social Psychology, 72,* 408–419.

Huesmann, L. R., Guerra, N. G., Zelli, A., & Miller, L. (1992). Differing cognitions relating to TV viewing and aggression among boys and girls. In K. Bjorkqvist & P. Niemela (Eds.), *Of mice and women* (pp. 77–87). New York: Academic Press.

Huesmann, L. R., Lagerspetz, K., & Eron, L. D. (1984). Intervening variables in the TV violence-aggression relation: Evidence from two countries. *Developmental Psychology, 20,* 746–775.

Huesmann, L. R., & Miller, L. S. (1994). Long-term effects of repeated exposure to media violence in childhood. In L. R. Huesmann (Ed.), *Aggressive behavior: Current perspectives* (pp. 153–186). New York: Plenum Press.

Huesmann, L. R., Moise-Titus, J., Podolski, C. L., & Eron, L. (2003). Longitudinal relations between children's exposure to TV violence and their aggressive and violent behavior in young adulthood: 1977–1992. *Developmental Psychology, 39,* 201–221.

Hunter, J. P., & Csikszentmihalyi, M. (2003). The positive psychology of interested adolescents. *Journal of Youth and Adolescence, 32,* 27–35.

Hurley v. Irish-American Gay, Lesbian and Bisexual Group, 515 U.S. 557 (1995).

Institute for Social Research, University of Michigan. (1999). *Monitoring the future study, 1999.* Ann Arbor, MI: University of Michigan.

Interactive Digital Software Association v. St. Louis County, 329 F.3d 954 (2003).

Irving, L. M. (1990). Mirror images: Effects of the standard of beauty on the self- and body-esteem of women exhibiting varying levels of bulimic symptoms. *Journal of Social and Clinical Psychology, 9,* 230–242.

Irving, L. M., DuPen, J., & Berel, S. (1998). A media literacy program for high school females. *Eating Disorders: The Journal of Treatment and Prevention, 6,* 119–132.

Irwin, R., & Gross, A. (1995). Cognitive tempo, violent video games and aggressive behavior in young boys. *Journal of Family Violence, 10,* 337–350.

Jackson, C. (1997). Initial and experimental stages of tobacco and alcohol use during late childhood: Relation to peer, parent, and personal risk factors. *Addictive Behavior, 22,* 685–698.

Jackson, C. (1998). Cognitive susceptibility to smoking and initiation of smoking during childhood: A longitudinal study. *Preventative Medicine, 27,* 129–134.

Jackson, L. A., von Eye, A., Biocca, F. A., Barbatsis, G., Zhao, Y., & Fitzgerald, H. E. (2006). Does home Internet use influence the academic performance of low-income children? *Developmental Psychology, 42,* 429–435.

James v. Meow Media, Inc., 300 F.3d 683 (2002).

Jansz, J. (2005). The emotional appeal of violent video games for adolescent males. *Communication Theory, 15,* 219–241.

Jason, L. A., Berk, M., Schnopp-Wyatt, D. L., & Talbot, B. (1999). Effects of enforcement of youth access laws on smoking prevalence. *American Journal of Community Psychology, 27,* 143–160.

Jason, L., Katz R, Vavra J, Schnopp–Wyatt, D. L., & Talbot, B. (1999). Long term follow-up on youth access to tobacco law's impact on smoking prevalence. *Journal of Human Behavior in the Social Environment, 2,* 1–13.

Jo, E., & Berkowitz, L. (1994). A priming effect analysis on media influences: An update. In J. Bryant & D. Zillman (Eds.), *Media effects: Advances in theory and research* (pp. 43–60). Hillsdale, NJ: Erlbaum.

Johnson, J. D., Adams, M. S., Ashburn, L., & Reed, W. (1995). Differential gender effects of exposure to rap music on African-American adolescents' acceptance of teen dating violence. *Sex Roles, 33,* 597–605.

Johnson, J. G., Cohen, P., Kasen, S., & Brook, J. S. (2002). Eating disorders during adolescence and the risk for physical and mental disorders during early adulthood. *Archives of General Psychiatry, 59,* 545–552.

Johnson, J. G., Cohen, P., Smailes, E. M., Kasen, S., & Brook, J. S. (2002). Television viewing and aggressive behavior during adolescence and adulthood. *Science, 295,* 2468–2471.

Johnson, J. D., Jackson, L. A., & Gatto, L. (1995). Violent attitudes and deferred academic aspirations: Deleterious effects of exposure to rap music. *Basic and Applied Social Psychology, 16,* 27–41.

Johnson, R. A., & Hoffmann, J. P. (2000). Adolescent cigarette smoking in US racial/ethnic subgroups: Findings from the National Education Longitudinal Study. *Journal of Health and Social Behavior, 41,* 392–407.

Jones, D. C. (2001). Social comparison and body image: Attractiveness comparison to models and peers among adolescent girls and boys. *Sex Roles, 45,* 645–664.

Jones, D. C. (2004). Body image among adolescent girls and boys: A longitudinal study. *Developmental Psychology, 40,* 823–835.

Jones, D. C., Vigfusdottir, T. H., & Lee, Y. (2004). Body image and the appearance culture among adolescent girls and boys: An examination of friend conversations, peer criticism, appearance magazines, and the internalization of appearance ideals. *Journal of Adolescent Research, 19,* 323–339.

Jordan, A. (2004). The role of media in children's development: An ecological perspective. *Journal of Developmental & Behavioral Pediatrics, 25,* 196–206.

Joseph Burstyn, Inc. v. Wilson, 343 U.S. 495 (1952).

Josephson, W. L. (1987). Television violent and children's aggression: Testing the priming, social script, and disinhibition predictions. *Journal of Personality and Social Psychology, 53,* 882–890.

Kaiser Family Foundation and Children Now (1997). *Talking with kids about tough issues: A national survey.* Palo Alto, CA: Henry J. Kaiser Family Foundation.

Kahn, J. A., Huang, B., Rosenthal, S. L., Tissot, A. M., & Burk, R. D. (2005). Coercive sexual experiences and subsequent human papillomavirus infection and squamous intra-epithelial lesions in adolescent and young adult women. *Journal of Adolescent Health, 36,* 363–371.

Kandel, D. B., & Davies, M. (1986). Adult sequelae of adolescent depressive symptoms. *Archives of General Psychiatry, 43,* 255–262.

Kandel, D. B., Chen, K., Warner, L. A., Kessler, R. C., & Grant, B. (1997). Prevalence and demographic correlates of symptoms of last year dependence on alcohol, nicotine, marijuana and cocaine in the U.S. population. *Drug and Alcohol Dependence, 44,* 11–29.

Kandel, D. B., Kiros, G.-E., Schaffran, C., & Mei-Chen, H. (2004). Racial/ethnic differences in cigarette smoking initiation and progression to daily smoking: A multilevel analysis. *American Journal of Public Health, 94,* 128–135.

Kaukinen, C., & DeMaris, A. (2005). Age at first sexual assault and current substance use and depression. *Journal of Interpersonal Violence, 20,* 1244–1270.

Kawaja, J. (1994). Process video: Self-reference and social change. In P. Riano (Ed.), *Women in grassroots communication: Furthering social change* (pp. 131–148). Newbury Park, CA: Sage Publications.

Keating, D. P. (2004). Cognitive and brain development. In R. M. Lerner & L. D. Steinberg (Eds.), *Handbook of adolescent psychology* (2nd ed., pp. 45–84). New York: Wiley.

Keel, P. K., Fulkerson, J. A., & Leon, G. R. (1997). Disordered eating precursors in pre- and early-adolescent girls and boys. *Journal of Youth and Adolescence, 26,* 203–216.

Keel, P. K., Heatherton, T. F., Harnden, J. L., & Hornig, C. D. (1997). Mothers, fathers and daughters: Dieting and disordered eating. *Eating Disorders, 5,* 216–228.

Keel, P. K., Klump, K. L., Leon, G. R., & Fulkerson, J. A. (1998). Disordered eating in adolescent males from a school-based sample. *International Journal of Eating Disorders, 23,* 125–132.

Kellner, D. (1995). *Media culture.* London: Routledge.

Kendler, K., Neale, M., MacLean, C., Health, A., Eaves, L., & Kessler, R. (1993). Smoking and major depression. *Archives of General Psychiatry, 50,* 36–43.

Kent, S. L. (2001). *The ultimate history of video games.* Roseville, CA: Prima Publishing.

Kerr, M., & Stattin, H. (2000). What parents know, how they know it, and several forms of adolescent adjustment: Further support for a reinterpretation of monitoring. *Developmental Psychology, 36,* 366–380.

Keyishian v. Bd. of Regents, 385 U.S. 589 (1967).

Killen, J. D., Taylor, C. B., Hayward, C., Haydel, K. F., Wilson, D. M., & Hammer, L. (1996). Weight concerns influence the development of eating disorders: A 4-year prospective study. *Journal of Consulting and Clinical Psychology, 64,* 936–940.

Kinsman, S. B., Romer, D., Furstenberg, F. F., & Schwarz, D. F. (1998). Early sexual initiation: The role of perceived norms. *Pediatrics, 102,* 1185–1192.

Kirby, D., Brener, N., Brown, N., Peterfreund, N., Hillard, P., & Harrist, R. (1999). The impact of condom availability [correction of distribution] in Seattle schools on sexual behavior and condom use. *American Journal of Public Health, 89,* 182–187.

Kirlin, M. (2002). Civic skill building: The missing component in service programs? *PS: Political Science & Politics, 35,* 571–575.

Kirsh, S. J. (1998). Seeing the world through "Mortal Kombat" colored glasses: Violent video games and the development of a short-term hostile attribution bias. *Childhood, 5,* 177–184.

Kleindienst v. Mandel, 408 U.S. 753 (1972).

Klitzke, M., Irwin, R., Lombardo, T., & Christoff, K. (1990). Self-monitored smoking motives. *Journal of Substance Abuse, 2,* 121–127.

Kobus, K. (2003). Peers and adolescent smoking. *Addiction, 98,* 37–55.

Koval, J. J., Pederson, L. L., Mills, C. A., McGrady, G. A., & Carvajal, S. C. (2000). Models of the relationship of stress, depression, and other psychosocial factors to smoking behavior: A comparison of a cohort of students in grades 6 and 8. *Preventive Medicine, 30,* 463–477.

Kubey, R. (1998). Obstacles to the development of media education in the United States. *Journal of Communication, 48,* 59–69.

Kumar, R., O'Malley, P. M., Johnston, L. D., Schulenberg, J. E., & Bachman, J. G. (2002). Effects of school-level norms on student substance use. *Prevention Science, 38,* 55–71.

Kunkel, D, Biely, E., Eyal, K., Cope-Farrar, K., & Donnerstein, E. (2003). *Sex on TV 3: A biennial report to the Kaiser Family Foundation.* Menlo Park, CA: The Henry J. Kaiser Family Foundation. Retrieved January 20, 2006, from http://www.kff.org/entmedia/3325-index.cfm

Kunkel, D., Cope, K. M., & Biely, E. (1999). Sexual messages on television: Comparing findings from three studies. *Journal of Sex Research, 36,* 230–236.

Kunkel, D., Cope-Farrar, K., Farinola, W., Biely, E., Rollin, E., & Donnerstein, E. (2001). *Sex on TV: A biennial report to the Kaiser Family Foundation.* Menlo Park, CA: The Henry J. Kaiser Family Foundation.

Kunkel, D., & Wilcox, B. (2001). Children and media policy. In D. S. Singer & J. L. Singer (Eds.), *Handbook of children and the media* (pp. 589–604). Thousand Oaks, CA: Sage.

Kuntsche, E. N. (2004). Hostility among adolescents in Switzerland? Multivariate relations between excessive media use and forms of violence. *Journal of Adolescent Health, 34,* 230–236.

Labre, M. P. (2002). Adolescent boys and the muscular male body ideal. *Journal of Adolescent Health, 30,* 233–242.

Lakkis, J., Ricciardelli, L. A., & Williams, R. J. (1999). The role of sexual orientation and gender-related traits in disordered eating. *Sex Roles, 41,* 1–16.

Lamkin, L., Davis, B., & Kamen, A. (1998). Rationale for tobacco cessation interventions for youth. *Preventive Medicine, 27,* A3–A8.

Lamont v. Postmaster General, 381 U.S. 301.

Landmark Communications, Inc. v. Virginia, 435 U.S. 829 (1978).

Landrine, H., Richardson, J. L., Klonoff, E. A, & Flay B. (1994). Cultural diversity in the predictors of adolescent cigarette smoking: The relative influence of peers. *Journal of Behavioral Medicine, 17,* 331–346.

Landry, D. J., Kaeser L., & Richards, C. L. (1999). Abstinence promotion and the provision of information about contraception in public school district sexuality education policies. *Family Planning Perspectives, 31,* 280–286.

Lanis, K., & Covell, K. (1995). Images of women in advertisements: Effects on attitudes related to sexual aggression. *Sex Roles, 32,* 639–649.

Lantz P. M., Jacobson, P. D., Warner, K. E., Wasserman, J., Pollack, H. A., Berson, J., et al. (2000). Investing in youth tobacco control: A review of smoking prevention and control strategies. *Tobacco Control, 9,* 47–63.

Larimer, M. E., & Cronce, J. M. (2002). Identification, prevention, and treatment: A review of individual-focused strategies to reduce problematic alcohol consumption by college students. *Journal of Studies on Alcohol, 14,* 148–163.

Larson, M. (1996). Sex roles and soap operas: What adolescents learn about single motherhood. *Sex Roles: A Journal of Research, 35,* 97–121.

Larson, R. W. (2000). Toward a psychology of positive youth development. *American Psychologist, 55,* 170–183.

Lauer, R. M., Akers, R. L., Massey, J., & Clarke, W. (1982). Evaluation of cigarette smoking among adolescents: The Muscatine Study. *Preventive Medicine, 11,* 417–428.

Lavin, M. A., & Cash, T. F. (2001). Effects of exposure to information about appearance stereotyping and discrimination on women's body images. *International Journal of Eating Disorders, 29,* 51–58.

Lavine, H., Sweeney, D., & Wagner, S. H. (1999). Depicting women as sex objects in television advertising: Effects on body dissatisfaction. *Personality & Social Psychology Bulletin, 25,* 1049–1058.

Lawrence, S., & Giles, C. L. (1999). Accessibility of information on the web. *Nature, 400,* 107–109.

Lee, E., & Leets, L. (2002). Persuasive storytelling by hate groups online: Examining its effects on adolescents. *American Behavioral Scientist. Special Issue: Cyberterrorism in the 21st Century, 45,* 927–957.

Lee, J. D. (2005). Do girls change more than boys? Gender differences and similarities in the impact of new relationships on identities and behaviors. *Self and Identity, 4,* 131–147.

Lee, R. G., Taylor, V. A., & McGetrick, R. (2004). Toward reducing youth exposure to tobacco messages: Examining the breadth of brand and nonbrand communications. *Journal of Health Communication, 9,* 461–479.

Lee v. Weisman, 505 U.S. 577 (1992).

Lefkowitz, M. M., Eron, L. D., Walder, L. O., & Huesmann, L. R. (1977). *Growing up to be violent: A longitudinal study of the development of aggression.* New York: Pergamon Press.

Leiberman, D. A., Chaffee, S. H., & Roberts, D. F. (1988). Computers, mass media, and schooling: Functional equivalence in uses of new media. *Social Science Computer Review, 6,* 224–241.

Lemon v. Kurtzman, 403 U.S. 602 (1971).

Leon, G. R., Fulkerson, J. A., Perry, C. L., & Early-Zald, M. B. (1995). Prospective analysis of personality and behavioral vulnerabilities and gender influences in the later development of disordered eating. *Journal of Abnormal Psychology, 104,* 140–149.

Leon, G. R., Fulkerson, J. A., Perry, C. L., Keel, P. K., & Klump, K. L. (1999). Three to four year prospective evaluation of personality and behavioral risk factors for later disordered eating in adolescent boys and girls. *Journal of Youth and Adolescence, 28,* 181–195.

Lerman, C., Caporaso, N., Main, D., Audrain, J., Boyd, N. R., Bowman, E. D., & Shields, P. G. (1998). Depression and self-medication with nicotine: The modifying influence of the dopamine D4 receptor gene. *Health Psychology, 17,* 56–62.

Lerner, R. M., & Castellino, D. R (2002). Contemporary developmental theory and adolescence: Developmental systems and applied developmental science. *Journal of Adolescent Health, 31,* 122–135.

Leventhal, H., & Avis, N. (1976). Pleasure, addiction, and habit: Factors in verbal report or factors in smoking behavior? *Journal of Abnormal Psychology, 85,* 478–488.

Leventhal, T., & Brooks-Gunn, J. (2000). The neighborhoods they live in: The effects of neighborhood residence on child and adolescent outcomes. *Psychological Bulletin, 126,* 309–337.

Levesque, R. J. R. (2000). *Adolescents, sex and the law: Preparing adolescents for responsible citizenship.* Washington, DC: American Psychological Association.

Levesque, R. J. R. (2002a). *Child maltreatment law: Foundations in science, law and policy.* Durham, NC: Carolina Academic Press.

Levesque, R. J. R. (2002b). *Dangerous adolescents, model adolescents: Shaping the role and promise of education.* New York: Plenum/Kluwer Academic.

Levesque, R. J. R. (2002c). *Not by faith alone: Religion, law and adolescence.* New York: New York University Press.

Levesque, R. J. R. (2003). *Sexuality education: What adolescents' rights require.* Hauppauge, NY: Nova Science Publishers.

Levesque, R. J. R. (2006). *The psychology and law of criminal justice processes.* Hauppauge, NY: Nova Science Publishers

Levine, M. P. (1999). Prevention of eating disorders, eating problems and negative body image. In R. Lemberg (Ed.), *Controlling eating disorders with facts, advice, and resources* (2nd ed., pp. 64–72). Phoenix, AZ: Oryx Press.

Levine, M. P., Piran, N., & Stoddard, C. (1999). Mission more probable: Media literacy, activism, and advocacy in the prevention of eating disorders. In N. Piran, M. P. Levine, & C. Steiner-Adair (Eds.), *Preventing eating disorders: A handbook of interventions and special challenges* (pp. 3–25). Philadelphia: Brunner/Mazel.

Levine, M. P., & Smolak, L. (1996). Media as a context for the development of disordered eating. In L. Smolak, M. P. Levine & R. Striegel-Moore (Eds.), *The developmental psychopathology of eating disorders: Implications for research, prevention, and treatment* (pp. 235–257). Mahwah, NJ: Erlbaum.

Levine, M. P., & Smolak, L. (1998). The mass media and disordered eating: Implications for primary prevention. In G. Van Noordenbos & W. Vanereycken (Eds.), *The prevention of eating disorders* (pp. 23–56). New York: New York University Press.

Levine, M. P., & Smolak, L. (2001). Primary prevention of body image disturbances and disordered eating in childhood and early adolescence. In J. K. Thompson & L. Smolak (Eds.), *Body image, eating disorders, and obesity in youth: Assessment, prevention and treatment* (pp. 237–260). Washington, DC: American Psychological Association.

Levine, M. P., Smolak, L., & Hayden, H. (1994). The relation of sociocultural factors to eating attitudes and behaviors among middle school girls. *Journal of Early Adolescence, 14*, 471–490.

Levine, M. P., Smolak, L., Moodey, A. F., Shuman, M. D., & Hessen, L. D. (1994). Normative developmental challenges and dieting and eating disturbances in middle school girls. *International Journal of Eating Disorders, 15*, 11–20.

Levy, S. R., Weeks, K., Handler, A., Perhats, C., Franck, J. A., Hedecker, D., et al. (1995). A longitudinal comparison of the AIDS-related attitudes and knowledge of parents and their children. *Family Planning Perspectives, 27*, 4–10.

Lewinsohn, P. M., Striegel-Moore, R. H., & Seeley, J. R. (2000). Epidemiology and natural course of eating disorders in young women from adolescence to young adulthood. *Journal of the American Academy of Child & Adolescent Psychiatry, 39*, 1284–1292.

Lewit, E., Hyland, A., Kerrebrock, N., & Cummings, K. M. (1997). Price, public policy and smoking in youth people. *Tobacco Control, 6* (Supp. 2), 17–24.

Linz, D., Fuson, I. A., & Donnerstein, E. (1990). Mitigating the negative effects of sexually violent mass communications through preexposure briefings. *Communication Research, 17*, 641–674.

Linz, D., Land, K. C., Williams, J. R., Paul, B., & Ezell, M. E. (2004). An examination of the assumption that adult businesses are associated with crime in surrounding areas: A secondary effects study in Charlotte, North Carolina. *Law & Society Review, 38*, 69–104.

Littleton, H. L., & Ollendick, T. (2003). Negative body image and disordered eating behavior in children and adolescents: What places youth at risk and how can these problems be prevented? *Clinical Child and Family Psychology Review, 6*, 51–66.

Lobel, T. E., Nov-Krispin, N., Schiller, D., Lobel, O., & Feldman, A. (2004). Gender discriminatory behavior during adolescence and young adulthood: A developmental analysis. *Journal of Youth and Adolescence, 33*, 535–546.

Lock, J., Reisel, B., & Steiner, H. (2001). Associated health risks of adolescents with disordered eating: How different are they from their peers? Results from a high school survey. *Child Psychiatry and Human Development, 31*, 249–265.

Long, J. A., O'Connor, P. G., Gerbner, G., & Concato, J. (2002). Use of alcohol, illicit drugs, and tobacco among characters on prime-time television. *Substance Abuse, 23*, 95–103.

Lorillard Tobacco Co. v. Reilly, 533 U.S. 525 (2001).

Lucas, K., & Lloyd, B. (1999). Starting smoking: Girls' explanations of influence of peers. *Journal of Adolescence, 22*, 647–655.

Luke, A. (1997). Texts and discourse in education: An introduction to critical discourse analysis. In M. Apple (Ed.), *Review of research in education* (Vol. 21, pp. 3–48). Washington, DC: American Educational Research Association.

Luke, C. (1999). Media and cultural studies in Australia. *Journal of Adolescent and Adult Literacy, 42*, 622–626.

Lunner, K., Wertheim, E. H., Thompson, J. K., Paxton, S. J., McDonald, F., & Halvaarson, E. S. (2000). A cross-cultural examination of weight-related teasing, body image, and eating disturbance in Swedish and Australian samples. *International Journal of Eating Disorders, 28*, 430–435.

Luthar, S. S., Cicchetti, D., & Becker, B. (2000). The construct of resilience: A critical evaluation and guidelines for future work. *Child Development, 77*, 543–562.

Lyubomirsky, S., & Ross, L. (1997). Hedonic consequences of social comparison: A contrast of happy and unhappy people. *Journal of Personality and Social Psychology, 73*, 1141–1157.

McCabe, M. P., & Ricciardelli, L. A. (2001a). Body image and body change techniques among young adolescent boys. *European Eating Disorders Review, 9*, 1–13.

McCabe, M. P., & Ricciardelli, L. A. (2001b). The structure of the Perceived Sociocultural Influences on Body Image and Body Change Questionnaire. *International Journal of Behavioral Medicine, 8*, 19–41.

McCabe, M. P., & Ricciardelli, L. A. (2003a). A longitudinal study of body change strategies among adolescent males. *Journal of Youth and Adolescence, 32*, 105–113.

McCabe, M. P., & Ricciardelli, L. A. (2003b). Sociocultural influences on body image and body changes among adolescent boys and girls. *Journal of Social Psychology, 143*, 5–26.

McCabe, M. P., Ricciardelli, L. A., & Finemore, J. (2002). The role of puberty, media and popularity with peers on strategies to increase weight, decrease weight and increase muscle tone among adolescent boys and girls. *Journal of Psychosomatic Research, 52*, 145–153.

McCabe, M. P., & Vincent, M. A. (2003). The role of bio-developmental and psychological factors in the prediction of body dissatisfaction and disordered eating in adolescents. *European Eating Disorders Review, 11*, 315–328.

McCool, J., Cameron, L., & Petrie, K. (2001). Adolescent perceptions of smoking imagery in film. *Social Science and Medicine, 52*, 1577–1587.

McCool, J., Cameron, L., & Petrie, K. (2003). Interpretations of smoking images in film among older teens. *Social Science and Medicine, 56*, 1023–1032.

McCool, J., Cameron, L., & Petrie, K. (2004). Stereotyping the smoker: Adolescents' appraisals of smokers in film. *Tobacco Control, 13*, 308–314.

McDevitt, M., & Chafee, S. (2000). Closing gaps in political communication and knowledge: Effects of a school intervention. *Communication Research, 27*, 259–292.

McGuire, W. J. (1960). Cognitive consistency and attitude change. *Journal of Abnormal & Social Psychology, 60*, 345–353.

McIntosh, W. D., Bazzini, D. G., Smith, S. M., & Wayne, S. M. (1998). Who smokes in Hollywood? Characteristics of smokers in popular films from 1940 to 1989. *Addictive Behaviors, 23*, 395–398.

McIntyre, J. J., & Teevan, J. J., Jr. (1972). Television violence and deviant behavior. In G. A. Comstock & E. A. Rubinstein (Eds.), *Television and social behavior: Vol. 3. Television and adolescent aggression* (pp. 383–435). Washington, DC: U.S. Government Printing Office.

McLatchie, R. (1997). Psychological adjustment and school performance in immigrant children. *Journal of Psychological Practice, 3*, 34–46.

McLeod, J. M., Atkin, C. K., & Chaffee, S. H. (1972). Adolescents, parents, and television use: Adolescent self-report measures from Maryland and Wisconsin samples. In G. A. Comstock & E. A. Rubinstein (Eds.), *Television and social behavior: A technical report to the Surgeon General's Scientific Advisory Committee on Television and Social Behavior: Vol. 3. Television and adolescent aggressiveness* (DHEW Publication No. HSM 72-9058, pp. 173–238). Washington, DC: U.S. Government Printing Office.

McLeod, J. M., Scheufele, D. A., & Moy, P. (1999). Community, communication, and participation: The role of mass media and interpersonal discussion in local political participation. *Political Communication, 16,* 315–336.

McLoyd, V. C., & Steinberg, L. (Eds.). (1998). *Studying minority adolescents: Conceptual, methodological, and theoretical issues.* Mahwah, NJ: Erlbaum.

McRobbie, A. (1997). *Back to reality? Social experience and cultural studies.* Manchester, UK: Manchester University Press.

MacKay, N. J., & Covell, K. C. (1997). The impact of women in advertisements on attitudes toward women. *Sex Roles, 36,* 573–583.

Madsen v. Women's Health Center, 512 U.S. 753 (1994).

Malamuth, N. M., & Check, J. V. P. (1981). The effects of mass media exposure on acceptance of violence against women: A field experiment. *Journal of Research in Personality, 15,* 436–446.

Malamuth, N. M., & Impett, E. A. (2001). Research on sex in the media: What do we know about effects on children and adolescents? In D. S. Singer & J. L. Singer (Eds.), *Handbook of children and the media* (pp. 269–287). Thousand Oaks, CA: Sage.

Malkin, A. R., Wornian, K., & Chrisler, J. C. (1999). Women and weight: Gendered messages on magazine covers. *Sex Roles, 40,* 647–655.

Maney, D. W., Vasey, J. J., Mahoney, B. S., Gates, S. C., & Higham-Gardill, D. A. (2004). The tobacco-related behavioral risks of a nationally representative sample of adolescents. *American Journal of Health Studies, 19,* 71–83.

Mares, M.-L., & Woodard, E. (2005). Positive effects of television on children's social interactions: A meta-analysis. *Media Psychology, 7,* 301–322.

Markham, R., Howie, P., & Hlavacek, S. (1999). Reality monitoring in auditory and visual modalities: Developmental trends and effects of cross-modal imagery. *Journal of Experimental Child Psychology, 72,* 51–70.

Markstrom, C. A., Li, X., Blackshire, S. L., & Wilfong, J. J. (2005). Ego strength development of adolescents involved in adult-sponsored structured activities. *Journal of Youth and Adolescence, 34,* 85–95.

Markus, H., Hamill, R., & Sentis, K. P. (1987). Thinking fat: Self-schemas for body weight and the processing of weight relevant information. *Journal of Applied Social Psychology, 17,* 50–71.

Martin, J. A., Hamilton, B. E., Sutton, P. D., Ventura, S. J., Menacker, F., & Munson, M. L. (2003). Births: Final data for 2002. *National Vital Statistics Reports, 25,* 10.

Martin, M. C., & Gentry, J. W. (1997). Stuck in the model trap: The effects of beautiful models in ads on pre-adolescents and adolescents. *The Journal of Advertizing, 26,* 19–33.

Martin, M. C., & Kennedy, P. F. (1993). Advertising and social comparison: Consequences for female pre-adolescents and adolescents. *Psychology and Marketing, 10,* 513–530.

Martin v. City of Struthers, 319 U.S. 141 (1943).

Martino, S. C., Collins, R. L., Kanouse, D. E., Elliott, M., & Berry, S. H. (2005). Social cognitive processes mediating the relationship between exposure to television's sexual content and adolescents' sexual behavior. *Journal of Personality and Social Psychology, 89*, 914–924.

Martz, D., & Bazzini, D. (1999). Eating disorders prevention programming may be failing: Evaluation of two one-shot programs. *Journal of College Student Development, 40*, 32–42.

Matsuda, M. (1989). Public response to racist speech: Considering the victim's story. *Michigan Law Review, 87*, 2320–2381.

Meiklejohn, A. (1948). *Free speech and its relation to self-government.* New York: Harper.

Meiklejohn, A. (1965). *Political freedom: The constitutional powers of the people.* New York: Oxford University Press.

Menezes, I. (2003). Participation experiences and civic concepts, attitudes and engagement: Implications for citizenship education projects. *European Educational Research Journal, 2*, 430–445.

Meyer, I. H. (2003). Prejudice, social stress, and mental health in lesbian, gay, and bisexual populations: Conceptual issues and research evidence. *Psychological Bulletin, 129*, 674–697.

Meyer v. Nebraska, 262 U.S. 390 (1923).

Miami Herald Publishing Co. Division of Knight Newspapers, Inc. v. Tornillo, 418 U.S. 241 (1974).

Michell, L. (1997) Pressure groups: Young people's accounts of peer pressure to smoke. *Social Sciences in Health, 3*, 3–16.

Michell, L., & West, P. (1996). Peer pressure to smoke: The meaning depends on the method. *Health Education Research, 11*, 39–49.

Milavsky, J. R., Kessler, R., Stipp, H., & Rubens, W. S. (1982). Television and aggression: Results of a panel study. In D. Pearl, L. Bouthilet, & J. Lazar (Eds.), *Television and behavior: Ten years of scientific progress and implications for the eighties: Vol. 2. Technical reviews* (pp. 138–157). Washington, DC: U. S. Government Printing Office.

Milk Wagon Drivers Union v. Meadowmoor Dairies, 312 U.S. 287 (1941).

Mill, J. S. (1859/1985). *On liberty.* New York: Penguin.

Miller, B. C., Benson, B., & Galbraith, K. A. (2001). Family relationships and adolescent pregnancy risk: A research synthesis. *Developmental Review, 21*,1–38.

Miller v. California, 413 U.S. 15 (1973).

Millstein, S. G., & Halpern-Felsher, B. L. (2002). Judgments about risk and perceived invulnerability in adolescents and young adults. *Journal of Research on Adolescence, 12*, 399–422.

Minneapolis Star & Tribune Co. v. Minnesota Commissioner of Revenue, 460 U.S. 575 (1983).

Mitchell, K. J, Finkelhor, D., & Wolak, J. (2003). The exposure of youth to unwanted sexual material on the Internet: A national survey of risk, impact, and prevention. *Youth & Society, 34*, 330–358.

Mitchell, K. J., Finkelhor, D., & Wolak, J. D. (2005a). The Internet and family and acquaintance sexual abuse. *Child Maltreatment, 10*, 49–60,

Mitchell, K. J., Finkelhor, D., & Wolak, J. D. (2005b). Protecting youth online: Family use of filtering and blocking software. *Child Abuse & Neglect, 25*, 753–765.

Mizerski, R. (1995). The relationship between cartoon trade character recognition and attitude toward product category in young children. *Journal of Marketing*, *59*, 58–71.

Moeller, T. G. (2001). *Youth aggression and violence: A psychological approach*. Mahwah, NJ: Erlbaum.

Moffit, T., Caspi, A., Harrington, H., & Milne, B. (2002). Males on the life-course-persistent and adolescence-limited antisocial pathways: Follow-up at age 26 years. *Development and Psychopathology*, *14*, 179–207.

Moore, K. A., & Glei, D. (1995). Taking the plunge: An examination of positive youth development. *Journal of Adolescent Research*, *10*, 15–40.

Moreno, A., & Thelen, M. H. (1993). Parental factors related to bulimia nervosa. *Addictive Behaviors*, *18*, 681–689.

Moretti, M. M., Odgers, C. L., & Jackson, M. A. (Eds.). (2004). *Girls and aggression: Contributing factors and intervention principles*. New York: Kluwer Academic/ Plenum.

Morgan, M., & Shanahan, J. (1997). Two decades of cultivation research: An appraisal and meta-analysis. *Communication Yearbook*, *20*, 1–45.

Morgan, W., & Streb, M. (2001). Building citizenship: How student voice in service-learning develops civic values. *Social Science Quarterly*, *82*, 154–169.

Moscicki, A.-B. (2005). Impact of HPV infection in adolescent populations. *Journal of Adolescent Health*, *37*, S3–S9.

Mowery, P. D., Farrelly, M. C., Gable, J. M., Wells, H. E., & Haviland, M. L. (2004). Progression to established smoking among U.S. youths. *American Journal of Public Health*, *94*, 128–135.

Mueller, C., Field, T., Yando, R., Harding, J., Gonzalez, K. P., & Bendell, D. (1995). Under eating and over eating concerns among adolescents. *Journal of Child Psychology and Psychiatry*, *36*, 1019–1025.

Murnen, S. K., & Smolak, L. (1997). Femininity, masculinity, and disordered eating: A meta-analytic review. *International Journal of Eating Disorders*, *22*, 231–242.

Murray, D. M., Prokhorov, A. V., & Harty, K. C. (1994). Effects of a statewide anti-smoking campaign on mass media messages and smoking beliefs. *Preventive Medicine*, *23*, 54–60.

Murphy-Hoefer, R., Alder, S., & Higbee, C. (2004). Perceptions about cigarette smoking and risks among college students. *Nicotine and Tobacco Research*, *6* (Supp. 3), 371–374.

Myers, P. N., & Biocca, F. A. (1992). The elastic body image: The effect of television advertising and programming on body image distortions in young women. *Journal of Communication*, *42*, 108–133.

Nansel, T. R., Overpeck, M., Pilla, R. S., Ruan, W. J., Simons-Morton, B., & Scheidt, P. (2001). Bullying behaviors among U.S. youth: Prevalence and association with psychosocial adjustment. *Journal of the American Medical Association*, *285*, 2094–2100.

Nathanson, A. I. (1999). Identifying and explaining the relationships between parental mediation and children's aggression. *Communication Research*, *26*, 124–143.

Nathanson, A. I. (2001). Parents versus peers: Exploring the significance of peer mediation of antisocial television. *Communication Research*, *28*, 251–275.

Nathanson, A. I. (2002). The unintended effects of parental mediation of television on adolescents. *Media Psychology*, *4*, 207–230.

Nathanson, A. I. (2004). Factual and evaluative approaches to modifying children's responses to violent television. *Journal of Communication,* 54, 321–336.

Nathanson, A. I., & Botta, R. (2003). Shaping the effects of television on adolescents' body image disturbance: The role of parental mediation. *Communication Research,* 30, 304–331.

Nathanson, A. I., & Cantor, J. (2000). Reducing the aggression-promoting effect of violent cartoons by increasing children's fictional involvement with the victim. *Journal of Broadcasting & Electronic Media,* 44, 125–142.

National Association of Attorneys General. (1998). *Master Settlement Agreement, November 23, 1998, National Conference of State Legislatures.* Retrieved, February 6, 2006, from http://www.ncsl.org/statefed/tmsasumm.htm

National Endowment for the Arts v. Finley, 524 U.S. 596 (1998).

National Television Violence Study. (1998). *National television violence study* (Vol. 3). Santa Barbara: University of California, Santa Barbara, Center for Communication and Social Policy.

Neuman, S. B. (1995). *Literacy in the television age* (2nd ed.). Norwood: NJ: Ablex.

Neumark-Sztainer, D., & Hannan, P. J. (2000). Weight-related behaviors among adolescent girls and boys: Results from a national survey. *Archives of Pediatrics and Adolescent Medicine,* 154, 569–577.

Neumark-Sztainer, D., Story, M., Falkner, N. H., Beuhring, T., & Resnick, M. D. (1999). Sociodemographic and personal characteristics of adolescents engaged in weight loss and weight/muscle gain behaviors: Who is doing what? *Preventative Medicine: An International Journal Devoted to Practice and Theory,* 28, 40–50.

Neumark-Sztainer, D., Story, M., & French, S. A. (1996). Covariations of unhealthy weight loss behaviors and other high-risk behaviors among adolescents. *Archives of Pediatrics and Adolescent Medicine,* 150, 304–310.

Neumark-Sztainer, D., Story, M., Hannan, P. J., Beuhring, T., & Resnick, M. D. (2000). Disordered eating among adolescents: Associations with sexual/physical abuse and other familial/psychological factors. *International Journal of Eating Disorders,* 28, 249–258.

New York Times Co. v. Sullivan, 376 U.S. 254 (1964).

New York v. Ferber, 458 U.S. 747 (1982).

Newman, D. L., Moffitt, T. E., Silva, P. A., Caspi, A., Magdol, L., & Stanton, W. R. (1996). Psychiatric disorder in a birth cohort of young adults: Prevalence, comorbidity, clinical significance, and new case incidence from ages 11 to 21. *Journal of Consulting and Clinical Psychology,* 64, 552–562.

Nichter, M., Nichter, M., Vuckovic, N., Quintero, G., & Ritenbaugh, C. (1997). Smoking experimentation and initiation among adolescent girls: Qualitative and quantitative findings. *Tobacco Control,* 6, 285–295.

Nixon v. Shrink Missouri Government PAC, 528 U.S. 377 (2000).

Ng, C., & Dakake, B. (2002). *Tobacco at the movies: Tobacco use in PG-13 films.* Retrieved, February 6, 2006, from http://masspirg.org/MA.asp?id2=8330&id3=MA

Noble State Bank v. Haskell, 219 U.S. 104 (1911).

Noland, M. P., Kryscio, R. J., Riggs, R. S., Linville, L. H., Ford, V. Y., & Tucker, T. C. (1998). The effectiveness of a tobacco prevention program with adolescents living in a tobacco-producing region. *American Journal of Public Health,* 88, 1862–1865.

Norris, P. (1996). Does television erode social capital? A reply to Putnam. *PS: Political Science & Politics, 293*, 474–480.

O'Dea, J. A., & Abraham, S. (1999). Onset of disordered eating attitudes and behaviors in early adolescence: Interplay of pubertal status, gender, weight, and age. *Adolescence, 34*, 671–679.

Ogbu, J. I. (1981). Origins of human competence: A cultural-ecological perspective. *Child Development, 52*, 413–429.

Ohring, R., Graber, J. A., & Brooks-Gunn, J. (2002). Girls' recurrent and concurrent body dissatisfaction: Correlates and consequences over 8 years. *International Journal of Eating Disorders, 31*, 404–415.

Olivardia, R., Pope, H. G., & Hudson, J. I. (2000). Muscle dysmorphia in male weightlifters: A case-control study. *American Journal of Psychiatry, 157*, 1291–1296.

O'Loughlin, J., Paradis, G., Renaud, L., & Gomez, L. S. (1998). One year predictors of smoking initiation and of continued smoking among elementary schoolchildren in multiethnic, low-income, inner-city neighborhoods. *Tobacco Control, 7*, 268–275.

Olson, C. K. (2004). Media violence research and youth violence data: Why do they conflict? *Academic Psychiatry, 28*, 144–150.

Orlando, M., Ellickson, P. L., & Jinnett, K. (2001). The temporal relationship between emotional distress and cigarettes during adolescence and young adulthood. *Journal of Consulting and Clinical Psychology, 69*, 959–70.

Osborne v. Ohio, 495 U.S. 103 (1990).

O'Sullivan, L. F., & Brooks-Gunn, J. (2005). The timing of changes in girls' sexual cognitions and behaviors in early adolescence: A prospective, cohort study. *Journal of Adolescent Health, 37*, 211–219.

Owen, P. R., & Laurel-Seller, E. (2000). Weight and shape ideals: Thin is dangerously in. *Journal of Applied Social Psychology, 30*, 979–990.

Paik, H., & Comstock, G. A. (1994). The effects of television violence on antisocial behavior: A meta-analysis. *Communication Research, 21*, 516–546.

Pardun, C. J., L'Engle, K. L., & Brown, J. D., (2005). Linking exposure to outcomes: Early adolescents' consumption of sexual content in six media. *Mass Communication and Society, 8*, 75–91.

Paris Adult Theatre I v. Slaton, 413 U.S. 49 (1973).

Parke, R. D., Berkowitz, L., Leyens, J. P., West, S. G., & Sebastian, R. J. (1977). Some effects of violent and nonviolent movies on the behavior of juvenile delinquents. In L. Berkowitz (Ed.), *Advances in experimental social psychology* (Vol. 10, pp. 135–172). New York: Academic Press.

Patten, C. A., Choi, W. S., Gillin, J. C., & Pierce, J. P. (2000). Depressive symptoms and cigarette smoking predict development and persistence of sleep problems in US adolescents. *Pediatrics, 106*, E23.

Patton, G., Hibbert, M., Rosier, M., Carlin, J., Caust, J., & Bowes, G. (1996). Is smoking associated with depression and anxiety in teenagers? *American Journal of Public Health, 86*, 225–230.

Patton, G. C., Selzer, R., Coffey, C., Carlin, J. B., & Wolfe, R. (1999). Onset of adolescent eating disorders: Population based cohort study over 3 years. *British Medical Journal, 318*, 765–768.

Paul, B., Linz, D., & Shafer, B. J. (2001). Government regulation of "adult" businesses through zoning and anti-nudity ordinances: Debunking the legal myth of negative secondary effects. *Communication Law and Policy, 6*, 355–399.

Paulson, K. A. (2004). Regulation through intimidation: Congressional hearings and political pressure on America's entertainment media. *Vanderbilt Journal of Entertainment Law & Practice, 7,* 61–89.

Paxton, R. J., Valois, R. F., Drane, J., & Wanzer, J. (2004). Correlates of body mass index, weight goals, and weight-management practices among adolescents. *Journal of School Health, 74,* 136–143.

Paxton, S. J., Schutz, H., Wertheim, E. H., & Muir, S. L. (1999). Friendship clique and peer influences on body image concerns, dietary restraint, extreme weight-loss behaviors, and binge eating in adolescent girls. *Journal of Abnormal Psychology, 108,* 255–266.

Pechmann, C., & Knight, S. J. (2002). An experimental investigation of the joint effects of advertising and peers on adolescents' beliefs and intentions about cigarette consumption. *Journal of Consumer Research, 29,* 5–19.

Pechmann, C., & Shih, C. F. (1999). Smoking scenes in movies and antismoking advertisements before movies: Effects on youth. *Journal of Marketing, 63,* 1–13.

Pelham, B. W., & Wachsmuth, J. O. (1995). The waxing and waning of the social self: Assimilation and contrast in social comparison. *Journal of Personality and Social Psychology, 69,* 825–838.

Perkins, D., Brown, B., & Taylor, R. (1996). The ecology of empowerment: Predicting participation in community organizations. *Journal of Social Issues, 52,* 85–110.

Perry, C., Murray, D., & Klepp, K. (1987). Predictors of adolescent smoking and implications for prevention. *Morbidity and Mortality Weekly Report, 35* (Suppl. 4S), 41S–45S.

Pesa, J. A., Syre, T. R., & Jones, E. (2000). Psychosocial differences associated with body weight among female adolescents: The importance of body image. *Journal of Adolescent Health, 26,* 330–337.

Petersen, A. C., & Taylor, B. (1980). The biological approach to adolescence: Biological change and psychological adaptation. In J. Adelson (Ed.), *Handbook of psychology* (pp. 117–158). New York: Wiley.

Peterson, D. L., & Pfost, K. S. (1989). Influence of rock videos on attitudes of violence against women. *Psychological Reports, 64,* 319–322.

Phillips, B. J., & Stavchansky, L. (1999). Camels and cowboys: How junior high students view cigarette advertising. In M. C. Macklin & L. Carlson (Eds.), *Advertising to children: Concepts and controversies* (pp. 229–249). Thousand Oaks, CA: Sage.

Pierce v. Society of Sisters, 268 U.S. 510 (1925).

Pierce, J. P., Choi, W. S., Gilpin, E. A., Farka, A. J., & Merritt, R. K. (1996). Validation of susceptibility as a predictor of which adolescents take up smoking in the United States. *Health Psychology, 15,* 355–61.

Pierce, J. P., Choi, W. S., Gilpin, E. A., Farkas, A. J., & Berry, C. C. (1998). Tobacco industry promotion of cigarettes and adolescent smoking. *Journal of the American Medical Association, 279,* 511–520.

Pierce, J. P., Distefan, J. M., Jackson, C., White, M. M., & Gilpin, E. A. (2002). Does tobacco marketing undermine the influence of recommended parenting in discouraging adolescents from smoking? *American Journal of Preventive Medicine, 23,* 73–81.

Pierce v. Society of Sisters, 268 U.S. 510 (1925).

Pike, K. M., & Rodin, J. (1991). Mothers, daughters, and disordered eating. *Journal of Abnormal Psychology, 100,* 198–204.

Pogarsky, G., Lizotte, A. J., & Thornberry, T. P. (2003). The delinquency of children born to young mothers: Results from the Rochester Youth Development Study. *Criminology, 41*, 1249–1286.

Polce-Lynch, M., Myers, B. J., Kliewer, W., & Kilmartin, C. (2001). Adolescent self-esteem and gender: Exploring relations to sexual harassment, body image, media influence, and emotional expression. *Journal of Youth and Adolescence, 30*, 225–224.

Polivy, J., & Herman, C. P. (1999). The effects of resolving to diet on restrained and unrestrained eaters: The "false hope syndrome." *International Journal of Eating Disorders, 25*, 223–226.

Polivy, J., & Herman, C. P. (2002). Causes of eating disorders. *Annual Review of Psychology, 53*, 187–213.

Pope, H. G., Jr., & Gruber, A. J. (1997). Muscle dysmorphia: An under recognized from of body dysmorphic disorder. *Psychosomatics, 38*, 548–557.

Pope, H. G., Jr., Phillips, K. A., & Olivardia, R. (2000). *The Adonis Complex: The secret crisis of male body obsession.* New York: Free Press.

Posavac, H. D., Posavac, S. S., & Posavac, E. J. (1998). Exposure to media images of female attractiveness and concern with body weight among young women. *Sex Roles, 38*, 187–201.

Posavac, H. D., Posavac, S. S., & Weigel, R. G. (2001). Reducing the impact of media images on women at risk for body image disturbance: Three targeted interventions. *Journal of Social & Clinical Psychology, 20*, 324–340.

Potter, W. J. (1999). *On media violence.* Thousand Oaks, CA: Sage Publications.

Potter, W. J., & Chang, I. C. (1990). Television exposure measures and the cultivation hypothesis. *Journal of Broadcasting and Electronic Media, 34*, 313–333.

Potter, W. J., Pashupati, K., Pekurny, R. G., Hoffman, E., & Davis, K. (2002) Perceptions of television: A schema explanation. *Media Psychology, 4*, 27–50.

Prince v. Massachusetts, 321 U.S. 158 (1944).

Proman, J. M. (2004). Liability of media companies for the violent content of their products marketed to children. *St. John's Law Review, 78*, 427–491.

Pumariega, A. J., Rogers, K., & Rothe, E. (2005). Culturally competent systems of care for children's mental health: Advances and challenges. *Community Mental Health Journal, 41*, 539–555.

Putnam, R. (2000). *Bowling alone: The collapse and revival of American community.* New York: Simon and Schuster.

Radke-Yarrow, M., & Brown, E. (1993). Resilience and vulnerability in children of multiple risk families. *Development & Psychopathology, 5*, 581–592.

Raghavan, R., Bogart, L. M., Elliot, M. N., Vestal, K. D., & Schuster, M. A. (2004). Sexual victimization among a national probability sample of adolescent women. *Perspectives on Sexual and Reproductive Health, 36*, 225–232.

Ramey, C. T., & Ramey, S. L. (1998). Early intervention and early experience. *American Psychologist, 53*, 109–120.

Raphael, F. J., & Lacey, J. H. (1992). Cultural aspects of eating disorders. *Annals of Medicine, 21*, 293–296.

Raudenbush, B., & Zellner, D. A. (1997). Nobody's satisfied: Effects of abnormal eating behaviors and actual and perceived weight status on body image satisfaction in males and females. *Journal of Social Clinical Psychology, 16*, 95–110.

R.A.V. v. City of St. Paul, 505 U.S. 377 (1992).

Raz, J. (1991). Free expression and personal identification. *Oxford Journal of Legal Studies, 11,* 303–324.

Redish, M. (1982). The value of Free Speech. *University of Pennsylvania Law Review, 130,* 591–645.

Red Lion Broadcasting v. Federal Communications Commission, 395 U.S. 367 (1969).

Regan v. Taxation with Representation of Washington, 461 U.S. 540 (1983).

Reis, O., & Youniss, J. (2004). Patterns in identity change and development in relationships with mothers and friends. *Journal of Adolescent Research, 19,* 31–44.

Reno v. American Civil Liberties Union, 521 U.S. 844 (1997).

Rieves, L., & Cash, T. F. (1996). Social developmental factors and women's body-image attitudes. *Journal of Social Behavior and Personality, 11,* 63–78.

Ricciardelli, L. A., & McCabe, M. P. (2001a). Dietary restraint and negative affect as mediators of body dissatisfaction and bulimic behaviors in adolescent girls and boys. *Behavior Research and Therapy, 39,* 1317–1328.

Ricciardelli, L. A., & McCabe, M. P. (2001b). Self-esteem and negative affect as moderators of sociocultural influences on body dissatisfaction, strategies to decrease weight, and strategies to increase muscles among adolescent boys and girls. *Sex Roles, 44,* 189–207.

Ricciardelli, L. A., & McCabe, M. P. (2003). A longitudinal analysis of the role of psychosocial factors in predicting body change strategies among adolescent boys. *Sex Roles, 45,* 349–360.

Ricciardelli, L. A., & McCabe, M. P. (2004). A biopsychosocial model of disordered eating and the pursuit of muscularity in adolescent boys. *Psychological Bulletin, 130,* 206–227.

Ricciardelli, L. A., McCabe, M. P., & Banfield, S. (2000). Body image and body change methods in adolescent boys: Roles of parents, friends and the media. *Journal of Psychosomatic Research, 49,* 189–197.

Richardson, C. R., Resnick, P. J., Hansen, D. L., Derry, H. A., & Rideout, V. J. (2002). Does pornography-blocking software block access to health information on the Internet? *Journal of the American Medical Association, 288,* 2887–2894.

Rimal, R. N., Flora, J. A., & Schooler, C. (1999). Achieving improvements in overall health orientation: Effects of campaign exposure, information seeking, and health media use. *Communication Research, 26,* 322–348.

Roberts, D. F., Chirstenson, P. G., & Gentile, D. A. (2003). The effects of violent music on children and adolescents. In D. A. Gentile (Ed.), *Media violence and children: A complete guide for parents and professionals* (pp. 153–170). Westport, CT: Praeger.

Roberts, D. F., & Foehr, U. G. (2004). *Kids and media in America: Patterns of use at the millennium.* New York: Cambridge University Press.

Roberts, D. F., Foehr, U. G., Rideout, V. J., & Brodie, M. (1999). *Kids and media at the new millennium.* Menlo Park, CA: Kaiser Family Foundation Report.

Robinson, T. N., Wilde, M. L., Navracruz, L. C., Haydel, K. F., & Varady, A. (2001). Effects of reducing children's television and video game use on aggressive behavior: A randomized controlled trial. *Archives of Pediatrics and Adolescent Medicine, 155,* 17–23.

Rooney, B. L., & Murray, D. M. (1996). A meta-analysis of smoking prevention programs after adjustment for errors in the unit of analysis. *Health Education Quarterly, 23,* 48–64.

Rose, J. S., Chassin, L., Presson, C. C., & Sherman, S. J. (1999). Peer influences on adolescent cigarette smoking: A prospective sibling analysis. *Merrill-Palmer Quarterly, 45*, 62–84.

Rosenblum, G. D., & Lewis, M. (1999). The relations among body image, physical attractiveness, and body mass in adolescence. *Child Development, 70*, 50–64.

Rosenkoetter, L. I., Rosenkoetter, S. E., Ozretich, R. A., & Acock, A. C. (2004). Mitigating the harmful effects of violent television. *Journal of Applied Developmental Psychology, 25*, 25–47.

Rosenthal, R. (1990). How are we doing in soft psychology? *American Psychologist, 45*, 775–777.

Rosenthal, R., & DiMatteo, M. R. (2001). Meta-analysis: Recent developments in quantitative methods for literature reviews. *Annual Review of Psychology, 52*, 59–82.

Roskos-Ewoldsen, D., Roskos-Ewoldsen, B., & Carpenter, F. (2002). Media priming: A synthesis. In J. Bryant & D. Zillmann (Eds.), *Media effects: Advances in theory and research* (pp. 97–120). Mahwah, NJ: Erlbaum.

Ross, H. E., & Ivis, F. (1999). Binge eating and substance use among male and female adolescents. *International Journal of Eating Disorders, 26*, 245–260.

Roper v. Simmons, 543 U.S. 551 (2005).

Roth v. United States, 354 U.S. 476 (1957).

Rubin, A. M., West, D. V., & Mitchell, W. S. (2001). Differences in aggression, attitudes towards women, and distrust as reflected in popular music preferences. *Media Psychology, 3*, 25–42.

Ruble, D. N., & Martin, C. L. (1998). Gender development. In W. Damon (Series ed.), & N. Eisenberg (Vol. ed.), *Handbook of child psychology: Vol. 3. Social, emotional, and personality development* (pp. 933–1016). New York: Wiley.

Rudman, L. S., & Borgida, E. (1995). The afterglow of construct accessibility: The behavioral consequences of priming men to view women as sexual objects. *Journal of Experimental Social Psychology, 31*, 493–517.

Rust v. Sullivan, 500 U.S. 173 (1991).

Rutter, M. (1987). Psychosocial resilience and protective mechanisms. *American Journal of Orthopsychiatry, 57*, 316–331.

Ryan, R. M. (1993). Agency and organization: Intrinsic motivation, autonomy and the self in psychological development. In J. Jacobs (Ed.), *Nebraska symposium on motivation: Developmental perspectives on motivation* (Vol. 40, pp. 1–56). Lincoln, NE: University of Nebraska Press.

Ryan, R. M., & Deci, E. L. (2000). Self-determination theory and the facilitation of intrinsic motivation, social development and well-being. *American Psychologist, 55*, 68–78.

Sable Communications of California, Inc., v. FCC, 492 U.S. 115 (1989).

Sanders v. Acclaim Entertainment, Inc., 188 F. Supp. 2d 1264 (2002).

Santa Fe Independent School District v. Doe, 530 U.S. 290 (2000).

Santelli, J. S., Kaiser, J., Hirsch, L., Radosh, A., Simkin, L., & Middlestadt, S. (2004). Initiation of sexual intercourse among middle school adolescents: The influence of psychosocial factors. *Journal of Adolescent Health, 34*, 200–208.

Sapiro, V. (2004). Not your parents' political socialization: Introduction for a new generation. *Annual Review of Political Science, 7*, 1–23.

Sargent, J. D., Beach, M. L., Dalton, M. A., Mott, L. A., Tickle, J. J., Ahrens, M. B., et al. (2001). Effect of seeing tobacco use in films on trying smoking among adolescents: Cross sectional study. *British Medical Journal, 323*, 1394–1397.

Sargent, J. D., Dalton, M., Beach, M., Bernhardt, A., Heatherton, T., & Stevens, M. (2000). Effect of cigarette promotions on smoking uptake among adolescents. *Preventive Medicine, 30,* 320–327.

Sargent, J. D., Dalton, M. A., Beach, M. L., Mott, L. A., Tickle, J. J., Ahrens, M. B., et al. (2002). Viewing tobacco use in movies: Does it shape attitudes that mediate adolescent smoking? *American Journal of Preventive Medicine, 22,* 137–145.

Saunders, K. W. (2003). *Saving our children from the First Amendment.* New York: New York University Press.

Saunders, K. W. (2005). A disconnect between law and neuroscience: Modern brain science, media influences, and juvenile justice. *Utah Law Review, 2005,* 695–741.

Savage, J. (2004). Does viewing violent media really cause criminal violence? A methodological review. *Aggression and Violent Behavior, 10,* 99–128.

Savin-Williams, R. C. (2005). *The new gay teenager.* Cambridge, MA: Harvard University Press.

Schad v. Borough of Mount Ephraim, 452 U.S. 61 (1981).

Scharrer, E. (2003). Making a case for media literacy in the curriculum: Outcomes and assessment. *Journal of Adolescent & Adult Literacy, 46,* 354–358.

Schenck v. United States, 249 U.S. 47 (1919).

Schutz, H. K., Paxton, S. J., & Wertheim, E. H. (2002). Investigation of body comparison among adolescent girls. *Journal of Applied Social Psychology, 32,* 1906–1937.

Scott, E. S., Reppucci, N. D., & Woolard, J. L. (1995). Evaluation adolescent decision making in legal contexts. *Law and Human Behavior, 19,* 221–244.

Seidman, S. A. (1999). Revisiting sex-role stereotyping in MTV videos. *International Journal of Instructional Media, 26,* 11–23.

Seligman, M. P., & Csikszentmihalyi, M. (2000). Positive psychology. *American Psychologist, 55,* 5–14.

Semmer, N., Cleary, P., Dwyer, J., Fuchs, R., & Lippert, P. (1987). Psychosocial predictors of adolescent smoking in two German cities: The Berlin-Bremen Study. *Morbidity and Mortality Weekly Report, 36* (Suppl. 4S), 3S-10S.

Shah, D. V. (1998). Civic engagement, interpersonal trust, and television use: An individual level assessment of social capital. *Political Psychology, 19,* 469–496.

Shah, D. V., Cho, J., Eveland, W. P., Jr., & Kwak, N. (2005). Information and expression in a digital age: Modeling Internet effects on civic participation. *Communication Research, 32,* 531–565.

Shah, D. V., Kwak, N., & Holbert, R. L. (2001). "Connecting" and "disconnecting" with civic life: Patterns of Internet use and the production of social capital. *Political Communication, 18,* 141–162.

Shaw, J., & Waller, G. (1995). The media's impact on body image: Implications for prevention and treatment. *Eating Disorders: The Journal of Treatment and Prevention, 3,* 115–123.

Shields, D., Balbach, E., & McGee, S. (1990). Hollywood on tobacco: How the entertainment industry understands tobacco portrayal. *Tobacco Control, 8,* 378–386.

Sherman, B. L., & Dominick, J. R. (1986). Violence and sex in music videos: TV and rock 'n' roll. *Journal of Communication, 36,* 79–93.

Sherrod, L. R. (2003). Promoting the development of citizenship in diverse youth. *PS: Political Science & Politics, 36,* 287–292.

Sherry, J. L. (2001). The effects of violent video games on aggression: A meta-analysis. *Human Communication Research, 27,* 409–432.

Shidler, J. A., & Lowry, D. T. (1995). Network TV sex as a counterprogramming strategy during a sweeps period—An analysis of content and ratings. *Journalism and Mass Communication Quarterly, 72,* 147–157.

Shin, N. (2004). Exploring pathways from television viewing to academic achievement in school age children. *Journal of Genetic Psychology, 165,* 367–381.

Shisslak, C. M., & Crago, M. (2001). Risk and protective factors in the development of eating disorders. In J. K. Thompson & L. Smolak (Eds.), *Body image, eating disorders, and obesity in youth* (pp. 103–125). Washington, DC: American Psychological Association.

Siegel, J. M., Yancey, A. K., Aneshensel, C. S., & Schuler, R. (1999). Body image, perceived timing, and adolescent mental health. *Journal of Adolescent Health, 25,* 155–165.

Siegel, M., & Biener, L. (2000). The impact of anti-smoking media campaigns on progression to established smoking: Results of a longitudinal youth study in Massachusetts. *American Journal of Public Health, 90,* 380–386.

Signorielli, N., McLeod, D., & Healy, E. (1994). Gender stereotypes in MTV commercials: The best goes on. *Journal of Broadcasting and Electronic Media, 38,* 91–101.

Silverblatt, A. (1995). *Media literacy: Keys to interpreting media messages.* Westport, CT: Praeger.

Silverman-Watkins, L. T., & Sprafkin, J. N. (1983). Adolescents' comprehension of televised sexual innuendos. *Journal of Applied Developmental Psychology, 4,* 359–369.

Simmons, R. G., & Blyth, D. A. (1987). *Moving into adolescence: The impact of pubertal change and school context.* Hawthorne, NJ: Aldine.

Singer, D. G., & Singer, J. L. (1998). Developing critical viewing skills and media literacy in children. *Annals of the American Academy of Political and Social Sciences, 557,* 164–180.

Singer, J. L., & Singer, D. G. (1986). Family experiences and television viewing as predictors of children's imagination, restlessness, and aggression. *Journal of Social Issues, 42,* 107–124.

Singhal, A., & Rogers, E. M. (1999). *Entertainment-education: A communication strategy for social change.* Mahwah, NJ: Erlbaum.

Skinner, H., Biscope, S., & Poland, B. (2003). Quality of Internet access: Barrier behind Internet use statistics. *Social Science & Medicine, 57,* 875–880.

Smith, E. S. (1999). Effects of investment in the social capital of youth on political and civic behavior in young adulthood: A longitudinal analysis. *Political Psychology, 20,* 553–580.

Smith, K. H., & Stutts, M. A. (1999). Factors that influence adolescents to smoke. *Journal of Consumer Affairs, 33,* 321157.

Smith, S. L. (2003). Popular video games: Quantifying the presentation of violence and its context. *Journal of Broadcasting & Electronic Media, 47,* 58–76.

Smith, S. L., & Boyson, A. R. (2002). Violence in music videos: Examining the prevalence and context of physical aggression. *Journal of Communication, 52,* 61–83.

Smolak, L., Levine, M. P., & Gralen, S. (1993). The impact of puberty and dating on eating problems among middle school girls. *Journal of Youth and Adolescence, 22,* 355–368.

Smolak, L., Levine, M. P., & Schermer, F. (1998). Lessons from lessons: An evaluation of an elementary school prevention program. In W. Vandereyken & G. Noordenbos (Eds.), *The prevention of eating disorders: Ethical, legal, and personal issues* (pp. 137–172). New York: New York University Press.

Smolak, L., Levine, M. P., & Thompson, J. K. (2001). The use of the Sociocultural Attitudes Towards Appearance Questionnaire with middle school boys and girls. *International Journal of Eating Disorders, 29*, 216–223.

Smolak, L., & Murnen, S. K. (2001). Gender and eating problems. In R. H. Striegel-Moore & L. Smolak (Eds.), *Eating disorders: Innovative directions in research and practice* (pp. 91–110). Washington, DC: American Psychological Association.

Snyder, H. (2000). *Juvenile arrests, 1999.* Washington, DC: Office of Juvenile Justice and Delinquency Prevention.

Snyder, H., & Sickmund, M. (1995). *Juvenile offenders and victims: A national report.* Washington, DC: Office of Juvenile Justice and Delinquency Prevention.

Snyder, H., & Sickmund, M. (1999). *Juvenile offenders and victims: 1999 national report.* Washington, DC: Office of Juvenile Justice and Delinquency Prevention.

Sommers-Flanagan, R., Sommers-Flanagan, J., & Davis, B. (1993). What's happening on music television? A gender role content analysis. *Sex Roles, 28*, 745–753.

Speiser v. Randall, 357 U.S. 513 (1958).

Stanley v. Georgia, 394 U.S. 557 (1969).

Stead, L. F., & Lancaster, T. (2000). A systematic review of interventions for preventing tobacco sales to minors. *Tobacco Control, 9*, 169–176.

Steele, J. R., & Brown, J. D. (1995). Adolescent room culture: Studying media in the context of everyday life. *Journal of Youth and Adolescence, 24*, 551–576.

Steiger, H., Stotland, S., Trottier, J., & Ghadiriam, A. M. (1996). Familial eating concerns and psychopathological traits: Causal implications of transgenerational effects. *International Journal of Eating Disorders, 19*, 147–157.

Steinberg, L. (2005). Cognitive and affective development in adolescence. *Trends in Cognitive Sciences, 9*, 69–74.

Steinberg, L., & Cauffman, E. (1996). Maturity of judgment in adolescence: Psychosocial factors in adolescent decision making. *Law and Human Behavior, 20*, 249–272.

Stewart, D. A., Carter, J. C., Drinkwater, J., Hainsworth, J., & Fairburn, C. G. (2001). Modification of eating attitudes and behavior in adolescent girls: A controlled study. *International Journal of Eating Disorders, 29*, 107–118.

Stice, E. (1998). Modeling of eating pathology and social reinforcement of the thin-ideal predict onset of bulimic symptoms. *Behavior Research and Therapy, 36*, 931–944.

Stice, E. (2002). Risk and maintenance factors for eating pathology: A meta-analytic review. *Psychological Bulletin, 128*, 825–848.

Stice, E., Akutagawa, D., Gaggar, A., & Agras, W. S. (2000). Negative affect moderates the relation between dieting and binge eating. *International Journal of Eating Disorders, 27*, 218–229.

Stice, E., & Bearman, S. K. (2001). Body image and eating disturbances prospectively predict growth in depressive symptoms in adolescent girls: A growth curve analysis. *Developmental Psychology, 37*, 597–607.

Stice, E., Cameron, R. P., Hayward, C., Taylor, C. B., & Killen, J. D. (1999). Naturalistic weight-reduction efforts prospectively predict growth in relative weight and onset of obesity among female adolescents. *Journal of Consulting and Clinical Psychology, 67*, 967–974.

Stice, E., Hayward, C., Cameron, R., Killen, J. D., & Taylor, C. B. (2000). Body image and eating disturbances predict onset of depression in female adolescents: A longitudinal study. *Journal of Abnormal Psychology, 109*, 438–444.

Stice, E., Mazotti, L., Weibel, D., & Agras, W. S. (2000). Dissonance prevention program decreases thin-ideal internalization, body dissatisfaction, dieting, negative affect, and bulimic symptoms: A preliminary experiment. *International Journal of Eating Disorders, 27*, 206–217.

Stice, E., Nemeroff, C., & Shaw, H. (1996). A test of the dual pathway model of bulimia nervosa: Evidence for restrained-eating and affect-regulation mechanism. *Journal of Social and Clinical Psychology, 15*, 340–363.

Stice, E., Presnell, K., & Bearman, S. K. (2001). Relation of early menarche to depression, eating disorders, substance abuse, and comorbid psychopathology among adolescent girls. *Developmental Psychology, 37*, 608–619.

Stice, E., Presnell, K., & Spangler, D. (2002). Risk factors for binge eating onset in adolescent girls: A 2-year prospective investigation. *Health Psychology, 21*, 131–138.

Stice, E., Schupak-Neuberg, E., Shaw, H. E., & Stein, R. I. (1994). Relation of media exposure to eating disorder symptomatology: An examination of mediating mechanisms. *Journal of Abnormal Psychology, 103*, 836–840.

Stice, E., & Shaw, H. E. (1994). Adverse effects of the media portrayed thin-ideal on women and linkages to bulimic symptomatology. *Journal of Social and Clinical Psychology, 13*, 288–308.

Stice, E., & Shaw, H. E. (2004). Eating disorder prevention programs: A meta-analytic review. *Psychological Bulletin, 130*, 206–227.

Stice, E., Shaw, H. E., & Nemeroff, C. (1998). Dual pathway model of bulimia nervosa: Longitudinal support for dietary restraint and affect-regulation mechanisms. *Journal of Social and Clinical Psychology, 17*, 129–149.

Stice, E., Spangler, D., & Agras, W. S. (2001). Exposure to media-portrayed thin-ideal images adversely affects vulnerable girls: A longitudinal experiment. *Journal of Social and Clinical Psychology, 20*, 270–288.

Stice, E., & Whitenton, K. (2002). Risk factors for body dissatisfaction in adolescent girls: A longitudinal investigation. *Developmental Psychology, 38*, 669–678.

Stice, E., Ziemba, C., Margolis, J., & Flick, P. (1996). The dual pathway model differentiates bulimics, subclinical bulimics, and controls: Testing the continuity hypothesis. *Behavior Therapy, 27*, 531–549.

Stockwell, T. F., & Glantz, S. A. (1997). Tobacco use is increasing in popular films. *Tobacco Control, 6*, 282–284.

Stolle, D., & Hooghe, M. (2004). The roots of social capital: Attitudinal and network mechanisms in the relation between youth and adult indicators of social capital. *Acta Politica, 39*, 422–441.

Strasburger, V. C. (1995). *Adolescents and the media: Medical and psychological impact.* Thousand Oaks, CA: Sage.

Strasburger, V. C., & Donnerstein, E. (1999). *Children, adolescents, and the media: Issues and solutions. Pediatrics, 103*, 129–139.

Strasburger, V. C., & Wilson, B. J. (2002). *Children, adolescents, and the media.* Thousand Oaks, CA: Sage.

Striegel-Moore, R. H., & Cachelin, F. (1999). Body image concerns and disordered eating in adolescent girls: Risk and protective factors. In N. Johnson, M. Roberts,

& J. Worell (Eds.), *Beyond appearance: A new look at adolescent girls* (pp. 85–108). Washington, DC: American Psychological Association.

Striegel-Moore, R. H., Schreiber, G. B., Lo, A., Crawford, P., Obarzanek, E., & Rodin, J. (2000). Eating disorder symptoms in a cohort of 11- to 16-year-old Black and White girls. *International Journal of Eating Disorders, 27,* 49–66.

Striegel-Moore, R. H., & Steiner-Adair, C. (1998). Primary prevention of eating disorders: Further consideration from a feminist perspective. In W. Vandereycken & G. Noordenbos (Eds.), *The prevention of eating disorders* (pp. 1–22). New York: University Press of America.

Strouse, J. S., & Buerkel-Rothfuss, N. L. (1987). Media exposure and the sexual attitudes and behaviors of college students. *Journal of Sex Education and Therapy, 13,* 43–51.

Strouse, J., Buerkel-Rothfus, N., & Long, E. (1995). Gender and family mediators of the relationship between music video exposure and adolescent sexual permissiveness. *Adolescence, 30,* 505–521.

Sussman, S. (2002). Effects of sixty six adolescent tobacco use cessation trials and seventeen prospective studies of self-initiated quitting. *Tobacco Induced Diseases, 1,* 35–81.

Sussman, S., Dent, C. W., Mestel-Rauch, J., Johnson, C. A., Hansen, W. B., & Flay, B. R. (1988). Adolescent nonsmokers, triers, and regular smokers' estimates of cigarette smoking prevalence: When do overestimations occur and by whom? *Journal of Applied Social Psychology, 18,* 537–551.

Sutton, M. J., Brown, J. D., Wilson, K. M., & Klein, J. D. (2002). Shaking the tree of knowledge for forbidden fruit: Where adolescents learn about sexuality and contraception. In J. D. Brown, J. R. Steele, & K. Walsh-Childers (Eds.), *Sexual teens, sexual media: Investigating media's influence on adolescent sexuality* (pp. 25–55). Mahwah, NJ: Erlbaum.

Swarr, A. E., & Richards, M. H. (1996). Longitudinal effects of adolescent girls' pubertal development, perceptions of pubertal timing, and parental relations on eating problems. *Developmental Psychology, 32,* 636–646.

Tamborini, R, Eastin, M. S., Skalski, P., Lachlan, K., Fediuk, T. A., & Brady, R. (2004). Violent virtual video games and hostile thoughts. *Journal of Broadcasting & Electronic Media, 48,* 335–357.

Tan, A. S. (1979). TV beauty ads and role expectations of adolescent female viewers. *Journal of Social and Clinical Psychology, 20,* 270–288.

Taylor, C. B., Sharpe, T., Shisslak, C., Bryosn, S., Estes, L. S., Gray, N., et al. (1998). Factors associated with weight concerns in adolescent girls. *International Journal of Eating Disorders, 24,* 31–42.

Taylor, L. D. (2005). Effects of visual and verbal sexual television content and perceived realism on attitudes and beliefs. *Journal of Sex Research, 42,* 130–137.

Telch, C. F., Agras, W. S., & Linehan, M. M. (2001). Dialectical behavior therapy for binge eating disorder. *Journal of Consulting and Clinical Psychology, 69,* 1061–1065.

Texas v. Johnson, 491 U.S. 397 (1989).

Thomas v. Collins, 323 U.S. 516 (1945).

Thompson, J. K., Coovert, L. J., & Stormer, S. (1999). Body image, social comparison, and eating disturbance: A covariance structure modeling investigation. *International Journal of Eating Disorders, 26,* 43–51.

Thompson, J. K., & Heinberg, L. J. (1999). The media's influence on body image disturbance and eating disorders: We've reviled them, now can we rehabilitate them? *Journal of Social Issues, 55,* 339–353.

Thompson, J. K., Heinberg, L. J., Altabe, M., & Tantleff-Dunn, S. (1999). *Exacting beauty: Theory, assessment, and treatment of body image disturbance.* Washington, DC: American Psychological Association.

Thompson, J. K., & Smolak, L. (2001). *Body image, eating disorders, and obesity in childhood and adolescence.* Washington, DC: American Psychological Association.

Thompson, J. K., & Stice, E. (2001). Thin-ideal internalization: mounting evidence for a new risk factor in body-image disturbance and eating pathology. *Current Directions in Psychological Science, 10,* 181–183.

Thompson, K. M. (2005). Addicted media: Substances on screen. *Child and Adolescent Psychiatric Clinics of North America, 14,* 473–489.

Tickle J. J., Sargent, J. D., Dalton, M. A., Beach, M. L., & Heatherton, T. F. (2001). Favorite movie stars, their tobacco use in contemporary movies and its association with adolescent smoking. *Tobacco Control, 10,* 16–22.

Tiggemann, M. (2003). Media exposure, body satisfaction and disordered eating: Television and magazines are not the same! *European Eating Disorders Review, 11,* 418–430.

Tiggemann, M., & Pickering, A. S. (1996). Role of television in adolescent women's body dissatisfaction and drive for thinness. *International Journal of Eating Disorders, 20,* 199–203.

Tiggemann, M., & Slater, A. (2003). Thin ideals in music television: A source of social comparison and body dissatisfaction. *International Journal of Eating Disorders, 35,* 45–58.

Tinker v. Des Moines Independent Community School District, 393 U.S. 503 (1969).

Tomeo, C. A., Field, A. E., & Berkey, C. S. (1999). Weight concerns, weight control behaviors, and smoking initiation. *Pediatrics, 104,* 918–924.

Tomori, M., & Rus-Makovec, M. (2000). Eating behavior, depression, and self-esteem in high school students. *Journal of Adolescent Health, 26,* 361–367.

Took, K. S., & Weiss, D. S. (1994). The relationship between heavy metal and rap music and adolescent turmoil: Real or artifact? *Adolescence, 29,* 613–621.

Tremblay, R. E. (2000). The development of aggressive behavior during childhood: What have we learned in the past century? *International Journal of Behavioral Development, 24,* 129–141.

Troiano, R. P., Flegal, K. M., Kuczmarski, R. J., Campbell, S. M., & Johnson, C. L. (1995). Overweight prevalence and trends for children and adolescents. *Archives of Pediatric Adolescent Medicine, 149,* 1085–1091.

Turner Broadcasting System, Inc. v. FCC, 512 U.S. 622 (1994).

Turner Broadcasting System, Inc. v. FCC, 520 U.S. 180 (1997).

Tyas, S., & Pederson, L. (1998). Psychological factors related to adolescent smoking: A critical review of the literature. *Tobacco Control, 7,* 409–420.

United States v. American Library Association, Inc., 539 U.S. 194 (2003).

United States v. O'Brien, 391 U.S. 367 (1968).

United States v. Playboy Entertainment Group, 529 U.S. 803 (2000).

Uhlmann, E., & Swanson, J. (2004). Exposure to violent video games increase implicit aggressiveness. *Journal of Adolescence, 27,* 41–52.

United States Department of Health and Human Services. (1998). *Tobacco use among US racial/ethnic minority groups—African Americans, American Indians and Alaska Natives, Asian Americans and Pacific Islanders, and Hispanics: A report of the Surgeon General*. Atlanta, GA: Centers for Disease Control and Prevention, National Center for Chronic Disease Prevention and Health Promotion, Office of Smoking and Health.

United States Department of Health and Human Services. (2000). *Preliminary results from the 1999 National Household Survey on Drug Abuse*. Rockville, MD: Research Triangle Institute.

United States Department of Health and Human Services. (2001a). *Changing adolescent smoking prevalence*. Bethesda, MD: National Institutes of Health, National Cancer Institute; 2001. Smoking and Tobacco Control Monograph No. 14. Retrieved February 6, 2006, from http://cancercontrol.cancer.gov/tcrb/monographs

United States Department of Health and Human Services. (2001b). *The Surgeon General's call to action to prevent and decrease overweight and obesity*. Rockville, MD: U.S. Department of Health and Human Services, Public Health Service, Office of the Surgeon General. Retrieved February 1, 2006, from http://www.surgeon general.gov/library

United States Department of Health and Human Services. (2001c). *Youth violence: A report of the Surgeon General*. Rockville, MD: U.S. Department of Health and Human Services; Centers for Disease Control and Prevention, National Center for Injury Prevention; Substance Abuse and Mental Health Services Administration, Center for Mental Health Services; and National Institutes of Health, National Institute of Mental Health.

Urberg, K. A., Degirmencioglu, S. M., & Pilgrim, C. (1997). Close friend and group influence on adolescent cigarette smoking and alcohol use. *Developmental Psychology, 33*, 834–844.

Utman, C. H. (1997). Performance effects of motivational state: A meta-analysis. *Personality and Social Psychology Review, 1*, 170–182.

Valkenburg, P. M. (2000). Media and youth consumerism. *Journal of Adolescent Health, 27*, 52–56.

Valkenburg, P. M., Schouten, A. P, & Peter, J. (2005). Adolescents' identity experiments on the Internet. *New Media & Society, 7*, 383–402.

van den Berg, P., Thompson, J. K., Obremski-Brandon, K., & Coovert, M. (2002). The tripartite influence model of body image and eating disturbance: A covariance structure modeling investigation testing the mediational role of appearance comparison. *Journal of Psychosomatic Research, 53*, 1007–1020.

van den Berg, P., Wertheim, E. H., Thompson, J. K., & Paxton, S. J. (2002). Development of body image, eating disturbance, and general psychological functioning in adolescent females: A replication using covariance structure modeling in an Australian sample. *International Journal of Eating Disorders, 32*, 46–51.

Van Den Bulck, J. (2000). Is television bad for your health? Behavior and body image of the adolescent "couch potato." *Journal of Youth and Adolescence, 29*, 273–288.

van Hoeken, D., Lucas, A. R., & Hoek, H. W. (1998). Epidemiology. In H. W. Hoek, J. L. Treasure, & M. A. Katzman (Eds.), *Neurobiology in the treatment of eating disorders* (pp. 97–126). New York: Wiley.

Vandewater, E. A., Lee, J. H., & Shim, M.-S. (2005). Family conflict and violent electronic media use in school-aged children. *Media Psychology, 7*, 73– 87.

Verba, S., Schlozman, K. L., & Brady, H. E. (1995). *Voice and equality, civic voluntarism in American politics*. Cambridge, MA: Harvard University Press.

Video Software Dealers Association v. Webster, 968 F.2d 684 (1992).

Villarruel, F. A., Perkins, D. F., Borden, L. M., & Keith J. G. (2003). *Community youth development: Practice, policy, and research*. Thousand Oaks, CA: Sage.

Vincent, M. A., & McCabe, M. P. (2000). Gender differences among adolescents in family and peer influences on body dissatisfaction, weight loss and binge eating behaviors. *Journal of Youth and Adolescence, 29*, 205–221.

Virginia State Board of Pharmacy v. Virginia Citizens Consumer Council, Inc., 425 U.S. 748 (1976).

Virginia v. Black, 538 U.S. 343 (2003).

Vogel, J. S., Hurford, D. P., Smith, J. V., & Cole, A. K. (2003). The relationship between depression and smoking in adolescents. *Adolescence, 38*, 57–74.

Vooijs, M. W., & van der Voort, T. H. A. (1993). Learning about television violence: The impact of a critical viewing curriculum on children's attitudes and judgments of crime series. *Journal of Research and Development in Education, 26*, 133–142.

Wakefield, M., & Chaloupka, F. J., (1999). Effectiveness of comprehensive tobacco control program in reducing teenage smoking in the United States. *Tobacco Control, 9*, 177–186.

Wakefield, M., Flay, B., Nichter, M., & Giovino, G. (2003). Role of the media in influencing trajectories of youth smoking. *Addiction, 98* (Suppl 1), 79–103.

Wakefield, M. A., Ruel, E. E., Chaloupka, F. J., Slater, S. J., & Kaufman, N. J. (2002). Association of point of purchase tobacco advertising and promotions with choice of usual brand among teenage smokers. *Journal of Health Communication, 7*, 113–121.

Wallack, L., Dorfman, L., Jernigan, D., & Themba, M. (1993). *Media advocacy and public health: Power for prevention*. Newbury Park: Sage Publications.

Waller, G., Hamilton, K., & Shaw, J. (1992). Media influences on body size estimation in eating disordered and comparison subjects. *British Review of Bulimia and Anorexia Nervosa, 6*, 81–87.

Walsh, D. A., & Gentile, D. A. (2001). A validity test of movie, television, and videogame ratings. *Pediatrics, 107*, 1302–1308.

Walsh-Childers, K., & Brown, J. D. (1993). Adolescents' acceptance of sex-role stereotypes and television viewing. In B. S. Greenberg, J. D. Brown, & N. L. Buerkel-Rothfuss (Eds.), *Media, sex and the adolescent* (pp. 117–133). Cresskill, NJ: Hampton Press.

Walsh-Childers, K., Gotthoffer, A., & Lepre, C. R. (2002). From "just the facts" to "downright salacious": Teens' and women's magazine coverage of sex and sexual health. J. D. Brown, J. R. Steele, & K. Walsh-Childers (Eds.), *Sexual teens, sexual media: Investigating media's influence on adolescent sexuality* (pp. 153–171). Mahwah, NJ: Erlbaum.

Ward, L. M. (2002). Does television exposure affect emerging adults' attitudes and assumptions about sexual relationships? Correlational and experimental confirmation. *Journal of Youth and Adolescence, 31*, 1–15.

Ward, L. M. (2003). Understanding the role of entertainment media in the sexual socialization of American youth: A review of empirical research. *Developmental Review, 23*, 347–388.

Ward, L. M., & Rivadeneyra, R. (1999). Contributions of entertainment television to adolescents' sexual attitudes and expectations: The role of viewing versus viewer involvement. *Journal of Sex Research, 36,* 237–249.

Watson, D., Clark, L. A., & Tellegen, A. (1988). Development and validation of brief measures of positive and negative affect: The PANAS scales. *Journal of Personality and Social Psychology, 54,* 1063–1070.

Watson, N. A, Clarkson, J. P, Donovan, R. J, & Giles-Corti, B. (2003). Filthy or fashionable? Young people's perceptions of smoking in the media. *Health Education Research, 18,* 554–567.

Watts v. United States, 394 U.S. 705 (1969).

Weinstein, N. D., Slovic, P., & Gibson, G. (2004). Accuracy and optimism in smokers' beliefs about quitting. *Nicotine & Tobacco Research, 6* (Supp. 3), 375–380.

Weinstock, H., Berman, S., & Cates, W. (2004). Sexually transmitted diseases among American youth: Incidence and prevalence estimates. *Perspectives in Sexual and Reproductive Health, 36,* 6–10.

Weisz, M. G., & Earls, C. M. (1995). The effects of exposure to filmed sexual violence on attitudes towards rape. *Journal of Interpersonal Violence, 10,* 71–84.

Wentzel, K., & McNamara, C. (1999). Interpersonal relationships, emotional disturbance and pro-social behavior in middle school. *Journal of Early Adolescence, 19,* 114–125.

Werner-Wilson, R. J., Fitzharris, J. L., & Morrissey, K. M. (2004). Adolescent and parent perceptions of media influence on adolescent sexuality. *Adolescence, 39,* 303–313.

Wertheim, E. H., Koerner, J., & Paxton, S. J. (2001). Longitudinal predictors of restrictive eating and bulimic tendencies in three different age groups of adolescent girls. *Journal of Youth and Adolescence, 30,* 69–81.

Wertheim, E. H., Martin, G., Prior, M., Sanson, A., & Smart, D. (2002). Parent influences in the transmission of eating and weight related values and behaviors. *Eating Disorders: The Journal of Treatment and Prevention, 10,* 321–334.

Wertheim, E. H., Paxton, S. J., Maude, D., Szmukler, G. I., Gibbons, K., & Hiller, L. (1992). Psychosocial predictors of weight loss behaviors and binge eating in adolescent girls and boys. *International Journal of Eating Disorders, 12,* 151–160.

West Virginia State Board of Education v. Barnette, 319 U.S. 624 (1943).

Whalen, C. K., Jamner, L. D., Henker, B., & Delfino, R. J. (2001). Smoking and moods in adolescents with depressive and aggressive dispositions: Evidence from surveys and electronic diaries. *Health Psychology, 20,* 99–111.

Wichstrom, L. (1995). Social, psychological and physical correlates of eating problems: A study of the general adolescent population in Norway. *Psychological Medicine, 25,* 567–579.

Wichstrom, L. (2000). Psychological and behavioral factors unpredictive of disordered eating: A prospective study of the general adolescent population in Norway. *International Journal of Eating Disorders, 28,* 33–42.

Wiegman, O., & van Schie, E. G. M. (1998). Video game playing and its relations with aggressive and prosocial behavior. *British Journal of Social Psychology, 37,* 367–378.

Wilfley, D. E., Welch, R. R., Stein, R. I., Spurrell, E. B., Cohen, L. R., & Saelens, B. E. (2002). A randomized comparison of group cognitive-behavioral therapy and group interpersonal psychotherapy for the treatment of overweight individuals with binge eating disorder. *Archives of General Psychiatry, 59,* 713–721.

Will, K. E., Porter, B. E., Geller, E. S., & DePasquale, J. P. (2005). Is television a health and safety hazard? A cross-sectional analysis of at-risk behavior on primetime television. *Journal of Applied Social Psychology, 35,* 198–222.

Willemsen, M. C., & de Zwart, W. M. (1999). The effectiveness of policy and health education strategies for reducing adolescent smoking: A review of the evidence. *Journal of Adolescence, 22,* 587–599.

Williams, J. M., & Currie, C. (2000). Self-esteem and physical development in early adolescence: Pubertal timing and body image. *Journal of Early Adolescence, 20,* 139–149.

Williams, R. J., & Ricciardelli, L. A. (2003). Negative perceptions about self-control and identification with gender-role stereotypes relate to binge eating, problem drinking, and to comorbidity among adolescents. *Journal of Adolescent Health, 32,* 66–72.

Williamson, I., & Hartley, P. (1998). British research into the increased vulnerability of young gay men to eating disturbance and body dissatisfaction. *European Eating Disorders Review, 6,* 160–170.

Wilson, B. J., Colvin, C. M., & Smith, S. (2002). Engaging in violence on American television: A comparison of child teen, and adult perpetrators. *Journal of Communication, 52,* 36–60.

Wilson, B. J., Kunkel, D., Linz, D., Potter, J., Donnerstein, E., Smith, S. L., et al. (1997). Violence in television programming overall: University of California, Santa Barbara study. In M. Seawall (Ed.), *National Television Violence Study* (Vol. 1, pp. 3–184). Thousand Oaks, CA: Sage Publications.

Wilson, B. J., Kunkel, D., Linz, D., Potter, J., Donnerstein, E., Smith, S. L., et al. (1998). Violence in television programming overall: University of California, Santa Barbara study. In M. Seawall (Ed.), *National Television Violence Study* (Vol. 2, pp. 3–204). Thousand Oaks, CA: Sage Publications.

Wilson, B. J., Linz, D., Donnerstein, E., & Stipp, H. (1992). The impact of social issue television programming on attitudes towards rape. *Human Communication Research, 19,* 179–208.

Wilson, B. J., Linz, D., Federman, J., Smith, S., Paul, B., & Nathanson, A. (1999). *The choices and consequences evaluation: A study of Court TV's antiviolence curriculum.* Santa Barbara: Center for Communication and Social Policy, University of California.

Wilson, B. J., Smith, S. L., Potter, W. J., Kunkel, D., Linz, D., Colvin, C. M., et al. (2002). Violence in children's television programming: Assessing the risks. *Journal of Communication, 52,* 5–36.

Wilson, D. K., Rodrigue, J. R., & Taylor, W. C. (Eds.) (1997). *Health-promoting and health-compromising behaviors among minority adolescents.* Washington, DC: American Psychological Association.

Wilson v. Midway Games, Inc.,198 F. Supp. 2d 167 (2002).

Wingood, G. M., DiClemente, R. J., Harrington, K., Davies, S., Hook, E. W., III, & Oh, M. K. (2001). Exposure to X-rated movies and adolescents' sexual and contraceptive-related attitudes and behaviors. *Pediatrics, 107,* 1116–1119.

Winkel, F. W., & deKluever, E. (1997). Communication aimed at changing cognitions about sexual intimidation: Comparing the impact of perpetrator-focused versus a victim-focused persuasive strategy. *Journal of Interpersonal Violence, 12,* 513–529.

Winters v. New York, 333 U.S. 507 (1948).

Wisconsin v. Mitchell, 505 U.S. 377 (1992).

Wisconsin v. Yoder, 406 U.S. 205 (1972).

Wood, J. V. (1989). Theory and research concerning social comparisons of personal attributes. *Psychological Bulletin, 106,* 231–248.

Woodhouse, B. B. (2004). Reframing the debate about the socialization of children: An environmentalist paradigm. *The University of Chicago Legal Forum, 2004,* 85–149.

Worden, J. K., Flynn, B. S., Solomon, L. J., & Secker-Walker, R. H. (1996). Using mass media to prevent cigarette smoking among adolescent girls. *Health Education Quarterly, 23,* 453–468.

Yang, N., & Linz, D. (1990). Movie rating and the content of adult videos: The sex-violence ratio. *Journal of Communication, 40,* 28–42.

Yates, M., & Youniss, J. (1998). Community service and political identity development in adolescence. *Journal of Social Issues, 54,* 495–512.

Ybarra, M. L., & Mitchell, K. J., (2004). Online aggressor/targets, aggressors, and targets: A comparison of associated youth characteristics. *Journal of Child Psychology and Psychiatry, 45,* 1308–1316.

Youniss, J., McLellan, J., Su, Y., & Yates, M. (1999). The role of community service in identity development. *Journal of Adolescent Research, 14,* 248–261.

Yoon, J. S, & Somers, C. L. (2003). Aggressive content of high school students' TV viewing. *Psychological Reports, 93,* 949–953.

Zelman v. Simmons-Harris, 536 U.S. 639 (2002).

Zhu, S., Sun, J., Billings, S. C., Choi, W. S., & Malarcher, A. (1999). Predictors of smoking cessation in U.S. adolescents. *American Journal of Preventive Medicine, 16,* 202–207.

Zillmann, D. (1979). *Hostility and aggression.* Hillsdale, NJ: Erlbaum.

Zillmann, D. (1983). Transfer of excitation in emotional behavior. In J. T. Cacioppo & R. E. Petty (Eds.), *Social psychophysiology: A sourcebook* (pp. 215–240). New York: Guilford Press.

Zillmann, D. (1991). Television viewing and physiological arousal. In J. Bryant & D. Zillmann (Eds.), *Responding to the screen: Reception and reaction process* (pp. 103–133). Hillsdale, NJ: Lawrence Erlbaum.

Zillman D., & Bryant J. (1988a). Effects of prolonged consumption of pornography on family values. *Journal of Family Issues, 9,* 518–544

Zillman D., & Bryant J. (1988b). Pornography's impact on sexual satisfaction. *Journal of Applied Social Psychology, 18,* 438–453.

Zillmann, D., & Weaver, J. B. (1999). Effects of prolonged exposure to gratuitous media violence on provoked and unprovoked hostile behavior. *Journal of Applied Social Psychology, 29,* 145–165.

Zimring, F. E., & Hawkins, G. (1997). *Crime is not the problem: Lethal violence in America.* New York: Oxford University Press.

Index